16.95

D0392137

COMMENTARY

on the

OCCASIONAL SERVICES

COMMENTARY

on the

OCCASIONAL SERVICES

PHILIP H. PFATTEICHER

FORTRESS PRESS   Philadelphia

Library of Congress Cataloging in Publication Data

Pfatteicher, Philip H.
  Commentary on the occasional services.

  Bibliography: p.
  Includes indexes.
  1. Occasional services—Lutheran Church. 2. Lutheran
Church—Liturgy. I. Title
BX8067.A1P45 1983   264′.04133   82–48542
  ISBN 0-8006-0697-3

9767K82   Printed in the United States of America   1–697

ACKNOWLEDGMENTS

Material from the following sources is acknowledged:

Excerpts from *The Book of Occasional Services* published by the Church Hymnal Corporation, New York, New York, copyright © 1979 by The Church Pension Fund; and from *The Book of Offices for Certain Occasions not provided in the* Book of Common Prayer, copyright © 1960 by The Church Pension Fund, are used by permission.

From *The Book of Worship for Church and Home.* Copyright © 1964, 1965 by The Board of Publication of The Methodist Church, Inc. Used by permission.

From *Commentary on the American Prayer Book* by Marion Hatchett. Copyright © 1980 by Marion Hatchett. Used by permission of The Seabury Press, Inc.

Passages from *Liturgy and Worship,* edited by W. K. Lowther Clarke and Charles Harris, copyright © 1932, reprinted 1964; *The Treatise on the* Apostolic Tradition *of St. Hippolytus of Rome,* edited by Gregory Dix, copyright © 1968; *The Ordination Prayers of the Western Churches* by H. Boone Porter, copyright © 1967 are used by permission of the publisher and copyright holder, SPCK, London, England.

Excerpts from the *Pastor's Manual* of the Church of the Brethren, copyright © 1978 by The Brethren Press, Elgin, Illinois, are used by permission.

Excerpts from the English translation of the *Rite of Funerals* © 1970, International Committee on English in the Liturgy, Inc. (ICEL); excerpts from the English translation of *Rite of Anointing and Pastoral Care of the Sick* © 1973, ICEL; excerpts from the English translation of *The Roman Missal* © 1973, ICEL; excerpts from the English translation of *Holy Communion and Worship of the Eucharist outside Mass* © 1974, ICEL; excerpts from the English translation of *Rite of Penance* © 1974, ICEL; excerpts from the *Ordination of Deacons, Priests, and Bishops* © 1975, ICEL; excerpts from the English translation of *Dedication of a Church and an Altar* © 1978, ICEL. All rights reserved.

Passages from *The Roman Ritual: Complete Edition,* copyright © 1964, are used with the permission of Philip T. Weller, the translator and editor.

Excerpts from the 1975 revised edition of *The Service Book of the Holy Orthodox Catholic Apostolic Church,* translated by Isabel Hapgood, are printed with the permission of the Antiochian Orthodox Christian Archdiocese of North America.

Excerpts reprinted from *The Worshipbook—Services and Hymns.* Copyright © MCMLXX, MCMLXXII, The Westminster Press. Used by permission.

Biblical quotations, unless otherwise noted, are from the Revised Standard Version of the Bible, copyright 1946, 1952 © 1971, 1973 by the Division of Christian Education of the National Council of the Churches of Christ in the U.S.A., and are used by permission.

CONTENTS

CONTENTS

To Lois

PREFACE

Liturgy is the focus and expression of the church's history, theology, and piety. Those who experience this pervasive and public manifestation of the church's life, as well as those who study it, are entitled to a statement of the intentions which motivated the formation of revised services and to an account of their development. This commentary, therefore, is for those pastors and laity who seek to understand the occasional services and to use them responsibly and intelligently.

The arrangement of this commentary, it will be noticed, does not follow the arrangement of the rites in *Occasional Services* (1982). Related rites are gathered under one heading in each chapter as an alternate way of grouping the several services and rites. Such a rearrangement may suggest more relationships than simply reproducing the order of *Occasional Services* (1982).

The careful reader of this commentary may detect at certain points what may seem to be an implied criticism of those who drafted the occasional services. If any such criticism is to be made, however, I must include myself, since I was part of the committee. In certain cases (none, I think, serious) we simply did not know as much as we should have, and that is no one person's fault, for the time was short and we all wanted *Occasional Services* to appear as close to the publication of the *Lutheran Book of Worship* as possible.

I must record my debt to my colleagues on the Task Force on Occasional Services. Many of their insights, comments, and observations have helped shape this book. I have tried to reflect their ideas and decisions accurately; indeed, some of their very phrases have been incorporated into this commentary.

I am particularly grateful for the attention of representatives of the worship departments of three of the cooperating churches, who read the manuscript and made helpful suggestions: Ralph Van Loon and S. Anita Stauffer of the Lutheran Church in America; Mons Teig of the American Lutheran Church; and Mark Bangert of the Association of Evangelical Lutheran Churches.

Eugene L. Brand was engaged by the American Lutheran Church's

Division for Life and Mission in the Congregation to provide a theological and liturgical review of the occasional services at a late stage of the manuscript's development. The report of that study (August 1981) was important to the American Lutheran Church review committee and to the manuscript committee as well. It has also been of considerable value in writing this commentary. A great many of Brand's insights and several of his phrases have been shamelessly borrowed and appear in the following pages. Acknowledgment of that dependence must be made here since it is not otherwise noted in this book.

Acknowledgment must also be made of a debt to the detailed records of sources of the prayers in the 1979 *Book of Common Prayer* which Marion Hatchett has maintained and published in his *Commentary on the American Prayer Book* (New York: Seabury Press, 1981). The information given in this book concerning the prayers in the *Lutheran Book of Worship* and in *Occasional Services* (1982) which have been borrowed from the American Prayer Book is drawn from Hatchett's book. Massey Shepherd's *The Oxford American Prayer Book Commentary* (New York: Oxford University Press, 1950) has also been useful in providing background for prayers borrowed from the 1928 American Prayer Book. Looking back on our work on the *Lutheran Book of Worship* and *Occasional Services* (1982), it is to be regretted that such detailed records were not kept of the authors of the prayers and texts included in those books. In defense it may be observed that in most cases the prayers and texts have undergone such revision in the course of the development and review of the manuscript that the authors might no longer recognize them and, in some cases, might no longer care to acknowledge them as their own. A general acknowledgment of the names of those who in various capacities contributed to the book is recorded on page 5 of *Occasional Services* (1982).

The index correlating the prayer numbers and page numbers in the *Lutheran Book of Worship*, given as Appendix III, was initially the work of Elizabeth A. Davey. It has been revised and expanded by Philip Pfatteicher for this book.

At the urging of the publisher, we have generally used the designation *LBW* for the *Lutheran Book of Worship*.

Work on this commentary on the occasional services has increased my regard for the achievement of those nineteenth-century Lutheran liturgists who in the *Church Book* made a contribution to the whole church. I am pleased to record that one of them, Adolph Spaeth, was the brother of my great-grandmother.

The occasional services provide more than helpful and even necessary forms for ministerial acts. Properly understood and employed, the services provide an entire course in pastoral theology for those who use them and a comprehensive expression of the church's care to those who are recipients of the ministry which they embody. It is the author's hope that this book will contribute to the enrichment of such ministry.

East Stroudsburg, Pa.
Advent I 1982
Maranatha!

INTRODUCTION

The *Lutheran Book of Worship* made available to Lutherans in North America the services of the church that are used most regularly—Holy Baptism, Holy Communion, and Daily Prayer of the Church. The full liturgy is in the Ministers Edition; selections from it—those most useful to congregations—appear in the pew edition, which also includes the hymnal.

However, the services which appear in the Ministers Edition do not comprise the entire liturgy of the church, its whole body of liturgical materials and services. There are also other services in the church's store-house which are used from time to time as occasion demands. With the publication of *Occasional Services* (1982), the new liturgy of the Lutheran church in North America is now complete.

With the publication of the *Church Book* in 1868, an important advance in Lutheran liturgy was achieved. When work began on a collection of what were then called "Ministerial Acts" for inclusion in the *Church Book*, a leading scholar Beale Melanchthon Schmucker was reluctant to enter upon the work. Henry Eyster Jacobs described the process in "The Making of the *Church Book*," a paper read at the annual meeting of the Lutheran Church Book and Liturgical Society in April 1912. The basic form of the orders for public worship was substantially laid in the Ministerium of Pennsylvania's liturgy of 1860, and general agreement upon it had been obtained. These orders were rooted in the ancient mass, and its historical roots were traceable for a thousand years. But the orders for Ministerial Acts has no such thoroughly elaborated foundation. The underlying principles needed to be understood before such services could be prepared. However, the church could not wait for this careful preparation to be completed, and the work had to go forward without the scholarly groundwork that the best Lutheran students of the liturgy of the time knew was essential.

So has it always been. The occasional services receive short shrift while the churches give major attention, time, and support to the preparation of the weekly and daily services, building upon foundations that ecumenical liturgical scholarship has laid. By the time the service book appears, the church rejoices and hastens to complete the collection.

Pastors and people expect the supplementary services soon after the publication of the basic book. The church seeks to capitalize on the mood and the momentum. Those charged with the preparation of the occasional services seldom have the leisure to research and reflect upon the remainder of the collection of services. Moreover, substantial scholarship on the occasional services is rare; practical advice and comment is nearly nonexistent. This commentary, therefore, seeks to offer a modest redress of that situation.

The history of the development of the occasional services to be outlined here and reflected in the following pages is admittedly deficient. Many will note that there is little reference to the several Scandinavian traditions or to the various German orders prepared for use in North America. (Friedrich Lochner, for example, prepared some orders for use by pastors in the Missouri Synod, and Wilhelm Loehe in Germany prepared an *Agenda* for use by pastors in North America.) Nonetheless, this book attempts to trace the principal ancestry of *Occasional Services* (1982), which is derived principally from *Occasional Services* (1962), which in turn was heavily dependent upon *Occasional Services* (1930 and 1943). The latter was based upon the work done on the Ministerial Acts in the *Church Book* of 1891–92, which was drawn from sixteenth-century German sources. A full account of the development of the North American Lutheran rites remains to be written.

HISTORICAL DEVELOPMENT

The major tradition of occasional services in North American Lutheranism began with the preparation of the 1877 edition of the *Kirchenbuch*, which included for the first time in North America the full offices of matins and vespers and nineteen occasional services (called *Kirchliche Handlungen*) in German. In the summer of 1884 a committee of Beale Melanchthon Schmucker, Adolph Spaeth, Edward F. Moldehnke, and Sigmund Fritschel, later joined by the young Henry Eyster Jacobs, met at the summer home of Adolph Spaeth in Cape May Point, New Jersey. That summer, despite Schmucker's objections that the orders for Ministerial Acts "could not successfully pass the same critical tests" as the orders for public worship in the *Liturgy for the Use of the Evangelical Lutheran Church* of 1860,[1] a draft in English of four orders was completed: Infant Baptism, Adult Baptism, Confession and Absolution, and Confirmation. The work was based upon the services in German in the

---

1. Henry E. Jacobs, "The Making of the Church Book" (Philadelphia, 1912), p. 22. This is a separate printing of an article with the same title in the *Lutheran Church Review* 31 (1912):597–622.

1877 *Kirchenbuch*, which in turn was based upon the German Agendas of the sixteenth century.[2]

Of the work, Adolph Spaeth wrote:

> The remembrance of this joint work, with brethren who were of one heart and one soul, involving the valuation of our old liturgical treasures, and how best to turn them to account, is to this day one of the most delightful recollections of my life.
>
> Much of the preparatory work was done in the summer vacation at Cape May Point. Dr. Schmucker came down from Pottstown with the great, heavy trunk containing the most valuable treasures of our liturgical library. From the West came our never-to-be-forgotten friend Sigmund Fritschel, and, in our modest seaside home, the work was industriously carried on for weeks. When we were tired of the old folios, and high tide brought the longed-for bathing hour, we dropped everything and hurried to the beach, where we older ones renewed our youth with the boys.[3]

In 1886 the committee indicated that none of the orders as then adopted should be regarded, until tested by use, as anything other than provisional. The pressure for a complete book, however, was strong from the pastors of the General Council. In 1887, Matrimony and Private Baptism of Infants in Cases of Necessity were prepared. In July 1888, Schmucker, Spaeth, Moldehnke, and Fritschel met again at Cape May Point and completed the Visitation of the Sick, Communion of the Sick, Commendation of the Dying, and Burial of the Dead. This was the last part of the work on which Schmucker was directly engaged, "and more than once he expressed with unusual warmth his satisfaction with this part of our liturgical work. Could he have thought that before many weeks this service would be used for the first time at his own coffin, and over his grave!"[4] The orders were "hurried into the book without reference to the purely provisional character."[5] Schmucker's sudden death in 1888 and the ill health of Spaeth delayed the work. Still to be done were the orders for ordination, installation of pastors, installation of church officers, dedication of churches, opening and closing of synods. The completed orders for Ministerial Acts were finally copyrighted in 1891 and published in 1892. The doctrinal and rubrical statements before each of the orders were gathered by Spaeth mostly from standard German church orders of the sixteenth century.

---

2. Adolph Spaeth, "Erinnerungen," *Life of Adolph Spaeth, D.D., LL.D.,* ed. H. R. Spaeth (Philadelphia: General Council Publication House, 1916), p. 171.

3. Ibid.

4. Ibid., p. 172.

5. Jacobs, "Making of the Church Book," p. 23.

Meanwhile, in 1888, the United Synod in the South, the General Synod, and the General Council had published the Common Service. (This important work had taken precedence so that work on the Ministerial Acts was put aside for a time.) In the revision of the Common Service in preparation for the *Common Service Book* with Hymnal (1917), the Ministerial Acts of the *Church Book* were studied, revised, and given a new name: The Occasional Services. The title has not always been understood. "Occasional," used this way, does not have to do with any relative infrequency of the use of these services, but rather with the purpose for which they are designed. The occasional services—like "occasional verse" in poetry—are services designed for specific occasions. They are therefore to be distinguished from services of worship of a more general character such as the Holy Communion and the Daily Prayer of the Church.

The work on the occasional services was done by Jacobs, who had served on the committee which had prepared the Ministerial Acts for the *Church Book*. At the time of the publication of the *Common Service Book* (1917) not all of the work on the occasional services had been completed, and in the music edition only two services were included: the Order for Public Confession and the Order for the Burial of the Dead. In the text edition of the *Common Service Book* (1919) all the occasional services were included:

Order for the Baptism of Infants
Confirmation of Lay Baptism
Order for the Baptism of Adults
Order for Confirmation
Order for Public Confession
Order for Private Confession and Absolution
Order for the Communion of the Sick
Lessons and Prayers for the Sick
Order for the Commendation of the Dying
Order for the Burial of the Dead
Order for Marriage
Order for Ordination
Order for the Installation of a Pastor
Order for Laying the Corner-stone of a Church
Order for the Dedication of a Church
Order for the Opening of Synods
Order for the Closing of Synods
Order for the Installation of a Church Council

The arrangement of these orders which by placing Marriage immediately following Burial of the Dead caused merriment in some quarters had nonetheless a rational explanation. The first orders were those used for every Christian: Baptism, Confirmation, Confession, Death, and Burial. Then followed two orders which were less than universal: Marriage and Ordination. Finally, there were orders for the life and governing of a congregation: Installation of a Pastor, Laying the Corner-stone and Dedication of a Church, Opening and Closing of Synods, and Installation of a Church Council.

A revision of the *Common Service Book* was authorized at the Erie convention of the United Lutheran Church in America in 1928. This revised edition was published in 1929 and 1930. (Paul Zeller Strodach said of this edition, "It is the first edition published under the *direct order* of the Church and therefore is the 'Authorized Edition.' "[6]) At the Erie convention, the Common Service Committee also presented for consideration and approval thirty new orders and offices for the inclusion in the occasional services (the list is given in Appendix I), which were "approved, adopted, and ordered included unanimously."[7] These "additional orders and offices" were prepared by a subcommittee of the Common Service Book Committee consisting of J. J. Scherer, Harvey D. Hoover, and Paul Z. Strodach "to meet the increasing needs of the Church, in historic literary form for ministerial actions and Church offices."[8]

> The necessity of providing for occasional services other than those already included in *The Common Service Book* inspired the action of the United Lutheran Church at Erie in 1928 authorizing the Common Service Book Committee to prepare and issue such liturgical forms as would meet the needs of congregations and Synods.
>
> The Committee therefore presents to the Church this group of Orders and Offices, which have historic precedent and represent historic usage, in the hope that they will serve unto edification and promote desirable unity.[9]

Strodach wrote of this work with justifiable pride: "With these joined to the older Occasional Services the Church possesses as complete a *Rituale* as exists, and in its evangelical forms and actions is as historic, full, and complete as is its older predecessor. No other Communion possesses as complete a *vade mecum* for pastoral acts."[10] In 1943 a new edition of the

---

6. Paul Zeller Strodach, *Manual on Worship* (Philadelphia: Muhlenberg Press, 1946), p. 195.

7. Ibid.

8. Ibid.

9. *Occasional Services* (Philadelphia: Board of Publication of the United Lutheran Church in America, 1930), p. 102.

10. Strodach, *Manual on Worship*, p. 195.

5

Occasional Services was published, identical with the 1930 book except for the addition to the additional orders and offices of an "Office for Reception into Synod of a Minister from Another Denomination."

As the Common Service was increasingly accepted into the various Lutheran hymnals and service books in North America, each church body continued to publish and use its own series of ministerial acts.[11] When work began on a new service book in 1945, despite the substantial agreement in the cooperating churches on the structure of the Holy Communion, there were few common traditions and no agreement on the number or the character of the occasional services.

The difficulties in arriving at agreed-upon texts are described in the report of the Commission on Worship to the 1950 convention of the United Lutheran Church in America:

> The . . . Occasional Services, for the most part, represent extensive revisions of the ancient Manual or Ritual, the service book for parish priests, and the Pontifical, the service book for bishops. These differed greatly in different areas in medieval times. Many diocesan, provincial, or national peculiarities persisted in the different European countries after the Reformation and were preserved in translation in the service books of our various Lutheran Churches in America.
>
> Other differences are explained by the fact that when the confessional and liturgical revival of the middle of the nineteenth century swept across Europe, some Lutheran countries made quite full recoveries of lost or neglected materials, while other countries made partial recoveries. Much new material, also, largely hortatory in character, was improvised. As a result of these factors, a perplexing variety of forms and traditions developed in the co-operating Churches, some of their Orders being simple, even rudimentary in form, while others were fully developed.

Eventually, however, "an indomitable will to agree" led to the adoption by the Joint Commission on the Liturgy in Easter Week 1950 of these occasional services, which (together with the Prayer of the Church, General Prayers, and the Holy Communion) were presented to the cooperating churches in 1950 and approved by them:[12]

Baptism of Infants

Baptism of Adults

---

11. Luther D. Reed, *The Lutheran Liturgy*, rev. ed. (Philadelphia: Muhlenberg Press, 1960), p. 206.

12. Ibid., pp. 217–18. The list given on these pages, however, is defective, because it omits Confirmation and the Dedication of a Church. See the *Bulletin of Reports: Seventeenth Biennial Convention of the United Lutheran Church in America* (Philadelphia: United Lutheran Publishing House, 1950), pp. 36–37. The booklet *Liturgical Texts* was presented as "part of the report."

Confirmation
Adult Baptism and Confirmation at the Same Service
Brief Order for Public Confession
Public Confession
Private Confession and Absolution
Burial of the Dead
Marriage
Visitation of the Sick
Communion of the Sick
Commendation of the Dying
Ordination
Setting Apart of a Deaconess
Laying the Cornerstone of a Church
Dedication of a Church
Blessing of a Cemetery
Installation of a Pastor
Sending Forth of a Missionary
Induction of a President
Installation of a Church Council
Opening of Synods
Closing of Synods
Induction of Office-Bearers

These services were published in a booklet *Liturgical Texts* (n.p.: United Lutheran Publication House, n.d.) and "approved by the Joint Commission on the Liturgy, Easter Week, 1950, and proposed for adoption by the co-operating Churches."

The *Service Book and Hymnal* (music edition) was published in 1958, but "only the most necessary and generally used services" were included.[13] These services were the Baptism of Infants, Confirmation, A Brief Order for Public Confession, Public Confession, and the Burial of the Dead. Luther Reed observed, "The importance of this body of material, now for the first time in common form and use, cannot be over-estimated, perhaps not even fully understood at the moment."[14]

In 1962 the *Occasional Services* was published. The book was divided into two sections. The first 153 pages were the twenty-four occasional services approved by the cooperating churches in 1950 plus Lay Baptism and the Blessing of a Dwelling. The Foreword observes regarding these twenty-six orders: "They are a part of the Common Liturgy. With The

---

13. Reed, *Lutheran Liturgy*, p. 218.
14. Ibid.

Service, the Offices, the Propers and Prayers they comprise the Service Book of the Church." These occasional services were all included in the text edition of the *Service Book and Hymnal* when it was finally published in November 1967 as the standard edition of the complete text of the Common Liturgy. The second part of *Occasional Services* (1962) begins with this Foreword (p. 156):

> The Additional Orders and Offices which follow have been prepared by the Commission on the Liturgy and Hymnal at the request of Churches and pastors. They are supplementary to The Occasional Services. It is hoped that they will meet the needs of liturgical and pastoral work.

The Foreword is dated Pentecost 1962. The description of this second category of services as "Additional Orders and Offices" is drawn from the *Occasional Services* of 1930, which also divided the book into two parts.

THE PRESENT BOOK

With the publication of the *Lutheran Book of Worship* in 1978, the cooperating churches recognized that the liturgy was not yet complete. In the following year a Task Force on Occasional Services was appointed representing the four cooperating churches:

The American Lutheran Church
    Vernon E. Anderson
    Durwood Buchheim
    Walter Huffman
    Fred Lee
    Ralph W. Quere
    Bruno Schlachtenhaufen
    Mons A. Teig
The Association of Evangelical Lutheran Churches
    Mark Bangert
The Evangelical Lutheran Church of Canada
    James Buenting
    Irvin Hohm
The Lutheran Church in America
    Herbert W. Chilstrom
    Janice C. Jenson
    Philip H. Pfatteicher
    Elizabeth A. Platz
    Virginia Trendel
    Ralph R. Van Loon

An observer from The Lutheran Church—Missouri Synod, which had participated in the preparation of the *Lutheran Book of Worship* (although not its adoption), was present for part of the first meeting of the Task Force.

The Inter-Lutheran Task Force met for the first time on 4–5 May 1979 in Chicago. Mark Bangert was elected chairperson; Janice Jenson, recorder. A nineteen-member drafting committee was appointed to assist in the preparation of the first draft of the various orders.[15] The drafting committee met with the task force in December 1979. In May 1980 a manuscript committee was selected by the task force to prepare the drafts for review by the whole task force. The drafts would then be submitted to the review committees of the churches. During 1981 the manuscript committee revised the rites according to the responses by the review committees. The whole task force met on 21–22 May 1981 in Minneapolis to make the decisions referred to it by the manuscript committee, to review the entire corpus, and to "submit the total corpus of manuscripts to the churches for testing and review." The manuscript committee was charged with the preparation of the final manuscript for approval by the churches following the testing period.

After extensive testing and theological, liturgical, and linguistic review of the proposed services, the final manuscript, revised on the basis of the review and testing, received general affirmation from the committees responsible for approval. Concurrent meetings for the purpose of final review and approval were held by the management committee of the Lutheran Church in America's Division for Parish Services and the *Occasional Services* review group of the American Lutheran Church. On 29 January 1982 agreement was reached to approve the publication of the proposed book of occasional services. Proposals for a small number of revisions were negotiated by telephone by representatives of the four participating church bodies. *Occasional Services* was published in September 1982.

As Lutherans were recovering and adapting their liturgical heritage during the nineteenth century, similar work was being done in the Episcopal Church. To supplement the *Book of Common Prayer*, a Book of Offices was proposed for publication to the General Convention of 1889. *Offices for Special Occasions* appeared in 1916. The General Convention

---

15. From the Association of Evangelical Lutheran Churches: The Revs. James L. Clark and Leonard R. Klein. From the American Lutheran Church: The Revs. R. David Berg, Fred Gaiser, Paul Gilbertson, Lowell H. Mays, Martha Myers, Byron Souder, Gary A. Wilkerson, and Donald M. Wisner. From the Evangelical Lutheran Church of Canada: The Rev. Oscar Sommerfeld. From the Lutheran Church in America: The Revs. Paul F. Bosch and John R. Cochran, Sister Sophie Damme, Dr. Charles A. Ferguson, The Revs. Louis G. Golder, Henry E. Horn, Frank C. Senn, and Charles D. Trexler.

of 1937 authorized a revised Book of Offices. It was prepared by the Liturgical Commission and published in 1940. Its use in a diocese was conditioned upon the approval of the bishop. It contained "Offices for the many specific purposes which occur in the work of Bishops and other Clergy: Offices for the Dedication of Buildings of one kind or another, or the Blessing of articles of Church furniture, and the like."[16] A second edition of the *Book of Offices* appeared in 1949, an "extensive revision in light of actual use." The third edition was compiled by the Standing Liturgical Commission and published in 1960. It included Benedictions for Certain Occasions in the Church Year and "forms for certain traditional ceremonials of the Church Year that have had a widespread revival throughout the Church in recent times." Many of these were incorporated into the 1979 *Book of Common Prayer*.

To complement and supplement the new *Book of Common Prayer*, the General Convention of 1976 directed the preparation of a new edition of the *Book of Offices*. The name of the book was changed to the *Book of Occasional Services*, in order "to express more specifically the contents of the book, and to avoid confusion with that section of the Prayer Book called the Daily Office."[17]

Behind the Lutheran *Occasional Services* and the Episcopal *Book of Occasional Services* and their predecessors lie the traditions embodied in the Roman Pontifical and Sacramentary.

In ancient times several liturgical books were related to the celebration of the Mass: the Antiphonary, containing the parts of the Daily Prayer and the Mass which were sung by the choir antiphonally; the Gradual, a chant sung between the Epistle and the Gospel; the Epistolary, containing the Epistles for the Mass; the Evangeliary, containing the Gospels; the Ordo, containing ceremonial directions; and the Sacramentary, containing the Canon of the Mass and the proper collects, prefaces, and other prayers needed by the celebrant (presiding minister). From the tenth century forward, as the custom of saying private masses spread, the several books were combined into one—the Missal—containing everything to be sung or said with ceremonial directions for the celebration of Mass throughout the year.

The sacramentaries developed as collections of texts used by the bishops and priests of Rome during the early period of the Roman liturgy. The Roman Ordinals (manuals for priests with the office to be recited in ac-

---

16. From the commission's report to the convention, quoted in the Preface to the 1940 book.
17. *The Book of Occasional Services* (New York: Church Hymnal Corp., 1979), p. 5.

cordance with variations throughout the year) developed at the same time during the mid-eighth century and contained directions for the celebrant and other ministers. They originally described the papal celebration of Mass, the sacraments, and the liturgical year. Eventually they were adapted for the use of bishops outside Rome.

Several pontificals were composed in Europe in the twelfth and thirteenth centuries. At the end of the thirteenth century a book was composed by the Bishop of Mende William Durand, which was noteworthy for its clear organization and its exclusion of all elements for presbyters (priests). It was a book for bishops, the first true pontifical. Its threefold division became standard: Part I — the blessing and consecration of persons (e.g., Confirmation, Ordination); Part II — the blessing and consecration of things (e.g., churches and altars); Part III — certain ecclesiastical offices and special functions (e.g., visitation of dioceses, excommunication, blessing of oils, councils).

Pope Innocent VIII commissioned an edition of the pontifical, published in 1485. It was twice revised in 1520 and 1561, and in 1596 the edition was made obligatory for the whole Latin church by Clement VIII. The work remained virtually the same with minor revisions until 1961. In that year a revision appeared which had been prepared by a commission appointed by Pius XII. It was a reform of Part II in which some rites were reduced and placed into more logical order, and from which other repetitious, obsolete, or seldom-used ceremonies were eliminated. The Second Vatican Council ordered a revision of Parts I and III. The English translation of Part I of the new Roman Pontifical appeared in 1978. Parts II (except for Dedication of a Church and an Altar) and III have not yet been translated.

The resources gathered and presented in *Occasional Services* (1982) are more than a collection of things for a pastor to say in certain situations. In the occasional services a distillation of the church's wisdom and experience is found, which has been achieved through centuries of ministering to people at important stages of their lives. The occasional services are rites of passage; they are the way the church takes its people through the world. *Occasional Services*, therefore, is not only a useful — indeed indispensable — handbook for liturgical actions, but also a textbook and guide in pastoral theology as well.

Joseph A. Jungmann in his book *Pastoral Liturgy* wrote, "For centuries, the liturgy, actively celebrated, has been the most important form of pastoral care."[18] So it remains today — not the liturgy as words to read

---

18. Joseph A. Jungmann, *Pastoral Liturgy* (New York: Herder & Herder, 1962), p. 380.

or as a form to be gotten through, but the liturgy actively celebrated with participation, compassion, and understanding by the whole assembly.[19] Thus *Occasional Services* supplements and guides the prayers of the pastor and the congregation as the work of ministry is carried forward. This commentary is intended to assist in the active celebration of the occasional services and thus in the pastoral care of God's people.

FOR FURTHER READING

Arnold, William V. *Introduction to Pastoral Care.* Philadelphia: Westminster Press, 1982.

Burkhart, John E. *Worship.* Philadelphia: Westminster Press, 1982.

Campbell, Alastair V. *Rediscovering Pastoral Care.* Philadelphia: Westminster Press, 1981.

Capps, Donald. *Biblical Approaches to Pastoral Counseling.* Philadelphia: Westminster Press, 1981.

_____. *Pastoral Care: A Thematic Approach.* Philadelphia: Westminster Press, 1979.

_____. *Pastoral Counseling and Preaching: A Quest for an Integrated Ministry.* Philadelphia: Westminster Press, 1980.

Cobb, John B., Jr. *Theology and Pastoral Care.* Philadelphia: Fortress Press, 1977.

Davies, J. G., ed. *The Westminster Dictionary of Worship.* Philadelphia: Westminster Press, 1979.

Eliade, Mircea. *The Sacred and the Profane.* New York: Harcourt, Brace & World, 1959.

Fischer, Balthasar. *Signs, Words, Gestures: Short Homilies on the Liturgy.* New York: Pueblo Publishing Co., 1981.

Hiltner, Seward. *Preface to Pastoral Care.* Nashville: Abingdon Press, 1958.

Hulme, William. *Pastoral Care and Counseling: Using the Unique Resources of the Christian Tradition.* Minneapolis: Augsburg Publishing House, 1981.

Jungmann, Josef A. *Pastoral Liturgy.* New York: Herder & Herder, 1962.

McNeill, John T. *A History of the Cure of Souls.* New York: Harper & Row, 1977.

Nouwen, Henri J. M. *Intimacy.* New York: Harper & Row, 1981.

Oates, Wayne. *Pastoral Counseling.* Philadelphia: Westminster Press, 1974.

Oglesby, William B. *Biblical Themes for Pastoral Care.* Nashville: Abingdon Press, 1980.

Peterson, Eugene H. *Five Smooth Stones for Pastoral Work.* Atlanta: John Knox Press, 1980.

Power, David N. *Liturgy and Human Passage.* New York: Seabury Press, 1979.

Tripp, D. H. "Worship and Pastoral Care." In *The Study of Liturgy,* edited by

---

19. Some hymns to assist the congregation to know itself as a caring community are: "Christ is Alive! Let Christians Sing" (363); "Lord of All Nations, Grant Me Grace" (419); "Lord, Whose Love in Humble Service" (423); "O God of Earth and Altar" (428); "O God, Empower Us" (422); "The Son of God, Our Christ" (434).

Cheslyn Jones, Geoffrey Wainwright, and Edward Yarnold, S. J., pp. 510–32. New York: Oxford University Press, 1978.

Turner, Victor. *The Ritual Process.* Chicago: Aldine Publishing Co., 1969.

Van Gennep, Arnold. *Rites of Passage.* Translated by Monika B. Vizedon and Gabrielle L. Caffee. Chicago: University of Chicago Press, 1960.

Westerhoff, John, and Gwen K. Neville. *Learning Through Liturgy.* New York: Seabury Press, 1978.

Westerhoff, John, and William Willimon. *Liturgy and Learning Through the Life Cycle.* New York: Seabury Press, 1980.

White, James F. *Introduction to Christian Worship.* Nashville: Abingdon Press, 1980.

Williams, Daniel Day. *The Minister and the Care of Souls.* New York: Harper & Row, 1961.

Willimon, William H. *Worship as Pastoral Care.* Nashville: Abingdon Press, 1979.

Winstone, Harold, ed. *Pastoral Liturgy.* London: William Collins & Co., 1975.

Worgul, George S. *From Magic to Metaphor: A Validation of Christian Sacraments.* New York: Paulist Press, 1980.

1
THE SERVICES
RELATED TO BAPTISM

INTRODUCTION

In Lutheran theology, baptism occupies a central place. Indeed, as Eugene Brand and Anita Stauffer observe, "No theological tradition is richer in baptismal emphasis than the Lutheran tradition."[1] The emphasis began with Luther himself, and a central document for understanding this emphasis is Luther's essay of 1519 "The Holy and Blessed Sacrament of Baptism." Baptism, Luther says, is an effective sign which accomplishes what it signifies and makes the baptized a different kind of person.

> Baptism is an external sign or token, which so separates us from . . . all not baptized that we are thereby known as a people of Christ, our Leader, under whose banner of the holy cross we continually fight against sin.[2]

> The significance of baptism is a blessed dying unto sin and a resurrection in the grace of God, so that the old man, conceived and born in sin, is there drowned, and a new man, born in grace, comes forth and rises.[3]

Baptism thus commits those who are washed by it to a lifelong struggle.

> This significance of baptism — the dying or drowning of sin — is not fulfilled completely in this life. Indeed this does not happen until man passes through bodily death and completely decays to dust. As we can plainly see, the sacrament or sign of baptism is quickly over. But the spiritual baptism, the drowning of sin, which it signifies, lasts as long as we live and is completed only in death. Then it is that a person is completely sunk in baptism, and that which baptism signifies comes to pass.
>
> Therefore this whole life is nothing else than a spiritual baptism which does not cease till death, and he who is baptized is condemned to die.[4]

---

1. Eugene L. Brand and S. Anita Stauffer, *By Water and the Spirit*, Pastor Guide (Philadelphia: Parish Life Press, 1979), p. 5.

2. *Luther's Works*, vol. 35, ed. E. Theodore Bachmann (Philadelphia: Fortress Press; St. Louis: Concordia Publishing House, 1960), p. 29; hereafter referred to as *LW*.

3. Ibid., p. 30.

4. Ibid.

> For in baptism we all make one and the same vow: to slay sin and to become holy through the work and grace of God, to whom we yield and offer ourselves, as clay to the potter [Jer. 18:4-6].[5]

> The spiritual birth and the increase of grace and righteousness — even though it begins in baptism, lasts until death, indeed, until the Last Day. Only then will that be finished which the lifting up out of baptism signifies.[6]

In this long struggle, the baptized have God's help and strength for support.

> This blessed sacrament of baptism helps you because in it God allies himself with you and becomes one with you in a gracious covenant of comfort.[7]

With such a promise of God's alliance with his people, the baptized gladly and confidently go forth to live their new life.

Baptism is nothing less than a dramatic presentation of the gospel and the Christian life. As Luther puts it in the Large Catechism: "Thus a Christian life is nothing else than a daily Baptism, once begun and ever continued."[8] It is death and resurrection, and it is the center of life and therefore the center of the church's liturgy. The lives of Christians are constantly related to the foundation upon which they are built, the sacrament by which we are adopted as children of God. "In Baptism, therefore, every Christian has enough to study and to practice all his life."[9]

Such a rich baptismal theology requires, for adequate expression, a rite of initiation which shows clearly and dramatically its centrality, importance, and richness and which enables its participants to see and to sense the central importance of Holy Baptism. Thus, "the service of Holy Baptism has several parts which together constitute the fullness of the sacrament of initiation into the community of faith: presentation, thanksgiving, renunciation and profession of faith, baptism with water, laying on of hands and signation, welcome into the congregation."[10]

The depth of this understanding of what it means to be brought into the Christian community suggests the appropriateness of remembering the event that changed one's relationship to God and to the world. Most

---

5. Ibid., p. 41.

6. Ibid., p. 31.

7. Ibid., p. 33.

8. *The Book of Concord*, trans. and ed. Theodore G. Tappert (Philadelphia: Fortress Press, 1959), p. 445.

9. Ibid., p. 441.

10. *Lutheran Book of Worship*, Ministers Ed. (Philadelphia: Fortress Press; Minneapolis: Augsburg Publishing House, 1978), p. 30; hereafter referred to as *LBW*, Min. Ed.

of all we remember and make use of our baptismal covenant by returning to it through daily repentance.

> Repentance, therefore, is nothing else than a return and approach to Baptism, to resume and practice what had earlier been begun but abandoned.

> Therefore let everybody regard his Baptism as the daily garment which he is to wear all the time. Every day he should be found in faith and amid its fruits, every day he should be suppressing the old man and growing up in the new. If we wish to be Christians, we must practice the work that makes us Christians.[11]

Observing the anniversary of one's baptism can help one remember that event and impel one to practice what it requires. The general and public remembrance of baptism is done at the Easter Vigil, which relates our baptismal dying and rising to Christ's death and resurrection. There we renew the vows we once made (or which were made by our sponsors) and bind ourselves anew to the faith and life of the church. A private remembrance may be made in the home on the actual date of one's entrance into the church by baptism.

In addition, of course, we remember that we have been baptized whenever we make the sign of the cross, confess our sins and receive absolution, celebrate evening and morning prayer, and struggle valiantly and confidently to live the life God expects of his children — drawing strength from the knowledge "I have been baptized."[12]

Christians are recovering the central importance of baptism, and the new baptismal rites reflect this renewed understanding and appreciation. The situation in which Christians find themselves is changing. No longer do they live in a Christian society and culture which supports their faith and practice. "Christendom" is gone, and instead Christians live in a pluralistic and secular culture in which many religions and no religion compete for attention and shape human life. To an ever-decreasing degree Christians may expect that nearly everyone will be born into a practicing Christian family, and more and more they will find that those who seek entrance into the church have no church connection at all, no knowledge of the faith, no baptism. In some ways the present situation has come to resemble the situation which faced the early church as it spread across the Roman Empire and beyond.

We can increasingly expect that candidates for baptism will be older people with little or no experience of Christianity. If the church is more

11. Large Catechism, *Book of Concord*, p. 446.
12. Ibid., p. 442.

than a society or club one joins because one finds like-minded people there; if baptism is the dramatic turning once-for-all from darkness to light and from death to life; if entrance into the church is a permanent and radical transition from the old life to the new, from estrangement to adoption as children of God which lasts through death forever; then surely baptism requires serious and earnest preparation of those old enough to understand what is about to happen to them. And it requires instruction for those who were baptized as infants concerning what happened to them in infancy while they were too young to understand what they were doing and what was being done to them.

This requires the most careful preparation of candidates, involving not only extensive instruction but encouragement by word and example of the new life to which followers of the Way (Acts 9:2) are committed. When people move from inquiry to a serious commitment to prepare for baptism, a formal public rite can help them and the congregation mark this step toward the Christian life. Such a public rite can, moreover, enhance the congregation's understanding of Christian initiation as a corporate action involving the entire community. So the ancient practice of the Enrollment of Candidates for Baptism is being revived in many places in many denominations.

For Further Reading

Brand, Eugene L. *Baptism: A Pastoral Perspective*. Minneapolis: Augsburg Publishing House, 1975.

Brand, Eugene L., and S. Anita Stauffer. *By Water and the Spirit*. Philadelphia: Parish Life Press, 1979.

Brockopp, Daniel C., Brian Helge, and David G. Truemper, eds. *Christian Initiation: Reborn of Water and the Spirit*. Valparaiso, Ind.: Institute of Liturgical Studies, 1981.

Couratin, A. H. *The Pelican Guide to Modern Theology*, vol. 2, 131–239. Harmondsworth, Middlesex: Penguin Books, 1969.

Dujarier, Michel. *A History of the Catechumenate: The First Six Centuries*. Translated by Edward J. Hassl. New York: William H. Sadlier, 1979.

———. *The Rites of Christian Initiation: Historical and Pastoral Reflections*. Translated by Kevin Hart. New York: William H. Sadlier, 1979.

Eliade, Mircea. *Myths, Dreams, and Mysteries: The Encounter between Contemporary Faiths and Archaic Realities*. New York and Evanston: Harper & Row, 1960.

———. *Rites and Symbols of Initiation: The Mysteries of Birth and Rebirth*. New York: Harper & Row, 1965. (First published as *Birth and Rebirth*. New York: Harper & Row, 1958.)

"Initiation." Part III in *The Study of Liturgy*, edited by Chesyln Jones, Geoffrey Wainwright, Edward Yarnold, pp. 79-146. New York: Oxford University Press, 1978.

Kavanagh, Aidan. *The Shape of Baptism: The Rite of Christian Initiation*. New York: Pueblo Publishing Co., 1978.

Kemp, Raymond B. *A Journey in Faith: An Experience of the Catechumenate*. New York: William H. Sadlier, 1979.

Made, Not Born: New Perspectives on Christian Initiation and the Catechumenate. Edited by the Murphy Center for Liturgical Research. Notre Dame, Ind.: University of Notre Dame Press, 1976.

Marty, Martin E. *Baptism*. Philadelphia: Fortress Press, 1962.

Meltzer, David, ed. *Birth: An Anthology of Ancient Texts, Songs, Prayers, Stories*. San Francisco: North Point Press, 1981.

Riley, Hugh M. *Christian Initiation: A Comparative Study of the Interpretation of the Baptismal Liturgy in the Mystagogical Writings of Cyril of Jerusalem, John Chrysostom, Theodore of Mopsuestia, and Ambrose of Milan*. Washington, D.C.: Catholic University of America Press, 1974.

Schlink, Edmund. *The Doctrine of Baptism*. Translated by Herbert J. A. Bouman. St. Louis: Concordia Publishing House, 1972.

Schmeiser, James, ed. *Initiation Theology: Ecumenical Insights*. Toronto: Anglican Book Centre, 1978.

Schmemann, Alexander. *Of Water and the Spirit*. Tuckahoe, N.Y.: St. Vladimir's Seminary Press, 1974.

Searle, Mark. *Christening: The Making of Christians*. Collegeville, Minn.: Liturgical Press, 1980.

Senn, Frank C. *The Pastor as Worship Leader*. Minneapolis: Augsburg Publishing House, 1977. Esp. chapter 3, "Initiation into Worship."

Stookey, Laurence H. *Baptism: Christ's Act in the Church*. Nashville: Abingdon Press, 1982.

Wagner, Johannes, ed. *Adult Baptism and the Catechumenate*. Concilium, vol. 22. New York: Paulist Press, 1967.

Wainwright, Geoffrey. *Christian Initiation*. London: Lutterworth Press, 1969.

_____. "The Rites and Ceremonies of Christian Initiation: Developments in the Past." *Studia Liturgica* 10 (1974): 2-24.

Whitaker, E. C. *The Baptismal Liturgy: An Introduction to Baptism in the Western Church*. London: SPCK, 1965.

_____. *Documents of the Baptismal Liturgy*. 2d ed. London: SPCK, 1970.

Willimon, William H. *Remember Who You Are: Baptism, A Model for Christian Life*. Nashville: Upper Room, 1980.

Worship 56: 4 (July 1982): 309-43. Responses to the Roman Catholic Rite of Christian Initiation of Adults after ten years of its use.

Yarnold, E. J. *The Awe-Inspiring Rites of Initiation*. Westminster, Md.: St. Paul Publications, 1972.

ENROLLMENT OF CANDIDATES
FOR BAPTISM
(*Occasional Services*, pp. 13-15)

Parallel Rites

Roman Catholic   Rite of the Catechumenate Received in Stages, *The Rites*, pp. 13-15, 40-93.[13]

Episcopal   Preparation of Adults for Holy Baptism, *Book of Occasional Services*, pp. 112-25.[14]

Orthodox   The Prayers at the Reception of Catechumens, *Service Book*, pp. 271-75.[15]
Prayer at the Signing of a Child When It Receives a Name on the Eighth Day After Its Birth, *An Orthodox Prayer Book,* pp. 36-37.
Prayers at the Making of a Catechumen, *An Orthodox Prayer Book*, pp. 46-54.[16]

Purpose

This service is for enrolling those who will be given instruction leading to Holy Baptism. It is an evidence of serious intent and a commitment to a new way of living. Pastors and congregations need to understand clearly the distinction between inquirers' classes and this prebaptismal instruction.

This service, therefore, is for neither infants nor for catechumens who have been baptized and who are beginning instruction leading to Affirmation of Baptism (Confirmation).

Characteristics

This service is new to Lutherans, as well as to those of other traditions, and does not reflect the general practice of the present. This recovery of the ancient progressive entrance into the Christian community is designed to teach and to lead congregations toward a more responsible and

13. *The Rites of the Catholic Church as Revised by Decree of the Second Vatican Ecumenical Council and Published by Authority of Pope Paul VI* (New York: Pueblo Publishing Co., 1976); hereafter cited as *The Rites*.

14. *The Book of Occasional Services* (New York: Church Hymnal Corp., 1979).

15. Isabel Florence Hapgood, *Service Book of the Holy Orthodox-Catholic Apostolic Church*, rev. ed. (Englewood, N.J.: Antiochian Orthodox Christian Archdiocese, 1975).

16. *An Orthodox Prayer Book*, ed. N. M. Vaporis (Brookline, Mass.: Holy Cross Orthodox Press, 1977).

useful baptismal practice. It is to meet a new, yet ancient, situation in which more and more unbaptized adults seek membership in the Christian community. By its movement and progress it suggests the spiritual journey of those who inquire into the Christian faith and who mature in it, moving forward as through a series of gates, up a series of steps.

The service provided here and the procedure suggested are somewhat more simple than those of the Roman Catholic and Episcopal churches. The intention is to make the introduction of a new practice and a new rite as straightforward and as understandable as possible.

Background

In popular Lutheran use "catechumen" has been applied to those who have been baptized and who are preparing for Affirmation of Baptism (Confirmation). In a more ancient sense, however, "catechumen" is the name given to those who are preparing for baptism.

Baptized Christians preparing to make affirmation of their baptism (such as members of confirmation classes, those being received into Lutheran churches from other denominations, and those who for a time had abandoned the practice of the Christian faith) are not thus considered catechumens in this older and more ecumenical sense, because baptism establishes an indissoluble relationship: "Child of God, you have been sealed by the Holy Spirit and marked with the cross of Christ forever."[17]

The systematic instruction and formation of its catechumens is a solemn responsibility of the Christian community. Traditionally in Lutheranism the preparation of confirmands and catechumens is a responsibility of the pastor, but lay people often assist in the instruction and formation.

The catechumenate leading to baptism is a period of training and instruction in Christian understandings of God, human relationships, and the meaning and purpose of life. The catechumenate culminates in the reception of baptism, the sacrament of Christian initiation. The period of training and instruction is marked by certain stages as one is brought progressively nearer to the Christian community.[18]

The precatechumenal period is marked by inquirers' classes for those who have been attracted to the Christian community. It is a time for the individuals to learn the basic outlines of the Christian life and faith and to examine and test their motives so that they may freely commit them-

---

17. *LBW*, Min. Ed., p. 311. See also *L W*, vol. 35, p. 31; and the Large Catechism, *Book of Concord*, p. 446, par. 77.

18. Much of this information is dependent upon "Concerning the Catechumenate," *Book of Occasional Services*, pp. 112-13.

selves to pursue a disciplined exploration of the implications of Christian living.

When inquirers are ready to make this commitment, it is appropriate for them to do so in a public liturgical act at the chief Sunday service. Their regular association with the worshiping community continues, and they begin more earnestly to live their life in accordance with the gospel, including service to the poor and neglected. They receive encouragement and instruction in the life of prayer and learn the history of salvation as revealed in the Holy Scriptures.

Each candidate is given a sponsor who normally accompanies the catechumen through the candidacy and serves as sponsor at baptism.

Admission to the catechumenate may be an appropriate time to choose the name by which one desires to be known in the Christian community. This may be one's given name, a new name legally changed, or an additional name of Christian significance. This ancient tradition has its roots in the biblical practice by which a change in status is signified by a change in name.

From the time of admission, a catechumen has traditionally been regarded as part of the Christian community. For example, a person who dies during the catechumenate receives a Christian burial.

The enrollment of candidates for baptism takes place several weeks before one of the stated days for baptism. When baptism is administered at Easter, enrollment normally takes place at the beginning of Lent; when baptisms are planned for the Baptism of Our Lord, the enrollment takes place at the beginning of Advent. (The old association of Lent with preparation for baptism is reflected in the three-year cycle of lessons for Lent, many of which have baptismal themes.)

In addition to the public liturgical act, the catechumenate has traditionally involved fasting and should include the private disciplines of examination of conscience and prayer. It also involves the purification of one's motives so that one will be spiritually and emotionally ready for baptism. In accordance with ancient custom, it is desirable that the sponsors support the candidates by joining them in prayer (and fasting).

The process is not finished with the administration of baptism. In the early church the period of postbaptismal instruction was a time for *mystagogia*, that is, entrance into the mysteries of the faith. This period is devoted to such learning and activities as will assist the newly baptized to experience the fullness of the corporate life of the church and to gain a deeper understanding of the meaning of the sacraments. In the case of those baptized at the Easter Vigil, the period extended through the fifty days of Easter.

In the modern, as well as ancient, Roman Catholic practice, the preparation begins when the candidate hears the first preaching of the gospel, makes inquiry, and receives initial instruction by the church.

The first stage of initiation is then marked by the Rite of Becoming Catechumens. This begins the catechumenate, which may last for years. When faith has grown and the catechumenate is nearly complete, the candidate is admitted to a more profound preparation for the sacraments. This second stage is marked by the Rite of Election or Enrollment of Names, usually done at the beginning of Lent. It is a period of purification and illumination or enlightenment.

During Lent (or at other times) the ancient practice of the scrutinies is being revived as a rite of purification and strengthening.[19] On the Third Sunday in Lent (the theme of the first Sunday is Jesus' Temptation; the theme of the second is Jesus' Transfiguration) the following propers are used:[20]

Prayer of the Day

Lord,
you call these chosen ones
to the glory of a new birth in Christ, the second Adam.
Help them to grow in wisdom and love
as they prepare to profess their faith in you.
Grant this through our Lord Jesus Christ . . .

Reading 1: Exod. 17:3-7
Resp. Ps.: Ps. 95:1-2, 6-7, 8-9
Reading 2: Rom. 5:1-2, 5-8
Verse: John 4:42; 15
Gospel: John 4:5-42 (or 4:5-15, 19b-26, 39a, 40-42)

After the sermon, the candidates (now called "the elect") and sponsors come before the presiding minister, who invites the congregation to pray for the candidates, who bow or kneel. The prayers are first in silence, then a series of petitions is said aloud. A prayer of exorcism referring to the Samaritan woman (see the Gospel for the day) is said by the presiding minister so that the elect may acknowledge their sin. A psalm may be sung, and the candidates are dismissed. After the elect depart, the Holy Communion is celebrated.

During the week after the first scrutiny (if it has not been done earlier in

---

19. Frank C. Senn prepared a modern adaptation of the Scrutiny of the Elect from the Gelasian Sacramentary for the Worship Supplement of *The Circle*, published by the Lutheran Council in the U.S.A. Division of Campus Ministry, February 1977.

20. *The Rites*, p. 161.

the catechumenate) at a weekday Mass after the sermon, the Apostles' Creed is given to the elect to memorize in preparation for the day of their baptism. The Nicene Creed may also be given to them. Thus the church entrusts the elect with a summary of the faith.

On the Fourth Sunday in Lent the second scrutiny takes place with these propers:[21]

Prayer of the Day

> Almighty and eternal God,
> may your Church increase in true joy.
> May these candidates for baptism
> and all the family of man
> be reborn into the life of your kingdom.
> We ask this through our Lord Jesus Christ . . .

> *Reading 1:*   1 Sam. 16:1b, 6-7, 10-13a
> *Resp. Ps.:*   Psalm 23
> *Reading 2:*   Eph. 5:8-14
> *Verse:*   John 8:12b
> *Gospel:*   John 9:1-41 (or 9:1, 6-9, 13-17, 34-38)

Again, as before, after the sermon the elect and sponsors come before the presiding minister for prayer and exorcism, making reference to the man born blind (see the Gospel reading). After the elect depart, the Holy Communion continues.

On the Fifth Sunday in Lent the third scrutiny takes place with these propers:[22]

Prayer of the Day

> Lord,
> enlighten your chosen ones with the word of life.
> Give them a new birth
> in the waters of baptism
> and make them living members of the Church.
> Grant this through our Lord Jesus Christ . . .

> *Reading 1:*   Ezek. 37:12-14
> *Resp. Ps.:*   Psalm 130
> *Reading 2:*   Rom. 8:8-11

---

21. Ibid., p. 164.
22. Ibid., p. 167.

Verse: John 11:25a, 26
Gospel: John 11:1–45

After the sermon, silent prayer and then spoken prayer are offered for the elect. A prayer of exorcism is said, making reference to the Gospel account of the raising of Lazarus. The elect are dismissed and the Holy Communion continues.

During the week after the third scrutiny, if it has not been done earlier in the catechumenate, at a weekday Mass (after the Gospel) the Lord's Prayer is given to the elect and is explained in the sermon. Since ancient times this prayer has belonged to those who in baptism have received the Spirit of adoption as children of the heavenly Father.

The modern liturgy of the Roman Catholic church also provides a series of optional preparatory actions for use on Holy Saturday by the elect in preparation for their baptism at the Easter Vigil: the recitation of the Creed, the symbolic opening of the ears and mouth ("the rite of Ephphetha"), the choosing of a Christian name, anointing with the oil of catechumens.

Major Moments of Initiation

ROMAN CATHOLIC *The Rites,* pp. 19–106	EPISCOPAL *Book of Occasional Services,* pp. 112–30	LUTHERAN *Occasional Services* (1982), pp. 13–15
Precatechumenate	Inquirer's class	Inquirer's class
First Stage: Rite of Becoming Catechumens	Admission of Catechumens	
The Catechumenate	Prayers during the Catechumenate	
Second Stage: Rite of Election or Enrollment of Names (at beginning of Lent)	Enrollment of Candidates for Baptism (at beginning of Lent or Advent)	Enrollment of Candidates for Baptism
Scrutinies and Presentation	Prayers during candidacy	Instruction
Preparatory rites	Vigil for the Eve of Baptism	
Holy Baptism	Holy Baptism	Holy Baptism
Postbaptismal Mystagogia (Fifty days of Easter)	Incorporation	Incorporation

Detailed Comparison of Roman Catholic and Episcopal Rites of Becoming a Catechumen

ROMAN CATHOLIC	EPISCOPAL
Rite of Becoming Catechumens	Admission of Catechumens
The Rites	*Book of Occasional Services*
pp. 40–61	pp. 115–17

I. Introductory rite
(outside the church)

Greeting and first instruction

Opening dialogue
What is your name? *N.*
What do you ask . . . ? Faith.
What does faith offer?   What do you seek? Life in
Eternal life.   Christ.

First promise   Promises
Address*   by candidate
Are you ready to enter on this   acceptance of New Testament
path?   summary of the law
regular attendance
openness to Word of God and
the Lord Jesus
Sponsors: ready to help?   by sponsors
support and help

Exorcism† (and renunciation of
non-Christian worship)
Sponsors: testimony to resolve
Thanksgiving for answering the   Blessing: power to Holy Spirit to
call to faith   persevere

---

*Text of the first promise:

God enlightens every man who comes into the world. Through the world he has created, he makes known the unseen wonders of his love so that every man may learn to give thanks to his Creator.

You have followed his light. Now the way of the Gospel opens before you, inviting you to make a new beginning by acknowledging the living God who speaks his words of truth to men. You are called to walk by the light of Christ and to trust in his wisdom. He asks you to submit yourself to him more and more and to believe in him with all your heart. This is the way of faith on which Christ will lovingly guide you to eternal life. Are you ready to enter on this path today under the leadership of Christ? (*The Rites*, p. 42; "optional formulas more suitable for other circumstances" are given on pp. 151–52)

†Text of the exorcism:

Breathe your Spirit, Lord, and drive out the spirits of evil: command them to depart, for your kingdom is drawing near. (*The Rites*, p. 43)

Signing of forehead with cross
    by celebrant
    (and sponsors)
N., receive this cross on your
    forehead:
by this sign of his love
    (*or:* of his triumph)
Christ will be your strength.
Learn now to know and follow
    him.
    (signing of senses: ears, eyes,
    lips, breast, shoulders)
Prayer for catechumens

(Giving the new name)

Entering into the church

II. Celebration of the Word of God

Readings

Sermon

(Presentation of the Gospels to
    the candidates)

Prayer for the catechumens

Dismissal of the catechumens

III. Celebration of Holy Communion
    beginning with Prayers of
    Intercession

Signing of forehead by
    celebrant and sponsors

N., receive the sign of the Cross
on your forehead and in your
heart, in the Name of the
Father, and of the Son,
and of the Holy Spirit.

(Creed and)

Prayers of the people

The Catechumenate and Its Rites
  Instruction and worship
  Minor exorcisms
    to show battle between
      flesh and spirit
    to underscore self-denial
  Blessing the catechumens
    to show the love of God
    to show the care of the
      church
  Rites between the stages of the
  catechumenate
    anointing with oil of
      catechumens
Election or Enrollment of Names

During the Catechumenate
Instruction
At conclusion of each session:
  silent prayer
  a spoken prayer
  laying on of a hand
    in silence

Enrollment of Candidates for
Baptism

THE SERVICES RELATED TO BAPTISM

Survey of the Service

The first note under "The Service in Detail" departs from a general principle of the *Lutheran Book of Worship* and permits the use of this rite with the Service of the Word. The *LBW* principle is to include occasional services only within the Holy Communion, as the second note at the beginning of this service suggests.

Following the Creed in the Holy Communion (or following the opening hymn of the Service of the Word), each candidate is brought forward and is presented by a sponsor (or sponsors) to the minister. The wording of the presentation makes clear the intention of the action and of the service.

The minister's brief address to the candidates acknowledges the fundamental work of the Holy Spirit who calls, gathers, enlightens, and sanctifies each of us as he calls, gathers, enlightens, and sanctifies the whole Christian church on earth, as Luther teaches in his explanation of the third article of the creed.[23]

The Spirit calls each candidate to walk in the light of Christ, to live as he has shown us, and to trust in the wisdom of God. Each candidate is called to commit himself or herself to "the pioneer and perfecter of our faith" (Heb. 12:2), Jesus Christ, who is Holy Wisdom, whose teaching the candidate gradually learns. (See also Hymn 446 "Whatever God Ordains Is Right.") The address at least indirectly alludes to what has been accomplished by the Spirit so far: some contact with the gospel and the community, a positive response to the inquirers' class, the establishment of a relationship with a sponsor, and the desire for baptism.

The minister next addresses the sponsors who have presented the candidates and elicits from them the commitment to support the candidates by prayer and example, by word and deed, encouraging their growth in the knowledge and love of God (see Col. 1:10; 2 Pet. 1:2). This last phrase in the address, however, is more exactly from the blessing in The Holy Eucharist: Rite One in the *Book of Common Prayer*: "The peace of God, which passeth all understanding, keep your hearts and minds in the knowledge and love of God, and of his Son Jesus Christ our Lord."

Third, the minister addresses the congregation and asks them to support the nurture of the candidates, reminding the congregation of the obligation to build up one another (Eph. 4:12–16).

The presiding minister's prayer ⟨429⟩ appropriately asks two gifts: peace (the peace of God which passes all understanding—see the fourth stanza of Hymn 449—which echoes the earlier reference in the address to

---

23. Small Catechism, *Book of Concord*, p. 345. See also 1 Cor. 12:3.

the sponsors to "the knowledge and love of God") and steadfastness in faith. The prayer is a new composition.

An additional prayer—⟨430⟩ or ⟨431⟩—may be said. Both of the prayers which are provided are new compositions and refer to the time of candidacy, the catechumenate, as a period of growth, purification, and struggle. See the Ash Wednesday exhortation to the congregation which sounds the same themes.[24]

The candidates and their sponsors return to their places, and the service continues with the prayers (with the Old Testament canticle if it is the Service of the Word).

The final rubric (p. 14, no. 11) is there not only to make absolutely clear that only the baptized have access to the Holy Communion, but also to indicate that the Enrollment of Candidates for Baptism is part of a continuing ministry of the church leading to even fuller incorporation into its life. Candidates for baptism, catechumens in that older sense of the term, do not yet participate in the Lord's Supper. The desire to seek baptism is an important step, but it is not the radical change which Holy Baptism effects. There is no parallel here with the practice of admitting confirmands to Holy Communion before they have been confirmed. Confirmation adds nothing to what has already been done in baptism, and Holy Communion is "the birthright of the baptized."[25]

BAPTISM IN AN EMERGENCY
(*Occasional Services,* pp. 16–22)

Parallel Rites

Roman Catholic   Simple Rite of Adult Initiation (by a priest or deacon), *The Rites,* pp. 107–16.

Short Rite of Adult Initiation in Proximate Danger of Death (especially for use by catechists and laypersons), *The Rites,* pp. 118–26.

Rite of Baptism for Children Administered by a Catechist When No Priest or Deacon Is Available, *The Rites,* pp. 238–49.

Rite of Baptism for Children in Danger of Death When No Priest or Deacon Is Available, *The Rites,* pp. 193, 250–61.

---

24. *LBW,* Min. Ed., p. 129.
25. Ibid., p. 31.

Episcopal	Emergency Baptism, *Book of Common Prayer*, pp. 313–14.
Lutheran	Order for Lay Baptism, *Occasional Services* (1962), pp. 10–11.
	Lay Baptism; Confirmation of Lay Baptism, *Common Service Book* (text ed.), pp. 393–94.
	A Short Form for Holy Baptism in Cases of Necessity, *Lutheran Hymnal*, p. 858.

Purpose

This form is for the baptism of one in danger of death. The candidate is a child born into a Christian family or an older person who has expressed a clear desire for baptism. Indiscriminate baptism can cause mischief in the church and in society, and the pastor must be aware of this danger. While a spirit of legalism is inappropriate in making decisions about emergency baptisms, neither should this sacrament be celebrated indiscriminately for any person near death.

Characteristics

Theological and pastoral justification for such a rite is a debated issue among Lutherans and others. For an argument against emergency baptism see Eugene L. Brand, *Baptism: A Pastoral Perspective* (Minneapolis: Augsburg Publishing House, 1975), pp. 43–44. The rite is provided in *Occasional Services* (1982) out of pastoral concern for the dying and for their families. It is not included to encourage the baptism of anyone near death, regardless of the person's condition or desires. The inclusion of Baptism in an Emergency is not intended to further or support a mechanistic view of baptism, let alone a magical understanding of the sacrament.

In those cases where such a baptism seems indicated, the rite is simple. The full baptismal rite of the *LBW* is stripped to its essential core: the washing with water in the threefold name. To this essential action is added the Lord's Prayer and, if possible or desired, other prayers.

If the person survives, the newly baptized person is brought to the church and the remainder of the baptismal service is performed. This is called in *Occasional Services* (1982) "Public Recognition of Baptism," but it is much more than a formal acknowledgment and ratification of what was done privately, perhaps by a layperson. It is in fact the completion of the baptismal liturgy, a recognition that "the service of Holy Baptism has several parts which together constitute the fullness of the sacrament of initiation into the community of faith: presentation, thanksgiving, renunciation and profession of faith, baptism with water, laying on of hands and signation, welcome into the congregation.''[26] All that rich complex of actions is important to suggest the manifold dimensions of the entrance into the Christian community, and one who was near death should not be deprived of these dimensions.

The leadership of Baptism in an Emergency may be "any baptized person"; a pastor is not required. Because *Occasional Services* is primarily for pastors and others who regularly share the leadership of worship, ways need to be found to inform the congregation of this possibility and to teach them what to do should a baptism be necessary.

Background

Emergency baptism by clergy or by laity has long been a practice of the Christian church. But with the renewal of interest in the theology of baptism, a deeper understanding of the theology of the sacraments and of the liturgy, and a changed social setting, serious questions have been raised about its legitimacy. Generally speaking, the form for Baptism in an Emergency is preserved not out of theological necessity but out of pastoral concern. Such a practice may be contrary to the best theological insight but may nonetheless be required by a concern for the welfare of the living who request baptism for a dying loved one.

In any case a mechanistic or magical understanding of baptism ought to be rejected, an understanding which suggests that the sacrament is effective and meaningful in whoever is baptized under whatever circumstances. Rather, the purpose of baptism is to begin and confirm a relationship.

Survey of the Service

Prayer ⟨432⟩ is an adaptation of a model provided in the 1979 *Book of Common Prayer* (p. 314) for a prayer following Emergency Baptism. When baptism is administered by a layperson, the baptism is to be reported to the pastor of the congregation so that it may be properly recorded in the register of the congregation and so that the person baptized can be included in the congregation's prayers.

If the baptized person survives, instruction of the person (or the parents and sponsors of an infant) is necessary, leading to the completion of the baptismal initiation in the public act. As the Notes on the Liturgy in the Ministers Edition of the *LBW* (p. 30) observe:

---

26. Ibid., p. 30.

The service of Holy Baptism has several parts which together constitute the fullness of the sacrament of initiation into the community of faith: presentation, thanksgiving, renunciation and profession of faith, baptism with water, laying on of hands and signation, welcome into the congregation.

One who is baptized under emergency conditions and who survives deserves the fullness of the baptismal action.

ANNIVERSARY OF A BAPTISM
(*Occasional Services*, pp. 23–26)

Parallel Rites

Episcopal   Vigil for the Eve of the Baptism of Our Lord, *Book of Occasional Services*, pp. 49–50.

Vigil for the Eve of the Baptism of Our Lord, *Book of Occasional Services*, pp. 104–5.

Purpose

This service is for use in a home rather than in the church. It is not intended that the pastor be invited to lead this service. The service is informal, and the leader is not strictly bound to the language provided. All that the rubrics require is the lighting of the baptismal candle, prayers, and the blessing.

Public remembrance of baptism and renewal of the baptismal vows are done at the Easter Vigil (*LBW*, Min. Ed., p. 152).

Background

Congregations often give a candle to the baptized person, sometimes with the suggestion that it be lighted on the anniversary of the baptism. This rite gives guidance for doing that. The rite is in relatively simple language because it will often be used with children.

The candle that is a central symbol of this rite is the candle given to the person at the time of baptism (*LBW*, Min. Ed., p. 311, no. 16). The candle is related also to the paschal candle, the great candle which in the Easter Vigil through the Day of Pentecost symbolizes the risen Lord present among his people, and which afterward is often placed by the font as a sign of the relationship between Christ's dying and rising and the death and resurrection that each of his people experience in Holy Baptism.

Survey of the Service

Hymn singing at home may be unfamiliar to many families, but it has long been a tradition among Lutherans and may be worth reviving in places where it has fallen into disuse.

The sign of the cross and the use of the name of the triune God here as elsewhere in the liturgy recall baptism. (See the opening of the Brief Order for Confession and Forgiveness, *LBW*, Min. Ed., p. 195). Its use is optional, for not everyone may find this action comfortable.

The candle is lighted; words may accompany the action, although they are not necessary. The verse and response (no. 5) are from the Service of Light at the beginning of Evening Prayer (*LBW*, Min. Ed., p. 58; see John 1:4); it is appropriate when the family knows the response to the verse or has a text of the rite from which to read. The alternate text is from the Sermon on the Mount (Matt. 5:16) and emphasizes the obligations of witness which are placed upon the baptized. It is used at the giving of the candle in Holy Baptism (*LBW*, Min. Ed., p. 311).

A lesson from the Bible may be read. Although the first reading provided (Rom. 6:3-4) is a central text, it may be a difficult lesson, especially for children, and should not be understood as the preferred reading. Different members of the family may read several texts.

The suggested introduction to the discussion of baptism (p. 25, no. 6) is in deliberately simple language, for the rite is primarily for children. The discussion of baptism may be a time for storytelling and may include recollections of one's baptism and reflections on its meaning. The Small Catechism is an excellent basis for such discussion, especially for children. For older people, the Large Catechism (Fourth Part: Baptism) or Luther's "The Holy and Blessed Sacrament of Baptism" (*LW*, vol. 35, pp. 23-43) are very good. These will not be easily accessible to most families, and considerate pastors will provide copies of them or selections from them to the baptized and their families, perhaps as a gift on the anniversary of the baptism.

The prayer provided ⟨434⟩ is an adaptation of the prayer in Affirmation of Baptism (*LBW*, Min. Ed., p. 327).

The blessing is from the Service of the Word. The alternate blessing is from Morning Prayer (*LBW*, Min. Ed., pp. 52, 57).

The greeting which may conclude the service, although resembling the peace, is a less formal, familial greeting in words and actions. The peace is used primarily with the Eucharist and secondarily with rites of reconciliation which restore a broken relationship. (See Individual Confession and Forgiveness, *LBW*, Min. Ed., p. 323.) Care must be taken that the peace not degenerate into a mere sentimental gesture and debase the eucharistic connection.

Because most members of the congregation will not usually have access to *Occasional Services*, the pastor will need to make this service available to them. Note the permission granted on page 4 of *Occasional Services:*

Permission to reproduce an individual order from this book for a specific service is hereby granted to any congregation, national unit, district, synod, agency, or institution affiliated with one of the copyright holders, provided that no part of such reproduction is sold and provided that the following credit is used: Reprinted from *Occasional Services*, copyright 1982, by permission.

Leaflets or folders may be prepared for distribution to the congregation, or to parents and to sponsors. The form may be reproduced in congregational papers and newsletters. On the anniversary of a child's baptism, the pastor could send a letter to the parents and sponsors and enclose a copy of the order for the Anniversary of a Baptism to encourage its observance.

An alternate means for celebrating baptismal anniversaries is the Paschal Blessing from Morning Prayer (*LBW*, Min. Ed., pp. 53–57). It is a detachable section of Morning Prayer, which can stand alone. "The Paschal Blessing is an appropriate remembrance of Baptism. As such it may be used separately, particularly on baptismal anniversaries" (*LBW*, Min. Ed., p. 16, no. 16). When it is so used, the focus is not a candle — although that may be lighted also — but a bowl of water to recall the baptismal washing. The Paschal Blessing is therefore especially appropriate when a baptismal candle has not been given to the baptized.

The Episcopal Church provides in the *Book of Occasional Services* (pp. 49–50) a Vigil for the Eve of the Baptism of Our Lord. It is a reflection of the Easter Vigil and provides a setting for baptism, confirmation, or the renewal of baptismal vows. The vigil begins with the Service of Light *(Book of Common Prayer*, p. 109; the parallel in the *LBW*, Min. Ed., pp. 58–60), substituting if desired "Glory to God in the highest" for "O gracious light" ("Joyous light of glory" is the translation in the *LBW*). The salutation and prayer of the day are said, followed by three or more lessons, each followed by silence and a psalm, canticle, or hymn. The lessons provided are:

The Flood	Gen. (7:1–5, 11–18); 8:6–18; 9:8–13
	Ps. 25:3–9 or Psalm 46
The Lord Who Makes	Isa. 43:15–19
a Way in the Sea	Psalm 114
Anointing of Aaron	Lev. 8:1–12
	Psalm 23 or 133
Anointing of David	1 Sam. 16:1–13
	Ps. 2:1–8 or Ps. 110:1–5
Naaman	2 Kings 5:1–14
	Ps. 51:8–13

Salvation for All	Isa. 55:1–11 Canticle 9: The First Song of Isaiah (Isa. 12:2–6)
A New Heart	Ezek. 36:24–28 Psalm 42
The Spirit of the Lord	Isa. 61:1–9
or	
Behold My Servant	Isa. 42:1–9 (First Lesson for the Baptism of Our Lord) Ps. 89:20–29
God's Patience	1 Pet. 3:15b–22
or	
God Anointed Jesus	Acts 10:34–38 (Second Lesson for the Baptism of Our Lord)

Then the Gospel is read, either the Gospel for the Baptism of Our Lord according to the appropriate year (A, B, C) or Matt. 28:1–10, 16–20. The sermon is preached, and after it the Renewal of Baptismal Vows (*Book of Common Prayer*, pp. 292–94) follows. The questions in the renewal go beyond those in the *LBW*, which involve a renunciation of evil and a profession of the three articles of the creed, and treat the practice of the Christian life as well. The Renewal of Vows concludes with a blessing:

> May almighty God, the Father of our Lord Jesus Christ, who has given us a new birth by water and the Holy Spirit, and bestowed upon us the forgiveness of sins, keep us in eternal life by his grace, in Christ Jesus our Lord. *Amen.*

The *Book of Occasional Services* (pp. 104–5) also makes similar provision for a baptismal vigil for the eve of All Saints' Day or the Sunday after All Saints' Day. The order is the same as that for the Vigil for the Eve of the Baptism of Our Lord: the Service of Light with *Gloria in excelsis* instead of *phos hilaron* if desired, and the salutation and prayer of the day. Three or more lessons are read:

The Call of Abraham	Gen. 12:1–8 Psalm 113
Daniel in the Lion's Den	Dan. 6:(1–15), 16–23 Canticle 2 (Song of the Three Young Men: *Benedictus es, Domine*)

Death of Mattathias	1 Macc. 2:49–64 Psalm 1
Martyrdom of the Seven Brothers	2 Macc. 6:1–2; 7:1–23 Psalm 111
Eulogy of the Ancestors	Ecclus. 44:1–10, 13–14 (First Lesson for All Saints) Psalm 116
Cloud of Witnesses	Heb. 11:32(33–38), 39–12:2 Psalm 149 (Psalm for All Saints)
The Reward of the Saints	Rev. 7:2–4, 9–17 (Second Lesson for All Saints)

The Gospel follows (Matt. 5:1–12—the Gospel for All Saints—or Matt. 11:27–30 or Matt. 28:1–10, 16–20). The Renewal of Baptismal Vows (or baptism or confirmation) follows the sermon.

These resources provided by The Episcopal Church may offer helpful suggestions also to Lutherans who seek to remember their baptism.

2

THE SERVICES RELATED TO MARRIAGE

INTRODUCTION

Marriage is an institution in crisis in modern society. Divorce is frequent and relatively easy; those entering marriage seldom see it as a lifelong commitment. At the same time, those who enter marriage often do so with unrealistic expectations of what married life will and should be like.

The address in the marriage service in the *Lutheran Book of Worship* is an attempt to outline a biblical and realistic view of marriage: God's intention of joy for his people since creation, the human fall into sin which distorts all relationships, the continuing presence and support of the Creator who is always at work renewing what he has made.

Rites to support those who enter marriage are more important than ever, and so too are resources to assist pastors in ministering responsibly to those who encounter trouble in marriage. *Occasional Services* (1982) therefore provides not only a form for the Blessing of a Civil Marriage, which one would perhaps expect to find in the collection, since it was in the preceding book of 1962, but the 1982 book also provides for the anniversary of marriage, for the ministry to those undergoing separation or divorce, and for the affirmation of marriage vows after a time of strain or separation.

For Further Reading

Achtemeier, Elizabeth. *The Committed Marriage.* Philadelphia: Westminster Press, 1982.

Arnold, William V., et al. *Divorce: Prevention or Survival.* Philadelphia: Westminster Press, 1982.

Atkinson, David. *To Have and To Hold: The Marriage Covenant and the Discipline of Divorce.* Grand Rapids: Wm. B. Eerdmans, 1982.

Baab, Otto J. "Divorce," "Marriage." *The Interpreter's Dictionary of the Bible.* New York and Nashville: Abingdon Press, 1952.

Barth, Karl. *On Marriage.* Philadelphia: Fortress Press, 1968.

Bassett, William, and Peter Huizing. *The Future of Christian Marriage.* Concilium, vol. 87. New York: Seabury Press, 1976.

Batey, Richard A. *New Testament Nuptial Imagery.* Leiden: E. J. Brill, 1971.

Clinebell, Howard J. *Growth Counseling for Marriage Enrichment: Pre-Marriage and the Early Years.* Philadelphia: Fortress Press, 1975.

Kennedy, Eugene. *Crisis Counseling: The Essential Guide for Non-Professional Counselors.* New York: Continuum, 1981.

Kysar, Myrna, and Robert Kysar. *The Asundered: Biblical Teachings on Divorce and Remarriage.* Atlanta: John Knox Press, 1978.

Likness, L. R. *With Your Promises.* Minneapolis: Augsburg Publishing House, 1980.

Pfatteicher, Philip H. *In Love and Faithfulness: Planning for Marriage.* Philadelphia: Parish Life Press, 1982.

Sheridan, Kathleen. *Living with Divorce.* Chicago: Thomas More Press, 1978.

Sittler, Joseph. *Grace Notes and Other Fragments.* Philadelphia: Fortress Press, 1981.

Stone, Howard W. *Crisis Counseling.* Philadelphia: Fortress Press, 1976.

Switzer, David K. *The Minister as Crisis Counselor.* Nashville: Abingdon Press, 1974.

Weiss, Robert S. *Marital Separation.* New York: Basic Books, 1975.

BLESSING OF A CIVIL MARRIAGE
(*Occasional Services,* pp. 32–36)

Parallel Rites

Episcopal   The Blessing of a Civil Marriage, *Book of Common Prayer*, pp. 433–34.

Lutheran   The Blessing of a Civil Marriage, *Occasional Services* (1962), pp. 193–96. One of the "Additional Orders and Offices."

The Order of the Consecration of a Civil Marriage, *Lutheran Agenda,* pp. 53–57.

Presbyterian   A Service for the Recognition of a Marriage, *Worshipbook*, pp. 69–70.

Purpose

The purpose of this service is to ask God's blessing upon a marriage previously contracted before a secular official.

Characteristics

The Blessing of a Civil Marriage is not a remarriage or a true marriage which replaces an inferior one. According to Lutheran theology, marriage is not a peculiarly Christian institution, for it existed in the Old Testament since the beginning of the race, and it exists around the world in a variety of religious and secular situations.[1]

---

1. See, for example, the Apology of the Augsburg Confession, Article XIII, *The Book of Concord,* trans. and ed. Theodore G. Tappert (Philadelphia: Fortress Press, 1959), p. 213, pars. 14–15.

The marriage has already taken place. The general notes direct the pastor to make this clear to the couple, and the documentation required is to assure the pastor that the couple is in fact married. In many parts of the Lutheran world there is only a civil marriage which may then be blessed in a church. While quite different from marriage patterns in North America, this reflects the situation of marriage in Luther's time. In Luther's Order of Marriage for Common Pastors of 1529,[2] the regulation of marriage is left to the secular authorities. In the order itself, reflecting general medieval practice, there are two parts to the action: a civil ceremony which takes place at the entrance of the church, and the blessing which takes place at the altar. The rubric before the civil ceremony begins "marrying them at the entrance to the church" and explicitly makes this the marriage. The rubrics in the religious ceremony "before the altar" read: "Before the altar he shall read God's word over the bridegroom and bride . . . speak to them . . . and pray."[3] The reading over the couple is Gen. 2:18, 21-24, which for Luther serves as a sort of "words of institution" for marriage. Thus, until comparatively recent times, marriage consisted of a civil espousal — remnants of which appear in the marriage service in the *Service Book and Hymnal* — and the religious reinforcement of the marriage.

In the 1979 *Book of Common Prayer* the title of the rite — Celebration and Blessing of a Marriage — reflects this two-part practice.

In the Roman Catholic liturgy the rite of marriage is in three parts: declaration of consent, blessing and exchange of rings, and the nuptial blessing. When marriage is celebrated during Mass, the nuptial blessing is separated from the rest of the rite and is said over the couple following the Lord's Prayer and before the peace, which is immediately prior to the reception of Holy Communion. The blessing is introduced with this introduction:

> My dear friends, let us turn to the Lord and pray
> that he will bless with his grace this woman (or *N.*)
> now married in Christ to this man (or *N.*)
> and that (through the sacrament of the body and blood of Christ,)
> he will unite in love the couple he has joined in this holy bond.

All pray silently for a while. Then the priest extends his hands and prays:

> Father, by your power you have made everything out of nothing.
> In the beginning you created the universe
> and made mankind in your own likeness.
> You gave man the constant help of woman

---

2. *LW,* vol. 53, pp. 113-15.

3. Ibid., pp. 113, 114.

so that man and woman should no longer be two, but one flesh,
and you teach us that what you have united may never be divided.

or,

Father, you have made the union of man and wife so holy a mystery
that it symbolizes the marriage of Christ and his Church.

or,

Father, by your plan man and woman are united,
and married life has been established
as the one blessing that was not forfeited by original sin
or washed away in the flood.
Look with love upon this woman, your daughter,
now joined to her husband in marriage.
She asks your blessing.
Give her always the grace of love and peace.
May she always follow the example of the holy women
whose praises are sung in the scriptures.

May her husband put his trust in her
and recognize that she is his equal
and the heir with him to the life of grace.
May he always honor her and love her
as Christ loves his bride, the Church.

Father, keep them always true to your commandments.
Keep them faithful in marriage
and let them be living examples of Christian life.

Give them the strength which comes from the gospel
so that they may be witnesses of Christ to others.
(Bless them with children
and help them to be good parents.
May they live to see their children's children.)
And, after a happy old age,
grant them fullness of life with the saints
in the kingdom of heaven.

We ask this through Christ our Lord.[4]

The priest blesses the bride and bridegroom again at the end of the Mass before the blessing of the people.[5]

In Roman Catholic and Eastern Orthodox theology marriage is accounted a sacrament and therefore to be contracted before a priest as

---

4. *The Rites,* pp. 543–45.
5. Ibid., pp. 569–70.

the principal witness. Those who are joined in marriage before a civil authority come to the church for a separate, sacramental service.

Background

The Blessing of a Civil Marriage did not appear in North American Lutheran service books before the middle of the twentieth century. The *Lutheran Agenda* of the Synodical Conference, undated but published in the 1940s, provided for the Consecration of a Civil Marriage. The basic order is the Order of a Marriage (the congregation participating) with only slight alterations, chiefly those required by the different situation, the marriage having already taken place.

There is no giving of the bride to the groom. The declaration of intent ("*N.*, wilt thou have this woman . . .") becomes a declaration that a marriage has occurred ("*N.*, thou hast taken . . ."); the vows ("I, *N.*, in the presence of God and these witnesses take thee, *N.* . . .") are omitted; the rings are given; the pronouncement of marriage is omitted; and the minister blesses the couple with a form of the marriage blessing:

> May the almighty and eternal God look down from His exalted throne in heaven upon you with His favor and sanctify and bless you with the benediction first spoken to Adam and Eve in Paradise, that you may please Him both in body and soul, and live together in holy love until life's end. (p. 56)

Curiously, perhaps, this blessing does not conclude with the trinitarian conclusion of the marriage service ("The eternal God, the Father of our Lord Jesus Christ, bestow upon you his Holy Spirit and be with you and richly bless you forevermore") but with the alternate conclusion from the marriage service:

> The God of Abraham, the God of Isaac, the God of Jacob,
> be with you and richly bless you forevermore. Amen.

One might have expected the consecration of a civil marriage to mention explicitly the name of the Holy Trinity, one of the principal reasons for seeking such a consecration presumably being to receive the blessing of the Christian church on the marriage.

In the Episcopal tradition, the *Book of Offices* (2d ed., 1949) for the first time included a form designed for the blessing of civil marriages called The Blessing of Married Persons and adapted from the marriage rite in the 1928 American *Book of Common Prayer*. From its introduction there it has been incorporated into the 1979 *Book of Common Prayer*, the first Episcopal Prayer Book to include such a blessing among the pastoral offices.[6]

---

6. Marion J. Hatchett, *Commentary on the American Prayer Book* (New York: Seabury Press, 1981), p. 439.

The Blessing of a Civil Marriage in *Occasional Services* (1962), like the rite in the *Lutheran Agenda* and in the *Book of Offices*, is a close adaptation of the marriage rite, in this case the one in the *Service Book and Hymnal*. It begins with the trinitarian invocation and moves directly to the two lessons, one of which is required in the marriage rite, Eph. 5:25, 28b-29, 22-23a and 1 Pet. 3:1a, 4b, 7a. (The introductory address in the marriage rite, which quotes Gen. 2:18 and Matt. 19:4b-6 and acknowledges the existence of "many a cross" that burdens marriage, is omitted in the Blessing of a Civil Marriage.) The declaration of intent is divided into two questions:

> *N.*, dost thou acknowledge this Woman to be thy wedded wife, to live together after God's ordinance in the holy estate of Matrimony? *I do.*
> Wilt thou love her, comfort her, honor and keep her in sickness and in health, and, forsaking all others, keep thee only unto her, so long as ye both shall live? *I will.* (pp. 193-94)

Then "first the man and then the woman" acknowledge their vows, saying to each other:

> I, *N.*, acknowledge thee, *N.*, as my wedded (wife, *or,* husband), to have and to hold from this day forward, for better for worse, for richer for poorer, in sickness and in health, to love and to cherish, till death us do part, according to God's holy ordinance; and thereto I plight thee my troth. (p. 194)

There is no provision for the exchange of rings in this rite, and following the acknowledgment of the vows the minister says:

> Forasmuch as *N.*, and *N.*, have, before God (and in the presence of this company), confirmed and acknowledged their union in the holy estate of Matrimony, I invoke upon their marriage the Blessing of Almighty God: In the Name of the Father and of the Son and of the Holy Ghost. Amen.
>
> What God hath joined together, let not man put asunder. (pp. 194-95)

The marriage blessing may follow:

> The Lord God, who created our first parents and sanctified their union in Marriage: Sanctify and bless you, that ye may please him both in body and soul, and live together in holy love until life's end. Amen. (p. 195)

The first prayer of the *Service Book and Hymnal* marriage service, with the opening address altered, follows. (In the marriage service the prayer begins, "Almighty and most merciful God, who hast now united this Man and this Woman in the holy estate of Matrimony: Grant them grace"; in the Blessing of a Civil Marriage the prayer begins, "Almighty

God, send thy blessing upon this Man and this Woman in the holy estate of Matrimony; grant them grace.'') The prayer for children and the prayer for all families and homes may be added but the text is not given. The rite concludes with the Lord's Prayer and the Aaronic benediction or the forceful and evocative alternate from the marriage service: "God Almighty send you his light and truth to keep you all the days of your life. The hand of God protect you; his holy Angels accompany you. God the Father, God the Son, and God the Holy Ghost, cause his grace to be mighty upon you."

Throughout the *Occasional Services* (1962) rite—the declaration of intent, the acknowledgment of the vows, the invocation of God's blessing by the minister—the implication is that something new is beginning with the blessing of the civil marriage, and, by implication, some doubt is cast upon the character of the secular marriage as if it had not been contracted before God.

Survey of the Service

The Blessing of a Civil Marriage in *Occasional Services* (1982) follows the pattern of its few predecessors and is deliberately parallel to the marriage service in the *LBW*. There are differences, however. There is no entrance hymn or procession, because it is assumed that this will be a relatively private service for the couple and some friends. The "witnesses" spoken of in the first rubric are present as representatives of the congregation which supports the marriage and prays for the couple, as it is obliged to support and to pray for all married people. These "witnesses" have no legal status in this service since this is not a marriage.

The opening prayer ⟨435⟩ is reworked from the marriage service. In place of the vows, there is a question by the presiding minister about the couple's intention to continue to live together as husband and wife. The presiding minister asks those who are gathered, referred to as "friends and family of *N.* and *N.*," if they are willing to pledge their support.

Almost always rings will have been exchanged in connection with the civil ceremony. If they have not been given, this may be done at the blessing of the marriage. In the text of the blessing only one word is changed from the *LBW* marriage service. Instead of "establish and sustain you" God is asked to "bless and sustain you" since the marriage has already taken place and its establishment has been accomplished.

The second of the three prayers ⟨436⟩ has been slightly altered by the deletion of "fulfill the vows they have made this day."

ANNIVERSARY OF A MARRIAGE
(*Occasional Services*, pp. 37–40)

Parallel Rites

Roman Catholic   Votive Mass of Thanksgiving, *Sacramentary*,[7] pp. 851–53.

Episcopal   Anniversary of a Marriage, *Book of Occasional Services*, pp. 144–46 (". . . intended for use in the context of a celebration of the Holy Eucharist").

Lutheran   Prayer "For a Wedding Anniversary," *Occasional Services* (1962), p. 214.
Order for the Anniversary of a Marriage, *Lutheran Agenda*, pp. 58–61.

Purpose

Anniversary of a Marriage is for use at home or in a parish house. Family members or persons who participated in the couple's marriage service may be appropriate leaders of this service. It is not intended that the pastor be invited to lead this service. Because *Occasional Services* (1982) is primarily a book for pastors and others who share the leadership of worship, ways must be found to make this service available to couples for their use. The pastor, for example, may choose to send copies of this rite to couples in the congregation on their anniversary.

Note that when it is desirable to mark an anniversary of a marriage within the corporate worship of the church, the prayer (no. 4) from this service may be used for that purpose during the prayers (no. 22) in the Holy Communion.

Characteristics

Many pastors receive requests for some kind of commemoration of twenty-fifth, fiftieth, and similar wedding anniversaries. These are undeniably important anniversaries of a personal rite of passage, yet they are not anniversaries of a peculiarly Christian sacrament as, for example, a baptismal anniversary.

This service reflects the *LBW* marriage service, adapted for the less formal setting of a home or hall. The structure is simple: prayer, lessons and comment or conversation, concluding prayers. The blessing is taken from the Service of the Word.

---

7. *The Sacramentary* (New York: Catholic Book Publishing Co., 1974).

There is no provision for a repetition of the marriage vows. Such an act seems appropriate when there has been a rupture of the relationship which the vows express (as it is appropriate to repeat one's baptismal vows yearly) and when the marriage has come near to collapse (see the Affirmation of Marriage Vows). But to renew vows that have been faithfully honored for decades seems an essentially hollow act, strong on sentiment, perhaps, but weak on meaning.

Background

The *Lutheran Agenda* (pp. 58-61) provides the one Lutheran antecedent of this rite. The order provided there may be used privately, but the expectation of the rubrics is that it will be used within a church service (after the offering in Holy Communion or after the canticle in Matins or Vespers).

A hymn of praise is sung. The minister says the psalm verse traditional before blessings,

> Our help is in the name of the Lord
> Who made heaven and earth. (124:8)

addresses the couple, and prays for them:

> O Thou faithful and merciful God, heavenly Father, who hast instituted the estate of matrimony, hallowed it by the presence of Thy Son at the marriage in Cana of Galilee, and protected and preserved it until this day: we thank Thee for Thy goodness and heartily beseech Thee, Thou wouldst evermore maintain Thine ordinance by Thy gracious and almighty presence, and grant unto these, and all others united in marriage, peace and unity, and comfort and hope in the day of trouble; through Jesus Christ our Lord.

Another hymn may be sung. An address follows, for which a text may be selected from a list provided (Gen. 32:10; 1 Sam. 7:12; 2 Sam 7:18; Job 10:12; Ps. 9:1-2; Ps. 40:5; Ps. 64:9-10; Ps. 71:17-18; Ps. 92:13; Ps. 115:13, 15; Ps. 128:5; Prov. 16:16; Isa. 46:4; Zech. 8:4; 1 Cor. 15:10). After the sermon, there is an introduction and a prayer, "the celebrating couple kneeling":

> Lord God, heavenly Father, we give Thee thanks for the fatherly love and grace which Thou hast bestowed upon us Thine unworthy servants, in such rich measure since the days of our youth and especially during these _____ years of holy wedlock. Thou hast accompanied us with loving-kindnesses and tender mercies, visited us with Thy comfort, strengthened us in sorrow and sickness, and hast crowned our life with every blessing. To Thee alone, O most merciful God, belong all honor and praise, for Thou hast helped us to walk in marital love and fidelity without forsaking each

other; nor didst Thou forsake us in sickness or health, in weal or woe, in adversity or prosperity, but didst grant us comfort and strength, patience and faithfulness. Be Thou with us in the future, O Lord, until the end of our days. Be Thou our Guide as Thou hast guided us in the past. Be Thou our Light though the light of our eyes begins to dim. Be Thou our Strength though our strength departs. Be Thou our Support though earthly supports fall. Be Thou our Health in sickness and infirmity. Be Thou our Refuge and our Life in the hour of death. When the days of our pilgrimage on earth shall cease, graciously bring us to the marriage supper of Thy Son and our Lord Jesus Christ, that we may dwell with Thee and rejoice in Thy joy forever.

The minister may then bless the couple:

May the merciful God and Father, who hath hitherto sustained and blessed you by His grace in your wedded life, grant unto you the continuance of His divine protection and blessing and cause your hearts to remain united in faithful love unto the end +. *Amen.* Peace be with you.

The minister prays for them again:

O almighty God, most merciful Father, we bless and praise Thee for all Thy loving-kindness and tender mercies which, for so many years, Thou hast bestowed upon these Thy servants, providing for them by Thy bounty, defending them by Thy power, and guiding them by Thy mercy. We beseech Thee, let the sacrifice of thanksgiving which they offer to Thee be acceptable in Thy sight, and give ear to their humble requests. During the days which still remain of their pilgrimage on earth, even to their old age, be Thou their Strength and their Deliverer in every infirmity and peril of body and soul. Let them at all times know the comfort and peace of Thy Holy Spirit. Be Thou with them, and fulfill in them Thy promise that the house of the righteous shall stand and the tabernacle of the upright shall flourish forevermore. And finally, let them depart this life in joy and peace and with rejoicing meet in Thy heavenly kingdom to laud and praise Thee and Thy Son and the Holy Ghost, world without end.

Then the minister dismisses them:

Go your way, then, beloved in Christ, whom we have blessed in the name of the Lord and commended to His gracious keeping. May your hearts continue to be united in love and truth and your home to be a dwelling place of the Lord, that, at the end of your sojourning here on earth, you may together see God face to face and enjoy that glory which He hath promised unto all who abide in true faith unto the end.

A third hymn may be sung, after which the minister says or chants the Aaronic benediction.

Occasional Services (1962) provides one prayer "For a Wedding Anniversary":

> O Lord Jesus Christ, who in the mystery of thy sacrificial love for the Church didst reveal the mystery of the union of man and woman in marriage: Let thy blessing rest upon those who are living together in holy wedlock. Keep these thy servants in remembrance of their solemn vows exchanged in thy presence on this day in years now past, so that, enabled by thy love, they may never cease to love and honor each other; and serving thee with a pure faith, may together become heirs of the grace of life; who, with the Father and the Holy Ghost, livest and reignest, one God, world without end. (p. 214)

The Roman Catholic church provides prayers for The Anniversaries of Marriage for use with the Votive Mass of Thanksgiving or for use at a weekday mass in "ordinary time" (that is, seasons after Epiphany and after Pentecost, days for which the color is green). A prayer of the day ("Opening Prayer"), an offertory prayer ("Prayer over the Gifts"), and a postcommunion prayer are provided for The Anniversary, The Twenty-fifth Anniversary of Marriage, and The Fiftieth Anniversary of Marriage.

Opening Prayer

THE ANNIVERSARY	TWENTY-FIFTH ANNIVERSARY	FIFTIETH ANNIVERSARY
God our Father, you created man and woman to love each other in the bond of marriage. Bless and strengthen N. and N. May their marriage become an increasingly more perfect sign of the union between Christ and his Church. We ask this through . . .	Father, you have blessed and sustained N. and N. in the bond of marriage. Continue to increase their love throughout the joys and sorrows of life, and help them to grow in holiness all their days. Grant this through . . .	God, our Father, bless N. and N. We thank you for their long and happy marriage (for the children they have brought into the world) and for all the good they have done. As you blessed the love of their youth, continue to bless their life together with gifts of peace and joy. We ask this through . . .

Prayer Over the Gifts

THE ANNIVERSARY	TWENTY-FIFTH ANNIVERSARY	FIFTIETH ANNIVERSARY

Father,
the blood and water
  that flowed
from the wounded heart
  of Christ your Son
was a sign of the
  mystery of our
  rebirth:
accept these gifts we
  offer in thanksgiving.
Continue to bless the
  marriage of *N.* and *N.*
  with all your gifts.
 	
Grant this . . .
	Father,
	accept these gifts which
	  we offer in thanks-
	  giving for *N.* and *N.*
	May they bring them
	  continued peace and
	  happiness.
	
	We ask this through . . .
		Lord,
		accept these gifts
		  we offer in
		  thanksgiving
		  for *N.* and *N.*
		With trust in you and
		  in each other
		they have shared
		  life together.
		Hear their prayers,
		and keep them in your
		  peace.
		
		We ask this . . .

Prayer After Communion

THE ANNIVERSARY	TWENTY-FIFTH ANNIVERSARY	FIFTIETH ANNIVERSARY

Lord,
you give us food and
  drink from heaven.
Bless *N.* and *N.* on
  their anniversary.
Let their love grow
  stronger
that they may find
  within themselves
a greater peace and joy.
Bless their home
that all who come to it
  in need
may find in it an
  example of goodness
and a source of
  comfort.
 	
We ask this through
  Christ our Lord.
	Father,
	you bring *N.* and *N.*
	  (and their children
	  and friends) together
	at the table of your
	  family.
	Help them to grow in
	  love and unity,
	that they may rejoice
	  together
	in the wedding feast
	  of heaven.
	
	Grant this through
	  Christ our Lord.
		Lord,
		as we gather at the table
		  of your Son,
		bless *N.* and *N.* on their
		  wedding anniversary.
		Watch over them in the
		  coming years,
		and after a long and
		  happy life together
		bring them to the feast
		  of eternal life.
		
		Grant this through
		  Christ our Lord.

The readings appointed for a mass of thanksgiving are:

Old Testament
  1 Kings 8:55-61
  Ecclus. 50:24-26
  Isa. 63:7-9
  Zeph. 3:14-15

New Testament
  1 Cor. 1:3-9
  Eph. 1:3-14
  Col. 3:12-17

Responsorial Psalm
  1 Chron. 29:10-12
  Psalm 113
  Ps. 138:1-5
  Ps. 145:1-11

Alleluia Verse
  Eph. 1:3
  1 Thess. 5:18

Gospel
  Mark 5:18-20
  Luke 17:11-19

This provision is a modern addition to the liturgy. The *Roman Ritual* (1950), edited by Philip T. Weller, noted the need for the modern world to see and learn from the witness of a man and woman, married many years, who give praise to God and receive the church's blessing.[8] The 1952 *Roman Ritual* made provision for the "celebration of a Silver or a Golden Anniversary." The rite consisted of an allocution to the jubilarians, Psalm 128 or 117, an optional blessing of a red and a white lei (for sacrifice and for fidelity), and the renewal of the marriage vows. The Te Deum, a prayer, a blessing, and the dismissal concluded the rite.

The Episcopal *Book of Occasional Services* (pp. 144-46) provides for the observance of the Anniversary of a Marriage within the context of the Holy Communion. The propers for the day are used; at times other than a Sunday or major holy day, the psalm and readings are chosen from those recommended for use at the Celebration and Blessing of a Marriage (*Book of Common Prayer*, pp. 422-32); three prayers of the day are provided in the *Book of Occasional Services:*

> O gracious and everliving God, look mercifully on *N.* and *N.,* who come to renew the promises they have made to each other. Grant them your blessing, and assist them with your grace, that with true fidelity and steadfast love they may honor and keep their promises and vows; through Jesus Christ our

---

8. *The Roman Ritual,* trans. and ed. Philip T. Weller, vol. 1 (Milwaukee: Bruce Publishing Co., 1950), p. 594. See the *Roman Ritual: Complete Edition,* ed. Philip T. Weller (Milwaukee: Bruce Publishing Co., 1964), pp. 290-96.

Savior, who lives and reigns with you, in the unity of the Holy Spirit, one God, for ever and ever.

or,

O God, you have so consecrated the covenant of marriage that in it is represented the spiritual unity between Christ and his Church: Send your blessing upon *N.* and *N.,* who come to renew their promises to each other, and grant them your grace, that they may so love, honor, and cherish each other in faithfulness and patience, in wisdom and true godliness, that their lives together may be a witness to your love and forgiveness, and that their home may be a haven of blessing and peace; through Jesus Christ our Lord, who lives and reigns with you and the Holy Spirit, one God, now and for ever.

or,

Grant, O God, in your compassion, that *N.* and *N.,* having taken each other in marriage, and affirming again the covenant which they have made, may grow in forgiveness, loyalty, and love; and come at last to the eternal joys which you have promised through Jesus Christ our Lord; who lives and reigns with you, in the unity of the Holy Spirit, one God, for ever and ever.

After the sermon (and the Creed), "the husband and wife present themselves before the celebrant," who announces the intention of the celebration ("to give thanks to God for his blessing upon this marriage, and to reaffirm the marriage covenant") and asks the man and the woman, "*N.,* do you here, in the presence of God and of this congregation, renew the promises you made when you bound yourself to *N.* in holy matrimony?" The husband and wife say together a prayer of thanksgiving:

We thank you, most gracious God, for consecrating our marriage in Christ's Name and presence. Lead us further in companionship with each other and with you. Give us grace to live together in love and fidelity, with care for one another. Strengthen us all our days, and bring us to that holy table where, with those we love, we will feast for ever in our heavenly home; through Jesus Christ our Lord.

The celebrant then dismisses them with a blessing:

May God the Father, who at creation ordained that man and woman become one flesh, keep you one. *Amen.*

May God the Son, who adorned this manner of life by his first miracle, at the wedding in Cana of Galilee, be present with you always. *Amen.*

May God the Holy Spirit, who has given you the will to persevere in your love and in your covenant with each other, strengthen your bond. *Amen.*

And may God the Holy Trinity, the source of all unity, bless you this day and for ever. *Amen.*

The service continues with the peace.

Survey of the Service

Contrary to the Roman Catholic and Episcopal suggestions, the *Occasional Services* (1982) form for the Anniversary of a Marriage is not for use in a public service in the church but for an informal celebration in a parish house or home. It is desirable that the leader not be the pastor but a friend or member of the family.

Prayer ⟨437⟩, "Eternal God, our Creator and Redeemer . . . ," and prayer ⟨438⟩, "God of love . . . ," are new compositions, but are reminiscent of language in the *LBW*.

If it is desirable to mark the anniversary of a marriage (such as the fiftieth anniversary) within a service of worship in the congregation, the prayer ⟨438⟩, "God of love . . . ," may be included in the prayers of intercession, or another appropriate petition may be offered.

AFFIRMATION OF MARRIAGE VOWS
(*Occasional Services,* pp. 41–44)

Parallel Rites

Episcopal   Anniversary of a Marriage, *Book of Occasional Services,* pp. 144–46, has this final rubric: "When this form is used as an act of reconciliation, the celebrant may adapt it in consultation with the parties."

Purpose

Affirmation of Marriage Vows is intended primarily for use in informal situations of two sorts. First, it is for use with a couple when there has been a strain or a breach of vows. Second, it is for use in groups on marriage-enrichment occasions such as the conclusion of a retreat or a series of classes dealing with the enrichment of married life, or at such times as the Second Sunday after the Epiphany in year C when the Gospel is the wedding at Cana or the First Sunday after Christmas in all three years when the Gospels deal with the Holy Family.

Characteristics

The dual use intended for this service requires careful preparation so that the rite will speak to the needs of the participants. The Affirmation of Marriage Vows is on the border between a service and a resource.

The order is generally parallel to the structure of the marriage service in the *LBW,* but this material may be modified freely to fit the particular circumstances. It must be clear to all that this is not a remarriage but rather a return to the original vows and an affirmation of them. It is a reflection of the nature of marriage as a commitment to one another in a covenant of fidelity.

Survey of the Service

Individual Confession and Forgiveness may be appropriate if a couple, after a strain or separation, is returning to the marriage covenant. It may also be appropriate if an emphasis of a marriage-enrichment occasion has been on overcoming weaknesses and shortcomings.

The prayers ⟨439⟩, ⟨440⟩ are adaptations of prayers in the order for marriage.

The lessons must be selected with special care so that they will be appropriate to the occasion.

The promises, the "affirming statement," should be prepared by the couple (together with the pastor) to say what they intend, whether it is a renewal of forgotten promises or a statement of general and continuing commitment.

It may be appropriate for the couple to offer prayers for each other and for their families, but the pastor must be sensitive to the situation and not force such acts or encourage merely formal gestures and language.

PRAYERS DURING THE TIME OF SEPARATION OR DIVORCE
(*Occasional Services,* pp. 287–89)

Parallel Rites

Episcopal	[See David Ulrich, Frederick Bender, Faith Whitfield, "Service of Affirmation When Parents Are Separating," (Cincinnati: Forward Movement Publications, 1980).]
Methodist	[See "Rituals for the Divorced," *Ritual in a New Day* (Nashville: Abingdon Press, 1976), pp. 73–96.]
Presbyterian	Prayer "For Those in Marital Difficulty"; prayer "For the Divorced or Separated," *Worshipbook* (Philadelphia: Westminster Press, 1970), p. 186.

Purpose

This section of *Occasional Services* is not a service as such but rather resources and suggestions for use in counseling.

The inclusion of these prayers is not intended to depreciate marriage or to condone, encourage, or facilitate divorce. The church remains committed to preserving the sanctity and the permanence of marriage as a lifelong covenant of faithfulness and selfless love.

These prayers are included to encourage honesty, to recognize reality, and to meet a clear and increasing pastoral need by giving guidance to those who minister to people in troubled marriages.

The rubrics and the prayers may also serve to suggest to the pastor and to the couple dimensions of pastoral concern: the individuals, the children, the parents of the couple, and other family members.

Characteristics

These resources are designed to encourage pastors to be understanding and not judgmental, for those who are divorcing are often already guilt-ridden.

Unlike the situations represented in other rites of passage, a great variety of situations will be represented by those who are separating or divorcing. Both individuals may be present; they may or may not be on speaking terms with one another; one may have abandoned the other; one may have suffered abuse and violence. No one form, prayer, or approach can cover all of the possibilities, and a concerned pastor will need to understand the particular situation clearly so that it can be dealt with responsibly and sensitively.

The grief process in a broken marriage often parallels that which follows the death of a loved one. Support for the individual(s) during and after the division is essential, and the pastor should not provide this support alone. Often individuals and groups in the congregation can be encouraged to assist in this ministry as a pledge of present and future support.

Survey of the Notes and the Prayers

Individual Confession and Forgiveness may be appropriate if one or both of the individuals have something to confess. The pastor must be certain, however, that the person is not simply taking undue personal blame for matters that are far larger and more complex. Nor are people to be forced to confess. They must desire to declare their sins to God and yearn for the message of forgiveness.

Corporate Confession and Forgiveness may be appropriate as two people (together with their friends, perhaps) seek in the presence of a pastor to work through the troubles which beset them. This requires careful preparation by the pastor who must know the service thoroughly and be able to use it effectively.

The list of sections from Psalms, Lessons, and Prayers—anxiety, apprehension, fear; guilt; loneliness; impending death or irreversible illness; anger, bitterness, self-pity, turmoil—is not only to guide the pastor to particular resources, but also to alert the pastor to the kinds of emotions which may be at work in the individuals who are being counseled.

The prayers are drawn from the following sources:

"God of compassion and grace . . ." ⟨554⟩. New

"Loving God and Father of our Lord Jesus Christ . . ." ⟨551⟩. New.

"God of all grace . . ." ⟨552⟩. New.

"Hear us good Lord . . ." ⟨553⟩. New.

"O God, by whom your people . . ." ⟨554⟩ is an adaptation of an original prayer printed in the appendix of William Bright's *Ancient Collects and Other Prayers* ([Port Washington, N.Y.: Regency Press, 1976], p. 234), which makes allusion to Ps. 25:8; Isa. 11:2; Ps. 36:9; and Jer. 31:9. The prayer was included in the 1928 American *Book of Common Prayer* and is in the 1979 Prayer Book as no. 58, "For Guidance" (p. 832).

Book of Common Prayer (1979)	*Occasional Services* (1982)
O God, by whom the meek are guided in judgment, and light *riseth* up in darkness for the godly: Grant us, in all our doubts and uncertainties, the grace to ask what *thou wouldest* have us to do, that the Spirit of wisdom may save us from all false choices, and that in *thy* light we may see light, and in *thy* straight path may not stumble; through Jesus Christ our Lord.	O God, by whom your people are guided in judgment: Enable us in all our doubts and uncertainties to ask what you would have us to do, that the Spirit of wisdom may save us from all false choices, and that in your light we may see light, and in your straight path we may not stumble; through Jesus Christ our Lord.

"O God, you have bound us together . . . " ⟨555⟩. This prayer originated in *The Grey Book* (New York: Oxford University Press, 1923), a collection of proposals for the revision of the English Prayer Book. From there it came into the 1979 *Book of Common Prayer* as no. 28, "In Times of Conflict" (p. 824). It is slightly altered in *Occasional Services*.

"Grant, O God, that your holy and life-giving Spirit . . . " (167). This prayer, by an unknown author, was borrowed by the *LBW* from the *Draft Proposed Book of Common Prayer*. It is in the 1979 Prayer Book as no. 27, "For Social Justice" (p. 823). It is slightly altered in *Occasional Services*.

"O God, you made us in your own image . . ." (177). This prayer, drafted by Charles P. Price, who chaired the drafting committee for prayers and thanksgivings for the 1979 *Book of Common Prayer,* was borrowed by the *LBW* from the *Draft Proposed Book of Common Prayer*. It is included in the 1979 Prayer Book as no. 3, "For the Human Family" (p. 815). One phrase is inverted in *Occasional Services*.

"O God, the Lord of all . . . " (180). This is a revised form of a prayer from an anonymous correspondent printed in *The Living Church* (September 8, 1968). It was borrowed by the *LBW* from the *Draft Proposed Book of Common Prayer*. It is in the 1979 Prayer Book as no. 6, "For our Enemies" (p. 816). It is slightly simplified in the Lutheran form.

Book of Common Prayer (1979)	*Lutheran Book of Worship*
O God, the Father of all, whose Son commanded us to love our enemies:	O God, the Lord of all, your Son commanded us to love our enemies and to pray for them.
Lead them and us from prejudice to truth; deliver them and us from hatred, cruelty, and revenge; and in your good time enable us all to stand reconciled before you; through Jesus Christ our Lord.	Lead us from prejudice to truth; deliver us from hatred, cruelty, and revenge; and enable us to stand before you, reconciled through your Son, Jesus Christ our Lord.

"O most loving Father . . . " (204). This is a prayer by William Bright included in the 1928 American *Book of Common Prayer* (p. 596), drawing upon 1 Tim. 2:1; Phil. 3:8; and 1 Pet. 5:7. From the 1928 Prayer Book it was borrowed by the *LBW* and slightly altered.

Book of Common Prayer (1928)	*Lutheran Book of Worship*
O most loving Father, who willest us to give thanks for all things, to dread nothing but the loss of thee, and to cast all our care on	O most loving Father, you want us to give thanks for all things, to fear nothing except losing you, and to lay all our cares on you,

Book of Common Prayer (1928)	*Lutheran Book of Worship*
thee, who carest for us; Preserve us from faithless fears and worldly anxieties, and grant that no clouds of this mortal life may hide from us the light of that love which is immortal, and which thou hast manifested unto us in thy Son, Jesus Christ our Lord.	knowing that you care for us. Protect us from faithless fears and worldly anxieties, and grant that no clouds in this mortal life may hide from us the light of your immortal love shown to us in your Son, Jesus Christ our Lord.

"Lord, make us instruments of your peace . . ." (213). This prayer attributed to St. Francis is no. 62 in the *Book of Common Prayer* (p. 833). It was borrowed from the *Draft Proposed Book of Common Prayer* for the *LBW*. Marion Hatchett notes that it is by an unknown author and "cannot be traced back earlier than the present century."[9]

---

9. Hatchett, *Commentary on American Prayer Book,* p. 568.

3

THE SERVICES OF
THE MINISTRY OF HEALING

INTRODUCTION

St. Paul wrote to the Corinthians that God "through Christ reconciled us to himself and gave us the ministry of reconciliation; that is, in Christ God was reconciling the world to himself, not counting their trespasses against them, and entrusting to us the message of reconciliation."[1] This reconciliation was declared in Jesus' preaching, shown in his miracles of healing, and achieved by his death and resurrection. In Christ, God's kingdom of wholeness and peace has broken into this world. The church continues this work of reconciliation, and through its proclamation and ministry and service, Christ is still at work in the world.

The healing that God intends for his creation and that Christ brings to it is not limited to certain parts of the world or of the person. It is complete and total as the vision of Revelation suggests: "I saw a new heaven and a new earth. . . . And he who sat upon the throne said, 'Behold, I make all things new.' " (Rev. 21:1, 5).

This pervasive and total healing is experienced in confession and forgiveness by which we open ourselves to the searching brightness of God our Father, acknowledge what we are and what we have done, and hear the liberating and healing word of reconciliation.

It is experienced also in the ministry of the Word of God as the Scriptures bear his gospel to us and as the good news is made clear through the ancient record of God's mighty acts.

The healing that Christ came to bring is experienced in the laying on of hands (and anointing) as the church, in imitation and extension of the work of Christ, seeks healing of mental, physical, and spiritual sickness and infirmity.

The healing is experienced by sight, touch, smell, and taste in the Holy Communion as through the actions of eating and drinking God's people encounter the crucified and risen Lord, who is their peace.

This manifold healing of the whole person is part of the experience not only of an individual but of the entire church. When a member of the

---

1. 2 Cor. 5:18–19. See also Rom. 5:10; Col. 1:20.

body of Christ, the church, suffers pain, all the members suffer together, and the strength of Christ flows through the whole body to the afflicted member. The pastors and leaders of the congregation visit the sick person and bring the comfort and healing power of readings from the Scripture, prayer, and food from the table of the Lord. The pastor may hear the person's confession and give absolution and may lay hands on the person, perhaps anointing the person with oil. The visitors, by their presence, their words, and their actions declare to the sick person that as the church shares in the suffering of Christ and is baptized into his death, so the church also shares in the power of Christ's triumph over sickness and death. That triumph is made ours in baptism and will be complete after this life in the fullness of the kingdom.[2]

Anciently, insofar as liturgical forms reflect practice, the church, following the counsel of James 5:14-15, was involved in the ministry to the sick not simply to console them but in order to heal them. Because of the medicinal properties of oil, anointing was regularly a part of this ministry, as was also the ministration of Holy Communion—the "medicine of immortality"—to the sick person.

During the Middle Ages, the understanding of anointing (often called unction) was connected not with healing but with forgiveness. So anointing became increasingly reserved for the dying. In the visitation of the sick, prayers for healing became less frequent, and penitential actions multiplied. This changed understanding has left its mark on the rites for visiting the sick which have been included in Lutheran service books. For example, the rubrics at the head of Visitation of the Sick in the *Church Book,* themselves drawn from sixteenth-century German church orders, include this counsel:

> The Minister shall instruct the sick, as the need may be, how a Christian is to look upon his sickness, why it is sent upon him, what God intends thereby, and how to bear it in a Christian way. He should endeavor to give comfort, not only against bodily pains and weakness, but also against all manner of spiritual conflicts, that those in suffering may learn that God means it well with them, and become the more peacefully and patiently reconciled to their afflictions.[3]

The same paragraph is reproduced in the rubrics before the Visitation of the Sick in *Occasional Services* (1962). Compare that with the more lean, reticent, and helpful rubrics at the head of Lessons and Prayers for the Sick in the *Common Service Book* (text ed., p. 414):

---

2. M. Jennifer Glen, "Sickness and Symbol: The Promise of the Future," *Worship* 54:5 (September 1980): 397–411.

3. *Church Book for the Use of Evangelical Lutheran Congregations* (Philadelphia: General Council Publication Board, 1915), p. 378.

The Lessons and Prayers here following are intended for the guidance of the Minister in the visitation of the sick, and for private use by the afflicted.

In cases of illness the Minister should be informed, in order that he may visit the sick person and comfort and strengthen him with Word and Sacrament.

The Minister's visits should be brief.

The Minister may, at his discretion, read suitable passages of Scripture, as indicated below, and shall say one or more of the Prayers, or any other suitable prayer.

The general title "Ministry of Healing" has broad and positive implications and is therefore perhaps preferable to the older and more familiar title Visitation of the Sick from *Occasional Services* (1962) and the *Church Book* (1892). "Ministry of Healing" suggests that there is something that the church can do about the broken condition of humanity by being an instrument of healing and salvation. The older rite largely counseled the sick person to be submissive and to endure.

The many acts of healing that Jesus performed during his ministry were, at least in part, "enacted parables" which dramatically portrayed God's will that his people be whole and enjoy the fullness of life and salvation. As the early church extended the ministry of Jesus, it continued to heal as well as to preach and to celebrate the sacraments. The modern church—rejecting the division of the individual person into "body" and "soul," which too often seemed to imply that the church's concern was only with the soul, and returning after many centuries to a more biblical understanding of the individual—has begun to recover the totality of this ministry to the whole person.

The church's full ministry of healing, therefore, consists of several parts:

1. Confession and forgiveness
2. Psalms, lessons, and prayers
3. Laying on of hands and anointing
4. Holy Communion

The richness of this tradition invites creative use of its treasures: (1) The four parts may be used together in one unified liturgy on one occasion; (2) The four parts may be used as one liturgy but spread over several successive visits to the sick person; (3) The pastor may select one or more of the elements of the ministry of healing as appropriate to a particular person's condition at a given time.

This four-part approach to ministry to the sick and suffering outlined in *Occasional Services* (1982) is similar to that in the *Book of Common Prayer* (1979), which divides the Ministration to the Sick into three parts:

Part I. Ministry of the Word, with suggested lessons, psalms, and Gospels provided under four headings—general, penitence, when anointing is to follow, when Communion is to follow—and concluding, as in the eucharistic rites in the Prayer Book, with confession and absolution; Part II. Laying on of Hands and Anointing; Part III. Holy Communion.

The four-part approach of *Occasional Services* (1982) includes confession and forgiveness (usually individual) as a means of experiencing the ministry of reconciliation, that is, healing the broken relationship between humanity and God through a return to the baptismal covenant which God establishes with his people and to which his people have been unfaithful.

The second part—psalms, lessons, and prayers—is an anthology of resources for use with the sick and for use by the sick at various stages of their condition. It is a way of aiding them to confront their illness and respond to it.

The third part, the laying on of hands (and anointing), provides a form for those instances in which this ancient practice is desirable as a demonstration of God's concern for the total welfare of his people, physical as well as spiritual, and as an active prayer for that person.

The fourth part, the Holy Communion, is perhaps the clearest demonstration of God's concern for the total person as he feeds his people with spiritual food, the bread of heaven and the cup of salvation.

Of these four parts, the second and the fourth are the most familiar to Lutherans and are expected aspects of pastoral care. The first part, confession and forgiveness, is known in some forms to Lutherans, such as the Brief Order for Confession and Forgiveness before Holy Communion. The third part, laying on of hands (and anointing), is new to Lutheran service books, although some congregations have used the practice for many years.

With this four-part approach, the pastor and the congregation have rich resources for exercising the church's ministry of healing in various situations and in response to different needs.

For Further Reading

"Christian Healing," *New Catholic Encyclopedia,* vol. VI, pp. 960–62.

Crichton, J. D. *The Ministry of Reconciliation.* London: Geoffrey Chapman, 1974.

Dalbey, Gordon. "Recovering Healing Prayer." *Christian Century* 99:21 (June 9–16, 1982): 690–93.

Dearmer, Percy. "The Visitation and Communion of the Sick, and the Churching of Women." Chapter 16 in *The Parson's Handbook.* 12th ed., rev. New York: Oxford University Press, 1932.

Gerstenberger, Erhard S., and Wolfgang Schrage, eds. *Suffering*. Translated by John E. Steely. Nashville: Abingdon Press, 1980.

Grant, Brian W. *From Sin to Wholeness*. Philadelphia: Westminster Press, 1982.

Gusmer, Charles W. *The Ministry of Healing in the Church of England: An Ecumenical-Liturgical Study*. Alcuin Club Collection No. 56. Great Wakering, England: Mayhew-McCrimmon, 1974.

Harris, Charles. "Visitation of the Sick." In *Liturgy and Worship,* edited by W. K. Lowther Clarke and Charles Harris, pp. 472–540. London: SPCK, 1964 [1932].

Kelsey, Morton T. *Healing and Christianity*. New York: Harper & Row, 1973.

Knauber, Adolf. *Pastoral Theology of the Anointing of the Sick*. Translated by Matthew J. O'Connell. Collegeville, Minn.: Liturgical Press, 1975.

Letterman, Henry L., ed. *Healing and Health: Ministry of the Church*. Chicago: Wheatridge Foundation, 1980.

Liturgy 25:2 (March–April 1980). An issue devoted to "The Sick and the Dying."

Liturgy: Ministries to the Sick 2:2. Washington, D.C.: Liturgical Conference, 1982.

McNutt, Francis. *Healing*. Notre Dame, Ind.: Ave Maria Press, 1974. (But see the review by Charles Gusmer, *Worship* 49:3 [March 1975]: 183–84.)

Mitchell, Nathan, ed. *Background and Directions: The Rite of Penance: Commentaries*, vol. 3. Washington, D.C.: Liturgical Conference, 1978.

Nouwen, Henri J. M. *The Wounded Healer: Ministry in Contemporary Society*. Garden City, N.Y.: Doubleday & Co., 1979.

Nouwen, Henri J. M., and Walter J. Gaffney. *Aging: The Fulfillment of Life*. Garden City, N.Y.: Doubleday & Co., 1976.

O'Brien, John J. "Unto a New Creation: Anointing and Ministering to the Sick." *Liturgy* 24:2 (March–April 1979): 41–44.

Scharlemann, Martin. *Healing and Redemption*. St. Louis: Concordia Publishing House, 1965.

Schillebeeckx, Edward. *Sacramental Reconciliation*. Concilium, vol. 61. New York: Seabury Press, 1971.

Simundson, Daniel J. *Faith Under Fire: Biblical Interpretations of Suffering*. Minneapolis: Augsburg Publishing House, 1980.

"Unction," *Westminster Dictionary of Worship*. Philadelphia: Westminster Press, 1979.

Your Kingdom Come: Mission Perspectives. Report on the World Conference on Mission and Evangelism, Melbourne, Australia, 12–25 May 1980, pp. 199–200. Geneva: World Council of Churches, 1980.

INDIVIDUAL CONFESSION AND FORGIVENESS
(*Occasional Services,* pp. 45-47)

Parallel Rites

Roman Catholic — Rite of Reconciliation of Individual Penitents, *The Rites,* pp. 337-64.

Episcopal — The Reconciliation of a Penitent, *Book of Common Prayer,* pp. 446-52.

Lutheran — Order for Private Confession and Absolution, *Occasional Services* (1962), pp. 31-32.
Order for Private Confession and Absolution, *Common Service Book* (text ed.), p. 409.
Order for Private Confession and Absolution, *Church Book* (1915), pp. 364-67.

Orthodox — The Rite of Confession, *Service Book,* pp. 286-90.
The Sacrament of Holy Confession, *An Orthodox Prayer Book,* pp. 133-39.

Purpose

Individual Confession and Forgiveness is intended for use as a personal application of the gospel of the forgiveness of sins. It is a traditional use of what the Lutheran confessions call "the power (or office) of the keys," based on Matt. 16:19; 18:18; John 20:22-23, to disclose "a sure and firm consolation for the conscience."[4]

Characteristics

The form for Individual Confession and Forgiveness in the *Lutheran Book of Worship* is a simple one, based primarily on the model which Luther suggested in the Small Catechism, Part V, "Confession and Absolution. How Plain People Are to Be Taught to Confess."

The form is included in *Occasional Services* for the convenience of the pastor, since it is useful in several situations addressed by the book, such as before Holy Communion, in the Ministry of Healing, and in counseling the separated or divorced.

---

4. Apology of the Augsburg Confession, Article X, *The Book of Concord,* trans. and ed. Theodore G. Tappert (Philadelphia: Fortress Press, 1959), p. 180.

Background

In Lutheran service books, the form for Individual Confession and Forgiveness is basically a prayer of confession, which may or may not include an enumeration of particular sins and absolution. As the Small Catechism says:

> Confession consists of two parts. One is that we confess our sins. The other is that we receive absolution or forgiveness from the confessor as from God himself, by no means doubting but firmly believing that our sins are thereby forgiven before God in heaven.[5]

The Lutheran confessions, reacting to medieval abuses, frequently insist that "we should confess only those sins of which we have knowledge and which trouble us."[6] One should not "search for and invent other sins, for this would turn confession into torture."[7] So a rubric in the *Church Book* warns:

> The enumeration of sins in Private Confession is entirely free; and the Minister should not curiously inquire into special forms of transgression, or otherwise burden penitents by questions about what is not voluntarily confessed: for the ministry of divine Absolution is not appointed to investigate secret sins, neither is such investigation necessary to their forgiveness. But penitents should be encouraged to confess the sins which specially burden their souls, that proper direction and consolation may be given them.[8]

Luther intended confession and absolution especially for those who were about to receive Holy Communion,[9] and the Lutheran churches have maintained that connection. The initial rubric in the *Church Book* regarding private confession relates confession first to the reception of Holy Communion and then secondly to spiritual growth:

> It is of great importance that the Minister should have personal knowledge of those whom he admits to the Lord's Supper, and to this end should inquire into the spiritual condition especially of the young and inexperienced, that he may instruct and encourage them as need may be. Christian people also, for their growth in knowledge and grace, should use their privilege to confer personally with those appointed to watch over their souls, in order to

---

5. *Book of Concord*, pp. 349–50.
6. Ibid., p. 350.
7. Ibid.
8. *Church Book*, p. 365.
9. *Book of Concord*, p. 349 no. 5.

have the instructions and consolations of the Word of God ministered to them individually.[10]

The second rubric reflects traditional Lutheran insistence that on the one hand private confession is traditional and acceptable in evangelical use, but that on the other hand it is not required.

> Private Confession and Absolution is a service which has been used by the Church for such personal ministrations. It is not to be regarded as necessary, nor to be exacted of any one; but it is provided and recommended for such as are particularly distressed and burdened in conscience on account of sin.[11]

Confession is to be genuine, and it is to be free.

> Absolution is to be given only to such persons as are truly penitent, and sincerely determined to amend their ways; for without genuine repentance there is no forgiveness.

> The person making Confession may use his or her own words, or the words here given, or any other suitable words.[12]

The form in the *Common Service Book* and in *Occasional Services* (1962) which is derived from it is simple and straightforward: a confession, the absolution, and a blessing. *Occasional Services* (1962) permits the pastor to lay a hand on the head of the penitent as the absolution is said and includes the sign of the cross in the absolution. The form in both books is introduced with this rubric:

> Private Confession and Absolution has been used by the Church from ancient times, and persons who are burdened in conscience on account of sin may always seek the personal ministration of the Pastor before the Holy Communion or at any other time.[13]

The 1979 *Book of Common Prayer* gives two forms for what is called the Reconciliation of a Penitent. The first form is derived from general medieval practice and is like forms used in recent revisions in various Anglican provinces; the second is a fuller rite, closer to recent Roman Catholic reforms and to the Byzantine form for confession. It is "particu-

---

10. *Church Book*, pp. 364–65.

11. Ibid., p. 365.

12. Ibid.

13. *Common Service Book*, text ed. (Philadelphia: Board of Publication of the United Lutheran Church in America, 1919), p. 409.

larly appropriate when a person has turned or returned to the Christian faith, or at other possible 'crisis' points in a person's life.''[14]

The recent Roman Catholic revisions of penance provide a Rite for Reconciliation of Individual Penitents and a Rite for Reconciliation of Several Penitents. The latter rite emphasizes the relation of the sacrament to the community and places individual confession and absolution in the context of a celebration of the word of God.

Development of the Rite
Individual Confession and Forgiveness

Church Book (1892)	Common Service Book (1919)	Occasional Services (1962)	Lutheran Book of Worship (1978)
			Greeting
			Ps. 51:16–18, 1–2
			Invitation
Confession*	Confession†	Confession†	Confession
			Consolation from Scripture
			Ps. 51:1, 11–13
Absolution‡	Absolution§	Absolution§	Absolution
			Ps. 103:8–13
"The peace of the Lord be with thee."	Blessing	Blessing	Dismissal (The peace)

---

14. Marion J. Hatchett, *Commentary on the American Prayer Book* (New York: Seabury Press, 1981), p. 453.

*I confess before you, and before Almighty God, that I have greatly sinned against His holy commandments, in thoughts, words and deeds, and that I am by nature sinful and unclean, and deserve everlasting condemnation. On this account my heart is troubled. I sincerely lament that I have offended the Lord my God, and earnestly pray Him for Christ's sake graciously to forgive me and by His Holy Spirit to create in me a new heart, according as I believe

†O God, our Heavenly Father, I confess unto Thee that I have grievously sinned against Thee in many ways; not only by outward transgression, but also by secret thoughts and desires, which I cannot fully understand, but which are all known unto Thee. I do earnestly repent, and am heartily sorry for these my offences, and I beseech Thee of Thy great goodness to have mercy upon me, and for the sake of Thy dear Son, Jesus Christ our Lord, to forgive my sins,

Comparison of Rites
Individual Confession and Forgiveness

The Rites	*Book of Common Prayer* Form 1	Form 2	*Lutheran Book* *of Worship*
Reception of the Penitent			Greeting
		Ps. 51:1–3	Ps. 51:16–18, 1–2

---

and trust in His Word.

And inasmuch as you have command from the Lord Jesus, as a Minister of the Church, to absolve all that are truly penitent, I entreat of you to instruct and comfort me out of God's Word, to declare unto me in the Name of Jesus Christ the forgiveness of my sins, and to admit me to the Sacrament of his Body and Blood for the strengthening of my faith, as I purpose, with the help of God, to amend and better my sinful life. (pp. 365–66)

Or this:

I confess before God, my Maker and Redeemer, that I was conceived and born in sin, and that I have grievously sinned, in thoughts, words and deeds. But I flee for refuge to His infinite mercy, seeking and imploring pardon for Christ's sake. God be merciful to me! By his help I will live a better life. (p. 366)

‡Almighty God, our heavenly Father, is merciful and gracious, and ready to forgive thee all thy sins, for the sake of His Son Jesus Christ, Who suffered and died for thee; therefore, in His Name, in obedience to His command, and by virtue of His words: "Whose soever sins ye remit, they are remitted unto them," I declare thee, being penitent, absolved and free from all thy sins. They are forgiven, as abundantly and completely as Jesus Christ hath merited by His sufferings and death, and commanded to be preached by the Gospel throughout the world. Take to thyself, then, for thy comfort and peace, the assurance which I now give thee in the Name of the Lord Jesus, and believe without doubt that thy sins are forgiven thee, in the Name of the Father, and of the Son, and of the Holy Ghost. Amen. (pp. 366–67)

and graciously to help my infirmities. Amen. (*CSB*, pp. 409; *OS*, pp. 31–32)

§Almighty God, our Heavenly Father, hath had mercy upon thee, and for the sake of the sufferings, death, and resurrection of His dear Son Jesus Christ, our Lord, forgiveth thee all thy sins. Upon the confession which thou hast made, and in obedience to our Lord's command, I declare unto thee the entire forgiveness of all thy sins: In the Name of the Father, and of the Son, and of the Holy Ghost. (*CSB*, p. 409; *OS*, p. 32)

Comparison of Rites (continued)
Individual Confession and Forgiveness

| *The Rites* | *Book of Common Prayer* | | *Lutheran Book* |
	Form 1	Form 2	*of Worship*
(Scripture)		Scripture	
			Invitation to Confession
Confession	Confession	Confession	Confession
	(Consolation, direction, and comfort)	(Consolation, direction, and comfort)	
			Ps. 51:1, 11–13
Prayer of the penitent			
Expression of sorrow		Expression of sorrow	
		Questions to the penitent	
Absolution	Absolution	Absolution	Absolution
Praise of God		Praise	Ps. 103:8–13
Dismissal	Dismissal	Dismissal	Dismissal

Preparation for the Service

The introduction to the Roman Catholic rite of penance observes wisely:

> In order to fulfill his ministry properly and faithfully the confessor should understand the disorders of souls and apply the appropriate remedies to them. He should fulfill his office of judge wisely and should acquire the knowledge and prudence necessary for this task by serious study, guided by the teaching authority of the Church and especially by fervent prayer to God. Discernment of spirits is a deep knowledge of God's action in the hearts of men; it is a gift of the Spirit as well as the fruit of charity.[15]

The language of the passage is not inclusive enough for Lutherans, but the thought is worth pondering. A confessor must be a person of prayer and study as well as a person of sympathy.

The more immediate preparation for confession and forgiveness also requires prayer. Again, the Roman Catholic introduction observes:

---

15. *The Rites*, p. 348. A footnote to this section says see Phil. 1:9–10.

Priest and penitent should first prepare themselves by prayer to celebrate the sacrament. The priest should call upon the Holy Spirit so that he may receive enlightenment and charity. The penitent should compare his life with the example and commandments of Christ and then pray to God for the forgiveness of his sins.[16]

Lutherans will also recall Luther's advice in the Small Catechism, "Reflect on your condition in the light of the Ten Commandments."[17]

Physical preparations need also be made to insure privacy for the confession. The pastor may want to draw the curtain around the hospital bed as an indication that others should not intrude. In a home the pastor should sit next to the penitent. Kneeling should be encouraged if the person is able to do so, but many infirm people will not find this possible.

Survey of the Service

The purpose of the greeting is to set the penitent at ease and to set the proper tone for what follows. The Roman Catholic rite suggests several verses of Scripture as possible greetings: Ezek. 33:11; Luke 5:32; 1 John 2:1-2. Psalm 51 is used in the Orthodox confession, and phrases from it were used in the confession in the *Church Book*.

The pastor's invitation to the penitent (p. 45), "You have come to make confession before God. In Christ you are free to confess before me, a pastor in his Church, the sins of which you are aware and the sins which trouble you," is to clarify what is about to happen, especially for those to whom confession and absolution is unfamiliar.

In the Lutheran form the use and application of Scripture follows the confession as comfort and consolation. In the Roman Catholic rite, scriptural verses are used before the confession to proclaim God's mercy and to call people to conversion. The following verses are suggested: Isa. 53:4-6; Ezek. 11:19-20; Matt. 6:14-15; Mark 1:14-15; Luke 6:31-38; 15:1-7; John 10:19-23; Rom. 5:8-9; Eph. 5:1-2; Col. 1:12-14; 3:8-10, 12-17; and 1 John 1:6-7, 9. In the *Book of Common Prayer* the "comfortable words" from the confession in the Eucharist are used here: Matt. 11:28; John 3:16; 1 Tim. 1:15; 1 John 2:1-2.

Further verses from Psalm 51 conclude the act of confession which is thus surrounded by Scripture, beginning and ending with Psalm 51, the psalm of repentance.

The absolution follows. The pastor stands (it is almost always awkward to lay hands on a person's head while seated) and declares God's

---

16. Ibid., p. 350.
17. *Book of Concord*, p. 350.

forgiveness. (The Roman Catholic rite calls for the priest only to extend the hands, or at least the right hand, over the penitent's head as the absolution is pronounced. Form 1 in the Prayer Book does not mention a gesture; Form 2 allows either a hand on the head or over the head of the penitent.

Since the thirteenth century the absolution has been reserved to ordained ministers. Although any Christian can hear the confession of another, lay people make a declaration of grace rather than a pronouncement of absolution, for they do not have the same representative function as the ordained ministers.

A time of silence is appropriate as the penitent savors the words of absolution. The gratitude may be vocalized with the words of Ps. 103:8-13. The Roman Catholic rite concludes with

Give thanks to the Lord, for he is good.
His mercy endures forever. (Ps. 136:1)

which the *Common Service Book* and the *Service Book and Hymnal* appointed as the versicle before the postcommunion collect. The dismissal

Blessed are those whose sins have been forgiven,
whose evil deeds have been forgotten.
Rejoice in the Lord, and go in peace.

is from the Roman rite.[18]

PSALMS, LESSONS, AND PRAYERS
(*Occasional Services*, pp. 48-75)

Parallel Rites

Roman Catholic   Texts for Use in the Rites for the Sick, *The Rites*, pp. 629-36.
Mass For the Sick, *Sacramentary*, pp. 916-17.
See also "Human Sickness and Its Meaning in the Mystery of Salvation," *The Rites*, pp. 582-83.
Visiting the Sick, *The Rites*, pp. 593-94.

Episcopal   Ministration to the Sick. Part I. Ministry of the Word, *Book of Common Prayer*, pp. 453-55, 458-61.
Eucharist "For the Sick," *Book of Common Prayer*, pp. 260, 931.

18. *The Rites*, p. 364.

> Blessing of a Pregnant Woman, *Book of Occasional Services,* pp. 142–43.
>
> A Thanksgiving for the Birth or Adoption of a Child, *Book of Common Prayer,* pp. 439–45.

Lutheran   Order for the Visitation of the Sick, *Occasional Services* (1962), pp. 33–54.

> Thanksgiving After the Birth of a Child, *Occasional Services* (1962), pp. 171–72.
>
> Lessons and Prayers for the Sick and Dying, *The Pastor's Companion* (St. Louis: Concordia Publishing House, n.d.), pp. 109–46.
>
> Lessons and Prayers for the Sick, *Common Service Book* (text ed.), pp. 414–27.
>
> Order for the Visitation of the Sick, Lessons and Prayers for the Sick, *Church Book* (1915), pp. 378–99.

Orthodox   For a Woman on the Fortieth Day After Childbirth, *Service Book,* pp. 268–70; *An Orthodox Prayer Book,* pp. 38–45.

> Prayers for Various Occasions, *An Orthodox Prayer Book*, pp. 140–43, 148–49, 159–60.

Purpose

This collection is designed to serve as an anthology, providing an optional structure and resources for the variety of situations into which the pastor is called — hospital, homes, institutions, and other settings.

Characteristics

Following the pattern established in earlier Lutheran service books, the psalms, lessons, and prayers are gathered under several headings to facilitate their use by those who minister to the sick. The headings in *Occasional Services* (1982) reflect modern psychological understanding of the various responses a patient may experience in the face of the stages of sickness.

For each section one psalm is printed out for the convenience of the minister; additional psalms are cited by number.

For each section one lesson is printed out; additional readings are cited by chapter and verse. (In the first general section "Sickness" the pattern has been altered in the final process of negotiation between the churches and preparing the manuscript for publication. The intention of

70

the compilers of the book was that Psalm 91 be the psalm printed out for the "Sickness" section and that Luke 4:38–44 be the lesson which is printed out. All the other verses were intended to be gathered together as brief passages for the minister or for the sick person to remember and reflect upon. These Brief Lessons for the Sick would have been the brief lessons from Compline (the reading from Matt. 11:28–30 in the text of Compline is from the New English Bible to avoid the phrase "for your soul" in the Revised Standard Version; in Psalms, Lessons, and Prayers the translation is that of the New International Version), to which were added Pss. 27:1a and 42:1–3. The *Church Book* and the *Common Service Book* included a section called "Sentences" under each heading of Lessons and Prayers for the Sick which served in part a similar function.

It must be clear to the person visited as well as to the minister that healing does not always follow even the most earnest prayer for healing and that there is no clear and inevitable relationship between the prayers and a cure. The minister must also guard against implying that there is a direct correlation between the verdict of the physicians and the will of God. For example, in the second prayer under "Impending Death or Irreversible Illness" ("Almighty God, your love never fails . . ." ⟨469⟩), the phrase "your Word" is not to be confused with the announcement of the physicians.

The *Book of Common Prayer* (pp. 458–59) provides two prayers for a sick child:

> Heavenly Father, watch with us over your child *N.*, and grant that *he* may be restored to that perfect health which it is yours alone to give; through Jesus Christ our Lord.

> Lord, Jesus Christ, Good Shepherd of the sheep, you gather the lambs in your arms and carry them in your bosom: We commend to your loving care this child *N.* Relieve *his* pain, guard *him* from all danger, restore to *him* your gifts of gladness and strength, and raise *him* up to a life of service to you. Hear us, we pray, for your dear Name's sake.

Lutheran books in the past also have provided special prayers for children. *Occasional Services* (1962) included (p. 50) this:

> O God, upon whom we all depend for strength both in youth and in maturity: Stretch forth thy right hand upon thy loved one who, at this tender age, is sick; that, being restored to health and vigor, *he* may come to the fullness of *his* allotted years; and all the days of *his* life never fail to thank thee and serve thee faithfully; through Jesus Christ our Lord.

71

The *Common Service Book* (text ed., p. 427) included this prayer "For a Sick Child":

> O Almighty God and merciful Father, to Whom belong the issues of life and death: Look in mercy, we beseech Thee, upon this sick child; visit *him*, O Lord, with Thy salvation; deliver *him* from *his* bodily pain, and if it be Thy will, prolong *his* days, that *he* may live to Thee, and show forth Thy praise in a godly life; through Jesus Christ, Thy Son, our Lord.

None of these prayers, however, seems to be essentially different from the prayers for adults, and *Occasional Services* (1982) does not have a separate category of prayers for children. The visitor must, of course, be sensitive to the special needs, fears, and hopes of young patients and understand that they are as deeply affected by their condition as are older patients.

Background

Among its Ministerial Acts the *Church Book* (1892) included an Order for the Visitation of the Sick (pp. 379–81) in three parts: Part I. Order for the Visitation of the Sick, followed by a section of Lessons and Prayers for the Sick; Part II. Communion of the Sick; Part III. Commendation of the Dying. The order is heavily penitential, not to say pessimistic. There seems to be no expectation of recovery, and Commendation of the Dying is included as the third part of the Visitation of the Sick. It nonetheless contains several interesting features. The order may begin with the traditional greeting "Peace be to this house, and to all that dwell herein." The sixfold Kyrie is said:

Lord, have mercy.	*Lord, have mercy.*
Christ, have mercy.	*Christ, have mercy.*
Lord, have mercy.	*Lord, have mercy.*

It is followed by the Lord's Prayer without the doxology ("For thine is the kingdom and the power and the glory for ever and ever"). The final petition "But deliver us from evil" is given as a response leading into the preces, which conclude with a prayer for deliverance from "the bondage to sin." This use of the Lord's Prayer without the doxology served as a helpful reminder that the original text of the prayer probably did not include the doxology, which seems to have been a later liturgical addition. The Lord's Prayer without doxology and the last petition as a response appeared in the Suffrages in the *Common Service Book* (text ed., p. 242) and in the General Suffrages in the *Service Book and Hymnal* (p. 153). The practice was not carried into the *LBW*.

The *Church Book* order then provides a long optional exhortation making four points: (1) "Our bodily afflictions are from the hand of God, and come to us only by reason of sin"; (2) "Jesus Christ, the Son of God, is ready to free us from all sin, if we believe in His gracious promise"; (3) "Our blessed Lord sendeth us sickness, yea, even death . . . that He may thereby move us to true repentance and faith . . ."; (4) "Thus assured by the Gospel . . . know that God regardeth thee . . . as a righteous, holy and beloved child in Christ." The minister is then directed to "examine whether the sick person be in true penitence and in charity with his fellow-men, and have a good hope through grace of eternal life." Searching questions are provided (p. 381):

Dear Friend: Art thou heartily sorry that thou hast so often grieved and offended thy gracious God and loving Father, sincerely desiring that these thy sins be forgiven thee?

Believest thou that Jesus Christ, the Son of God, suffered for thee the painful death of the Cross, and hath redeemed thee with his precious blood?

Believest that thou canst not be saved by thine own merits or good works, but only through the bitter sufferings and death of thy Saviour, Jesus Christ?

The rubric before these questions counsels:

When these inquiries are made, the Minister may ask all others to withdraw, if he see cause, especially if the sick person desire to unburden his mind of any matter weighing upon the conscience.

After this examination of the sick person, "It is meet and salutary that . . . Private Confession and Absolution should follow." Suitable lessons and prayers may be read. Finally, ending with the word with which it began, the rite concludes with a sentence from the Holy Communion, "The peace of the Lord be with you alway."

The Lessons and Prayers are gathered under the following headings:
1. Afflictions and Their Uses (including a Litany for the Sick, an abbreviation and adaptation of The Litany)
2. Knowledge of Sin and Repentance
3. Assurance of Forgiveness Through Faith in Christ
4. Patience Under Suffering, and Trust in God's Help
5. Preparation for Death
6. Hope of Resurrection and Eternal Life

Under each heading appropriate psalms and lessons are cited; sentences — a series of appropriate verses — are printed out; and prayers are provided for use by the minister and by the individual. The collection of sentences —

73

carried into the *Common Service Book*, deleted from *Occasional Services* (1962), and restored in *Occasional Services* (1982), although not under that title—is a helpful list for a pastor so an appropriate verse or a few verses may be selected and given to the sick person to embrace and ponder.

The text of the Litany for the Sick provided in the *Church Book* (pp. 383-84) was:

Lord God, the Father in heaven,
Have mercy upon him.
Lord God, the Son, Redeemer of the world,
Have mercy upon him.
Lord God, the Holy Ghost,
Have mercy upon him.
    Be gracious to *him*.
        Spare him, *good Lord*.
    Be gracious to *him*.
      Help him, *good Lord*.
    From all sin,
      Good Lord, deliver him.
From all unbelief and doubt,
From Thy just and dreadful wrath,
From the crafts and assaults of the devil,
From the fear of eternal death,
From the anguish and pains of hell,
And from all evil,
    Defend him, *good Lord*.

By Thy holy Nativity,
By Thine Agony and Bloody Sweat,
By Thy Cross and Passion,
By Thy glorious Resurrection and Ascension,
    Help him, *O Lord*.
In the hour of death,
And in the day of Judgment,
    Help him, *good Lord*.

We poor sinners beseech Thee
    To hear us, O Lord God.
That Thou wouldest give *him* health of body and soul.
That *he* may confidently look to Thy fatherly goodness for whatsoever is needful.
That *he* may be enabled to call upon Thee in true faith.
That Thy good angel may defend, direct and conduct *him* in all *his* ways.
That, in steadfast faith, *he* may withstand and overcome all temptation.
That *he* may resign *himself*, body and soul, to Thy will.

That *he* may truly know and heartily repent of all *his* sins.
That *he* may find comfort in Thy goodness and mercy.
That *he* may willingly forgive all *his* enemies and persecutors.
That *he* may turn away from all lusts and pleasures of the world.
That *his* desire may be unto Thee and the treasures of Thy heavenly kingdom.
That *he* may await *his* last hour in patience.
That *he* may commit *his* spirit into Thy hands.
That *his* departure may be in peace.
That *he* may have part in the resurrection unto life.
That *he* may meet *his* Lord with joy.
That *he* may live for ever in Thy kingdom.
Hear us, good Lord.
O Lord Jesus Christ, Son of God;
Have mercy upon him.
O Lamb of God, that takest away the sin of the world.
Have mercy upon him.
O Lamb of God, that takest away the sin of the world.
Have mercy upon him.
O Lamb of God, that takest away the sin of the world.
Grant him *Thy peace.*

Amen.

The *Common Service Book* (1919) used the same divisions and titles and much of the same material in the section Lessons and Prayers for the Sick. Noteworthy, however, is the disappearance of the structure of a rite; only lessons and prayers are provided. The Litany for the Sick disappears. The tone of the sentences is less judgmental and more consoling, and the sentences themselves are drawn more from the New Testament than were the sentences in the *Church Book*. The order of the sentences remains the biblical order, although not slavishly so. At the conclusion of the anthology, divided into six sections as in the *Church Book*, there is a seventh section, "Additional Prayers," which concludes the Lessons and Prayers. There is a prayer "For the Sick," a prayer "For a Sick Child," and two prayers "After Recovery from Sickness."

The undated *Pastor's Companion authorized by the Synods constituting the Evangelical Lutheran Synodical Conference of North America*, published by Concordia Publishing House, St. Louis, reprinted material from the *Lutheran Agenda* in a more convenient pocket-sized book and added a section Lessons and Prayers for the Sick and the Dying. The titles of the categories and the lessons and sentences reflect the *Common Service Book:* Afflictions and Their Uses; Repentance and Assurance of Forgiveness; Patience Under Suffering and Trust in God's Help; Preparation for Death, and When the End Is at Hand; Gratitude for Recovery;

At the Sickbed of Children. The prayers in each section are cast in the first person for use by the one who is sick, except that the final section offers prayers for others to say for the child. Hymn stanzas (without music) are added to each section.

Occasional Services (1962) restored the *Church Book* framework: "Peace be to this house . . ."; sixfold Kyrie; "Our Father . . . deliver us from evil"; preces and prayer. "The blessing of Almighty God, the Father, the Son, and the Holy Ghost, be with you alway" concludes the section, and Private Confession and Absolution or the Communion of the Sick or a selection from Psalms, Lessons, and Prayers may follow. The structure of each subsection follows the general pattern established by the *Church Book*, but the subsections themselves are remarkably less penitential and gloomy:

1. Faith and Bodily Health
2. Comfort and Joy from Holy Scripture
3. God's Healing Power
4. In Time of Suffering and Mental Anguish
5. God Hears Our Prayers
6. The Christian Hope
7. Praise and Thanksgiving
8. Additional Prayers

In the Additional Prayers section the following are cited: For a Sick Child; For All Present at the Visitation of the Sick; For Those Who Minister to the Sick; For Those in a Hospital; For the Dying; Before an Operation; For a Happy Death; additional collects from the Collects and Prayers section of the *Service Book and Hymnal* are cited by number.

Under each subhead appropriate psalms are cited and appropriate lessons are indicated with a reference to their liturgical use, if any (for example, Mark 16:1-8 [Gospel for Easter]). As an alternate to these lessons, one or more readings are printed out. These are longer readings of several verses, and they represent a change in the state of biblical scholarship and understanding away from proof texts and fragmentation and toward taking passages in their context. The deficiency of this approach is that those who are weak may not be able to concentrate on such longer readings. The final rubric is curious: "A visit to a sick person may conclude with the Lord's Prayer [already said at the opening] and a Benediction." "The Blessing of Almighty God, the Father, the Son, and the Holy Ghost, be with thee alway" is provided once again, having already been used at the conclusion of the opening section of the visitation.

Development of the Rite
Psalms, Lessons, and Prayers

Church Book	*Common Service Book*	*Occasional Services* (1962)	*Occasional Services* (1982)
Peace . . .*		Peace . . .†	
Kyrie		Kyrie	
Our Father		Our Father	
Preces		Preces	
Prayer		Prayer	
Exhortation			
Examination			
		Blessing	
(Private confession)		(Private confession)	
Lessons and prayers	Lessons and prayers	Lessons and prayers	Lessons and prayers
1. Afflictions	1. Affliction	1. Faith and Health	1. Sickness
2. Knowledge of sin	2. Knowledge of sin	2. Comfort and joy	2. Gratitude
3. Forgiveness	3. Forgiveness	3. Healing	3, 4. Childbirth
4. Patience	4. Patience	4. Suffering	5. Stillbirth
5. Death	5. Death	5. God hears	6. Addiction
6. Resurrection	6. Resurrection	6. Hope	7. Anxiety
	7. Additional prayers	7. Praise	8. Guilt
		8. Additional prayers	9. Loneliness
			10. Impatience
			11. Death
			12. Anger
			13. Acceptance
			14, 15. Surgery
		Our Father	
The peace of the Lord be with you alway.		Benediction	Benedictions

---

*Peace be to this house, and to all that dwell herein.

Lord, have mercy.
Lord, have mercy.

Christ, have mercy.
Christ, have mercy.

†Peace be to this house, and to all that dwell therein.

Lord, have mercy.
Lord, have mercy.

Christ, have mercy.
Christ, have mercy.

The Roman Catholic church provides propers for a Mass For the Sick. The prayers and readings are these:

Opening Prayer

Father, your Son accepted our sufferings
to teach us the virtue of patience in human illness.
Hear the prayers we offer for our sick brothers and sisters.
May all who suffer pain, illness or disease
realize that they are chosen to be saints,
and know that they are joined to Christ
in his suffering for the salvation of the world,
who lives and reigns with you and the Holy Spirit,
one God, for ever and ever.

or,

Lord, have mercy.
Lord, have mercy.

Our Father, who art in heaven; Hallowed be Thy Name; Thy kingdom come; Thy will be done, on earth as it is in heaven; Give us this day our daily bread; And forgive us our trespasses, as we forgive those who trespass against us; And lead us not into temptation. *But deliver us from evil.*

O Lord, save Thy servant;

Who putteth his trust in Thee.

O Lord, send *him* help from the Sanctuary;

And strengthen him *out of Zion.*

Let the enemy have no advantage of *him.*

Nor the wicked approach to hurt him.

O Lord, strengthen *him;*

Upon the bed of languishing.

O Lord, hear our prayer;

And let our cry come unto thee.

Almighty God, to whom mercy belongeth, and Whose delight it is at all times to spare and save: Accept, we beseech Thee, our humble prayer, and set free Thy servants that lie under the bondage of sin, according to thy merciful goodness; through our Lord Jesus Christ. *Amen.* (pp. 378-79)

Lord, have mercy.
Lord, have mercy.

Our Father, who art in heaven, Hallowed be thy Name; Thy kingdom come; Thy will be done, on earth as it is in heaven. Give us this day our daily bread; And forgive us our trespasses, as we forgive those who trespass against us; And lead us not into temptation, But deliver us from evil.

For thine is the kingdom, and the power, and the glory, for ever and ever. Amen.

O Lord, save thy servant:

Who putteth his trust in thee. (86:2)

Send him help from the sanctuary:

And strengthen him out of Zion. (20:2)

Look upon his affliction and his pain.

And forgive all his sins. (25:18)

O Lord, strengthen him:

Upon the bed of languishing. (41:3)

O Lord, hear our prayer:

And let our cry come unto thee. (102:1)
The Lord be with you.

And with thy spirit.
Let us pray.

Almighty God, to whom mercy belongeth, and whose delight it is at all times to spare and save: Accept, we beseech thee, our humble prayer, deliver us and this thy servant from the bondage of sin, and according to thy merciful goodness, make known thy healing power; through our Lord Jesus Christ. *Amen.* (pp. 33-34)

All-powerful and ever-living God,
the lasting health of all who believe in you,
hear us as we ask your loving help for the sick;
restore their health,
that they may again offer joyful thanks in your Church.
Grant this through our Lord Jesus Christ, your Son,
who lives and reigns with you and the Holy Spirit,
one God, for ever and ever.

Old Testament reading
2 Kings 20:1-6   I have seen your tears, and I have cured you.
Isa. 53:1-5, 10-11   He is the one who bore our sufferings.

New Testament reading
Acts 28:7-10   All the people on the island who had sicknesses came
to the apostle Paul and were cured.
2 Cor. 4:10-18   We are consigned to death for the sake of Jesus.
2 Cor. 12:7b-10   My grace is enough for you: my power is at its best
in weakness.
James 5:13-16   The prayer of faith will save the infirm.

Responsorial Psalm
Isa. 38:10-12, 16
Ps. 102:1-3, 24-25, 19-21

Alleluia Verse
Matt. 8:17
2 Cor. 1:3b-4a
Col. 1:24b

Gospel
Matt. 8:14-17   He took our infirmities on himself.
Mark 16:15-20   They will place their hands on the sick and they will
recover.
Luke 22:39-43a   Father, let your will be done, not mine.
John 15:1-8   The Father prunes every branch that bears fruit to
make it bear even more.

Prayer Over the Gifts (offertory prayer)

God our Father,
your love guides every moment of our lives.
Accept the prayers and gifts we offer
for our sick brothers and sisters;
restore them to health
and turn our anxiety for them into joy.
We ask this in the name of Jesus the Lord.

Prayer After Communion

God our Father,
our help in human weakness,
show our sick brothers and sisters
the power of your loving care.
In your kindness make them well
and restore them to your Church.
We ask this through Christ our Lord.

For the sick who are dying, the Mass is celebrated with the following prayers:

Opening Prayer

God of power and mercy,
you have made death itself
the gateway to eternal life.
Look with love on our dying brother (sister),
and make him (her) one with your Son in his suffering and death,
that, sealed with the blood of Christ,
he (she) may come before you free from sin.
We ask this through our Lord Jesus Christ, your Son,
who lives and reigns with you and the Holy Spirit,
one God, for ever and ever.

Prayer Over the Gifts

Father,
accept this sacrifice we offer
for our dying brother (sister),
and by it free him (her) from all his (her) sins.
As he (she) accepted the sufferings you asked him (her) to bear in this life,
may he (she) enjoy happiness and peace for ever in the life to come.
We ask this through Christ our Lord.

Prayer After Communion

Lord,
by the power of this sacrament,
keep your servant safe in your love.
Do not let evil conquer him (her) at the hour of death,
but let him (her) go in the company of your angels
to the joy of eternal life.
We ask this through Christ our Lord.

A rubric in chapter 3 of the Rite of Anointing and Pastoral Care of the Sick advises: "The pastor and other priests who are entrusted with the spiritual care of the sick should do everything they can to insure that those in danger of death receive the body and blood of Christ in viaticum" (*The Rites,* p. 608). This reception of Holy Communion as food for one's journey from this world to the next may be at a celebration of mass, which may be the Mass For the Sick with the following prayers:

Opening Prayer

> Father, your Son, Jesus Christ, is our way, our truth, and our life.
> Our brother (sister) *N.* entrusts himself (herself) to you
>   with full confidence in all your promises.
> Refresh him (her) with the body and blood of your Son
> and lead him (her) to your kingdom in peace.
> We ask this through our Lord Jesus Christ, your Son,
> who lives and reigns with you and the Holy Spirit,
> one God, for ever and ever.

Prayer Over the Gifts

> Father,
> the suffering, death, and resurrection of Jesus,
> the true paschal Lamb,
> has opened heaven for us.
> May our offering become his sacrifice
> and lead our brother (sister) *N.* to eternal life.
> We ask this through Christ our Lord.

Prayer After Communion

> Lord,
> you are the source of eternal health
> for those who believe in you.
> May our brother (sister) *N.*,
> who has been refreshed with food and drink from heaven,
> safely reach your kingdom of light and life.
> We ask this through Christ our Lord.

The Roman Catholic church also provides a Mass For a Happy Death. The propers are these:

Opening Prayer

> Father, you made us in your own image
> and your Son accepted death for our salvation.
> Help us to keep watch in prayer at all times.
> May we be free from sin when we leave this world
> and rejoice in peace with you for ever.

We ask this through our Lord Jesus Christ, your Son,
who lives and reigns with you and the Holy Spirit,
one God, for ever and ever.

Old Testament Reading
Isa. 25:6–10a   He will destroy death for ever.

New Testament Reading
Rom. 14:7–9, 10b–12   Whether alive or dead, we belong to the
Lord.

Responsorial Psalm
Ps. 31:2, 6, 8b–9, 15–17, 25

Alleluia Verse
John 13:1

Gospel
Luke 23:39–46   Father, into your hands I commit my spirit.

Prayer Over the Gifts

Lord,
by the death of your Son,
you have destroyed our death.
By the power of this sacrament
keep us obedient to your will until death.
May we leave this world with confidence and peace
and come to share in the gift of his resurrection.
We ask this through Christ our Lord.

Prayer After Communion

Lord,
in receiving these sacred mysteries,
the pledge of unending life,
we pray for your loving help at the hour of our death.
Give us the victory over our enemy
and bring us to eternal peace in the glory of your kingdom.
We ask this through Christ our Lord.

The Roman Catholic liturgy for the sick centers, as in past ages, on
anointing, but other material is provided as well to guide the priest in
the care of the sick. An introductory section in the Rite of Anointing and
Pastoral Care of the Sick (*The Rites*, pp. 582–83) discusses "Human
Sickness and Its Meaning in the Mystery of Salvation." It suggests, first,
that the enigma of sickness and pain is shared by Christians and non-
Christians alike, but that Christians know from Christ's words that
"sickness has meaning and value for their own salvation and for the

world's." Second, while sickness is closely related to the sinful condition of humanity, it cannot be considered a punishment which one suffers for one's personal sins. Third, while we should struggle against sickness and seek health, we should always be prepared to fill up what is lacking in Christ's sufferings for the sake of the world (Col. 1:24; Rom. 8:19-21). Moreover, the sick have a role in the church: "to remind others not to lose sight of the essential or higher things." Finally, the sick person is not alone in the struggle against illness. "Doctors and all who are dedicated to helping the sick should consider it their duty to do whatever they judge will help the sick both physically and spiritually."

Moreover, chapter 1 of Anointing and Pastoral Care of the Sick provides introductory rubrics on "Visiting the Sick" (*The Rites*, pp. 593-94). It is the responsibility of all Christians to "share in the care and love of Christ and the Church for the sick," to visit them and to comfort them (no. 42). Pastors especially and others who care for the sick "should offer words of faith," explain the significance of human suffering in the mystery of salvation, and urge the sick to realize that through faith they are united with Christ's suffering. "It is the special task of priests to lead the sick step by step to the sacraments of penance and the eucharist, which they should receive often if their condition permits" (no. 43). The sick should be encouraged to pray, drawing primarily upon the Scriptures. "The sick should be helped in making this sort of prayer, and priests should always be ready to pray with them" (no. 44). The priest, together with the sick person and those present, should use "suitable elements of common prayer in the form of a brief liturgy of the word. As occasion permits, prayer drawn from the psalms or other prayers should be added to the word of God." The sick person should be blessed at the end, and the laying on of hands may be added (no. 45).

To guide those ministering to the sick, a list of Bible readings for use in the rites for the sick is provided for use in the Mass for the sick, in the visitation of the sick, or when praying for the sick whether they are present or not. Old Testament and New Testament readings, responsorial psalms, alleluia verses, and Gospels are provided.

The Episcopal Church offers fewer suggestions. Propers are provided for a votive Eucharist "For the Sick":

Collect for the Occasion

> Heavenly Father, giver of life and health: Comfort and relieve your sick servants, and give your power of healing to those who minister to their needs, that those (*or N., or NN.*) for whom our prayers are offered may be strengthened in *their* weakness and have confidence in your loving care; through Jesus Christ our Lord, who lives and reigns with you and the Holy Spirit, one God, now and for ever. *Amen.* (*Book of Common Prayer*, p. 260)

Psalms and Lessons (p. 931)
    Psalm 13 or 86:1-7
    2 Kings 20:1-5
    James 5:13-16
    Mark 2:1-12

Postcommunion prayer

> Gracious Father, we give you praise and thanks for this Holy Communion of the Body and Blood of your beloved Son Jesus Christ, the pledge of our redemption; and we pray that it may bring us forgiveness of our sins, strength in our weakness, and everlasting salvation; through Jesus Christ our Lord. *Amen.* (p. 457)

Under part one of Ministration to the Sick, "Ministry of the Word" (pp. 453-54), additional passages of Scripture are suggested:

General
    2 Cor. 1:3-5 God comforts us in affliction.
    Psalm 91 He will give his angels charge over you.
    Luke 17:11-19 Your faith has made you well.

Penitence
    Heb. 12:1-2 Looking to Jesus, the perfecter of our faith.
    Psalm 103 He forgives all your sins.
    Matt. 9:2-8 Your sins are forgiven.

When Anointing is to follow
    James 5:14-16 Is any among you sick?
    Psalm 23 You have anointed my head with oil.
    Mark 6:7, 12-13 They anointed with oil many that were sick.

When Communion is to follow
    1 John 5:13-15 That you may know that you have eternal life.
    Ps. 145:14-22 The eyes of all wait upon you, O Lord.
    John 6:47-51 I am the bread of life.

Comment on the readings, prayers, and confession may follow.

A series of Prayers for the Sick is given (pp. 458-60):
    For a Sick Person
    For Recovery from Sickness (two prayers)
    For a Sick Child (two prayers)
    Before an Operation (two prayers)
    For Strength and Confidence (two prayers)
    For the Sanctification of Illness
    For Health of Body and Soul

For Doctors and Nurses
Thanksgiving for a Beginning of Recovery

Four prayers are provided for use by a sick person (p. 461):
For Trust in God
In Pain
For Sleep
In the Morning

Survey of the Service

When visiting the sick, care should be taken so as not to tire the patient. (The rubric in the *Common Service Book* [p. 414] reads, "The Minister's visits should be brief.") On the other hand, the minister should not appear rushed, even if that is in fact the case. The visit must address the needs of each individual patient, and the visitor must avoid seeming to be too mechanical and too uncomfortable in the face of illness.

Although the resources provided in this collection are primarily for use by a pastor, lay people too should be encouraged to visit the sick, read Scripture to them, and pray with them. The love that unites us with God and with one another in him impels us to express our solidarity with infirm sisters and brothers by praying with them for God's strength and for confidence in God's care in this life and in the life to come.

Appropriate lessons and prayers are to be taken from the collection, and others may be added if the situation suggests. Pastors, therefore, need to study this section with great care and should come to know it intimately so that they may make use of the appropriate readings and prayers for each individual patient. The texts and prayers should always be appropriate to the physical and spiritual condition of the person visited. They should be read slowly and carefully, alternated with periods of silence.[19]

With the weak and the dying, significant, brief phrases may be repeated several times. The series of brief (one verse) lessons given under Acceptance of Inevitable Death (p. 73) and Ps. 31:5 are taken largely from the short texts from the Roman Catholic Rite for the Commendation of the Dying,[20] and may be used in such a way. (2 Cor. 4:7–18 is intended as the lesson for this section; it is out of place and interrupts the short texts.) One appropriate text from this list may be given to a weak or dying person to repeat over and over again, to hold onto, and to find strength in. Familiar hymn stanzas, especially for older people who know many hymns by heart, may also be useful.

---

19. *The Rites*, p. 622.
20. Ibid., pp. 623–24.

The person may be helped by clinging to a physical object. In the ministry to the dying, John Doberstein's advice, which he gave to his classes at Lutheran Theological Seminary at Philadelphia, may still be helpful: "Put a crucifix in their hands and preach the resurrection." The whole work of Christ is thus set before the person—death and resurrection. And that work of Christ was not for himself but for those who by baptism belong to him. Already they have died with him, and already they have been given eternal life by him.

Sources of the Prayers

Sickness

"O Lord, visit and restore your servant . . . " ⟨441⟩. *Occasional Services* (1962), pp. 35–36, altered; from the 1928 American *Book of Common Prayer,* this prayer was taken from the last of the nine collects following the suffrages in the Sarum office.

"O God, the strength of the weak . . ." ⟨442⟩. *LBW* (226), "Recovery from Sickness" with "sorrow" replaced by "anxiety"; from the 1928 American *Book of Common Prayer* (p. 312) and believed to be by Howard Baldwin St. George; it is in the 1979 Prayer Book, p. 458, "For Recovery from Sickness."

"O God of power and love . . . " ⟨443⟩. From the 1928 American *Book of Common Prayer,* p. 315; from William Bright's *Ancient Collects,* pp. 109–10, originally in the Gelasian Sacramentary (no. 1537) and the supplement to the Gregorian (no. 1390); it is in the 1979 Prayer Book, p. 458.

"Heavenly Father, giver of life and health . . . " ⟨444⟩. By John Dowden, bishop of Edinburgh (1886–1910), this prayer was included in the Scottish Prayer Book of 1912; abbreviated in the 1928 American Prayer Book, p. 597; and adapted by Charles M. Guilbert for the 1979 *Book of Common Prayer.*

"O Lord, look upon your servant . . . " ⟨445⟩. Liturgical Text committee of the Inter-Lutheran Commission on Worship, composed during the preparation of the *LBW.*

Gratitude

"Almighty and gracious God . . ." (228). The *LBW* adapted the thanksgiving "For the Restoration of Health" from the 1979 *Book of Common Prayer,* p. 841. The prayer first appeared in the Prayer Book in 1892, a variant of the thanksgiving in the rite for the Thanksgiving after Childbirth in the 1789 Prayer Book.

"O Lord our God, source of life . . . " ⟨446⟩. A free adaptation of a prayer in the 1928 American Prayer Book, p. 312:

O God, the strength of the weak and the comfort of sufferers: Mercifully accept our prayers, and grant to thy servant the help of thy power, that *his* sickness may be turned into health, and *his* sorrow into joy; through Jesus Christ our Lord.

Before Childbirth

"O God, the creator and sustainer . . . " ⟨447⟩. New.

"O Lord our God, creator of all . . ." ⟨448⟩. This prayer is altered from *Occasional Services* (1962), p. 172.

Following Childbirth

"Heavenly Father, you sent your Son . . . " (231). The *LBW* borrowed and slightly altered this prayer (by the addition of "as the child of Mary and Joseph") from the 1979 *Book of Common Prayer,* p. 841. It was originally drafted by Caroline Rose. This prayer is for the child, and it is especially appropriate for use by the parents.

"O gracious God, we give you thanks . . . " ⟨449⟩. This prayer is an abbreviation of the prayer of thanksgiving "For a safe delivery" in the 1979 *Book of Common Prayer,* p. 444. It has evolved from a prayer in the Sarum rite and was adapted for use in the 1549 Prayer Book. This prayer is a thanksgiving for the mother of the child.

"O God our creator, grant that the child . . . " ⟨450⟩. This prayer is taken, with slight change, from the 1928 American *Book of Common Prayer,* p. 307. It had been added to that book by the 1928 Revision Commission. This prayer is a prayer for the child.

"Almighty God, giver of life and love . . . " ⟨451⟩. This is an adaptation of a prayer "For the parents" in the 1979 *Book of Common Prayer,* p. 444. It was written by Angus Dun, bishop of Washington (1944–62).

Stillbirth or Death Shortly After Birth

"Lord God, Father of mercies . . ." ⟨452⟩. This is an adaptation of a prayer "Or, if the Child be dead" from the Thanksgiving after the Birth of a Child in *Occasional Services* (1962), p. 172.

"O God our Father, your beloved Son . . . " (283). This is a slight alteration of the collect "At the Burial of a Child" in the 1979 *Book of Common Prayer.* That prayer is a slightly revised version of a prayer first printed in the 1928 American Prayer Book. It was in turn based on a prayer by John Dowden, bishop of Edinburgh (1886–1910), which appeared in the Scottish Prayer Book of 1912.

"Merciful God, comfort your servants . . . " ⟨453⟩. This is an adaptation of a prayer from the 1928 English *Book of Common Prayer,* and the Scottish, Irish, and South African Prayer Books. The text is in *The Book of English Collects,* ed. John Wallace Suter, Jr. (New York and London: Harper & Brothers, 1940), p. 333, (no. 570).

Addiction

"O Lord, mercifully regard your servant . . . " ⟨454⟩. This prayer was originally composed by the Liturgical Text Committee of the Inter-Lutheran Commission on Worship in the course of the preparation of the *LBW.*

"O blessed Jesus, you ministered to all . . . " (227). This prayer from the *LBW* is a slight revision of a prayer "For the Victims of Addiction" (no. 56) in the 1979 *Book of Common Prayer,* p. 831. The prayer was drafted by Charles W. F. Smith.

Anxiety, Apprehension, Fear

"Almighty and merciful God, our only source of health . . . " ⟨455⟩. This prayer is an alteration of a prayer originally drafted by the Liturgical Text Committee of the Inter-Lutheran Commission on Worship in the course of the preparation of the *LBW.*

"Loving Lord, we entrust ourselves to your care . . . " ⟨456⟩. This is a revision of a prayer originally drafted by the Liturgical Text Committee of the Inter-Lutheran Commission on Worship.

"O most loving Father, you want us to give thanks . . . " ⟨457⟩. This prayer, adapted from the *LBW,* is a revision of a prayer "For Trustfulness" from the 1928 American *Book of Common Prayer,* p. 596. It was composed by William Bright and recalls phrases from 1 Tim. 2:1; Phil. 3:8; 1 Pet. 5:7; Matt. 6:25–34; and 1 John 4:7–21.

Guilt

"God of mercy, compassion, and healing . . . " ⟨462⟩. This is an adaptation of a prayer "For Use by the Afflicted" from *Occasional Services* (1962), p. 44, which takes phrases from Psalm 51.

"Almighty and everlasting God, comfort of the sad . . . " (223). This is a revision of a prayer in the *LBW* which was borrowed from the *Service Book and Hymnal* prayer "For Those in Affliction" (p. 223, no. 35). It is taken from the Gelasian Sacramentary, appointed for Good Friday (ed. Henry A. Wilson), p. 76.

Loneliness

"Merciful God, our Father, in the stillness of our souls . . . " ⟨463⟩. This is a revision of a prayer drafted by the Liturgical Text Committee of the Inter-Lutheran Commission on Worship.

"O Lord our God, you see and know and feel the pain . . . " ⟨464⟩.

This is a revision of a prayer "For God's Healing Power" from *Occasional Services* (1962), p. 40.

"Blessed Lord, in moments of pain . . . " ⟨465⟩. New.

Impatience or Boredom

"O Lord our God, we need your guidance . . ." ⟨466⟩. This is a revision of a prayer by Bishop Ashton Oxenden, collected in *A Chain of Prayer across the Ages,* ed. Selina Fitzherbert Fox (New York: E. P. Dutton, 1936), p. 77.

"Lord, do with us as seems best . . . " ⟨467⟩. This is a revision of a prayer by Archbishop William Laud (1573) collected in *A Chain of Prayer across the Ages,* p. 109.

Impending Death or Irreversible Illness

"O merciful Father, you teach us in your holy Word . . . " ⟨468⟩. This prayer from the *LBW* is a revision of prayer no. 55, "For a Person in Trouble or Bereavement" from the 1979 *Book of Common Prayer,* p. 831. It was introduced into the American Prayer Book in 1789, emended somewhat from a manuscript of prayers gathered by Bishop Samuel Seabury. See Lam. 3:33.

"Almighty God, your love never fails . . . " ⟨469⟩. This is a revision of a prayer from the Funeral Service in the Presbyterian *Worshipbook* (1972), p. 72.

"O blessed Lord, God of mercies and of comfort . . . " ⟨470⟩. This is a revision of a prayer "In Time of Suffering and Mental Anguish" from *Occasional Services* (1962), p. 43.

Anger, Bitterness, Self-Pity, Turmoil

"Our Lord and our God, grant us grace to see your love . . . " ⟨471⟩. This is a revision of a prayer "In Time of Suffering and Mental Anguish" from *Occasional Services* (1962), p. 44. The address is taken from the prayer "For Use by the Afflicted," which in turn is from John 20:28.

"Almighty God, to whom our needs are known . . . " (211). This prayer from the *LBW* is borrowed from the 1979 *Book of Common Prayer,* pp. 394–95. It is a contemporary adaptation of the collect by Thomas Cranmer which in the 1979 Prayer Book is appointed as the Collect for Proper 11, p. 231. The Cranmerian prayer was included in the *Service Book and Hymnal* as no. 122, "For Answer to Prayer."

"Merciful God, grant that the spirit of Jesus . . . " ⟨472⟩. This is an adaptation of a prayer in *The Daily Office,* ed. Herbert Lindemann (St. Louis: Concordia Publishing House, 1965), p. 482.

Acceptance of Inevitable Death

"O Lord, support us all the day long . . ." (260). This prayer from the *LBW* is borrowed from the 1979 *Book of Common Prayer* ("In the Evening," p. 833, no. 63). It was added to the 1928 American Prayer Book, having been found or composed by George W. Douglas in or before 1876 in connection with a passage in sermon XX of a collection of sermons by John Henry Newman, *Sermons on Subjects of the Day* (See *The Living Church,* June 8, 1935).

"God of all grace, you sent your Son . . . " (284). This prayer from the Burial of the Dead section in the *LBW* is a revision of a prayer for burial in the *Service Book and Hymnal* (1958). It first appeared in the *Book of Common Order* of the Church of Scotland (1940) in the Order for the Burial of the Dead on p. 175 of the 1962 printing.

"Lord God, you have brought us near . . . " ⟨473⟩. This prayer is from William Bright's *Ancient Collects,* p. 236. It is borrowed from there by the *Service Book and Hymnal* and included as no. 44 of the Collects and Prayers.

"Lord Jesus Christ, you have overcome death . . . " ⟨474⟩. This is a revision of a prayer in Hope of Resurrection and Eternal Life in Lessons and Prayers for the Sick in the *Common Service Book* (text ed., p. 426). The address recalls 2 Tim. 1:10.

"Lord Jesus Christ, Son of the living God . . . " ⟨475⟩. This is the first part of a prayer appointed for Good Friday in the 1979 *Book of Common Prayer,* p. 282. It is from the memorial of the cross which was frequently included in medieval primers, which were small books for lay people with devotions for various hours of the daily prayer of the church. The prayer in the Prayer Book is a slight revision of a translation in *A Procession of Passion Prayers,* ed. Eric Milner-White (London: SPCK, 1956), p. xiii. The full text in the Prayer Book is:

> Lord Jesus Christ, Son of the Living God, we pray you to set your passion, cross, and death between your judgment and our souls, now and in the hour of our death. Give mercy and grace to the living; pardon and rest to the dead; to your holy Church peace and concord; and to us sinners everlasting life and glory; for with the Father and the Holy Spirit you live and reign, one God, now and for ever. *Amen.*

Before Surgery

"Almighty God, our heavenly Father, graciously protect . . . " ⟨458⟩. This is a slight revision of a prayer "Before an Operation" from the 1979 *Book of Common Prayer,* p. 459. In turn it was a slight revision of a prayer "For One about to undergo an Operation," which appeared in the 1928 American Prayer Book, the work of the 1928 Revision Commission. The concluding phrase is from Ps. 56:3.

"Strengthen your servant . . . " ⟨459⟩. This is a revision of a prayer "Before an Operation" from the 1979 *Book of Common Prayer,* p. 459. It is a revision of a prayer by Robert N. Rodenmayer published in *The Pastor's Prayerbook* (New York: Oxford University Press, 1960), no. 252.

"Loving Lord, hold _____ in your care" ⟨460⟩. New.

Following Surgery

"Almighty and gracious God, we give you thanks . . . " ⟨461⟩. New.

Benedictions

"Now may our Lord Jesus Christ . . . " (2 Thess. 2:16–17).

"Now to him who by the power . . . " (Eph. 3:20–21).

"The almighty Lord, a strong tower . . . " This is an edited version of the blessing which concludes the Visitation of the Sick in the 1549 *Book of Common Prayer*. It is in the 1979 Prayer Book, pp. 456–57. It is based on Ps. 61:3; Phil. 2:10–11, and Acts 4:12. It seems to have no liturgical antecedents before 1549.

"The God of peace sanctify you . . . " (1 Thess. 5:23 with the Roman pontifical blessing).

"May the God of hope . . . " (Rom. 15:13).

LAYING ON OF HANDS AND ANOINTING THE SICK
(*Occasional Services,* pp. 99–102)

Parallel Rites

Roman Catholic	Rite of Anointing a Sick Person, *The Rites,* pp. 599–604.
	Rite of the Sacraments for Those Near Death, *The Rites,* pp. 615–20.
	Rite of Blessing of Oils, *The Rites,* pp. 513–27.
Episcopal	Ministration to the Sick. Part II. Laying on of Hands and Anointing, *Book of Common Prayer,* pp. 455–57.
Orthodox	The Office of Holy Unction, *Service Book,* pp. 332–59, 607–9.
Brethren	The Anointing Service, *Pastor's Manual,* pp. 63–71.

THE SERVICES OF THE MINISTRY OF HEALING

Purpose

The Laying on of Hands and Anointing the Sick is for use with an individual during the course of pastoral ministry to the sick. There is another rite, the Service of the Word for Healing, for corporate use.

This rite is a testimony to God's compassion and to his will for the wholeness of his creation. It is, moreover, a recognition that healing is more than a physical process.

When this rite is employed, care must be taken not to suggest that physical healing must follow from its use nor to suggest that those who do not experience physical healing have not found favor with God. The service is not to burden consciences, but to expand our understanding of God's goodness, care, and concern.

Characteristics

This service is new to Lutheran service books, although it is not new to Lutheran practice in many places, to Christianity at large, nor to Scripture.[21] The action of this service is a response to the direction of James 5:14-15, "Is any among you sick? Let him call for the elders of the church, and let them pray over him, anointing him with oil in the name of the Lord."

Laying on of hands is here a gesture of compassion, carried out in imitation of Jesus' touching the sick.

Oil, a common medical remedy in ancient times (see Isa. 1:6; Mark 6:13; Luke 10:34), is in the Epistle of James invested also with a spiritual significance through connection with the name of God. Its use has continued in Christian practice through all the centuries since. Although for many centuries anointing was almost exclusively associated with the dying,[22] recent years have witnessed a recovery of its earlier and biblical significance as a rite of healing.

---

21. The only reference to anointing in the Lutheran confessions is in the Apology of the Augsburg Confession, Article XIII, 6:

> Confirmation and extreme unction are rites received from the Fathers which even the church does not require as necessary for salvation since they do not have the command of God. Hence it is useful to distinguish these from the earlier ones which have an express command from God and a clear promise of grace. (*Book of Concord*, p. 212)

A statement on Anointing and Healing was adopted by the adjourned meeting of the 1960 convention of the United Lutheran Church in America (25-27 June 1962) in Detroit. It discouraged healing services and anointing with oil and accepted laying on of hands only "where it will readily serve as a sign of concern and as a sign of a desired blessing." The statement encouraged prayer, concern, and service for the sick.

22. The older name in the Roman Catholic tradition "extreme unction" was often

The oil bears a relationship to baptismal anointing (*LBW*, Min. Ed., p. 311: "14. The minister marks the sign of the cross on the forehead of each of the baptized. Oil prepared for this purpose may be used.") By baptism the person is already a citizen of that kingdom where there shall be neither suffering nor death.

In the Roman Catholic rite, the introduction to the Blessing of Oils and Chrism observes:

> The Christian liturgy has assimilated this Old Testament usage of anointing kings, priests, and prophets with consecratory oil because the name of Christ, whom they prefigured, means "the anointed of the Lord."

> Chrism is a sign: by baptism Christians are plunged into the paschal mystery of Christ; they die with him, are buried with him, and rise with him; they are sharers in his royal and prophetic priesthood.[23]

Background

In his ministry to the people around him, Jesus performed many acts of healing. Among them were the forgiveness of sins, casting out of demons, and curing physical disease. In these actions he used many different means, such as praying to the Father, laying his hands on people, touching the affected part of the body, and mixing his saliva with earth and applying it to the person. The Gospel accounts report that his disciples also performed acts of healing and made use of prayer, laying on of hands, and anointing the sick with oil. These practices continued as part of the church's ministry of healing.

The Roman Catholic church distinguishes between three oils: the oil for anointing the sick, which is olive oil, "or, according to circumstances, other plant oil";[24] the oil of catechumens, which is olive oil (by which "the effect of the baptismal exorcisms is extended. Before they go to the font of life to be reborn the candidates for baptism are strengthened to renounce sin and the devil");[25] and the chrism of baptism, which is olive (or other plant) oil to which balsam or perfume is added ("Chrism is made of oil and perfumes or other sweet smelling matter").[26] The containers of each of these oils are traditionally marked with Latin

---

understood to be an anointing *in extremis*, when one was near death, although its earlier intention was an anointing of the extremities of the body: the eyes, the ears, the nostrils, the mouth, the hands, the feet. The name "last anointing" became common only at the end of the twelfth century.

23. *The Rites*, p. 518. See Bo Reicke, *The Epistles of James, Peter, and Jude* (Garden City, N.Y.: Doubleday & Co., 1964), pp. 57–62.

24. *The Rites*, pp. 518–19.

25. Ibid., p. 518.

26. Ibid., p. 519.

abbreviations: OI (*oleum infirmorum*), oil of the sick; OC (*oleum catechumenorum*), oil of catechumens; CH, chrism.

In the history of the church, anointing the sick has taken various forms. In the fifth century, for example, it was generally customary for the local bishop to bless the oil, praying that through it the Holy Spirit would bring healing of body and soul. The anointing itself could be done by other clergy or by lay people, and in some places the sick took the oil home and administered it to themselves with prayer.

The Council of Florence (1438–45) described the essential elements of the anointing of the sick. It was the Council of Trent (1545–63), however, that declared its divine institution, declared that the priest is the proper minister of the sacrament of anointing, and said that "this anointing is to be administered to the sick, especially those who are in such a condition as to appear to have reached the end of their life, whence it is also called the sacrament of the dying."[27] The Second Vatican Council restored anointing to its ancient role as a rite not only for those who are at the point of death but for all those who are seriously ill. It also greatly simplified the rite.

When a Christian is near death, or is in danger of death, a unified rite of viaticum may be desirable, including confession and forgiveness, anointing, and Holy Communion. Olavus Petri's Manual (1529) provided such a rite, including all three elements: confession and forgiveness, Holy Communion, and anointing.

The 1549 *Book of Common Prayer* retained the optional use of anointing, but the practice was eliminated in 1552 and was not restored in the American Prayer Book until 1928. In the 1979 Prayer Book, provision is made for the blessing of the oil by the local priest in the presence of the people.

In the twentieth century, the church has been rediscovering and renewing various aspects of its ministry of healing; both the laying on of hands and the anointing with oil have been practiced in the visitation of the sick and in public services of healing. A number of Lutheran congregations have made use of these forms of healing.

Preparing for the Service

The oil used for anointing is olive oil, which is easily absorbed by the skin. The Roman Catholic church now permits the substitution of another plant oil. Pope Paul VI in the Apostolic Constitution on the Sacrament of Anointing the Sick wrote:

---

27. Ibid., p. 579.

Since olive oil, which had been prescribed until now for the valid administration of the sacrament, is unobtainable or difficult to obtain in some parts of the world, we decreed, at the request of numerous bishops, that from now on, according to the circumstances, another kind of oil could also be used, provided that it be obtained from plants, and thus similar to olive oil.[28]

The oldest form for blessing oil for the sick is found in the *Apostolic Tradition* of Hippolytus:

Sanctify this oil, O God, with which you anointed kings, priests, and prophets, you that would grant health to those who use it and partake of it, so that it may bestow comfort on all who taste it and health to all who use it.

The oil was offered with the bread and wine at the Holy Communion, blessed at the prayer, and returned for use to the one who offered it.[29] Eventually the Latin rite reserved the blessing of oil and chrism for the bishop. In the Roman Catholic church and in parts of the Anglican communion the oil used for anointing and the chrism is blessed by the bishop on Maundy Thursday morning at a Mass of the Chrism, which is distinct from the Mass of the Lord's Supper later that day. According to the tradition of the Latin rite, the blessing of the oil of the sick takes place within the eucharistic prayer just before the doxology; the blessing of the oil of catechumens and the consecration of the chrism take place after the Holy Communion.

The prayer provided for optional use at the preparation of the oil ⟨484⟩ is an abbreviated form of the blessing of the oil in the Roman Catholic rite.

Lord God, loving Father,
you bring healing to the sick
through your Son Jesus Christ.
Hear us as we pray to you in faith,
and send the Holy Spirit, man's Helper and Friend,
upon this oil, which nature has provided
to serve the needs of men.
May your blessing +
come upon all who are anointed with this oil,
that they may be freed from pain and illness
and made well again in body, mind, and soul.
Father, may this oil be blessed for our use
in the name of our Lord Jesus Christ
who lives and reigns with you for ever and ever.[30]

28. Ibid., p. 580.
29. Hatchett, *Commentary on American Prayer Book*, p. 463.
30. *The Rites*, pp. 522, 602.

The oil is conveniently kept in a small metal cylinder called a stock, with a securely fitting lid. To prevent spillage, cotton may be put in the stock and only enough oil poured in to moisten the cotton. A stock usually comes with a ring attached to its base; the ring may be worn on the middle finger, the cylinder resting in the palm of the left hand.

Instead of using a stock, an alternate practice is to pour oil from a vial onto a dish such as a deep paten or a shell (to suggest the connection with baptism). This method may be less neat than using a stock, but it allows more oil to be used and, by being a more significant sign of baptism, may perhaps be preferable.

A cloth for cleaning the pastor's hands is desirable.

The Service in Detail

The rubric observes that normally confession and forgiveness precede the Laying on of Hands and Anointing the Sick; however it does not prescribe that confession and forgiveness immediately precede the rite. The selection of the various parts of the ministry of healing will differ from situation to situation, but the pastor should always bear in mind that all four parts—confession and forgiveness; psalms, lessons, and prayers; laying on of hands (and anointing); Holy Communion—are available for use as the circumstances warrant. The sick, like the well, need the opportunity to be cleansed and to hear the liberating word of forgiveness.

In all but the most exceptional cases, the Laying on of Hands and Anointing the Sick is led by a pastor. This makes the association with baptismal anointing and sealing clear, for a pastor presides at Holy Baptism. Moreover, the text from James 5:14–15 directs that what appear to be the official representatives of the church—the "elders," that is, the presbyters/priests/pastors—are to be sent forth to anoint and to pray. The laying on of hands in other contexts—baptism, confirmation, ordination—is always done by a pastor. Although in the early church anointing was done by laypersons as well as by ordained persons, the limitation of the leadership to the ordained is in accord with ecumenical practice: the Roman Catholic (since Trent, chapter 3, canon 4) and the Episcopal rites each require a priest to preside.

Survey of the Service

The greeting is an appropriate beginning if the Laying on of Hands and Anointing the Sick is used as a separate service. The first form, "Peace to you from our Lord Jesus Christ," is based on a frequent New Testament greeting, "Grace to you and peace from God our Father and the Lord Jesus Christ" (Rom. 1:7; 1 Cor. 1:3; etc.). The second form, "The peace of the Lord be with you always," is the peace from the Holy Communion and familiar to Lutherans also from the Common Service (*Common Service Book, Service Book and Hymnal, Lutheran Hymnal*). It may be less useful here since it requires a response from the person visited. Neither greeting, however, is traditional at this point. The traditional text, in Lutheran use since the *Church Book* (and used in the 1979 *Book of Common Prayer,* p. 453, and in the Roman Catholic rite as well, *The Rites,* p. 600), "Peace be to this house and to all who dwell in it," is provided in the notes along with a second alternate, "Grace to you and peace" (1 Thess. 1:1).[31] All the rites allow for flexibility at this point.

The use of the word "peace," whatever form the greeting takes, is significant. It follows the admonition given by Jesus to the Seventy (Luke 10:5-6) and to the Twelve (Matt. 10:12-13). It recalls the greeting of the risen Lord to the Eleven (John 20:19, 21, 26). Peace is the work of Christ (Col. 1:19-20; John 14:27; 16:33), who is himself our peace (Eph. 2:14). Moreover, Susan Sontag in *Illness as Metaphor* observes that the language used to describe cancer is often military language using the terminology of warfare.[32] Thus in such cases, the healing power inherent in the word "peace" is especially apposite.

If another service or portion of the ministry of healing has immediately preceded this service, the greeting is pointless and should be omitted.

The address is taken from the Roman Catholic Rite of Anointing a Sick Person.[33] It is cast in the plural, and this suggests that when possible the pastor not be alone in this ministration. (The text of James 5:14 invites the sick to summon "the elders of the church.") If others accompany the pastor, the communal nature of the church is made more evident and the concern of the congregation is more clearly demonstrated. A rubric in the 1959 Canadian Prayer Book suggests, "Where possible, it is desirable that more than one Priest should take part in the administration."

Normally, confession and forgiveness are included in this rite. The appropriate form is Individual Confession and Forgiveness.

Care must be taken that the lessons which are read are appropriate to what follows. The first lesson provided, Luke 4:40, is appropriate when the laying on of hands takes place. If anointing is to follow, one or both of the other two lessons (the composite reading from Matt. 10:1, 5, 7-8a and Mark 6:12-13 and the reading from James 5) may be added to the first lesson or may be substituted for it. It is not desirable to substitute other readings for those provided in this rite.

---

31. There are further suggestions in ibid., p. 634.

32. Susan Sontag, *Illness as Metaphor* (New York: Farrar, Strauss & Giroux, 1978), pp. 64ff.

33. *The Rites,* p. 600. A prayer (pp. 637-38) expressing similar thoughts may be substituted for the address.

The minister then lays both hands on the person's head, and a time of silence is maintained. To be effective, this dramatic gesture must be more than a passing pause of a few seconds' duration; five to seven seconds is a minimum. In the Roman Catholic rite, the laying on of hands is carried out in silence. It is a powerful gesture.

Occasional Services (1982) has the pastor say:

> I lay my hands on you in the name of our Lord and Savior Jesus Christ, beseeching him to uphold you and fill you with grace, that you may know the healing power of his love.

This is a slightly altered form of the alternate formula for the laying on of hands given in the 1979 *Book of Common Prayer* (p. 456).[34]

If the person is to be anointed, the pastor dips a thumb in the oil and makes the sign of the cross on the sick person's forehead, saying, "*N.*, I anoint you with oil in the name of the Father, and of the Son, and of the Holy Spirit." This formula is from the *Book of Common Prayer* (p. 456). The formula with which the anointing of the sick is conferred in the Roman Catholic rite is:

> Through this holy anointing
> may the Lord in his mercy and love help you
> with the grace of his Holy Spirit.
> *Amen.*
> May the Lord who frees you from sin
> save you and raise you up.
> *Amen.*[35]

This form makes explicit the connection between the anointing with oil and the anointing with the Holy Spirit. It is divided into two parts because the Roman rite requires anointing on the forehead and on the hands.

The thumb is used in anointing for practical reasons: it is larger and more convenient than the tip of the index finger.

If the person's forehead is bandaged or if anointing the forehead would cause pain, the anointing may be done on another part of the body such as the breast or the back of a hand.

---

34. The Prayer Book uses the person's name at the beginning and has "fill you with his grace . . ." The other formula provided in the Prayer Book is:

> *N.*, I lay my hands on you in the Name of the Father, and of the Son, and of the Holy Spirit, beseeching our Lord Jesus Christ to sustain you with his presence, to drive away all sickness of body and spirit, and to give you that victory of life and peace which will enable you to serve him both now and evermore.

35. *The Rites*, p. 587.

The use of the phrases "I lay my hands upon you . . ." and "I anoint you with oil . . ." in the Lutheran and Episcopal rites may at first seem odd. It may appear unnecessary in a liturgical text to declare what is obviously being done, and normally this sort of description of the obvious is avoided in the liturgy. But the parallel here is again with baptism in which the minister says (in the traditional Western formula), "I baptize you . . ." Declaring clearly what is happening has the added benefit in an unfamiliar rite of telling the person exactly what is going on so that there will be no surprise, confusion, or fear.

The Church of the Brethren has a similar practice. The Anointing Service in the *Pastor's Manual* (pp. 70–71) provides this text at the anointing:

_____, upon your confession of faith in the love and power of God, your willingness to commit your life completely to God in sickness or in health, and your desire to live your life for God's glory, you are now being anointed with oil in the name of the Lord,

for the forgiveness of your sins,
for the strengthening of your faith,
and for the healing and wholeness according to God's grace and wisdom.

A few drops of oil may be placed on the fingers of the officiant, after which he or she will gently touch the forehead of the person three times, once as each purpose is stated.

Free prayer by those who lead the service brings the action to a close.

In *Occasional Services* (1982) the concluding prayer of thanksgiving ⟨483⟩ is a new composition. Prayer ⟨482⟩ in the Service of the Word for Healing is quite similar and is perhaps preferable because it is a superior text. The Roman rite provides six prayers from which to choose:

Lord Jesus Christ, our Redeemer,
by the power of the Holy Spirit,
ease the sufferings of our sick brother (sister)
and make him (her) well again in mind and body.
In your loving kindness forgive his (her) sins
and grant him (her) full health
so that he (she) may be restored to your service.

You are Lord for ever and ever.
Amen.

Lord Jesus Christ,
you shared in our human nature
to heal the sick and save all mankind.
Mercifully listen to our prayers
for the physical and spiritual health of our sick brother (sister)
whom we have anointed in your name.

May your protection console him (her)
and your strength make him (her) well again.
[Help him (her) find hope in suffering,
for you have given him (her) a share in your passion.]

You are Lord for ever and ever.
Amen.

When the illness is the result of advanced age.
Lord,
look kindly on our brother (sister)
who has grown weak under the burden of his (her) years.
In this holy anointing
he (she) asks for the grace of health in body and soul.
By the power of your Holy Spirit,
make him (her) firm in faith and sure in hope,
so that his (her) cheerful patience
may reveal your love to us.
We ask this through Christ our Lord.
Amen.

When the sick person is in great danger.
Lord Jesus Christ,
you took our weakness on yourself
and bore our sufferings in your passion and death.

Hear this prayer for our suffering brother (sister).
You are his (her) redeemer:
strengthen his (her) hope for salvation
and in your kindness sustain him (her)
in body and soul.
You live and reign for ever and ever.
Amen.

When anointing and viaticum are given together.
Lord God, merciful Father, comforter of the suffering,
look kindly on your son (daughter) *N.* who trusts in you.
May this anointing ease his (her) sufferings,
and may the food he (she) has received for his (her) journey,
the body and blood of your Son Jesus Christ,
refresh him (her) and lead him (her) to life.

We ask this through Christ our Lord.
Amen.

For those about to die.
Lord God, loving Father,
you are the source of all goodness and love,
and you never refuse forgiveness
to those who are sorry for their sins.

Have mercy on your son (daughter) *N.*,
who is about to return to you.
May this holy anointing,
and our prayer made in faith assist him (her):
relieve his (her) pain, in body and soul,
forgive all his (her) sins,
and strengthen him (her) with your loving protection.

We ask this, Father, through your Son Jesus Christ,
who conquered death
and opened for us the way to eternal life,
and who lives and reigns for ever and ever.
   Amen.[36]

The blessing is a revision of the blessing at the conclusion of the Holy
Communion. The Roman rite has two blessings:

May the Lord Jesus Christ be with you to protect you.
   Amen.
May he go before you to guide you and stand
behind you to give you strength.
   Amen.
May he look upon you, to keep you and bless you.
   Amen.
[And may almighty God,
the Father, and the Son, + and the Holy Spirit,
bless you all.
   Amen.]

or,

May the blessing of almighty God,
the Father, and the Son, + and the Holy Spirit,
come upon you and remain with you forever.
   Amen.[37]

The *Book of Common Prayer* provides this blessing, included in a revised
form in *Occasional Services* (1982) among the Psalms, Lessons, and
Prayers (p. 75):

The Almighty Lord, who is a strong tower to all who put their trust in him,
to whom all things in heaven, on earth, and under the earth bow and obey:
Be now and evermore your defense, and make you know and feel that the
only Name under heaven given for health and salvation is the Name of our
Lord Jesus Christ.[38]

---

36. Ibid., pp. 603-4, 639-41.
37. Ibid., p. 637.
38. *Book of Common Prayer* (New York: Seabury Press, 1979), pp. 456-57.

When the Laying on of Hands and Anointing the Sick is used in conjunction with the Distribution of Communion to Those in Special Circumstances as one continuous rite, the full form has this order:

Greeting

    Peace to you from our Lord Jesus Christ.

    or The peace of the Lord be with you always.

        And also with you.

    or Peace be to this house and to all who dwell in it.

    or Grace to you and peace.

[Psalm, Lesson, Prayer]

Laying on of Hands and Anointing the Sick

  Address

  Confession and forgiveness

  Lessons (Luke 4:40; Matt. 10:1, 5, 7–8a; Mark 6:12–13;

    James 5:14–16a)

  Laying on of hands

  Anointing

Distribution of Communion to Those in Special Circumstances

  Address

  Prayer of the day

  Gospel (comment)

  Preparation of the bread and wine

  Our Father

  "As often as we eat of this bread and drink from this cup,

    we proclaim the Lord's death until he comes."

  Ministration of the Holy Communion

  Silence

  Prayer—p. 79 (209) or (241) *or* p. 101 ⟨483⟩

  Blessing—p. 101

Comparison of Rites
Laying on of Hands and Anointing the Sick

ROMAN CATHOLIC	LUTHERAN	EPISCOPAL
Greeting	Peace to you from our Lord Jesus Christ.	
	or The peace of the Lord be with you always. *And also with you.*	
	or Peace be to this house and to all who dwell in it.	Peace be to this house (place) and to all who dwell in it.

Comparison of Rites (continued)
Laying on of Hands and Anointing the Sick

ROMAN CATHOLIC	LUTHERAN	EPISCOPAL
	or Grace to you and peace.	
(Sprinkling with holy water)		
Address or prayer with James 5:14–16	Address	
Confession and forgiveness	(Confession and forgiveness)	
Lesson Matt. 8:5–10, 13 or another	Lessons Luke 4:40 Matt. 10:1, 5, 7–8a Mark 6:12–13 James 5:14–16a	Ministry of the Word James 5:14–16 Psalm 23 Mark 6:7, 12–13
(Litany)*		Prayers
		(Confession and forgiveness)
		(Blessing of oil)
		Anthem
Laying on of hands in silence	Laying on of hands	Laying on of hands
Blessing of oil or prayer of thanksgiving if already blessed		
Anointing	Anointing	Anointing
Prayer	Prayer	
Our Father		Our Father
Blessing	Blessing	Blessing

*A brief litany may be said here or after the anointing or, according to circumstances, at some other point (*The Rites*, pp. 601, 638–39).

SERVICE OF THE WORD FOR HEALING
(*Occasional Services*, pp. 89-98)

Parallel Rites

Roman Catholic	Celebration of Anointing in a Large Congregation, *The Rites*, pp. 606-7.
Episcopal	A Public Service of Healing, *The Book of Occasional Services*, pp. 147-54.
Brethren	The Anointing Service, *Pastor's Manual*, pp. 63-71.

Purpose

The Service of the Word for Healing is for public and corporate use in a church as a "healing service." The Laying on of Hands and Anointing the Sick is for private use.

The service is an affirmation of God's concern for the whole person. It is, moreover, an occasion for those who suffer from various sicknesses and mental distresses to pray for themselves and for one another. The service further provides opportunity for the congregation to offer prayers of intercession for the sick and suffering in the congregation, the community, and the world.

Characteristics

In both the Roman Catholic and Episcopal liturgy this is a secondary service. In *The Rites* it is dealt with by rubrics, which describe how the ordinary rite of anointing a sick person may be adapted for use with a congregation in two settings: apart from Mass and during Mass. In The Episcopal Church, A Public Service of Healing (note the article: it is simply "a service") is not included in the *Book of Common Prayer* but in the supplementary *Book of Occasional Services*.

In the Lutheran book *Occasional Services* (1982), this service is set within the Service of the Word rather than within the Holy Communion. It is, therefore, a deviation from the principle of the *LBW* that occasional services be set within the Holy Communion as the chief service of the congregation. It is also a divergence from the Roman Catholic and Episcopal services for healing, both of which allow for—but do not require—a celebration of Holy Communion.

The Service of the Word for Healing, like the Laying on of Hands and Anointing the Sick, is new to Lutheran service books, but it is not new to Lutheran practice. In many places and for many years Lutherans have conducted healing services and established a tradition.

104

Because this is a corporate adaptation of the Laying on of Hands and Anointing the Sick, the Service of the Word for Healing departs from the general pattern of the Service of the Word and does not make provision for a layperson to preside. This service is led by a pastor as presiding minister and by assisting ministers.

Preparing for the Service

The oil used for anointing the sick is olive oil, to which some may choose to add a small amount of balsam or other fragrant oil. The oil for anointing may be conveniently kept in a small metal cylinder, called a stock, with a securely fitting lid. To prevent spillage cotton may be put in the stock and only enough oil poured in to moisten the cotton. In the absence of a stock, the oil may be poured on a shell (to suggest the connection with baptism), paten, or similar plate with a sufficiently deep shape.

A cloth for cleaning the pastor's hands after the anointing is desirable.

St. Luke's Day, October 18, is a traditional time for services of healing because Luke is described by St. Paul as "the beloved physician" (Col. 4:14). The Gospels for certain Sundays, listed under Notes on the Service, are not to imply that the Service of the Word for Healing is the principal Sunday Service.

In planning for this service, provision must be made for those who are not ambulatory and for those who cannot kneel.

Survey of the Service

For general comments on the Service of the Word see the *LBW*, Min. Ed., pp. 32–33 and the *Manual on the Liturgy*, pp. 253–62.

The Propers for the Service of the Word for Healing offer suggestions for the opening hymn. In addition to that list, the following hymns also have to do with healing:

  36 On Jordan's Banks the Baptist's Cry
162 Lord God, the Holy Ghost
164 Creator Spirit, by Whose Aid
188 I Bind unto Myself Today
189 We Know That Christ Is Raised
191 Praise and Thanksgiving Be to God
192 Baptized into Your Name Most Holy
194 All Who Believe and Are Baptized
195 This Is the Spirit's Entry Now
250 Open Now Thy Gates of Beauty
272 Abide with Me
290 There's a Wideness in God's Mercy

294 My Hope Is Built on Nothing Less
400 God, Whose Almighty Word
418 Judge Eternal, Throned in Splendor
438 Lord, Teach Us How to Pray Aright
439 What a Friend We Have in Jesus
440 Christians, While on Earth Abiding
441 Eternal Spirit of the Living Christ
442 O Thou, Who Hast of Thy Pure Grace
443 Rise, My Soul, to Watch and Pray
444 With the Lord Begin Your Task
448 Amazing Grace, How Sweet the Sound
475 Come, Gracious Spirit, Heavenly Dove
476 Have No Fear, Little Flock
499 Come, Thou Fount of Every Blessing
504 O God, My Faithful God
542 Sing Praise to God, the Highest Good

"The full participation of those present should be encouraged by the use of appropriate songs to foster common prayer and manifest the Easter joy proper to this sacrament."[39] Even though Lutherans do not count anointing among the sacraments, the counsel is nonetheless sound. Laying on of hands and anointing partakes of the Easter mystery of suffering, death, and resurrection.

The sources of the verses of the dialogue are biblical. The psalm translation is that of the *LBW* psalter.

Give thanks to the Lord, for he is good,
and his mercy endures forever.   Ps. 107:1

They cried to the Lord in their trouble,
and he delivered them from their distress.   Ps. 107:6

He sent forth his Word and healed them,
and saved them from the grave.   Ps. 107:20

The Lord is righteous in all his ways,
and loving in all his works.   Ps. 145:18

The Lord upholds all [those] who fall;
he lifts up those who are bowed down.   Ps. 145:15

The Lord sustains them on their sickbed,
and ministers to them in their illness.   Ps. 41:3

---

39. *The Rites*, p. 606.

The Lord is my strength and my song,
and he has become my salvation.   Exod. 15:2

Give thanks to the Lord, for he is good,
and his mercy endures forever.   Ps. 136:1

In the Apostles' Creed, unless there is a theological objection to the phrase, congregations should be encouraged to use the text in the footnote "He descended to the dead" (the translation of the International Committee on English Texts) instead of the reading "He descended into hell." This is the only instance in the *LBW* in which a text of the International Committee on English Texts was altered unilaterally. The change was made in response to strongly held theological opinions endorsed by some but not all of the participants in the Inter-Lutheran Commission on Worship.

The Old Testament canticles are given in the *LBW* (Canticles 14, 15, 16, 18, 19).

Suggestions for the lessons and the psalm are provided in the propers for the Service of the Word for Healing.

The prayers provided are drawn from these sources:

For all who suffer ⟨477⟩. New.

For recovery from sickness (226). This prayer in the *LBW* is taken from the 1979 *Book of Common Prayer* (p. 458). It entered the Prayer Book in 1928 and is apparently the work of Howard Baldwin St. George. In the Prayer Book and in the *LBW* it is cast in the singular; here it is made plural to be more appropriate for the Service of the Word for Healing.

For those in affliction (223). This prayer in the *LBW* also was included in the *Service Book and Hymnal* among the Collects and Prayers (no. 35). Its origin is the Gelasian Sacramentary appointed for Good Friday; it was translated by Eric Milner-White, *The Occasional Prayers in the 1928 Book Reconsidered* (London, 1930), p. 25.

For those who minister in healing ⟨478⟩. This is a revision of the prayer "For Doctors and Nurses" from the 1979 *Book of Common Prayer* (p. 460). It is an abbreviation of a prayer by John W. Suter, *Prayers of the Spirit* (New York: Harper & Row, 1943), p. 29.

For the ministry of family and friends ⟨479⟩. New.

For those who desire our prayers ⟨480⟩. New.

For those making decisions ⟨481⟩. New.

The conclusion to the prayers is a modest revision of the thanksgiving for the oil in the Roman Catholic Rite of Anointing and Pastoral Care of the Sick:

ROMAN CATHOLIC *The Rites*	LUTHERAN *Occasional Services* (1982)
Praise to you, almighty God and Father. You sent your Son to live among us and bring us salvation. *Blessed be God.*	Praise to you, almighty God and Father. You sent your Son to live among us and to bring us your salvation. *Blessed be God.*
Praise to you, Lord Jesus Christ, the Father's only Son. You humbled yourself to share in our humanity, and you desired to cure all our illnesses. *Blessed be God.*	Praise to you, Lord Jesus Christ, incomparable Son of the Father. You humbled yourself to share in our humanity, and you came to heal all our illnesses. *Blessed be God.*
Praise to you, God and Holy Spirit, the Consoler. You heal our sickness, with your mighty power. *Blessed be God.*	Praise to you, Holy Spirit, our defender and consoler. You heal our sickness with your mighty and life-giving power. *Blessed be God.* (p. 93)
Lord God, with faith in you our brother (sister) will be anointed with this holy oil. Ease his (her) sufferings and strengthen him (her) in his (her) weakness. We ask this through Christ our Lord. *Amen.* (pp. 602–3)	

The final portion of this prayer of thanksgiving in *Occasional Services* is a revision of the formula for the laying on of hands in the *Book of Common Prayer* (p. 456).

Book of Common Prayer (1979)	*Occasional Services* (1982)
N., I lay my hands upon you in the Name of the Father, and of the Son, and of the Holy Spirit, beseeching our Lord Jesus Christ to sustain you with his presence, to drive away all sickness of body and spirit, and to give you that victory of life and peace which will enable you to serve him both now and evermore.	Holy and blessed Trinity, sustain your servants, _____, with your presence; drive away their sickness of body and spirit, and give them that victory of life and peace which will enable them to serve you now and evermore.

Following the prayers, those who wish and who are able come to the altar and kneel if their condition permits. Those who are waiting in line to kneel—especially if they are to kneel one after another at a kneeling desk, or "station," at the communion rail—should be instructed to stand back from the one kneeling to allow for privacy in any conversation which may take place between the person kneeling and the pastor.

The minister lays both hands on the head of each person. The fullness of this gesture with both hands rather than one is important to maintain. It suggests the total concentration of energy upon that one person at that point. Timidity on the part of the minister has no place here. The popular evangelistic healers perhaps have something to teach traditional Christians in this regard.

If there are several pastors present, each one may lay hands on some of the sick (and anoint them). Two or more stations may be arranged with kneeling desks to facilitate the action.

The two actions of laying on of hands and anointing are complementary. To prevent duplication and redundancy in the words said during these actions, when anointing follows, the minister lays both hands on the person's head in silence. The minister will speak in connection with the anointing, and that is sufficient to make clear what is happening.

If only laying on of hands is to be done and if anointing does not follow, then the minister says the prayer for each person as both hands are laid on the person's head. Two prayers are provided. One is based on the confirmation prayer which has been dear to Lutherans since the *Church Book* (1868); it was preserved in the *Common Service Book* and in the *Service Book and Hymnal.*

> The Father in heaven, for Jesus' sake, renew and increase in thee the gift of the Holy Ghost, to thy strengthening in faith, to thy growth in grace, to thy patience in suffering, and to the blessed hope of everlasting life.

The formula was adapted for the Affirmation of Baptism in the *LBW* (Min. Ed., p. 327):

> Father in heaven, for Jesus' sake, stir up in _____ the gift of your Holy Spirit; confirm *his/her* faith, guide *his/her* life, empower *him/her* in *his/her* serving, give *him/her* patience in suffering, and bring *him/her* to everlasting life.

The first formula at the laying on of hands takes that opening phrase invoking the Spirit and combines it with phrases from the formula for the laying on of hands from the *Book of Common Prayer* as well as the additional text for the anointing with oil.

Book of Common Prayer

Occasional Services

N., I lay my hands upon you in the Name of the Father, and of the Son, and of the Holy Spirit, beseeching our Lord Jesus Christ to sustain you with his presence, to drive away all sickness of body and spirit, and to give you that victory of life and peace which will enable you to serve him both now and evermore.

As you are outwardly anointed with this holy oil, so may our heavenly Father grant you the inward anointing of the Holy Spirit. Of his great mercy, may he forgive you your sins, release you from suffering, and restore you to wholeness and strength. May he deliver you from all evil, preserve you in all goodness, and bring you to everlasting life; through Jesus Christ our Lord. (p. 456)

Father in heaven, for Jesus' sake, send your Holy Spirit upon your servant, _____; drive away all sickness of body and spirit; make whole that which is broken; deliver *him/her* from the power of evil; and preserve *him/her* in true faith, to share in the power of Christ's resurrection and to serve you with all the saints now and evermore. (p. 94)

The other prayer provided for the laying on of hands "I lay my hands upon you . . ." is the alternate formula for the laying on of hands from the *Book of Common Prayer* (p. 456).

If anointing follows, after the laying on of hands and prayer in silence (for a minimum of five to seven seconds; the action must have its own integrity), the minister dips a thumb in the oil (because a thumb is larger and more convenient than any other finger) and makes the sign of the cross with it on the person's forehead. The text which accompanies the anointing is an adaptation of the prayer at the optional blessing of the oil in the *Book of Common Prayer,* based on an old Roman form:

Book of Common Prayer

Occasional Services (1982)

O Lord, holy Father, giver of health and salvation: Send your Holy Spirit to sanctify this oil; that, as your holy apostles anointed many that were sick and healed them, so may those who in faith and repentance receive this holy unction be made whole; through Jesus Christ our Lord, who lives and reigns with you and the Holy Spirit, one God, for ever and ever. (p. 445)

O God, the giver of health and salvation: As the apostles of our Lord Jesus Christ, at his command, anointed many that were sick and healed them, send now your Holy Spirit, that _____, anointed with this oil, may in repentance and faith be made whole; through the same Jesus Christ our Lord. (p. 94)

A server should hold the book for the minister so that the minister's hands will be free for the anointing.

After all have returned to their places, the minister says the blessing, a revised form of the blessing in the *Book of Common Prayer* (pp. 456-57).

The prayer of thanksgiving after all have returned to their places is another version of the same prayer of thanksgiving which appears in the Laying on of Hands and Anointing the Sick. This version ⟨482⟩ is perhaps preferable because of the important added phrase "as we wait for that day when there will be no more pain." It is an acknowledgment that the service may not bring healing to all who participate in it, and it points to the eschatological fulfillment of God's promise of wholeness and joy in his kingdom.

The New Testament canticles are given in the *LBW* (Canticles 13, 17, 20, 21).

The Aaronic benediction, unlike the form printed in the text of the Service of the Word in the *LBW,* is here in the declarative form reserved for a pastor because a pastor is the leader of the Service of the Word for Healing. The declarative form is suggested for pastors in the Notes on the Liturgy (*LBW,* Min. Ed., p. 33, no. 17).

Comparison of Rites
Service of the Word for Healing

ROMAN CATHOLIC	LUTHERAN	EPISCOPAL
(Celebration of Anointing in a Large Congregation)	(Service of the Word for Healing)	(A Public Service of Healing)
I. Reception of the Sick	(hymn)	Beginning of Eucharist or Penitential Order or Greeting
	Dialogue	
Greeting	Apostles' Creed	
(Sprinkling)	Old Testament canticle	
Address or prayer	Prayer of the day	Collect
II. Penitential Rite		
III. Word of God		
Reading(s)	First lesson	1 or 2 lessons
	Psalm/hymn/anthem	Psalm/hymn/anthem
	Second lesson	Gospel
	Silence and sermon	Sermon and/or silence
Homily (silence)		

Comparison of Rites (continued)
Service of the Word for Healing

ROMAN CATHOLIC	LUTHERAN	EPISCOPAL
IV. Celebration of the Sacrament		
(Litany)	Prayers	Creed or prayers
		(Confession of Sin)
		Anthem
		Blessing
Laying on of hands	Laying on of hands	Laying on of hands
Blessing of oil or thanksgiving		
Anointing	(Anointing)	(Anointing)
(General intercessions)	Blessing	The peace
Prayer or Our Father	Prayer and Our Father (New Testament canticle)	Our Father
Blessing	Blessing	Blessing
(Hymn)		
Dismissal		Dismissal

4
THE COMMUNION OF
THOSE IN SPECIAL CIRCUMSTANCES

INTRODUCTION

The corporate nature of Christianity is clear from its earliest writings. St. Paul stresses the unity which the church has in Holy Communion: "Because there is one bread, we who are many are one body, for we all partake of the one bread" (1 Cor. 10:17). In the next century, Ignatius of Antioch (ca. 35–115) warns, "Take care to have but one Eucharist. For there is one flesh of our Lord Jesus Christ and one cup of unity in his blood." [1] The *Didache* or *Teaching of the Twelve Apostles* (ca. 140) says of the eucharistic bread:

> Just as the bread broken
> was first scattered on the hills,
> then was gathered and became one,
> so let your Church be gathered
> from the ends of the earth into your kingdom,
> for yours is glory and power through all ages. [2]

Unity was thus a central theme of the Holy Communion.

The absent (apparently whether sick or well) were included in the one meal at the one table of the Lord. Justin Martyr, who died ca. 165, reports that when the presiding minister has prayed the Great Thanksgiving,

> and the people have signified their assent [by saying "Amen"], those whom we call "deacons" distribute the bread and the wine and water over which the eucharist [i.e., the Thanksgiving] has been spoken, to each of those present; they also carry them to those who are absent. [3]

In some places it seems that communicants took home a portion of the eucharistic bread so that they could begin each day with communion from the Sunday Eucharist. This was an extension of the first day

---

1. Ignatius of Antioch, *The Letter to the Philadelphians* 4 in *Early Christian Fathers,* trans. and ed. Cyril C. Richardson (Philadelphia: Westminster Press, 1953), p. 108.

2. Lucien Deiss, *Springtime of the Liturgy* (Collegeville, Minn.: Liturgical Press, 1979), p. 75.

3. Ibid., p. 92.

throughout the week, allowing each weekday to partake of the resurrection character of Sunday. It was, moreover, an anticipation of the next Sunday as the "eighth day." This custom seems to have died out in the fourth century, but the ministers continued to carry the sacrament to those who were unable to be present at the congregational celebration.

The bread and wine which had been used in the eucharistic celebration were kept from one celebration to the next for use in communing the sick, especially those near death. Thus the unity of the one (weekly) Eucharist was preserved. Devotional practices eventually developed, however, which focused on the elements themselves apart from their use in the meal. During and after the thirteenth century, eucharistic piety centered more on seeing the sacrament than upon receiving it. In earlier centuries, as in some places in the East still, the sacrament was kept ("reserved" is the liturgical term) in the sacristy. When the church's tendency shifted to seeing the sacrament, the place of reservation was moved to the church itself: in a pyx, often in the shape of a dove, hung from the ceiling of the church; in a safe in the wall of the chancel called an "aumbry"; in parts of Germany in a "sacrament house," an elaborately carved shrine, free-standing in or near the chancel; or at length on the altar itself in a safe called a "tabernacle."

The Reformers for a time accepted the reservation of the elements of the Holy Communion for communicating the sick, but eventually, in reaction to the cult of adoration which had developed through the centuries, the practice gave way to separate celebrations of the sacrament in the houses of the sick. It was the zealous Carlstadt who forbade communion of the sick by means of the reserved elements and required a separate celebration in the sick room. This has remained normal practice in Lutheranism to the present. While this was not unknown in the medieval church, in the judgment of the British Presbyterian liturgist William D. Maxwell:

> On the whole, it was a practice to be deplored, and it soon spread far beyond Lutheranism. Communion of the sick by the reserved elements is as early as the second century. To hold a private celebration in the sick-room is to obscure the sense of fellowship.[4]

His observation was incisive.

Recent biblical, theological, and liturgical study has emphasized the communal nature of the sacrament, which had long been obscured in many churches. The Holy Communion is always personal. In the Small Catechism and elsewhere, Luther stressed the importance of the words

---

4. William D. Maxwell, *An Outline of Christian Worship: Its Development and Forms* (New York: Oxford University Press, 1936; rev. ed., 1945), p. 76 n. 1.

"for you," and Lutheran liturgies have always reserved these words in whatever formula accompanies the distribution. But while the Holy Communion is always personal, it is never private. It should never exclude an awareness of others, for the sacrament is always a communion with Christ and with his church. Indeed, St. Paul's warning against those who partake of the communion "without discerning the body" (1 Cor. 11:29) seems to have to do not only with the importance of perceiving the presence of Christ in the elements, but also with perceiving the unity of the people of God, the body of Christ which is his church, which eats and drinks together. When one eats of the bread and drinks of that cup, one not only proclaims the Lord's death, but one is united with one's sisters and brothers who are also eating and drinking. When the Apostles' Creed speaks of the "communion of saints," it may have been deliberately ambiguous for the original Latin may be either "the communion of holy people" (that is, the church) or "the communion in holy things" (that is, the Eucharist). A rubric in the Roman Catholic rite stresses this sense of unity:

> In fact it is proper that those who are prevented from being present at the community's celebration should be refreshed with the eucharist. In this way they may realize that they are united not only with the Lord's sacrifice but also with the community itself and are supported by the love of their brothers and sisters.[5]

Thus the Holy Communion establishes and nourishes the holy community, a community which is begun in Holy Baptism.

Despite the widespread use in our churches of the familiar term "private communion," there is in fact no such thing. The communion, even when administered by a pastor to a sick person with no one else present, is a communion with Christ and with his church. That church includes the whole congregation and all believers of all times and all places, the apostles and martyrs and confessors and teachers of the church throughout the centuries, the living and the dead, the church militant and the church triumphant. In the words of the Great Thanksgiving:

> And so, with the Church on earth and the hosts of heaven, we praise your name and join their unending hymn.

Thus, whether the communion is brought to the sick or whether it is celebrated for the sick in houses and hospitals, it ought always to be understood as an extension of the assembly, for it is in the gathering of the congregation around the altar that the existence of the church as the body of Christ is best seen.

---

5. *The Rites,* p. 459.

FOR FURTHER READING

Brilioth, Yngve. *Eucharistic Faith and Practice*. London: SPCK, 1965.

Cullmann, Oscar, and F. J. Leenhardt. *Essays on the Lord's Supper*. Translated by J. G. Davies. Richmond, Va.: John Knox Press, 1958.

Dix, Gregory. *The Shape of the Liturgy*. London: Dacre Press, 1945.

Elert, Werner. *Eucharist and Church Fellowship in the First Four Centuries*. Translated by N. E. Nagel. St. Louis: Concordia Publishing House, 1966.

Emminghaus, Johannes H. *The Eucharist: Essence, Form, Celebration*. Collegeville, Minn.: Liturgical Press, 1978.

"The Eucharist." In *The Study of Liturgy*, edited by C. Jones, G. Wainwright, E. Yarnold. New York: Oxford University Press, 1978.

Eucharist as Sacrifice. Lutherans and Catholics in Dialogue III. New York: Lutheran World Ministries; Washington, D.C.: Bishops' Committee for Ecumenical and Interreligious Affairs, 1967.

Harris, Charles. "Communion of the Sick." In *Liturgy and Worship*, edited by W. K. Lowther Clarke and Charles Harris, pp. 531–615. London: SPCK, 1964 [1932].

King, Archdale. *Eucharistic Reservation in the Western Church*. New York: Sheed & Ward, 1965.

Marty, Martin. *The Lord's Supper*. Philadelphia: Fortress Press, 1980.

Peters, E. F. "Nothing Has the Character of a Sacrament Outside of the Use." Diss., Concordia Seminary, St. Louis, 1968.

Pfatteicher, Philip H. *Distributing Communion to the Sick and Homebound*. Minneapolis: Augsburg Publishing House; Philadelphia: Board of Publication of the Lutheran Church in America, 1982.

Pfatteicher, Philip H., and Edward R. Zaiser. *Communion Practices Study Guide*. Edited by S. Anita Stauffer. Minneapolis: Augsburg Publishing House; Philadelphia: Fortress Press, 1980.

Schillebeeckx, Edward. *The Eucharist*. Translated by N. D. Smith. New York: Sheed & Ward, 1968.

Schmemann, Alexander. *For the Life of the World*. Tuckahoe, N.Y.: St. Vladimir's Seminary Press, 1971.

DISTRIBUTION OF COMMUNION TO THOSE IN SPECIAL CIRCUMSTANCES
(*Occasional Services*, pp. 76–81)

Parallel Rites

Roman Catholic   Administration of Communion and Viaticum to the Sick by an Extraordinary Minister (that is, a special minister, a layperson), *The Rites,* pp. 475–83.

| | Communion of the Sick (by priests and deacons), *The Rites,* pp. 594–98. |
| Episcopal | Communion under Special Circumstances (by a priest or deacon), *Book of Common Prayer,* pp. 396–99. |

Purpose

The purpose of the Distribution of Communion to Those in Special Circumstances is to bring the bread and wine of the eucharistic celebration of the congregation to those communicants who, for reasonable cause, cannot come to church. It is an extension of the distribution[6] of the Lord's Supper by trained lay ministers and by pastors to include the absent.

This rite is for use by pastors and by trained lay people. There is another form, Celebration of Holy Communion with Those in Special Circumstances, for use by pastors when it is necessary to celebrate the Holy Communion with those who cannot attend the congregational celebration.

Characteristics

In this service, the term "minister," as in the *Lutheran Book of Worship,* does not necessarily imply ordination. The service was prepared with lay people in mind, but it is also the appropriate service for use by pastors, especially in those congregations in which lay participation in the distribution of Holy Communion has not been introduced and in which the pastor is the one who is expected to bring the Holy Communion to the sick.

It is assumed that the Distribution of Communion to Those in Special Circumstances occurs within the context of pastoral ministry to the communicant. The use of this form of distribution by lay people supplements the ministry of the pastor; it is not a substitute for it.

Moreover, it is not desirable to commune those who suffer from an extended illness or confinement only by means of bringing them the elements from the congregational celebration. During certain seasons, especially Advent-Christmas and Lent-Easter, celebrations of the Lord's Supper should be scheduled in the homes of such persons with the con-

---

6. There has never been a consistent Lutheran tradition that describes this section of the Holy Communion. The *Lutheran Hymnal* called it "The Distribution." The *Common Service Book* used the title "The Administration of the Holy Sacrament." The *Service Book and Hymnal,* since "administration" had begun to take on unsavory bureaucratic connotations, called the action simply "The Communion." The *LBW* in no. 37 in the Holy Communion suggests "ministration."

gregation, or at least significant numbers from the congregation, invited to participate. Thus those who cannot attend church will at least occasionally have the benefit of a visible community and a fuller liturgy including hymns and a sermon. Special services may also be scheduled in the church for those who are able to be transported.

The use of this rite of the distribution of Holy Communion emphasizes the unity of the congregation by including all in the celebration and avoids the fragmentation and extreme individualism that separate bedside celebrations may imply.

If sufficient ministers are appointed so that the absent may receive communion on the same day as the congregational celebration, the centrality of Sunday, the day of resurrection, is emphasized. The ancient association of the Lord's Day and the Lord's Supper is underscored, and Sunday is more clearly the day of worship par excellence.

Even when the distribution of Holy Communion must be delayed for many hours or even many days (as it will be, for example, in those congregations in which the pastor must give all the communions alone without lay assistants), the ceremony helps keep the focus of each individual communion on the central congregational Eucharist.

The Distribution of Communion to Those in Special Circumstances is a way of involving lay people in significant ministry, clearly indicating both the dignity which baptism confers and the shared nature of the Christian ministry. When properly understood, this use of lay people does not undermine or devalue the role of the clergy. Rather, it enhances the totality of the ministry of the whole body of Christ.

Finally, and not incidentally, the practice of sending lay people with the Eucharist to the absent can provide help for the pastor in a large and busy parish. (Remember the two accounts of how Moses required help in judging the increasing numbers of Hebrews, in Exod. 18:13–25 and Deut. 1:9–18, and the selection of deacons in the early church, in Acts 6:1–6.) Congregations are celebrating the Holy Communion with greater frequency than in earlier decades and centuries, and the sick, the institutionalized, and the infirm should not be excluded—especially during the Easter season—from this opportunity for spiritual growth which frequent communion provides.

Background

Earlier Lutheran books included an order for the communion of the sick which required the leadership of a pastor. But the absent are not always sick; they may be aging, infirm, or in fact in excellent health but unable to join the congregational celebration because they are caring for one who cannot be left alone.

The Distribution of Communion to Those in Special Circumstances is new to Lutherans in North America; there was never such a service in previous service books. It was made necessary by the joint *Statement on Communion Practices* of 1978 by the American Lutheran Church and the Lutheran Church in America:

> II. B. 1. Sick and homebound members should be included in the Communion of the congregation. One way to provide such participation is through a visit during which the pastor administers the Communion to those who are present. Another way is by sending pastors or trained and designated lay members out from the corporate worship to the sick and the homebound. Elements from the congregation's celebration may be used. A rite used in these cases shall include the Words of Institution and the Lord's Prayer. The second method of ministering to the sick and homebound members is intended neither to suggest a concept of "reserved elements" nor depart from the traditional role of the pastor but is intended to be seen as an extension of the congregation's service of Holy Communion. It provides those persons an opportunity to be included in the worship of the congregation and to receive the benefits of the Sacrament.

There were existing orders for the celebration of Holy Communion with the sick (Order for the Communion of the Sick, *Occasional Services* [1962], pp. 56–60), but a new form was necessary for "the second method of ministering to the sick and homebound."

An important goal of the Reformation was to increase the frequency of the reception of the Sacrament of Holy Communion. In the Middle Ages there were many masses, but few communed. In Lutheran churches it eventually became the practice for nearly everyone to commune whenever the sacrament was celebrated. The peculiar Lutheran (and Protestant) problem, however, was that the frequency of celebrations of Holy Communion declined sharply in the seventeenth and eighteenth centuries so that people did not have the opportunity to commune often. Thus, before and after the Reformation, in Catholic and in Protestant churches, people did not receive Holy Communion frequently.

A second set of historical circumstances needs to be kept in mind. From time to time, especially in Scandinavia, Lutheranism has experienced an emphasis on lay preaching and lay leadership in worship. In North America—because of the shortage of clergy, the great distances between congregations, the influence of the less conservative Protestant churches which outnumbered Lutheran churches and which appeared to many to be the authentic American form of Christianity, and because of a (sometimes mistaken) understanding of the "priesthood of all believers"— lay responsibility for congregational management and ministry, and even worship leadership, became common. Moreover, in the twentieth century Lutherans have begun to recover their heritage of a rich baptismal theology which emphasized the responsibilities of all the baptized in the church.

In all this, Lutherans reflected what was happening not only in North America but elsewhere in Western Christianity. Even in the Roman Catholic church similar activity was occurring. In 1903, Pope Pius X issued a decree which called for reforms in sacred music and which also urged lay involvement in the liturgy. (Liturgy, after all, means "work of the people.") In 1910 the same pope, noting the long decline in the reception of Holy Communion, published his encyclical *"Quam singulari"* in which he sought to encourage frequent communion. As a result, children began receiving the sacrament at about the age of seven (the "age of reason"). In 1942, in an encyclical "The Mystical Body of Christ," Pius XII spoke of the church as the body of Christ and emphasized the dignity of each of its members.

By the middle of the twentieth century new understandings of the theology and practice of Holy Communion were developing across denominational lines. Lay people were again given significant roles in the service as assisting ministers with various duties: singing the Kyrie, reading lessons, leading the intercessions, sharing in the ministration of communion.

The renewal in the Roman Catholic church provided the specific impetus and model for the involvement of lay people in the distribution of Holy Communion. The new Roman liturgy was promulgated in the missal of Paul VI in 1969. In the following year the American Catholic bishops requested permission to use special ministers of Holy Communion, that is, those who were not ordained. Permission was given in 1971 for a period of one year; this was extended for a second year. On 29 January 1973, Paul VI issued an instruction, *"Immensae caritatis,"* on "Facilitating Sacramental Communion in Particular Circumstances." Official approval was given for the use of lay ministers of communion both in the celebration at the church and in the distribution of communion to the absent.

Within Lutheranism, the practice of using lay people to assist in communing the congregation and in carrying the sacrament to those who are absent, suggested by the *Statement on Communion Practices* (1978), is consistent with the *LBW*, which was introduced in Lutheran congregations at the beginning of Advent 1978. The book calls for an assisting minister for many parts of the Holy Communion in order to emphasize that leadership of worship is shared by pastors and laity. While an ordained pastor must preside, the pastor should not be the only leader.

The involvement of lay people in the distribution of communion has not been known for centuries in most churches, but it is nothing new in the long history of Christianity.

Until the fourth century the ancient association of the Lord's Day and the Lord's Supper dictated the celebration (and reception) of one Eucharist each Sunday. (Daily Mass was a later innovation.) The practice arose that people carried some of the eucharistic bread home to give to relatives and friends who were ill or in prison or who were isolated monks, so that all could commune from the one Eucharist.

For many centuries lay people were accustomed to handling the elements of communion. St. Cyril, bishop of Jerusalem, completing his instruction of the newly baptized on the Second Sunday of Easter in 348, described the way one should receive the Lord in Holy Communion:

> When you approach communion, do not come with your hands outstretched or with your fingers open, but make your left hand a throne for the right one, which is to receive the King. With your hand hollowed receive the body of Christ and answer Amen.[7]

In the next century Theodore of Mopsuestia (d. 428) wrote, "Everyone stretches out the right hand to receive the Eucharist, which is given, and puts the left hand under it."[8]

John Chrysostom in his fiery way admonished his congregation:

> You would not presume to kiss a king with an unclean mouth, and do you with an unclean soul kiss the king of heaven? It is an outrage. Tell me, would you choose to come to the Sacrament with unwashed hands? No, I suppose not. But you would rather choose not to come at all than to come with soiled hands. And then, as scrupulous as you are in this small matter, do you come with soiled soul and thus dare to touch it? And yet the hands hold it but for a time, whereas into the soul it is dissolved entirely.[9]

Canon 101 of the Trullan Council (692) directed: "If anyone wishes to . . . offer himself for the communion, let him draw near, arranging the hands in the form of a cross, and so let him receive the communion of grace."[10]

---

7. *Mystagogical Catechesis* V, 21, in *A Select Library of Nicene and Post-Nicene Fathers of the Christian Church*, vol. 7, 2d series, ed. Philip Schaff and Henry Wace (New York: Christian Literature Co., 1891–99), p. 156. See R. C. D. Jasper and G. J. Cuming, eds., *Prayers of the Eucharist: Early and Reformed*, 2d ed. (New York: Oxford University Press, 1980), p. 59. Cyril is apparently the earliest authority for thus placing the hands in the form of a cross.

8. A. Mingana, *Commentary of Theodore of Mopsuestia on the Lord's Prayer and on the Sacraments of Baptism and the Eucharist*, Woodbrooke Studies 6 (Cambridge, 1933), pp. 110–13.

9. John Chrysostom, *Homily III on Ephesians*, in *Nicene and Post-Nicene Fathers*, vol. 13, p. 63.

10. Canon 101 of the Council in Trullo, often called the Quinisext Council, in *Nicene and Post-Nicene Fathers*, vol. 14, pp. 407–8.

St. John of Damascus, called John Damascene, (d. ca. 749) in expounding the faith, issued the invitation, "Let us draw near to it [the Lord's Supper] with an ardent desire, and with our hands held in the form of the cross let us receive the body of the Crucified One."[11]

As late as the ninth century an altar book (sacramentary) contained an illustration showing the Eucharist placed into the hand of a communicant.

A change in eucharistic theology and piety led to a gradual change in practice, however. During the eighth and ninth centuries the laity were eliminated from the leadership in the liturgy, which became the prerogative of the clergy alone. Even handling the eucharistic elements became reserved to the clergy. The bread was placed directly into the mouth on the tongue by a priest—a practice still familiar to many Lutherans even now, centuries after the Reformation.

The *Statement on Communion Practices* and *Occasional Services* (1982) are careful to say nothing and to imply nothing about "reservation" of the sacrament, for it is a sensitive, not to say volatile, issue for many Lutherans. Consideration of the matter may nonetheless be inevitable as the practice of the Distribution of Communion to Those in Special Circumstances becomes more common.

Reservation is simply the practice of keeping, or reserving, the eucharistic elements from one celebration to the next so that they are available for those such as the sick and dying between celebrations of the Holy Communion. The celebration of the Holy Communion was always intended as as congregational act.

Throughout the early centuries of Christianity the eucharistic elements were kept in a movable vessel of one sort or another. The sacristy, as is still true in many of the Eastern Orthodox churches, was the usual place. A container called a pyx, suspended in the church and often in the shape of a dove suggesting not only the Holy Spirit but the coming down of the bread from heaven (see John 6:33, 41), gained considerable popularity. In Germany a free-standing, elaborately carved tower of wood or stone— a "sacrament house"—was a popular place for reservation of the communion elements. In England preference inclined toward a kind of wall safe—an aumbry.

The Brandenburg Church Order provided for reservation of the sacrament in churches of the Augsburg Confession.

The 1549 *Book of Common Prayer* allowed reservation for the communion of the sick on the day of a public celebration. The 1552 book eliminated reservation entirely. The 1979 *Book of Common Prayer* is the

---

11. John of Damascus, *Exposition of the Orthodox Faith*, IV, 13, in *Nicene and Post-Nicene Fathers*, vol. 9, p. 83.

first American Prayer Book to permit reservation of the sacrament, and the practice is carefully restricted.[12]

> If any of the consecrated Bread or Wine remain, apart from any which may be required for the Communion of the sick, or of others who for weighty cause could not be present at the celebration, or for the administration of Communion by a deacon to a congregation when no priest is available, the celebrant or deacon, and other communicants, reverently eat and drink it, either after the Communion of the people or after the Dismissal.[13]

One other occasion is permitted: Good Friday.

> Where it is desired to administer Holy Communion from the reserved Sacrament on Good Friday, the Sacrament for that purpose is consecrated at this service. [Maundy Thursday][14]

> [Good Friday] In places where Holy Communion is to be administered from the reserved Sacrament, the following order is observed . . . [15]

Only in the sixteenth century did a safe — the tabernacle — on the main altar begin to be the normal manner of reservation in the Roman Catholic church. It was prescribed by the Roman Ritual of 1614, but not until 1863 were all other ways of reservation forbidden in the Roman church. Following the reforms of the Second Vatican Council, when altars were moved out from the wall, reservation on the altar was difficult and undesirable, and therefore in the Roman church tabernacles were removed to side altars or to chapels.

The objection of the Reformers, both Lutheran and Anglican, to the practice of reservation had to do not with reservation as such, but with the abuses of the practice by which the elements were removed from their function as food and became objects of adoration and guarantees of the physical presence of Christ in churches at all times.

The statement of "one Eucharist," formulated by the Faith and Order Commission of the World Council of Churches meeting at Accra in 1974, recommends that differences over the reservation and disposal of the consecrated elements be treated in the light of the fact that the elements remain the sacramental reality which they have become for the sake of being consumed.[16]

---

12. Hatchett, *Commentary on American Prayer Book,* p. 409.

13. *Book of Common Prayer,* pp. 408-9.

14. Ibid., p. 275.

15. Ibid., p. 282.

16. *One Baptism, One Eucharist, and a Mutually Recognized Ministry* (Geneva: World Council of Churches, 1975).

Preparing the Congregation and Its Ministers of Communion

1. Teaching the Congregation. The training which is required before one introduces the Distribution of Communion to Those in Special Circumstances must be of two kinds: training the congregation and training the ministers. It is never adequate to train the ministers, no matter how carefully, unless the congregation first understands the practice and is prepared to participate in it.

The instruction therefore must begin with training the congregation. When the introduction of the practice of involving lay people in the distribution of Holy Communion has been decided upon by the church council and the congregation, the people must be prepared slowly and thoroughly for what will be a new experience for them.

Brief paragraphs of explanation and instruction should be inserted regularly in the newsletter. In addition, appropriate paragraphs from the *Statement on Communion Practices* would be useful.

Instructive and informative announcements should be made to the congregation at the Sunday services for several months. Church-school classes could focus on the Holy Communion and its extension from the congregational celebration to absent members, and on the text of the new rite. A sermon could be devoted largely to an explanation of the practice, or if the Sunday readings do not encourage such a treatment, the proposed practice may be brought into sermons on other texts and themes as a practical example.

The congregation needs to understand: (1) the theology of the Holy Communion; (2) the outline of liturgical history which brought us to where we are today; and (3) the practical value of the Distribution of Communion to Those in Special Circumstances. Nothing must be assumed. Of course every congregation should already know what the Lutheran church believes and teaches about the Holy Communion, but how many really do know? Is there any congregation that could not benefit from fresh examination of our understanding of the sacraments? Pastors too will find a new study of the Holy Communion valuable for themselves as well as for their people.

The entire congregation needs training. Shut-ins especially need instruction not only because they will be the primary beneficiaries of the new practice, but also because they will be unable to attend the congregational training and instruction. Special efforts need to be made to insure that shut-ins receive instruction. The pastor and other members of the congregation in regular visits should tell the homebound of the reasons for the "new" practice.

It may be helpful to have one or two proposed ministers of Holy Communion accompany the pastor on visits to homebound persons to familiarize them with the people who will exercise this ministry.

Be sure that it is clear to everyone—congregation, the homebound, the pastor(s)—that this ministry is an addition to the ministry of the pastor, who will continue to visit the sick and infirm regularly in the exercise of pastoral ministry.

There may be resistance to the practice on the part of some, especially those who are unfamiliar with lay people handling the eucharistic elements. Some people have been taught that the eucharistic elements are too sacred to be touched by anyone but a pastor. The answer is not to reduce the sense of the sacredness of the Holy Communion but to exalt the status that baptism confers on all the baptized.

The shut-ins and those who care for them, as well as the whole congregation, should also be taught how to prepare for the visit of a minister of Holy Communion. (One never knows, after all, when one will be in need of this ministry.) When the Holy Communion is expected by one who is hospitalized or homebound, a table should be prepared in the person's room with a clean white cloth covering, a candle, and perhaps a crucifix or cross. This is not only a practical help to the minister so that things will be ready upon arrival; it can be the occasion of spiritual preparation by the homebound person for the entrance of the Lord into the home and into the communicant.

The homebound (and the entire congregation) should also be taught how to receive the bread: lay the open right hand across the left, which makes a "throne" for the right hand which will receive the king. Both hands are then lifted to the mouth, and the bread is eaten. Such a practice must, of course, be modified by those with crippling diseases and those who are otherwise (because of intravenous tubes, for example) unable to move their arms and hands.

The education and preparation of ministers of communion from the congregation will take a minimum of possibly six months if an adequate job is to be done. Training is essential and cannot be abridged without serious difficulty. Perhaps in the most accepting congregation the practice can be introduced overnight, but even if there is no clear opposition to it, the purpose and meaning can never be clear to the pastors and people without proper training. Such an introduction without adequate preparation is disastrous, but it is more than a matter of avoiding trouble. Each congregation deserves the opportunity to examine and consider what it is about to do. The corporate time of study and reflection will be an opportunity for distinct growth in the congregation's awareness of itself—its history, theology, and mission.

When the preparatory study is well along, the selection of the ministers of Holy Communion can begin.

2. Selecting Ministers of Communion. "The harvest is plentiful, but the laborers are few; pray therefore the Lord of the harvest to send out laborers into his harvest," Jesus said (Matt. 9:37–38), and so we may imagine he says today. Before he chose the Twelve, according to Luke 6:12–13, Jesus continued all night in prayer to God. When selecting ministers of Holy Communion, prayer is a good place to begin.

As the early church grew it felt the need for helpers for the twelve apostles. The Twelve sought out seven "of good repute, full of the Spirit and of wisdom" to be appointed to the necessary ministry (Acts 6:1–6). This is still good advice. When the practice of using lay people to take the sacrament to the absent is being introduced, special care must be taken to select the most worthy and respected people for this task. People form their opinions about a new practice based upon their opinion of the people who do it and upon the performance of those people. The practice must be introduced, therefore, by responsible and respected people who know what they are doing.

Some in the congregation will come to mind at once—those who already serve as assisting ministers in the liturgy, seminarians, deaconesses. But the pastor and the appropriate committee should look over the entire church roster for candidates. Handicapped or disabled persons should not automatically be excluded. They may in fact be able to serve and thereby provide encouragement to others and an invaluable lesson to the congregation. Both men and women, young people and elderly are eligible and should be selected so that the royal priesthood which all the baptized share will be evident. Only the very young should be excluded on the basis of age; there is not an upper age limit.

"Let no one be chosen whose selection may cause scandal among the faithful," Pope Paul VI warned in his instruction establishing the practice of special ministers of communion in the Roman Catholic church. Those selected must be carefully instructed and should be distinguished by faith and a Christian life. They should strive to be worthy of this great office, cultivating devotion to the Holy Communion and acting as examples to others by reverence for the most holy Sacrament of the Altar.

To minimize criticism, involve the entire congregation in the initial selection process. Announce in the Sunday worship leaflet and parish newsletter that a certain number of people are to be selected as ministers of Holy Communion and invite nominations or recommendations. Seek further nominations from the church council and its committees. Always collect more names than are needed; some, when asked, will decline to serve.

The final selection should belong to the pastor, for the pastor may be the only one in the parish in possession of relevant information concerning the fitness of certain candidates.

Set a term of duty. It is usually best to appoint ministers of Holy Communion for a definite period such as the church year or a season of the church year. There is often value in establishing continuity in the relationship between the one who brings communion and the person visited. Consideration should be given, however, to scheduling the visits to the sick and shut-ins so that the absent may enjoy a variety of visitors from the parish, and so that the ministers may see a variety of members of the congregation.

3. Training the Ministers of Communion. When the congregation is well instructed in the extension of the congregational celebration of the Holy Communion to the absent and is prepared for the introduction of the new practice, then the ministers of Holy Communion who have been selected are ready for their special training. These ministers should be thoroughly familiar with their duties and carefully trained in this ministry. The pastor and other qualified instructors may collaborate in such training.

It is perhaps best to spread the training over three sessions of about two hours each. Those who are learning to be ministers of Holy Communion need time to assimilate the information they receive, to think over what they are about to do, to raise questions, to identify potential problems, to assess their own skills. Allowing sufficient time for the training to progress slowly and deliberately at this stage will minimize problems later.

It is a good idea to schedule these three sessions on a regular (yearly) basis at an appropriate time during the church year. The congregation may then expect this training to occur each year, for example, during the first three weeks of Advent.

These yearly training events will not only instruct newly chosen ministers of Holy Communion but will also serve as times of review and renewal for those who already serve. Experienced ministers of Holy Communion will welcome these sessions to review what they are doing. Moreover, the experienced ministers can provide effective help in the training of new ministers by offering advice and counsel from their own on-the-job experience.

Set a specific goal for the training/renewal program. Each minister should be expected to grow in love for the sacrament and to personify ever more deeply the self-giving love of Christ.

Enlist the help of those in your congregation or in neighboring parishes who have performed this ministry. You need not limit yourself necessarily to Lutheran parishes. Look around. Explore what others are doing.

Invite these experienced ministers to talk with your people, to encourage them, and to help prepare them for the surprises that will doubtless occur when their ministry begins.

Each of the three sessions should begin with a simple devotional act to set the tone of receptivity and service. Such a devotion could be:

Reading from Scripture (for example, from the Daily Lectionary)

Silent meditation

Hymn (for example, from the Holy Communion section of the Hymnal)

Collect or brief prayer (see *LBW,* Min. Ed., pp. 109–11, nos. 189, 190, 192, 202, 203)

Blessing

First session. The purpose of this session is instruction in the theology of the Holy Communion and its historical development. It is not simply to assemble facts but to lead to deepened love for the sacrament by increasing the understanding of its richness. In the review the pastor should also be learning. An outline might include:

a. the unity which the sacrament bestows

b. the unity which the sacrament builds

c. the unity of the Lord's Day and the Lord's Supper

d. the importance of the gathered church

e. the distribution of Holy Communion as a means of including the absent in the central action of the worshiping congregation

Second session. The purpose of this session is instruction in prayer as action as well as words and in the technique of the ministration of Holy Communion. Do a simulated demonstration with the members of the class playing the roles of the sick person and the family in two settings: at home and in the hospital. Have the people handle the actual vessels they will use in the Distribution of Communion to Those in Special Circumstances. Discuss with the class how to estimate the amount of bread and the quantity of wine necessary for the number of people who are to be communed, what to do when the supply runs short, what to do when the supply is more than enough.

Third session. This session should address matters of scheduling, including the names and addresses of those to whom Holy Communion will be distributed. First, answer any questions there may be concerning the material in the first two sessions. Then list the name and location of each hospitalized and homebound person. Work out the assignments with the class, inviting the members to offer suggestions for ministering to a distant person or ministry in an especially troublesome situation.

The final assignments may have to be made by the pastor, who may know good reasons why one individual is best for a particular place or should not be sent to a particular place. At the conclusion of this last session the ministers of Holy Communion should have a clear idea of what their own particular list will be like.

Preparing for the Service

Congregations should be carefully and frequently instructed that when a member becomes ill or is otherwise confined, the pastor should be notified promptly. Most of all, when a person is in danger of death, the pastor should be notified. Understandably, Christians have sought the solace of the Lord's Supper as death draws near.

To underscore the significance of bringing the congregational Eucharist to those unable to participate in the assembly, the sacrament should be carried to the absent without delay following the congregational celebration. Sufficient ministers should be appointed so that all who have expressed a desire to commune may receive Holy Communion within a few hours of the congregation's service.

The vessels which transport the Holy Communion need not be expensive or elaborate, but they should be worthy of what they contain. Thus, plastic or paper containers or jars that have been used for some other purpose are inappropriate. Glass cruets (so that one may see how much wine remains) with tight stoppers are appropriate for the wine. Metal, glass, or ceramic boxes are appropriate for the bread.

The minister should carefully estimate the amount of bread and wine needed for the absent so that the quantities are sufficient for each communicant and a great amount does not remain after all have communed. Bread and wine remaining after the last communicant has received may be consumed by the minister and by other communicants at the last place visited.

Lay ministers of Holy Communion should be appointed for a definite period, such as a year or a season of the church year.

A table covered with a clean, white cloth should be set near the person who is to receive Holy Communion. The following items may be placed on the table: wine glass to serve as a chalice; a lighted candle as a sign of Christ who comes in the sacrament; and perhaps a second candle and a crucifix or cross. Care must be taken, however, not to reproduce the altar of the church or to clutter the table with imposing decorations. The central objects are the bread and wine of the Holy Communion.

Survey of the Service

The prayer as the ministers go forth ⟨476⟩ makes use of several biblical figures. The image of God as a mother who loves humankind with parental solicitude is a biblical picture that has in the past often been overlooked.[17] (See Job 38:8-9; Deut. 32:11; Ruth 2:12; Pss. 17:8; 36:7; 57:1; 61:4; 63:7; 91:4; Matt. 23:37; Luke 13:34. See also Hymn 519 [LBW], stanza 3.) The image of God as mother is an image that has been employed in Christian devotional writing since the early Middle Ages. The second image in the prayer, Elijah's miraculous meals, is a reference to 1 Kings 17:1-6.

At the house or hospital the minister places on the table the containers of bread and wine, leaving them closed to indicate that the rehearsal of the biblical Words of Institution in the address which follows is not to be understood as a consecration of the elements. Nothing more happens to them than has already happened at the congregational celebration. The containers are opened just prior to the actual distribution.

The minister begins with a liturgical greeting, "Peace to you from our Lord Jesus Christ." The rubrics under "The Service in Detail" (p. 80, no. 5) allow an alternate greeting to be used: either the traditional "Peace to this house and to all who dwell in it" or "Grace to you and peace" (1 Cor. 1:3; Rom. 1:7; 2 Cor. 1:2; Gal. 1:3; Eph. 1:2; Phil. 1:2; Col. 1:2; 1 Thess. 1:1; 2 Thess. 1:2; Philem. 3).[18]

In the address the minister makes clear that this is not a new celebration of the Holy Communion but an extension of the congregation's celebration. The address includes the Words of Institution because the *Statement on Communion Practices* requires their use in this service: "A rite used in these cases shall include the Words of Institution and the Lord's Prayer." Lutherans sometimes understand the *verba institutionis* as a proclamation of the gospel. This solution to the problem created by following the direction of the *Statement on Communion Practices* while trying to avoid undesirable associations with a formula of consecration was suggested in an editorial by Colin Buchanan of the Church of England in *News of the Liturgy*.[19]

---

17. See Joan Engelsman, *The Feminine Dimension of the Divine* (Philadelphia: Westminster Press, 1979).

18. "The minister . . . may use this greeting:
    Peace to this house and to all who live in it.
Any other customary form of greeting from scripture may be used" *The Rites*, p. 475.

19. Colin Buchanan, in *News of the Liturgy* 56 (August 1979), wrote: "There are very positive good reasons for practising communion by extension. The most obvious one is that the sick are genuinely sharing in the same loaf as well. The ideal would be that, at a parish communion, laypersons should take with them the message of the sermon, and the kiss of peace, as well as the shared sacramental elements. . . . The liturgical question is: how can the actual administration be linked back to the point of the main celebration? I suggest that the 'satellite' administration should be introduced with words of this sort:

This is the bread and cup from the communion celebrated [half an hour ago] in St.

It should be carefully noted that since the Words of Institution are a recitation of an action performed in the congregational celebration the minister "does not touch or lift the bread and wine during the address." The biblical words are an echo of what was done in the congregation, a link between the celebration by the assembly and the distribution of Holy Communion to the sick person.

The confession which follows is perhaps to be regarded as an interim solution to the problem of confession and forgiveness. Congregations, as well as the church at large, need to search for pastorally more satisfying solutions, perhaps separating confession from Holy Communion. If that were done, the action of this rite would be less cluttered and more straightforward.

When a pastor is the minister of this service, the declaration of grace in the form reserved for pastors is used:

> In the mercy of Almighty God, Jesus Christ was given to die for you, and for his sake God forgives you all your sins. To those who believe in Jesus Christ he gives the power to become children of God and bestows on them the Holy Spirit. (p. 81)

Or the pastor may use the absolution:

> Almighty God, in his mercy, has given his Son to die for us and, for his sake, forgives us all our sins. As a called and ordained minister of the Church of Christ, and by his authority, I therefore declare to you the entire forgiveness of all your sins, in the name of the Father, and of the + Son, and of the Holy Spirit. (p. 81)

Individual Confession and Forgiveness may be used instead when the minister of Holy Communion is a pastor.

If some form of confession and forgiveness has been used, the peace may be exchanged as a demonstration of reconciliation. It is inappropriate to use the peace in this rite without confession and forgiveness, for the peace must not be allowed to degenerate into simply a warm greeting. It was because of such loss of significance and such abuse that the peace was removed from the liturgy of the Western church for many centuries.

The Prayer of the Day (*Occasional Services*, pp. 263–86) may be said. The prayers of the day for the commemorations are not given in *Occasional Services* because it is expected that the sacrament will be taken to

---

Agatha's Church. There we took the bread and cup in obedience to the Lord's command [who on the same night he was betrayed . . .] and gave thanks. Now we bring these to you to break the bread and to share the communion with you.

On the pattern of the present Series 3 there would follow the breaking of the bread, the Lord's Prayer, the invitation to communion, and the actual administration."

the absent on the day of the congregational celebration, which, in nearly all cases, will be a Sunday or a festival day. Sundays and festivals take precedence over the commemorations. If, however, the sacrament is brought to the absent on a day other than a Sunday or a festival, the minister should note the commemoration, should one occur, and use the appropriate prayer.

The brief Gospel text provided (John 6:35) is included for the convenience of those who use the rite.[20] The use of the Gospel for the day is encouraged. It may be abbreviated for the sick person if necessary. Other brief Gospels are given in the *Occasional Services* (p. 81, no. 10).

All of the foregoing has been simply preparation for the principal action of the visit: the actual ministration of Holy Communion. The minister opens the containers of bread and wine and pours some wine into the goblet.

The Lord's Prayer is required not only by the 1978 *Statement on Communion Practices* but by universal Christian use as the table prayer of the people of God.

The verse from 1 Cor. 11:26, "As often as we eat of this bread and drink from this cup, we proclaim the Lord's death until he comes," may be said as a statement of what the Holy Communion proclaims. It recalls the past and anticipates the future.[21] Then the bread and wine is given to the communicant. The *Statement on Communion Practices* allows that "the use of only one element is acceptable when there are special difficulties." If, for example, the person cannot swallow bread, a touch of wine to the lips is sufficient. It has always been the teaching of the church that the whole Christ is received under each element.

Ministers of the Holy Communion should be taught to say the words accompanying the administration of the sacrament precisely, without emendation or alteration:

---

20. *The Rites*, pp. 476–77, provides these other suggestions for "a brief passage from sacred scripture": John 6:54–58; 14:6; 14:23; 15:4; 15:5; 1 Cor. 11:26; 1 John 4:16.

21. The Roman Catholic invitation (*The Rites*, p. 477) is, the minister holding the bread:

This is the Lamb of God
who takes away the sins of the world.
Happy are those who are called to his supper.

The communicant responds:

Lord, I am not worthy to receive you,
but only say the word and I shall be healed.

The invitation (optional) in the *Book of Common Prayer* (p. 399) is:

The gifts of God for the people of God. (Take them in remembrance that Christ died for you, and feed on him in your hearts by faith, with thanksgiving.)

The body of Christ, given for you.
The blood of Christ, shed for you.

When only one element is given (when Holy Communion is received "under one kind"), the minister uses only the words pertaining to that element.

Communicants should be taught to respond "Amen" after each of the phrases that accompany the ministration of the elements as an affirmation of belief in Christ who comes to his people in the sacrament.

The silence for meditation which follows is an important part of the action and should not be passed over. It should be of sufficient duration so that real meditation can take place.

After the silence, the distribution concludes with dispatch. The first prayer of thanksgiving (209) was prepared by the Commission on the Liturgy for the *Service Book and Hymnal* (1958), based on a prayer in *The Kingdom, the Power, and the Glory.*[22] It was slightly altered for use in the *LBW*. The second prayer (241) is the *LBW* adaptation of Luther's postcommunion collect from his *German Mass.*[23]

The Benedicamus, "Let us bless the Lord," is the traditional ending of many of the services of the church. Historically, for example, that was the conclusion of morning and evening prayer, and no further benediction followed. When the communicant does not have the text of the service or cannot respond, it is desirable to eliminate these two lines. Such a dialogue is not effective if one person says both parts, for both lines express the same thought.

The benediction is from Responsive Prayer 2 and is identical to the blessing in the Roman Catholic rite.[24] It is deliberately different from the benediction at the conclusion of the Eucharist, for the Distribution of Communion to Those in Special Circumstances is not to be seen as a duplication of the congregational celebration of the Holy Communion.

When the Laying on of Hands and Anointing the Sick is combined with the distribution of Holy Communion in one continuous rite, see the outline previously provided, p. 102, for guidance.

---

22. *The Grey Book,* Part III, 3d ed. (London: Oxford University Press, 1925), p. 69.
23. *LW,* vol. 53, p. 84.
24. *The Rites,* p. 478. This alternate is also provided:

May the almighty and merciful God bless and protect us, the Father, and the Son, and the Holy Spirit.

Comparison of Rites
Distribution of Communion to Those
in Special Circumstances

ROMAN CATHOLIC (by an extraordinary minister) *The Rites* pp. 475–79	LUTHERAN *Occasional Services* pp. 76–81	EPISCOPAL *Book of Common Prayer* pp. 396–99
Greeting	Greeting	
	Address	
Penitential rite	(Confession)	
	(The peace)	
	(Prayer of the day)	
(Reading)	Gospel	Reading
	(comment)	(comment)
		(suitable prayers)
		(Confession of Sin)
		(The peace)
Our Father	Our Father	Our Father
This is the Lamb . . .*	(As often as we . . .)	(The gifts of God . . .)
Ministration*	Ministration	Ministration
(Silence)	Silence	
Prayer*	Prayer	Prayer
	Benedicamus	
Blessing	Blessing	Blessing or dismissal

---

*Elements of the "shorter rite" may be used when communion is given in different rooms of the same building, such as a hospital. The shorter rite begins with an appropriate antiphon, such as

How holy this feast
in which Christ is our food:
his passion is recalled,
grace fills our hearts,
and we receive a pledge of the glory to come. (*The Rites*, pp. 478–79)

CELEBRATION OF HOLY COMMUNION
WITH THOSE IN
SPECIAL CIRCUMSTANCES
(*Occasional Services*, pp. 83–88)

Parallel Rites

Episcopal   See An Order for Celebrating the Holy Eucharist, *Book of Common Prayer*, pp. 400–405. Also: "When persons are unable to be present for extended periods, it is desirable that the priest arrange to celebrate the Eucharist with them from time to time on a regular basis, using either the Proper of the Day or one of those appointed for Various Occasions. If it is necessary to shorten the service, the priest may begin the celebration at the Offertory, but it is desirable that a passage from the Gospel first be read" (*Book of Common Prayer*, p. 396).

Lutheran   Order for the Communion of the Sick, *Occasional Services* (1962), pp. 55–60.

Order for the Communion of the Sick, *Common Service Book* (1919), text ed., pp. 410–13.

The Order for the Communion of the Sick, *Pastor's Companion*, pp. 62–66.

Communion of the Sick, *Church Book* (1892), pp. 399–403.

The Order for the Communion of the Sick, *Lutheran Agenda* (194?), pp. 62–66.

Communion of the Sick, *Forms for Ministerial Acts* (General Synod, 1900), pp. 61–68.

Purpose

The Celebration of Holy Communion with Those in Special Circumstances is for use by pastors only. It provides for a celebration of the Holy Communion with the sick and infirm in places other than a church building. It is especially for use in those congregations which have not introduced the Distribution of Communion to Those in Special Circumstances or when such distribution is not possible or desirable.

Characteristics

This service is basically the *LBW* Holy Communion in its simplest weekday form. (See the Min. Ed., pp. 26-29, nos. 6, 8, 9, 20, 31.) The festive elaborations of the basic rite have been removed.

Background

A service such as this has been the usual means in Lutheran practice of communing those who are unable to come to church.

The Episcopal Church in the 1979 *Book of Common Prayer* provides a list in outline form of the elements considered essential for a eucharistic celebration. This provides freedom for those situations in which the Holy Communion forms of Rite One or of Rite Two, "designed for the Sunday gathering of the congregation, are too formal, too verbose, or too demanding." [25] In the outline, the people and priest (1) gather in the Lord's name; (2) proclaim and respond to the Word of God; (3) pray for the world and the church; (4) exchange the peace; (5) prepare the table; (6) make Eucharist; (7) break the bread; and (8) share the gifts of God. The rite requires careful preparation by all participants and "is not intended to provide license for a casually improvised service." [26]

Survey of the Service

The apostolic greeting begins the service and serves also as the salutation before the prayer of the day.

The Gospel is the principal reading and is always used. When conditions permit, another reading—the First (Old Testament) Lesson is next in order of preference—may precede the Gospel.

The intercessory prayers in this rite are optional, but normally when this rite is used the person should have the opportunity to pray for the church and the world. It is yet another way to indicate and express the communal nature of the sacrament.

After the peace, the Great Thanksgiving follows. The preface and the Sanctus are omitted, as in the 1962 *Occasional Services*, because the sick person may not have a text of the service to follow or may not be able to respond. The three options of the *LBW*—prayer of thanksgiving, Verba alone, prayer followed by the Verba—are preserved here. The first option, the brief prayer of thanksgiving, is a new composition. An alternate, provided in the notes on the service (p. 88, no 9), is the early third-century prayer of Hippolytus, given in the *LBW* as Eucharistic Prayer IV (Min. Ed., pp. 226, 262, 298). The second option is the *verba institutionis* by

---

25. Hatchett, *Commentary on American Prayer Book,* p. 411.
26. Ibid.

themselves. The third option, a prayer followed by the Verba, is derived from the 1942 *Massbook* of the Church of Sweden.[27] The Great Thanksgiving is concluded with the Our Father.

The first postcommunion prayer (209) is the *LBW* modernization (Min. Ed., p. 111) of a prayer prepared for the *Service Book and Hymnal* (1958) by the Commission on the Liturgy, based on a prayer in *The Kingdom, the Power, and the Glory*.[28] The alternate prayer (241) is a traditional Lutheran postcommunion prayer, given in the text of the Holy Communion in the *LBW*. It is a translation of a prayer in Luther's *German Mass* of 1526.[29]

For the benediction, the two alternatives of the *LBW* are provided.

Development of the Rite
Celebration of Holy Communion with Those
in Special Circumstances

Church Book*	GENERAL SYNOD (1900)	Common Service Book	Occasional Services (1962)	Lutheran Book of Worship
			Greeting	
Address	Address	Address	Address	
Confession	Confession	Confession	Confession	(Confession)
				Greeting
Introit (Psalm 25)	(Psalm 130)	Introit (Psalm 25)	(Introit Psalm 63)	
			Collect†	Prayer of the day
			Rom. 8:38–39	(Reading)
John 3:16		John 3:16	John 3:16 *or* 5:24	Gospel

---

27. In the Church of Sweden the prayer followed by the Verba has now been superseded by a eucharistic prayer which contains the Verba.

28. *Grey Book,* p. 69.

29. *LW,* vol. 53, p. 84.

* If the sick person be so weak, or in such peril of death, that the Order here given cannot be fully observed, it shall suffice to use the most essential parts, to wit: the Confession and Absolution, the Words of Institution, and the giving of the Bread and Wine. (p. 399)

† Assist us mercifully, O Lord, in these our supplications and prayers, and dispose the way of thy servant towards the attainment of everlasting salvation; that among all the changes of this mortal life, *he* may ever be defended by thy most gracious and ready help; through Jesus Christ our Lord.

Development of the Rite (continued)
Celebration of Holy Communion with Those in Special Circumstances

Church Book*	GENERAL SYNOD (1900)	Common Service Book	Occasional Services (1962)	Lutheran Book of Worship
Apostles' Creed		Apostles' Creed		
				(comment)
				(Prayers)
				(Peace)
				Great Thanksgiving
			Prayer‡	
Our Father	Verba	Our Father	Verba	
Verba and	Our Father	Verba and	Our Father	
Administration§		Administration§		
	Agnus Dei			
	Administration		Administration	Administration
(Psalm 103 or 111 or 117 or 118)	(Psalm 23 or 91 or 103; or Rom. 8:28–29; or Heb. 12:1–11)	Blessing	Blessing	Silence
Prayer//	Prayer//	Prayer//	(Prayer// or Psalm 117)	Prayer
Aaronic Benediction	Aaronic Benediction	Aaronic Benediction	Aaronic Benediction	Benediction

---

‡ O Lord God, who hast left unto us in a wonderful Sacrament a memorial of thy Passion: Grant, we beseech thee, that we may so partake of this Sacrament of thy Body and Blood, that the fruits of thy redemption may continually be manifest in us; who livest and reignest with the Father and the Holy Ghost, one God, world without end.

§The Words of Institution are divided so that the administration of the bread immediately follows the words relating to the bread and the administration of the wine immediately follows the words relating to the wine. This coincides with Luther's arrangement in the *Deutsche Messe.*

//Luther's postcommunion thanksgiving from the *German Mass* (no. 241 in the *LBW*) is emended in various ways and preceded by the versicle from Ps. 136:1, "O give thanks unto the Lord for he is good/And his mercy endureth for ever."

5

MINISTRY AT
THE TIME OF DEATH

INTRODUCTION

Ministry at the time of death is an expression of the church's support of an individual who makes the passage from life to life. Ritual passage takes place through prayer and through action. The most appropriate prayer form is often a litany with its repetition and insistence; the action often involves the gesture of touching the person, of retracing the cross made in baptism. It may involve movement and procession from place to place. The rites which accompany the church's ministry at the time of death thus form a kind of "stational" liturgy which pauses in its movement at the place of death, the home of the deceased, the church, the cemetery. Each place ("station" in liturgical language, from the Latin *statio,* a stop) has a reality which must be addressed by the Christian proclamation.

Ministry at the time of death helps the one who is dying. It also helps to guide the passage of the family and the community from grief and loss to a new life in which social configurations have been radically rearranged. It assists them in confronting the fact of death and in relinquishing a gift from God. By its physical and emotional movement, ministry at the time of death affirms the mortality of each human being, for mortals are created out of perishable material, the dust of the earth; but it also affirms that mortality is not the whole of what is real. The life and death of the deceased and of those who mourn are put within the larger framework of the death and resurrection of Christ. Thus, the Commendation of the Dying, Comforting the Bereaved, the Burial of the Dead (Entrance into the Church, Procession, Liturgy of the Word, Holy Communion, Commendation, Committal), the ministry to the mourners after the burial, and the commemoration of the anniversary of the death are all part of the movement from life to life.

The services provided for ministry at the time of death are for Christian people. In the case of non-Christians the forms provided may be altered and adapted to suit each situation. Identical claims cannot be made of the Christian and the non-Christian, for baptism makes a significant difference. The affirmation of God's mercy, however, remains constant for both Christian and non-Christian, for God desires "all to be saved and to come to the knowledge of the truth" (1 Tim. 2:4). The pastor must always be on guard against the two perils of claiming too much and of claiming too little.

Suicide presents a difficult problem, and no clear general rule can be formulated. In making decisions about the burial of a suicide the pastor should bear in mind that many "natural" deaths are the result of destructive relationships, the broken human community, and generally destructive life styles which are led without conscious self-destructive intent.

The remembrance of the anniversary of a death is not contrary to the evangelical faith. All Saints' Day (or the Sunday following) has long been associated with a general commemoration of the faithful departed, especially those in the congregation who have died during the previous year. Such a commemoration is a reminder of the communion of saints, the unity of the church on earth and in heaven. It is also appropriate to remember members of one's family on the day of their death, a kind of personal appropriation of the principle of the commemorations which the calendar suggests for the larger church.

FOR FURTHER READING

Aries, Philippe. *The Hour of Our Death*. Translated by Helen Weaver. New York: Alfred A. Knopf, 1981.

Bailey, Lloyd R. *Biblical Perspectives on Death*. Philadelphia: Fortress Press, 1979.

Becker, Ernest. *The Denial of Death*. New York: Free Press, 1973.

Benoit, Pierre, and Roland Murphy. *Immortality and Resurrection*. Concilium, vol. 60. New York: Seabury Press, 1970.

Bowers, Margaretta. *Counseling the Dying*. New York: Harper & Row, 1981.

Cope, Gilbert, ed. *Dying, Death, and Disposal*. London: SPCK, 1970.

Cullmann, Oscar. *Immortality of the Soul or Resurrection of the Dead? The Witness of the New Testament*. London: Epworth Press, 1958.

Curl, James Stevens. *A Celebration of Death: An Introduction to Some of the Buildings, Monuments, and Settings of Funerary Architecture in the Western European Tradition*. New York: Charles Scribner's Sons, 1980.

Fuller, Reginald H. "Lectionary for Funerals." *Worship* 56:1 (January 1982): 36–63.

Gundry, Robert H. *Soma in Biblical Theology*. Cambridge: Cambridge University Press, 1976.

Hauerwas, Stanley. *Truthfulness and Tragedy*. Notre Dame, Ind.: University of Notre Dame Press, 1977.

Herhold, Robert M. *Learning to Die, Learning to Live*. Philadelphia: Fortress Press, 1976.

Hoeffner, Robert J. "A Pastoral Evaluation of the Rite of Funerals." *Worship* 55:6 (November 1981): 482–99.

Jackson, Edgar. *Understanding Grief.* Nashville: Abingdon Press, 1967.

Kuebler-Ross, Elizabeth. *On Death and Dying.* New York: Macmillan Co., 1970.

Lewis, C. S. *A Grief Observed.* [by N. W. Clark, pseud.] Greenwich, Conn.: Seabury Press, 1963 [1961].

McManners, John. *Death and the Enlightenment: Changing Attitudes toward Death among Christians and Unbelievers in Eighteenth Century France.* New York: Oxford University Press, 1982.

Motter, Alton. *Preaching about Death.* Philadelphia: Fortress Press, 1975.

Muller, Alois. *The Experience of Dying.* Concilium, vol. 94. New York: Seabury Press, 1977.

Nouwen, Henri J. M. *A Letter of Consolation.* New York: Harper & Row, 1982.

Oates, Wayne E. *Pastoral Care and Counseling in Grief and Separation.* Philadelphia: Fortress Press, 1976.

Parabola: Myth and the Quest for Meaning 2:1 (Winter 1977). An issue devoted to death.

Parkes, Colin M. *Bereavement: Studies of Grief in Adult Life.* London: Tavistock Publications, 1972.

Pelikan, Jaroslav. *The Shape of Death: Life, Death, and Immortality in the Early Fathers.* New York: Abingdon Press, 1961.

Perrin, Norman. *The Resurrection According to Matthew, Mark, and Luke.* Philadelphia: Fortress Press, 1977.

Rahner, Karl. *On the Theology of Death.* New York: Seabury Press, 1973.

Rogness, Alvin, and Youth Research Center. *Appointment with Death.* New York: Thomas Nelson, 1972.

Rowell, Geoffrey. *The Liturgy of Christian Burial: An Introductory Survey of the Historical Development of Christian Burial Rites.* Alcuin Club no. 59. London: SPCK, 1977.

Rutherford, Richard. *The Death of a Christian: The Rite of Funerals.* New York: Pueblo Publishing Co., 1980.

Sabom, Michael B. *Reflections of Death: A Medical Investigation.* New York: Harper & Row, 1982.

Schwarz, Hans. *Beyond the Gates of Death: A Biblical Examination of Evidence for Life after Death.* Minneapolis: Augsburg Publishing House, 1981.

Spiegal, Yorick. *The Grief Process.* London: SCM, 1978.

Switzer, David K. *The Dynamics of Grief.* Nashville: Abingdon Press, 1970.

Thielicke, Helmut. *Death and Life.* Philadelphia: Fortress Press, 1970.

Wagner, Johannes, ed. *Reforming the Rites of Death.* Concilium, vol. 32. New York: Paulist Press, 1968.

Whytehead, Lawrence, and Paul Chidwick. *Dying: Considerations Concerning the Passage from Life to Death.* Toronto: Anglican Book Centre, 1982.

Young, Henry J., ed. *Preaching on Suffering and a God of Love.* Philadelphia: Fortress Press, 1978.

COMMENDATION OF THE DYING
(*Occasional Services*, pp. 103–7)

Parallel Rites

Roman Catholic	Rite for the Commendation of the Dying, *The Rites,* pp. 622–28.
Episcopal	Ministration at the Time of Death, *Book of Common Prayer,* pp. 462–65.
Lutheran	Order for the Commendation of the Dying, *Occasional Services* (1962), pp. 61–62.
	The Blessing of the Dying, *Pastor's Companion,* pp. 128–29.
	Order for the Commendation of the Dying, *Common Service Book* (1919), text ed., pp. 428–29.
	The Commendation of the Dying, *Church Book* (1892), pp. 403–6.
Orthodox	The Office at the Parting of the Soul from the Body, *Service Book,* pp. 360–67.

Purpose

The purpose of this rite is to commend a dying Christian to the mercy and care of God and to assist the dying across the threshold of death.

Provision is also made in this form for ministry when a life-support system is withdrawn.

Characteristics

The Commendation of the Dying is composed largely of optional portions for use at the discretion of the minister. Only four items are required: the opening prayer for God's comfort (although there is no rubric explicitly directing that this prayer must be said); the commendation itself, "Child of God, go forth . . . "; the prayer of commendation at the time of death, "Into your hands, O merciful Savior . . . "; and the blessing. The use of these four items will make a simple, straightforward rite for those occasions when such simplicity and directness is appropriate and desired. Thus, in its briefest form, the Commendation of the Dying is simply this:

> Almighty God, look on _____, whom you made your child in Baptism, and comfort *him/her* with the promise of life with all your saints in your eternal kingdom, the promise made sure by the death and resurrection of your Son, Jesus Christ our Lord.

Child of God, go forth in the name of God the Father almighty who created you; in the name of Jesus Christ, Son of the living God, who redeemed you; in the name of the Holy Spirit who was poured out upon you. May you rest in peace and dwell forever in the paradise of God.

Into your hands, O merciful Savior, we commend your servant, _____. Acknowledge, we humbly beseech you, a sheep of your own fold, a lamb of your own flock, a sinner of your own redeeming. Receive *him/her* into the arms of your mercy, into the blessed rest of everlasting peace, and into the glorious company of the saints in light.

May _____ and all the departed, through the mercy of God, rest in peace.

or,

Almighty God, Father, + Son, and Holy Spirit, bless you now and forever.

The additional items may be used as appropriate. Pastors sometimes find that when a death is protracted and the vigil is long, it is helpful to have a series of prayers to read to calm, support, and encourage the dying and those who keep vigil with the dying person. If still more material is desired, it has been traditional in Christianity in both East and West for the history of the passion of Christ to be read from one or more of the Gospels.

The Commendation of the Dying, except in the most extraordinary cases, is reserved for the pastor, who symbolizes the church to the dying person and to the family and who is the one who in other services represents the church in the laying on of hands. The pastor's presiding at the Commendation of the Dying will help recall those other occasions — Holy Baptism, Affirmation of Baptism, Laying on of Hands and Anointing the Sick.[1]

---

1. The Roman Catholic Rite for the Commendation of the Dying has this rubric:

   It is the responsibility of priests and deacons, whenever possible to assist the dying person and those who are with him and to recite the prayers of commendation and the prayer after death. The presence of these ministers clearly shows the Christian the meaning of death in the fellowship of the Church. When a priest or deacon is unable to be present because of other serious pastoral obligations, he should instruct the laity to assist the dying by reciting the prayers contained in this chapter or other prayers; texts of these prayers and readings should be made readily available to them. (*The Rites*, pp. 622–23)

   The *Book of Common Prayer* is less explicit, but the expectation is that the "minister of the congregation" will lead the prayers at the time of death. The first rubric under Ministration at the Time of Death is:

   When a person is near death, the Minister of the Congregation should be notified, in order that the ministrations of the Church may be provided. (p. 462)

   In the text of the ministration, however, the leader is called simply "the Officiant."

Background

By the time of the Council of Nicaea (325) the practice of giving Holy Communion to the dying as a viaticum (food for the journey) seems to have been regarded as an ancient custom. Prayers for the commendation of the dying and the departed are extant from the fourth century.

The order for the Commendation of the Dying seems to have entered North American Lutheran use with the recovery of sixteenth-century German practices in the *Church Book* (1892) and continued through the Common Service tradition. There is no corresponding rite in the *Lutheran Agenda* of the Synodical Conference.

Comparison of Texts
Commendation of the Dying

Church Book (1892)	Common Service Book (1919)	Occasional Services (1962)	Occasional Services (1982)
		The Lord be with you. *And with thy spirit.*	
Kyrie	Kyrie	Kyrie	
Our Father	Our Father	Our Father	
Prayer* (Psalms or Lessons)	Prayer† (Psalms or Lessons)	Prayer† (Psalms or Lessons)	Prayer
(Portion of the History of the Passion)			
	(Agnus Dei or		
(Nunc Dimittis)	Nunc Dimittis)		

Texts for the prayers, commendations, and blessings indicated in the chart now follow.

* O God, our heavenly Father: Thou hast promised us by Thy Son, "If two of you shall agree on earth as touching anything that they shall ask, it shall be done for them of My Father which is in heaven." Upon this Thy promise, we beseech Thee on behalf of Thy servant, who hath been baptized in the Name of Jesus, and hath openly confessed Thee the everlasting God, Father, Son and Holy Ghost. Graciously accept *him,* and forgive *him* all *his* sins; mercifully defend *him* against all temptations; and grant *him* everlasting life; through Jesus Christ, Thy Son, our Lord. Amen. (p. 403)

† O Lord God, our Heavenly Father, we beseech Thee graciously to accept this Thy servant, forgive *him* all *his* sins, mercifully defend *him* in the hour of *his* death, and grant *him* everlasting life; through Jesus Christ, Thy Son, our Lord. *Amen.* (p. 428)

Comparison of Texts (continued)
Commendation of the Dying

Church Book (1892)	Common Service Book (1919)	Occasional Services (1962)	Occasional Services (1982)
(Litany for the Dying)‡		(The Litany)	(Litany for the Dying)
			(Prayer)

‡ Lord, have mercy.
Lord, have mercy.
Christ, have mercy.
Christ, have mercy.
Lord, have mercy.
Lord, have mercy.
O God, the Father in heaven;
Have mercy upon him.
O God the Son, Redeemer of the world;
Have mercy upon him.
O God, the Holy Ghost;
Have mercy upon him.
Be gracious unto *him.*
Spare him, *good Lord.*
Be gracious unto *him.*
Help him, *good Lord.*
From Thy wrath;
From an evil death;
From the pains of hell;
From the power of the devil;
From all evil:
Good Lord, deliver him.
By Thy holy Nativity;
By Thine Agony and Bloody Sweat;
By Thy Cross and Passion;
By Thy Death and Burial;
By Thy glorious Resurrection and Ascension;
By the Grace of the Holy Ghost, the Comforter:
Help him, *good Lord.*
In the hour of death;
And in the day of judgment:
Help him, *good Lord.*
We poor sinners do beseech Thee;
To hear us, O Lord God.
That Thou wouldest spare *him*;
We beseech Thee to hear us, good Lord.
Lord, have mercy.
Lord, have mercy.
Christ, have mercy.
Christ, have mercy.
Lord, have mercy.
Lord, have mercy.

Comparison of Texts (continued)
Commendation of the Dying

Church Book (1892)	Common Service Book (1919)	Occasional Services (1962)	Occasional Services (1982)
(Commendation)§	(Commendation)//	Commendation# and Aaronic Benediction	Commendation
			(Nunc Dimittis) Prayer at the time of death
(Prayer after death)**	Prayer after death††	Prayer after death‡‡	(Prayer after death)

---

§ *When the soul is about to depart, the Minister may lay his hand on the head of the dying believer, and say:*
Depart in peace, Thou ransomed soul, in the Name of God the Father Almighty, Who created thee; in the Name of Jesus Christ, the Son of the Living God, Who redeemed thee; in the Name of the Holy Ghost, Who sanctified thee. Enter now into Mount Zion, the City of the Living God, the heavenly Jerusalem, to the innumerable company of angels, and to the General Assembly and Church of the firstborn, which are written in heaven. The Lord preserve thy going out and thy coming in, from this time forth, even for evermore. Amen.

// *Then may the Minister lay his hand on the head of the dying believer, and say:*
Depart in peace, thou ransomed soul. May God the Father Almighty, Who created thee; and Jesus Christ, the Son of the Living God, Who redeemed thee; and the Holy Ghost, Who sanctified thee, preserve thy going out and thy coming in, from this time forth, even for evermore. Amen.

The Minister may lay his hand on the head of the dying believer. Then shall he say:
Go forth from this world, O Christian soul: In the Name of God the Father Almighty, who created thee; In the name of Jesus Christ, Son of the living God, who suffered for thee; In the Name of the Holy Ghost, who hath been shed upon thee; in the company of saints and angels. May thy portion this day be in peace, and thy dwelling-place in Zion.

** We thank Thee, Lord Jesus, Thou Prince of Life that Thou hast kept this our *brother* steadfast in true repentance and faith, and hast granted *him* a blessed end. Now *he* is at home, and present with the Lord. All *his* sorrows are passed. God shall wipe away all tears from *his* eyes. Everlasting joy and gladness shall be on *his* head; and sorrow and sighing shall flee away. Comfort us, O Lord, who are still in this vale of tears. Help us, O Christ, to bear in patience to the end the burdens and trials of our earthly pilgrimage. Enable us to follow our *brother's* faith, and to stand ever ready, that, when our last hour shall come, we may also cease from our labor, depart in peace, and enter into Thy heavenly rest; Thou Who livest and reignest with the Father and the Holy Ghost, ever one God, world

Comparison of Texts (continued)
Commendation of the Dying

Church Book (1892)	Common Service Book (1919)	Occasional Services (1962)	Occasional Services (1982)
Blessing§§	Blessing// //	Blessing##	Blessing

The Commendation of the Dying only slowly entered the *Book of Common Prayer.* In 1932 Charles Harris said of "other necessary services" for the Prayer Book:

There are further required—

(1) *A Service for Assisting the Dying,* similar in character to that in the Roman *Rituale,* but fuller, and containing more matter suitable for the friends of the dying man to use by his bedside in the absence of the priest. In accordance with ancient precedent, the narratives of the Passion should be among the devotions used.

(2) *A Service for the Commendation of the Soul.* It is desirable that this should contain in full and unexpurgated form the greatest of all Commendatory Prayers, the *Profiscere anima Christiana de hoc mundo,* which is found in the Sarum Manual, and has been endeared to the whole English-speaking world by Newman's *Dream of Gerontius.* The abbreviated form, inserted in the 1928 Book, should be retained as an alternative; but the complete prayer ought certainly to be given.[2]

---

without end. Amen.

†† Lord Jesus, Thou prince of Life, we thank Thee that Thou didst keep this our *brother* steadfast in repentance and faith, and that Thou hast now taken *him* to Thyself. Comfort us who remain; help us to the end of life patiently to bear its burdens and trials; and when our last hour shall come, be Thou the strength of our heart and our portion forever; Who livest and reignest with the Father and the Holy Ghost, one God, world without end. *Amen.*

‡‡ O God, thou Source of life and being: We thank thee that thou didst keep this our *brother* steadfast in repentance and faith, and that thou hast now taken *him* to thyself. Comfort us who remain; help us to the end of life patiently to bear its burdens and trials; and when our last hour shall come, be thou the strength of our heart and our portion for ever; through Jesus Christ our Lord, who liveth and reigneth with thee in the unity of the Holy Ghost, God, blessed for evermore. *Amen.*

§§ The peace of the Lord be with us all. Amen.

// //The Blessing of Almighty God, the Father, the Son, and the Holy Ghost, be with us all, evermore. *Amen.*

The Blessing of Almighty God, the Father, the Son, and the Holy Ghost, be with you alway. *Amen.*

The 1979 *Book of Common Prayer* provides a form similar to the orders which Lutherans have come to expect in their service books.

The Roman Catholic liturgy provides not a form or a rite but a series of optional prayers and a recommended commendation "immediately after death."

Preparation for the Service

The first rubric (p. 103), "When a Christian is near death, the pastor should be notified so that the ministry of the Church may be extended," will be of no value if the book and its contents remain only in the hands of the pastor. Pastors should seek continually to teach the congregation their duties and obligations. In sermons, classes, service folders, and newsletters, information such as the counsel provided in this rubric should be frequently set before the congregation.

The congregation's responsibility does not, of course, end with the notification of the pastor. Christians are obliged to pray for one another and to support one another at all times, especially in times of crisis.

Survey of the Service

The resources provided in this form are to help the dying person imitate Christ in the face of the common human anxiety about death ("Father, take this cup from me," Jesus prayed in the Garden), for Christ by his power destroyed death by his own dying.

Even if the dying person is not conscious, those who are present can draw consolation from the texts and prayers and come to a better understanding of the paschal character of the death of a Christian. A vis-

---

2. *Liturgy and Worship: A Companion to the Prayer Books of the Anglican Communion*, ed. W. K. Lowther Clarke and Charles Harris (London: SPCK, 1932), p. 534. The *Proficiscere, anima Christiana, de hoc mundo* in its full and unexpurgated form is:

> Depart, O Christian soul, from this world, in the name of God the Father almighty who created you; in the name of Jesus Christ, Son of the living God, who suffered for you; in the name of the Holy Spirit who sanctified you; in the name of the glorious and blessed Virgin Mary, Mother of God; in the name of St. Joseph, her illustrious spouse; in the name of the Angels and Archangels, Thrones and Dominations, Principalities and Powers, Cherubim and Seraphim; in the name of the patriarchs and prophets, the holy apostles and evangelists, holy martyrs and confessors, the holy monks and hermits; in the name of the holy virgins and all the holy men and women of God. May you rest in peace this day and your abode be in holy Sion; through Christ our Lord. *Amen. (The Roman Ritual: Complete Edition*, trans. Philip T. Weller [Milwaukee: Bruce, 1964], pp. 236-37).

ible expression of this is making the sign of the cross on the forehead of the dying person, who was first signed with the cross in baptism.[3]

The elements of the rite should be selected with care and should be read in a slow, quiet voice, alternated with periods of silence.[4]

The first prayer "Almighty God, look on _____" ⟨485⟩ is a revision of the opening prayer for Ministration at the Time of Death in the *Book of Common Prayer*:

> Almighty God, look on this your servant, lying in great weakness, and comfort *him* with the promise of life everlasting, given in the resurrection of your Son Jesus Christ our Lord.[5]

The prayer in *Occasional Services* (1982) is a clear and explicit remembrance of baptism and the eternal life which begins at that time. The prayer sets the tone for the Commendation of the Dying: the emphasis is on life, not death; the community of the church militant; and the promise of fulfillment in the church triumphant. The eyes of the dying and of those who keep vigil are directed to the everlasting kingdom.

Then the attention turns to the immediate situation, the impending death of the person. The litany provided for optional use is the Litany at the Time of Death from the *Book of Common Prayer*,[6] slightly altered. The use of a litany in the Commendation of the Dying has ancient roots reaching back to Jewish practice, which bound a remembrance of God's deliverance of certain heroes of the tradition such as Noah and Daniel to the petition for his deliverance of the one for whom the prayer was offered. In the Roman tradition, the Litany of the Saints has often been used to assist the dying by asking the prayers of the cloud of witnesses. The present rite contains this rubric:

> If the dying person is not able to bear lengthy prayers it is recommended that, according to the particular circumstances, those present pray for him by reciting the litany of the saints, or at least some invocations from it, with the response "pray for him (her)." Special mention may be made of the patron saint or saints of the dying person or his family.[7]

Evangelical practice has avoided the invocation of the saints but has sometimes continued the use of the litany (a revision of the Litany of the

---

3. *The Rites*, p. 622.
4. Ibid.
5. *Book of Common Prayer* (1979), p. 462.
6. Ibid., pp. 462–64.
7. *The Rites*, p. 625.

Saints) with the dying. The result has been a change of emphasis, making the action more penitential (note also the continuing phrase in the prayer which began in the *Church Book* for keeping the person who has died "in repentance and faith"). The use of the litany does, however, have the benefit of binding the death of the Christian to the work of Christ, which is recalled stage by stage in the litany.

The introduction to the Lord's Prayer, the praying of which concludes the litany, is from Morning and Evening Prayer and is drawn from the plea of the penitent thief crucified with Christ (Luke 23:42) and the request of the disciples (Luke 11:1) which led Jesus to teach them the Our Father.

When praying the Lord's Prayer with the dying, the pastor must respect not only the practice of the congregation but also the needs and desires of the person so that these words which Jesus taught may be said in the translation which the person prefers. The pastor should understand that the older translation is not necessarily the "safe" one.

Following the Lord's Prayer, the first prayer for deliverance and freedom "Lord Jesus Christ, deliver your servant . . ." ⟨486⟩ is from the *Book of Common Prayer,* slightly revised. The text in the Prayer Book is:

> Deliver your servant, *N.,* O Sovereign Lord Christ, from all evil, and set *him* free from every bond; that *he* may rest with all your saints in the eternal habitations; where with the Father and the Holy Spirit you live and reign, one God, for ever and ever.[8]

This is a revision of a prayer in the 1928 American *Book of Common Prayer,* which in turn was a condensed form of a prayer in Charles Gore's *A Prayer Book Revised* (1913). Bishop Gore's prayer was based upon a translation of a prayer in the Eastern Orthodox Office at the Parting of the Soul from the Body, from William Bright's *Ancient Collects* (pp. 117–18). The prayer still reflects some of the imagery in the Orthodox prayer:

> O Lord God Almighty, the Father of our Lord Jesus Christ, . . . we pray and implore thee, absolve thou the soul of thy servant, *N.,* from every bond, and deliver him (her) from every curse . . . Yea, O Lord who lovest mankind, give thou command, and he (she) shall be released from the bonds of flesh and of sin; and receive thou in peace the soul of this thy servant, *N.,* and give it rest in the everlasting mansions, with thy Saints; through the grace of thine Only-begotten Son, our Lord, and God, and Saviour Jesus Christ.[9]

---

8. *Book of Common Prayer* (1979), p. 464.
9. *Service Book,* p. 366.

The alternate form in *Occasional Services* (pp. 105–6) is from the Roman Catholic Rite for the Commendation of the Dying.

ROMAN CATHOLIC	LUTHERAN
My brother (sister) in faith, I entrust you to God who created you. May you return to the one who formed you from the dust of this earth. May Mary, the angels, and all the saints come to meet you as you go forth from this life. May Christ who was crucified for you bring you freedom and peace. May Christ, the Son of God, who died for you take you into his kingdom. May Christ, the Good Shepherd, give you a place within his flock. May he forgive your sins and keep you among his people. May you see your Redeemer face to face and enjoy the sight of God for ever.[10]	_____, our *brother/sister* in the faith, we entrust you to God who created you. May you return to the one who formed us out of the dust of the earth. Surrounded by the angels and triumphant saints, may Christ come to meet you as you go forth from this life. Christ, the Lord of glory, who was crucified for you, bring you freedom and peace. Christ, the High Priest, who has forgiven all your sins, keep you among his people. Christ, the Son of God, who died for you, show you the glories of his eternal kingdom. Christ, the good shepherd, enfold you with his tender care. May you see your redeemer face to face and enjoy the sight of God forever.

The act of commendation, "Child of God, go forth . . . " (p. 106), is a modest revision of the form in the *Book of Common Prayer* and in the Roman Catholic Rite for the Commendation of the Dying:

ROMAN CATHOLIC	LUTHERAN	EPISCOPAL
In the name of God the almighty Father who created you, in the name of Jesus Christ, Son of the living God, who suffered for you, in the name of the Holy	Child of God, go forth in the name of God the Father almighty who created you; in the name of Jesus Christ, Son of the living God, who redeemed you; in the name of the Holy Spirit who was	Depart, O Christian soul, out of this world; In the Name of God the Father Almighty who created you; In the Name of Jesus Christ who

---

10. *The Rites*, pp. 625–26.

Roman Catholic	Lutheran	Episcopal
Spirit, who was poured out upon you, go forth, faithful Christian. May you live in peace this day, may your home be with God in Zion, with Mary the virgin Mother of God, with Joseph, and all the angels and saints.[11]	poured out upon you. May you rest in peace and dwell forever in the paradise of God.	redeemed you; In the Name of the Holy Spirit who sanctifies you. May your rest be this day in peace, and your dwelling place in the Paradise of God.[12]

The progress of the commendation in Lutheran use may be traced in the predecessor books described on page 144. The basic movement has been toward simplification of language and imagery.

The direction that the minister lay a hand on the head of the dying as these words are said is peculiar to the Lutheran rite. Predecessor rites permitted the minister to lay one hand "on the head of the dying believer." The Roman Catholic rite and the Episcopal *Book of Common Prayer* do not direct any gesture at this point.

The Commendation of the Dying is to be understood in relation to baptism. As Luther explained in "The Holy and Blessed Sacrament of Baptism" (1519):

> This significance of baptism—the dying or drowning of sin—is not fulfilled completely in this life. Indeed this does not happen until man passes through bodily death and completely decays to dust. As we can plainly see, the sacrament or sign of baptism is quickly over. But the spiritual baptism, the drowning of sin, which it signifies, lasts as long as we live and is completed only in death. Then it is that a person is completely sunk in baptism, and that which baptism signifies comes to pass.
>
> Therefore the life of a Christian, from baptism to the grave, is nothing else than the beginning of a blessed death. For at the Last Day God will make him altogether new. . . . Only then will that be finished which the lifting up out of baptism signifies. Then shall we arise from death, from sins, and from all evil, pure in body and soul, and then shall we live eternally. Then shall we be truly lifted up out of baptism and be completely born, and we shall put on the true baptismal garment of immortal life in heaven.[13]

11. Ibid., p. 625.
12. *Book of Common Prayer* (1979), p. 464.
13. *LW*, vol. 35, pp. 30-31.

The opening phrase of the commendation "Child of God" in the Lutheran rite is an echo of baptism. When the baptized is sealed with the cross of Christ (and oil), the minister says:

> *N.*, child of God, you have been sealed by the Holy Spirit and marked with the cross of Christ forever.[14]

The promise inherent in that sealing is now claimed by the church on behalf of the dying person.

The last phrase of the commendation, "dwell forever in the paradise of God," picks up "forever" from the baptismal sealing with which God's people can defy death; it also recalls Jesus' response to the plea of the dying penitent thief (the same plea was used to introduce the Lord's Prayer), "Today you will be with me in paradise" (Luke 23:43).

Jewish beliefs of Jesus' time concerning the next life were too varied to be reduced to a single consistent pattern. "Paradise" is a Persian word meaning "park" or "garden," but the commentators do not agree as to the proper understanding of the term in this context. On the one hand, like "Abraham's bosom" of Luke 16:22, "paradise" was understood to be the dwelling place of the righteous dead before the resurrection.[15] On the other hand, alongside of this hope was the belief that the righteous at death went immediately to heaven. In the commendation, "paradise" should be understood as a suggestive poetic reference to the royal garden reserved for the righteous (see Hymn 331, "Jerusalem, My Happy Home," for a meditation on the attractiveness of that heavenly garden). To earlier generations at least, a wealth of associations is suggested by the name "Zion": promise, heaven, rest, joy, reunion, the triumph of God, and the fulfillment of the kingdom. In a word, for us Zion and paradise are *home*.

When a life-support system is withdrawn, the minister may add to the words of commendation the prayer (p. 106, no. 5) that acknowledges not only physical weakness but the frailty and ignorance in which we must make decisions. It is a confession of our weakness as well as a confession of any sin which may be involved in the action. The prayer is newly composed.

To the commendation the minister may add the Nunc Dimittis, the Gospel Canticle for Prayer at the Close of the Day (Compline). The use of this canticle, which has long been a favorite with Lutherans from its use after Holy Communion and, in older books, sometimes at vespers, was an innovation of the *Church Book*. The *Common Service Book*

---

14. *LBW*, Min. Ed., p. 311.
15. Reginald H. Fuller, "Lectionary for Funerals," *Worship* 56:1 (January 1982): 36–63.

permitted either the Agnus Dei or the Nunc Dimittis after the words of commendation. (In the *Common Service Book* the Gloria Patri was not added to the Nunc Dimittis.) *Occasional Services* (1962) did not mention the use of either canticle. The use of one or both remains a possibility when the Commendation of the Dying needs to be prolonged.

At the time of death the minister says the prayer of commendation "Into your hands, O merciful Savior . . . ," which is also used in the Burial of the Dead (*LBW*, Min. Ed., p. 336). The prayer is borrowed from the *Book of Common Prayer* and in that book is used at this point in the Commendation of the Dying as well as in the Burial of the Dead.[16] The source is a prayer by John Cosin in *A Collection of Private Devotions* (1627), and it was included in the 1928 American Prayer Book. The opening phrase of the prayer recalls the Responsory in Prayer at the Close of the Day (Compline), which uses the last prayer of Jesus (Luke 23:46) as a refrain: "Into your hands, O Lord, I commend my spirit."[17] The phrase also recalls the conclusion of the prayers in the Holy Communion.

Immediately after the death, in line with previous Lutheran use and to mark a transition, two optional prayers are provided. The first, with yet another reference to baptism, asks the Savior to bring the departed from this life to God Most High. The prayer is an adaptation of the central stanza of a three-part prayer in the Roman Catholic rite:

> May Christ, who called you, take you to himself;
> may angels lead you to Abraham's side.
> *Receive his (her) soul and present him (her)*
> *to God Most High.*[18]

The prayer releases the departed from our care to the care of God.

---

16. *Book of Common Prayer* (1979), pp. 465, 483, 499.
17. *LBW*, Min. Ed., p. 73.
18. *The Rites*, p. 628. The full text of the prayer is:
Saints of God, come to his (her) aid!
Come to meet him (her), angels of the Lord!
  Receive his (her) soul and present
  him (her) to God the Most High.
May Christ, who called you, take you to himself;
may angels lead you to Abraham's side.
  Receive his (her) soul and present
  him (her) to God the Most High.
Give him (her) eternal rest, O Lord,
and may your light shine on him (her) for ever.
  Receive his (her) soul and present
  him (her) to God the Most High.
Let us pray.
We commend our brother (sister) *N.* to you, Lord.
Now that he (she) has passed from this life,

The second prayer (260) is for those who remain. It is the beloved prayer by John Henry Newman (or composed by George W. Douglas from a passage in Sermon XX in Newman's *Sermons on Subjects of the Day*)[19] included in the *LBW* in Compline (260). It begins the process, which will continue through the burial, of turning to life now without the departed.

Other prayers for the family may be appropriate and desirable. Those present may want to offer their own prayers also as they release the departed to God's care.

The minister then concludes the service either with the traditional prayer for the departed, adapted from the usage of the *Book of Common Prayer*[20] — the text was used in the Sarum rite at the commendation of the soul and as the dismissal after the service at the grave — or with the blessing from the Holy Communion. Although the rubric says "or," it is not redundant to use both concluding phrases if desired.

Comparison of Rites
Commendation of the Dying

ROMAN CATHOLIC *The Rites*	LUTHERAN *Occasional Services* (1982)	EPISCOPAL *Book of Common Prayer*
	Prayer for a person near death	Prayer for a person near death
Readings (Litany of the Saints)	Litany at the Time of Death and Our Father	Litany at the Time of Death and Our Father
	Prayer "deliver your servant . . ." *or*, "we entrust you to God . . ."	Prayer "Deliver your servant . . ."

may he (she) live on in your presence.
In your mercy and love,
forgive whatever sins he (she) may have committed
  through human weakness.
We ask this through Christ our Lord.
  Amen.

19. See Hatchett, *Commentary on American Prayer Book*, p. 568.

20. *Book of Common Prayer* (1979), p. 465:

May *his* soul and the souls of all the departed,
through the mercy of God, rest in peace. *Amen.*

Comparison of Rites (continued)
Commendation of the Dying

ROMAN CATHOLIC *The Rites*	LUTHERAN *Occasional Services* (1982)	EPISCOPAL *Book of Common* *Prayer*
Commendation	Commendation	Commendation
	(Prayer when life-support system is withdrawn)	
Litany		
	(Nunc Dimittis)	
Commendatory prayer	Commendatory prayer	Commendatory prayer
"Hail, Holy Queen"		
Prayer after death	Prayers after death	
	"May _____ and all the departed . . . " *or* "Almighty God . . . bless you . . . "	"May *his* soul . . . "

COMFORTING THE BEREAVED
(*Occasional Services*, pp. 108–12)

Parallel Rites

Roman Catholic   Vigil for the Deceased and Prayer When the Body is Placed on the Bier, *The Rites*, pp. 661–66.

Episcopal   Prayers for a Vigil, *Book of Common Prayer*, pp. 465–67.

Orthodox   The Trisagion for the Dead, *Service Book*, pp. 368–70; *An Orthodox Prayer Book*, pp. 97–101.

Purpose

"It is appropriate that the family and friends come together for prayers prior to the funeral."[21] This service is to provide suggestions for such prayers, a "wake" or vigil (by the side of the deceased) before burial. It functions as a ministry to those who mourn, giving them a way of expressing their sorrow and grief.

---

21. Ibid., p. 465.

Characteristics

The setting for this service is not usually a church but the place of death, the home of the deceased, or a funeral home.

This is intended to be an informal service and does not require the leadership of a pastor. Although it is entirely appropriate for the pastor to lead this service as a part of the ministry to the bereaved, in the absence of a pastor any layperson may lead the service.

The service is an opportunity for the family and close friends to acknowledge and confront death and loss, and to remember the life of the deceased. When this is done, the funeral can have a more pronounced resurrection character, without seeming to neglect the emotions of mourning.

Background

The Inter-Lutheran Commission on Worship intended that such a rite be provided but did not prepare a text.

The rite parallels rites in the Roman Catholic and Episcopal churches which serve two purposes: the vigil ("wake") before the funeral and the reception of the body when it is brought to the church and placed upon the bier.

Survey of the Service

The service begins with either the Western or the Eastern form of the Kyrie. The first form—"Lord, have mercy. Christ, have mercy. Lord, have mercy"—is from the Latin rite Mass and elsewhere, which Lutherans in the *Common Service Book* tradition know as the threefold Kyrie between the Introit and the Gloria in Excelsis as well as at the beginning of the prayers in Matins and Vespers:

> Lord, have mercy upon us.
> *Lord, have mercy upon us.*
> Christ, have mercy upon us.
> *Christ, have mercy upon us.*
> Lord, have mercy upon us.
> *Lord, have mercy upon us.*[22]

With the introduction of the *Service Book and Hymnal* (1958), an alternate Kyrie, "In peace let us pray to the Lord," was provided for the Holy Communion. It soon eclipsed the traditional form. In the *LBW*, the

---

22. The translation is by Thomas Cranmer. It has been suggested that Cranmer added "upon us" so that the number of syllables in English would equal the number in Greek, and thus the old melodies could be preserved.

phrase "Lord, have mercy" serves as a congregational response in the prayers of intercession in the Holy Communion and in Evening Prayer. Moreover, the Kyrie was used in many German penitential hymns, often retaining the Greek form "Kyrie eleison" or the elided form "Kyrieeleis."

The second form of the Kyrie, "Holy God, holy mighty One, holy immortal One, Have mercy on us," is the traditional form (the Trisagion) of the Eastern Orthodox churches. In that tradition the preliminary rite of burial opens and closes with this form of the Kyrie. An adaptation of this Trisagion is used in the *LBW* at the beginning of Responsive Prayer 1 and 2, in which the Eastern form is altered to "have mercy and hear us."

Psalm 121 or 130 is then said. Psalm 121 is more hopeful and is appropriate to joyful seasons of the church year; Psalm 130 is more penitential and is appropriate for Advent and Lent. However, both psalms express confidence in God's mercy and care. Usually the leader will read the psalm, but it is often more effective if the reading is shared by two persons who read it antiphonally. If those assembled have copies of the text, they may participate in the reading, but expecting them to do so at this occasion may be unrealistic. People should not be forced to speak when they do not feel like it.

After the lesson, which should be brief in keeping with the simple and quiet character of the service, the leader may comment on the reading or deliver an informal eulogy relating the life and character of the deceased to the lesson(s) just read. It is usually more desirable if the people share with one another what they remember of the deceased. The effective introduction of such conversation requires skill and sensitivity on the part of the leader. The conversation should be spontaneous and not forced. If the leader begins informally with some remembered events, others may be encouraged to add their own memories. The leader must be careful to be honest and not exalt the character of the deceased beyond measure.

The prayers follow. The prayers provided are from the following sources.

"Almighty God, source of all mercy . . . " (280).[23] This prayer is attributed to Bishop Charles Lewis Slattery of Massachusetts (d. 1930)

23. Philip H. Pfatteicher and Carlos R. Messerli, *Manual on the Liturgy* (Minneapolis: Augsburg Publishing House, 1979), p. 408:

NOTE: In the first printing of the *Lutheran Book of Worship* the ten prayers within the Burial rite, numbered 279–288, share the same numbers as the Psalm Prayers for Psalms 1–10. In the second printing the prayers within the burial rite are renumbered 429–438.

It was later decided that a renumbering would introduce still more confusion, and so the duplication stands.

and included in the 1928 American *Book of Common Prayer*, p. 342, for the Burial of a Child. It is included in the 1979 Prayer Book in the Prayers of the People in Burial Rite I, p. 481.

"Eternal God, you gave . . . " ⟨488⟩. New.

"With reverence and affection . . . " (235). This prayer was borrowed by the *LBW* from the *Service Book and Hymnal* where it was no. 43 "Thanksgiving for the Faithful Departed," p. 224 of the music edition. It was taken for that book from the *Book of Common Order* of the Church of Scotland (1940), p. 59.

"O most loving Father . . . " ⟨489⟩. This is an adaptation of prayer (204) in the *LBW*, which was borrowed from the 1928 American Prayer Book, p. 596. The prayer was written by William Bright and recalls phrases from 1 Tim. 2:1; Phil. 3:8; and 1 Pet. 5:7.

"Merciful Creator . . . " ⟨490⟩. New.

"O God our Father . . . " (283).[24] This is a prayer drawn from the *Book of Common Prayer*, "At the Burial of a Child," p. 494, slightly adapted by the *LBW*. It had appeared in the 1928 American Prayer Book. Its source was a prayer by John Dowden, bishop of Edinburgh (1886–1910), and it was in the 1912 Scottish Prayer Book.

The acclamation, "Blessed is the kingdom of the Father and of the Son and of the Holy Spirit, now and forever," is always said whatever other prayers are used. It is an expression by mortals of praise of the everlasting kingdom of the Triune God. It recalls the references to the kingdom of God in the ministry to the dying. The acclamation and variations of it are used frequently in the Eastern Orthodox churches. It is, for example, the opening of the Liturgy of the Catechumens.[25] (A more frequent form is "Blessed is our God always, now and ever, and unto ages of ages.") This acclamation of praise in this service for the bereaved recalls the confidence of Job, "the Lord gave and the Lord has taken away; blessed be the name of the Lord" (Job 1:21). It both teaches and expresses the duty of praise, even when we are deep in sorrow and grief. The mourner's kaddish in the Jewish tradition is likewise an expression of praise in the face of death.

The prayers conclude with the Lord's Prayer and the blessing, which is from Responsive Prayer 2 and points us toward the fulfillment of the promise of life which was declared to humankind in Christ Jesus.

---

24. See n. 23.
25. *Service Book*, p. 80.

Comparison of Rites
Comforting the Bereaved

ROMAN CATHOLIC The Rites pp. 662–66	LUTHERAN Occasional Services (1982)	EPISCOPAL Book of Common Prayer pp. 465–66
		It is appropriate that the family and friends come together for prayers prior to the funeral. Suitable Psalms, Lessons, and Collects (such as those in the Burial service) may be used. The Litany at the Time of Death may be said, or the following
Greeting Matt. 11:28 *or* Ecclus. 2:6 *or* 2 Cor. 1:3–4		
	Kyrie	
Psalm 130 or 23 or 114 – 115:12 or another	Psalm 121 or 130	
Prayer for the deceased* for mourners†		
Reading (Homily)	Reading (Reflection on readings)	Lessons
Intercessions	Prayers	Prayers
Lord's Prayer or other prayer	Our Father	
	Blessing	

---

*Lord, hear our prayers and be merciful
to your son (daughter) N., whom you have called from this life.
Welcome him (her) into the company of your saints,
in the kingdom of light and peace.
(We ask this) through Christ our Lord. (p. 663)
†Father,
God of all consolation,
in your unending love and mercy for us

ANNIVERSARY OF A DEATH
(*Occasional Services*, p. 295)

Parallel Rites

Roman Catholic   Propers for a Mass for the Dead (a) outside the Easter season, (b) during the Easter season, *Sacramentary*, pp. 956–60.

Episcopal   Propers for a Eucharist for the Departed, *Book of Common Prayer*, pp. 253, 928.

Lutheran   A Service of Commemoration, *Occasional Services* (1962), pp. 173–74.
Order of a Service of Commemoration, *Occasional Services* (1930), pp. 141–45.

Presbyterian   Prayer For Founders and Previous Leaders of a Congregation, *Worshipbook*, p. 198.

Purpose

The purpose of these two prayers is to maintain the unity of the church by providing a way for the church on earth to remember the church in heaven and by providing a link between the generations.

Background

In recent centuries Lutherans have been wary of anything that suggests prayers for the dead on the mistaken notion that the Reformers and the confessions are opposed to such prayer. What the Reformers and the confessions object to, however, is not the remembrance of the dead, but the misuse of the Holy Communion by reversing its direction and the attendant abuses of buying and selling masses.

---

you turn the darkness of death
into the dawn of new life.

Show compassion to your people in their sorrow.
(Be our refuge and our strength
to lift us from the darkness of this grief
to the peace and light of your presence.)

Your Son, our Lord Jesus Christ,
by dying for us, conquered death
and by rising again, restored life.
May we then go forward eagerly to meet him,
and after our life on earth
be reunited with our brothers and sisters
where every tear will be wiped away.
(We ask this) through Christ our Lord. (p. 664)

The *Occasional Services* of 1930 and 1962 provided propers for a Service of Commemoration for parochial and synodical use. The suggested time was the Sunday following All Saints' Day. Many congregations, however, followed the custom of remembering the departed on the last Sunday of the church year, the Sunday before Advent.

Comparison of Texts
A Service of Commemoration

Occasional Services
(1930)

Occasional Services
(1962)

Hymn

Invocation

Introit

I am the Way, the Truth, and the Life: no man cometh unto the Father, but by me. Alleluia.

I am the Resurrection and the Life: he that believeth in me, though he were dead, yet shall he live. Alleluia.

I am Alpha and Omega, the beginning and the ending: which is, and which was, and which is to come, the Almighty. Alleluia. Alleluia.

Psalm. Blessed are the dead which die in the Lord: Yea, saith the Spirit, that they may rest from their labors. Glory be to the Father . . .

Introit

Praise ye the Lord. Sing unto the Lord a new song: and his praise in the congregation of saints. The Lord taketh pleasure in his people: he will beautify the meek with salvation. *Psalm.* He that dwelleth in the secret place of the most High: shall abide under the shadow of the Almighty. Glory be to the Father . . .

Collect

O God, Eternal Author and Giver of life, Who didst give us Thy Son Jesus that in Him we might have the Life that knows no ending: Of Thy mercy, we beseech Thee, finish our faith in the victory that overcometh the world, that, of Thy grace and not of our deserving, we may be with Thee for evermore, and with all the adoring Host praise Thee, Father, Son, and Holy

Collect

O Lord most High, we give thee thanks for all thy saints, martyrs and confessors; for all thy faithful servants who in their lives have witnessed a good confession; and for all dear to us whom thou hast taken to thy nearer presence. Grant us grace to follow them as they followed Christ; and bring us, with them, to those things which eye hath not seen, nor ear heard, which

Comparison of Texts (continued)
A Service of Commemoration

Occasional Services (1930)	*Occasional Services* (1962)
Ghost in the Home of life, love, light and peace eternal.	thou hast prepared for them that love thee; through thy Son, Jesus Christ our Lord, who liveth and reigneth with thee and the Holy Ghost, one God, world without end.
	Lesson: Daniel 12:1–3
Epistle: 1 Thess. 4:13–18 *or* Rom. 8:31–39	Epistle: 1 Thess. 4:13–18 *or* Rev. 19:1–16
Gradual	Gradual
Gospel: John 14:1–6	Gospel: John 14:1–6 *or* John 5:24–29
Three prayers of commemoration replace the General Prayer	An optional petition for inclusion in the prayer of the church
Our Father	
Hymn	
The grace of our Lord Jesus Christ . . .	
Benediction	
(Hymn)	
	Preface of All Saints

In some parts of Christianity the "month's mind," the custom of observing the conclusion of thirty days of mourning, has been maintained. The custom was known to the Jews (Num. 20:29; Deut. 34:8).

On the anniversary of a death, the two prayers provided in *Occasional Services* may be made into a brief office by beginning with:

> Blessed is the kingdom of the Father, and of the Son, and of the Holy Spirit, now and always, and for ever and ever.

Then the two prayers may be said:

> With reverence and affection we remember before you, O everlasting God, all our departed friends and relatives, especially _____. Keep us in union with them here through faith and love toward you, that hereafter we

may enter into your presence and be numbered with those who serve you and look upon your face in glory everlasting, through your Son, Jesus Christ our Lord.

God, the generations rise and pass away before you. You are the strength of those who labor; you are the rest of the blessed dead. We rejoice in the company of your saints. We remember all who have lived in faith, all who have peacefully died, and especially those most dear to us who rest in you. Give us in time our portion with those who have trusted in you and have striven to do your holy will. To your name, with the Church on earth and the Church in heaven, we ascribe all honor and glory, now and forever.

Finally this ascription of praise from Rev. 1:5–6 may conclude the devotion:

To him who loves us and has freed us from our sins by his blood and made us a kingdom, priests to his God and Father, to him be glory and dominion for ever and ever. Amen.

Prayer (235) is also found in Comforting the Bereaved. Prayer (285) is from the Burial of the Dead, adapted for that rite from the *Service Book and Hymnal* burial office.

6

THE ORDINAL

INTRODUCTION

Through Moses the Lord gave to his people of the original covenant a system of daily and yearly sacrifices, a priesthood to offer the sacrifices, and a temple in which to offer them. The New Testament understands that Christ has fulfilled the old Levitical cult (Heb. 7:12). The temple has been replaced with the new temple, the body of Jesus (John 2:19-21); the old sacrifices disappear before the sacrificial death of Christ, the Lamb of God, on the cross (Heb. 10:5-7). Moses could beg for pardon for his people (Exod. 17:8-16; 32:11-14; Deut. 9:18-19); Christ, by shedding his blood, forgives sins (Rom. 3:24-26; 5:15-17; Eph. 2:4-7). The ministry of the New Testament is thus centered in Jesus Christ, the High Priest. He is the priest, the sacrifice, the temple of the new covenant.

This ministry is extended to the church in Holy Baptism, by which the baptized participate in the priestly ministry of Christ. The commission which Jesus gave to the apostles (Matt. 28:19-20; John 20:22-23) belongs to the whole church, and baptism establishes the participation of the baptized in that priesthood. This is made evident in 1 Pet. 2:9, which echoes Exod. 19:6:

> But you are a chosen race, a royal priesthood, a holy nation, God's own people, that you may declare the wonderful deeds of him who called you out of darkness into his marvelous light.

(It should not be overlooked that the idea of the nation as a priestly people was not the discovery of the New Testament; it was an Old Testament idea which functioned alongside the Levitical priesthood.)

To serve this priestly community, as the Lutheran confessions make clear (for example, Article V of the Augsburg Confession), the pastoral office has been established by which the apostolic ministry of proclaiming the gospel and administering the sacraments is exercised. The function of the ministry, therefore, is to equip God's people for their service in the world and to build up the body of Christ.

The New Testament presents a series of references to the work of the ministry which suggests its richness and variety. St. Paul instructs the Corinthian congregation, "God has appointed in the church first apostles, second prophets, third teachers . . . " (1 Cor. 12:28). He tells the Ephesians that God's "gifts were that some should be apostles, some prophets, some evangelists, some pastors and teachers . . . " (Eph. 4:11). Bishops, elders (presbyters), and deacons are all mentioned in the New Testament, but it is difficult to distinguish clearly their offices and functions.[1]

The earliest extant ordination rite, that of the *Apostolic Tradition* of Hippolytus (ca. 215), which seems to be representative of the early rites in Rome,[2] reflects the variety of the ministry in the early church. After dealing with the ordering of the offices of bishop, presbyter, deacon, subdeacon, widow, reader, and virgin, Hippolytus says of a gift of healing:

> If anyone among the laity appear to have received a gift of healing by a revelation, hands shall not be laid on him, because the matter is manifest.[3]

Historically, therefore, ordination referred to ministries that are arranged and regulated by the church. Ministries raised up by the Holy Spirit without the regulation of the church, usually called "charismatic," have been thought not to need validation by the public action of the church. The validity of such ministers, as in the case of the "prophets" in the New Testament, is apparent to all.

Ministries that the church has sought to order are those which assume particular responsibilities for the church and within the church. In the early years of Christianity, the bishop ("overseer" or "superintendent") emerged as the chief pastor, liturgical officer, the president of the college of presbyters or elders. Episcopacy, therefore, is a ministry of supervision, of overseeing, of looking over and seeing to the work of the church.

Deacons functioned as assistants to the bishop and represented the role

---

1. The preface to the Ordinal in the American *Book of Common Prayer* (1792), which remained through the 1928 Prayer Book, could assert:

> It is evident unto all men, diligently reading Holy Scripture and ancient Authors, that from the Apostles' time there have been these Orders of Ministers in Christ's Church, — Bishops, Priests, and Deacons. (American Prayer Book [1928], p. 529)

In the 1979 Prayer Book the preface begins:

> The Holy Scriptures and ancient Christian writers make it clear that from the apostles' time, there have been different ministries within the Church. In particular, since the time of the New Testament, three distinct orders of ordained ministers have been characteristic of Christ's holy catholic Church. (p. 510)

2. Hatchett, *Commentary on American Prayer Book,* p. 504.

3. *The Treatise on the Apostolic Tradition of St. Hippolytus of Rome,* ed. Gregory Dix (London: SPCK, 1968), p. 22.

of servanthood after the model of Christ, who came not to be served but to serve. The diaconate therefore is a ministry of service.

The presbyters or elders recall the concept of elders or leading men of the community of Judaism, who constituted a collegiate ruling body.[4] The ministry of these presbyters or elders seems not to have been a liturgical ministry in the early church but one of counsel and advice, in keeping with the traditional function of the elders of the community. The presbyters shared with the bishop the responsibilities for the governance of the church. The ordination prayer for presbyters in the *Apostolic Tradition* of Hippolytus asks for "the spirit of grace and counsel that he may share in the presbyterate and govern your people with a pure heart."[5]

Since it is often true that what is everyone's responsibility becomes no one's responsibility, the church charged its ordained leaders with leadership, administration, and service. As the years passed, the role of presiding at the Eucharist came to be associated with the bishop and, by the bishop's delegation, with the presbyters.[6] Deacons, who assisted the bishop in matters concerning the supervision of the church, were given roles of assisting the bishop at the Eucharist also.

By virtue of his presiding at the Eucharist, the bishop came to be regarded as the "high priest" within the priestly community of the new covenant. As presbyters were delegated to tend to the pastoral needs of Christian communities remote from the center of the diocese, they also assumed responsibility for Word and Sacrament and by extension were called "priests."

In western and northern Europe, where bishops and deacons were not plentiful in the early Middle Ages, presbyters (now "priests") served as pastors of congregations and exercised the ministerial responsibilities of oversight, Word and Sacrament, and service. The bishops of these large dioceses had to divert more and more attention to matters of administration and finance and focused less attention on preaching the word and administering the sacraments. The diaconate had become merely a steppingstone to the priesthood. As the Middle Ages advanced, so did the acquisition of temporal power by the bishops, and the stage was set for the Reformation criticism of the episcopate.

The Reformers understood the primary function of bishops to be one of teaching, preaching, and sacramental celebration. Because of this, they saw little difference between the offices of bishop and pastor, except

---

4. Hatchett, *Commentary on American Prayer Book,* p. 503.

5. *Apostolic Tradition,* p. 13.

6. See Raymond E. Brown, *Priest and Bishop: Biblical Reflections* (New York: Paulist Press, 1970), pp. 40ff.

in the scope of administrative responsibility.[7] Laurentius Petri recognized the historical reasons for the functional difference between bishop and priest in his Swedish Church Order (1561; authorized 1571). He went on to say:

> As this arrangement proved itself useful and without doubt was inspired by God the Holy Spirit, from whom all good gifts come, it was approved and accepted in all Christendom. Thus it came to be, and must be as long as the world lasts.[8]

The Swedish church retained the offices of bishop (and archbishop) and priest as did the other Scandinavian churches. The Lutheran churches of continental Europe, however, eventually combined the office of bishop and pastor into one and understood the purpose of the resulting pastoral office to be the proclamation of the gospel through preaching, the administration of the sacraments, and the exercise of "the power of the keys" (confession and absolution). Luther summarized this in an article on the gospel, saying:

> We shall now return to the Gospel, which offers counsel and help against sin. . . . First, through the spoken word, by which the forgiveness of sin (the peculiar office of the Gospel) is preached to the whole world; second, through Baptism; third, through the holy Sacrament of the Altar; fourth, through the power of the keys. . . .[9]

In this ministry, the pastor as servant of the Word represents Christ and the whole church.

Although all Christians through baptism are members of the royal priesthood, the pastor is one who is called through the action of the church. The Lutheran confessions declare:

> Our churches teach that nobody should preach publicly in the church or administer the sacraments unless he is regularly called.[10]

The intention of the authors in that last phrase is a debated point. The regular call may mean, as it is usually understood in North American Lutheran practice, the work of the Holy Spirit through the orderly proc-

---

7. See The Augsburg Confession, Articles IV, XIV, XXVIII; Apology of the Augsburg Confession, Articles XIII, XIV, XXVIII; The Smalcald Articles, Part II, Article IV, and Part III, Articles IX, X; and Treatise on the Power and Primacy of the Pope.

8. Conrad Bergendoff, "The Unique Character of the Reformation in Sweden," in *Symposium on Seventeenth Century Lutheranism* (St. Louis: Symposium on Seventeenth Century Lutheranism, 1962), p. 98.

9. The Smalcald Articles, Part III, Article IV.

10. The Augsburg Confession, Article XIV, *Book of Concord,* p. 36.

ess of pastoral selection. It may have been intended to mean, however, called by episcopal ordination, which through the centuries was the way ministers were called to the church's ministry. This is still the meaning of "call" in the Roman Catholic ordination rites. In either case, because the pastoral office is given to the whole church, no one can assume it for oneself. One becomes a pastor in an orderly way, as Luther reminds us in a classic observation: "One is born to be a priest, one becomes a minister."[11] The pastoral office is therefore a gift of the Spirit, as St. Paul exhorted Timothy: "Do not neglect the gift you have, which was given you by the prophetic utterance when the elders laid their hands upon you" (1 Tim. 4:14).

Ordination is the rite by which the church confers the pastoral office on one who has been led to prepare according to the requirements of the church and who has accepted the church's call. Ordination is simultaneously a recognition of that office by the church and a reception of that person upon whom it is conferred. The authority for ordination comes from Jesus Christ, the Head of the church and the great High Priest. It is he who instituted the office, and it is he who calls his servants to it.

In recognizing both the authority and the purpose of the pastoral office, the confessions observe:

> In order that we may obtain this faith, the ministry of teaching the Gospel and administering the sacraments was instituted. For through the Word and the sacraments, as through instruments, the Holy Spirit is given, and the Holy Spirit produces faith, where and when it pleases God, in those who hear the Gospel.[12]

Ordination thus expresses the church's recognition of the special duties and accountability belonging to the pastoral office.

Throughout its history Lutheranism has struggled with the doctrine of the ministry. It has maintained an episcopacy in some areas, devised other forms in other places. To the dismay of some and the bewilderment of others, clarity has never been achieved. There was in fact no compelling reason for Lutheranism to formulate a consistent and peculiar doctrine of the ministry so long as it understood itself to be not a separate and distinct organization but rather a confessing movement within the catholic church. Moreover, because it is not tied to a particular form of the pastoral office, Lutheranism may be in an advantageous position with regard to ecumenical conversation and union.

11. *LW*, vol. 40, p. 18.
12. The Augsburg Confession, Article V, *Book of Concord*, p. 31.

In the twentieth century there has been a new appraisal of ecclesiology and ministry, largely as a result of New Testament and patristic studies and the missionary needs of the modern church at home and abroad. Ministry has been expanded and is understood as something that belongs to all the baptized people of God. To locate all ministerial functions and responsibilities in one office is unnecessarily restrictive and limiting and is at variance with the New Testament understanding of the diversity of the ministry and with the emerging ecumenical consensus. Lutherans in North America are willing to use the title "bishop" (although there is not total agreement as to what the title implies) and are willing to experiment with forms of the diaconate (at least in some places), calls to special service, and tent-making ministries. The exploration of the richness and diversity of the ministry has just begun.

Note. The use of the word "ordinal" to refer to the body of liturgical rites relating to ordination and installation, although not uncommon in Lutheran circles, is borrowed from the Church of England and dates only from ca. 1600.

For Further Reading

Anderson, Ray S., ed. *Theological Foundations for Ministry: Selected Readings for a Theology of the Church in Ministry.* Edinburgh: T. & T. Clark; Grand Rapids: Wm. B. Eerdmans, 1979.

Baptism, Eucharist and Ministry. Faith and Order Paper No. 111. Geneva: World Council of Churches, 1982.

Barnett, James Monroe. *The Diaconate: A Full and Equal Order.* New York: Seabury Press, 1981.

Bradshaw, Paul F. *The Anglican Ordinal: Its History and Development from the Reformation to the Present Day.* London: SPCK, 1971.

Brown, Raymond E. *Priest and Bishop: Biblical Reflections.* New York: Paulist Press, 1970.

Cooke, Bernard. *Ministry to Word and Sacraments: History and Theology.* Philadelphia: Fortress Press, 1976.

The Deaconess: Service of Women in the World Today. World Council of Churches Studies No. 4. Geneva: World Council of Churches, 1966.

Empie, Paul, and T. Austin Murphy, eds. *Eucharist and Ministry.* Lutherans and Catholics in Dialogue IV. Minneapolis: Augsburg Publishing House, 1979.

Episkope and Episcopate in Ecumenical Perspective. Faith and Order Paper No. 102. Geneva: World Council of Churches, 1980.

Fink, Peter E. "The Sacrament of Orders: Some Liturgical Reflections." *Liturgy* 56:6 (November 1982): 482–502.

Firminger, Walter Kelly. "The Ordinal." In *Liturgy and Worship*, edited by W. K. Lowther Clarke and Charles Harris, pp. 626–82. London: SPCK, 1964 [1932].

Garrett, T. S. "The Ordinal of the Church of South India." *Scottish Journal of Theology* 12 (1959).

Holmes, Urban T. *The Priest in Community*. New York: Seabury Press, 1978.

Iersel, Bas van, and Roland Murphy. *Office and Ministry in the Church*. Concilium, vol. 80. New York: Seabury Press, 1972.

James, E. O. *The Nature and Function of Priesthood: A Comparative Anthropological Study*. New York: Vanguard Press, 1955.

Jenson, Robert W. "Ministries Lay and Ordained." *Partners* 3:5 (October 1981): 11–15, 32; and responses in succeeding issues.

Kilmartin, E. J. "Apostolic Office: Sacrament of Christ." *Theological Studies* 36 (1975).

Kirk, K. E., ed. *The Apostolic Ministry: Essays on the History and Doctrine of Episcopacy*. London: Hodder & Stoughton, 1946.

Küng, Hans, and Walter Kasper. *The Plurality of Ministries*. Concilium, vol. 74. New York: Seabury Press, 1972.

Lemaine, A. *Ministry in the Church*. London: SPCK, 1977.

Liturgy 2:4 (Fall 1982). Liturgy: Diakonia.

The Ministry of Deacons. World Council of Churches Studies No. 2. Geneva: World Council of Churches, 1965.

Moore, Peter, ed. *Bishops: But What Kind? Reflections on Episcopacy*. London: SPCK, 1982.

Occasional Papers 2: Church and Ministry. Edited by Daniel C. Brockopp. Valparaiso, Ind.: Institute of Liturgical Studies, 1982.

One Baptism, One Eucharist, and a Mutually Recognized Ministry. Faith and Order Paper No. 73. Geneva: World Council of Churches, 1975.

The Ordination of Bishops, Priests, and Deacons. Prayer Book Studies 20. New York: Church Hymnal Corp., 1970.

Parvey, Constance F., ed. *Ordination of Women in Ecumenical Perspective: Workbook for the Church's Future*. Geneva: World Council of Churches, 1980.

Porter, H. Boone. *The Ordination Prayers of the Ancient Western Churches*. London: SPCK, 1967.

Quere, Ralph W. "The Spirit and the Gifts are Ours: Imparting or Imploring the Spirit in Ordination Rites?" *Lutheran Quarterly* 27:4 (November 1975): 322–46.

Sabourin, Leopold. *Priesthood: A Comparative Study*. Leiden: E. J. Brill, 1973.

Schillebeeckx, Edward. *Ministry: Leadership in the Community of Jesus Christ*. New York: Crossroad, 1981.

_____. *The Unifying Role of the Bishop*. Concilium, vol. 71. New York: Seabury Press, 1971.

Shelp, Earl E., and Ronald Sunderland, eds. *A Biblical Basis for Ministry*. Philadelphia: Westminster Press, 1982.

Telfer, William. *The Office of Bishop*. London: Darton, Longman & Todd, 1962.

Vos, Wiebe, and Wainwright, Geoffrey, eds. "Ordination Rites. Papers read at the 1979 Congress of Societas Liturgica." *Studia Liturgica* 13:2, 3, 4 (1979).

Weiser, Frederick S. *Love's Response: A Study of Lutheran Deaconesses in America*. Philadelphia: Board of Publication, United Lutheran Church in America, 1962.

ORDINATION
(*Occasional Services*, pp. 192–203)

Parallel Rites

Roman Catholic	The Admission to Candidacy for Ordination as Deacons and Priests, *The Rites*, pp. 746–50.
	Ordination of Deacons, Ordination of a Deacon; Ordination of Priests, Ordination of a Priest; Ordination of a Bishop, Ordination of Bishops, *Roman Pontifical*, vol. 1, pp. 155–254.[13]
Orthodox	The Form Which Is Used at the Ordination of a Deacon, The Form and Manner of Ordaining a Priest, The Order of Electing and Consecrating a Bishop, *Service Book*, pp. 311–14, 316–18, 323–31.
Episcopal	The Ordination of a Bishop, The Ordination of a Priest, The Ordination of a Deacon, *Book of Common Prayer*, pp. 511–55.
Lutheran	Order for Ordination, *Occasional Services* (1962), pp. 90–99.
	The Order for Ordination, *Common Service Book* (text ed.), pp. 454–60.
	The Order for the Ordination of a Minister, *Lutheran Agenda*, pp. 104–9.
Methodist	The Order for the Ordination of Deacons, The Order for the Ordination of Elders, The Order for the Consecration of Bishops, *Book of Worship*, pp. 44–58;[14] *An Ordinal*, pp. 26–156.
Presbyterian	A Service for Ordination and Installation, *Worshipbook*, pp. 89–95.
Brethren	Ordination of Ministers, *Pastor's Manual*, pp. 85–91.[15]

---

13. *Roman Pontifical,* vol. 1 (Washington, D.C.: International Commission on English in the Liturgy, 1978).

14. *The Book of Worship for Church and Home* (Nashville: United Methodist Publishing House, 1964); *An Ordinal: The United Methodist Church Adopted for Official Alternative Use by the 1980 General Conference* (Nashville: United Methodist Publishing House, 1980).

15. *Pastor's Manual: Church of the Brethren* (Elgin, Ill.: Brethren Press, 1978).

Church of   The Ordinal, *Book of Common Worship*, pp.
South India   160-79.[16]

Purpose

The purpose of this service of ordination is to call upon the Holy Spirit
to fill a candidate with his gifts for the ministry of Word and Sacrament
and to receive the candidate into the college of pastors.

Characteristics

The chief divergence from the predecessor rite in the 1962 *Occasional
Services* is what occurs at the time of the laying on of hands. The 1962 rite
had the ordainer say:

> The Lord bestow upon thee the Holy Ghost for the office and work of a
> Minister in the Church of God, now committed unto thee by the authority
> of the Church through the imposition of our hands: In the Name of the
> Father, and of the Son, and of the Holy Ghost.[17]

The *Common Service Book* (1918) before it was still more direct and
explicit:

> I now commit unto thee the Holy Office of the Word and Sacraments:
> I ordain and consecrate thee a Minister of the Church: In the Name of the
> Father, and of the Son, and of the Holy Ghost.[18]

The earlier *Church Book* (1892) used similar words, but the formula was
cast in the plural:

> We now commit unto thee the Holy Office of the Word and Sacraments of
> the Triune God, and Ordain and Consecrate thee a Minister of the Church of
> Christ, In the Name of the Father, and of the Son, and of the Holy Ghost.[19]

In the 1982 *Occasional Services*, however, at the laying on of hands, the
ordainer, continuing the thanksgiving, says:

> Eternal God, through your Son, Jesus Christ, pour out your Holy Spirit
> upon _____ and fill *him/her* with the gifts of grace [for the ministry
> of Word and Sacrament]. (p. 196)

Although this formulation for various reasons may trouble some, it is
closer to the broad Lutheran tradition from which the twentieth-century

---

16. *The Book of Common Worship* (London: Oxford University Press, 1963).
17. *Occasional Services* (1962), p. 98.
18. *Common Service Book,* text ed. (1919), p. 458.
19. *Church Book,* p. 424.

American rites were a deviation.[20] Ordination, as Luther declared, is not by proclamation but by the laying on of hands and prayer. That understanding of ordination is crucial. It is, moreover, in harmony with the ecumenical trends of recent decades in the Roman Catholic, Episcopal, and Orthodox churches, and the various Protestant churches.

In the Roman Catholic rite for the Ordination of a Priest, after the Litany of the Saints the bishop prays:

> Hear us, Lord our God,
> and pour out upon this servant of yours
> the blessing of the Holy Spirit
> and the grace and power of the priesthood.
> In your sight we offer this man for ordination:
> support him with your unfailing love.
> We ask this through Christ our Lord.

Then follows the laying on of hands in silence and then the "Prayer of Consecration":

> Come to our help,
> Lord, holy Father, almighty and eternal God . . .
> When you had appointed high priests to rule your people,
> you chose other men next to them in rank and dignity
> to be with them and to help them in their task . . .
> In the desert
> you extended the spirit of Moses to seventy wise men
> who helped him to rule the great company of his people.
> . . . Lord,
> grant also to us such fellow workers . . .
> Almighty Father,
> grant to this servant of yours
> the dignity of the priesthood.
> Renew within him the Spirit of holiness.
> As a co-worker with the order of bishops
> may he be faithful to the ministry
> that he receives from you, Lord God,
> and be to others a model of right conduct.[21]

In the 1979 *Book of Common Prayer* form for the ordination of a priest, the bishop prays in the course of the "Prayer of Consecration":

---

20. See the important historical study by Ralph Quere, "The Spirit and the Gifts Are Ours," *Lutheran Quarterly* 27:4 (November 1975): 322–46. See also *An Ordinal: The United Methodist Church,* pp. 13–14.

21. *Roman Pontifical,* vol. 1, pp. 212–13.

Therefore, Father, through Jesus Christ your Son, give your Holy Spirit to
N.; fill *him* with grace and power, and make *him* a priest in your Church.[22]

In the Eastern Orthodox Form and Manner of Ordaining a Priest, the
bishop lays his hand on the head of the ordinand and says:

The grace divine, which always healeth that which is infirm, and completeth
that which is wanting, elevateth through the laying on of hands, *N.,* the most
devout Deacon, to be a Priest. Wherefore, let us pray for him, that the grace
of the all-holy Spirit may come upon him.[23]

And the prayers are said.

In the ordination rite in the Presbyterian *Worshipbook,* this prayer is
said at the laying on of hands:

Almighty God: in every age you have chosen servants to speak your word
and lead your loyal people. We thank you for *this man* whom you have
called to serve you. Give *him* special gifts to do *his* special work; and fill *him*
with Holy Spirit, so that *he* may have the same mind that was in Christ
Jesus, and be *a* faithful *disciple* as long as *he* shall live.[24]

The order for the Ordination of Ministers in the *Pastor's Manual* of the
Church of the Brethren contains this rubric:

Here the candidate shall kneel (with his or her spouse, if so desired), while
the officiant and several other representatives of the District and the local
congregation lay hands upon him or her, offering appropriate prayers.[25]

In the Ordination rite in *Occasional Services* (1982), as in many
modern ordination rites, there is no explicit statement of a "moment of
ordination," a precise time at which the office is transmitted to the
ordinand. A "moment of baptism" is no longer seen as a useful understanding of the richness of the sacrament of initiation into the Christian
community. A "moment of consecration" is no longer accepted as helpful in understanding the action of celebrating the Lord's Supper. So to
isolate a "moment" at which the ordination takes place also seems misleading. The ordination is "by the laying on of hands and prayer" (Acts
6:6; 13:3; 1 Tim. 4:14; 2 Tim. 1:6).

This is the first Lutheran ordination rite in North America which
makes provision for the possibility of the ordinand being a woman. It is

---

22. *Book of Common Prayer* (1979), p. 533.

23. *Service Book,* p. 316.

24. *Worshipbook* (Philadelphia: Westminster Press, 1970), p. 93.

25. *Pastor's Manual,* p. 89.

the first ordination rite which has been prepared since the ordination of women was approved by the churches.

The service of Ordination is cast in the singular because that is the practice of the majority of the participating churches. In the Lutheran Church in America the custom in most places has been to ordain a group of individuals, usually in connection with a synod convention. The use of the singular in Ordination also follows the practice of the 1979 *Book of Common Prayer*. (In earlier Prayer Books the title and the texts were in the plural.) The Roman Catholic church provides two forms: a rite for the ordination of one person and a rite for the ordination of more than one. The basic rite is the same in either case.

Background

The Ordination service in the *Occasional Services* (1982) is a revision of the Ordination service prepared by the Liturgical Text Committee of the Inter-Lutheran Commission on Worship at the conclusion of the work on the *Lutheran Book of Worship* and published in 1977, but which was never given general approval by the participating churches.

The essential elements of ordination rites in the early church consisted of approval by the church, usually in the form of election or at least of opportunity to reject the candidate; prayer, including the litany or bid to the people and the ordination prayer itself; and the laying on of hands.

The decisive influence of the *Apostolic Tradition* of Hippolytus on the ordination rites of East and West has long been recognized. In the rubrics for the ordination of a bishop the people are asked to pray in silence for the "descent of the Spirit." Then, during the laying on of hands, the ordaining bishop prays:

> Pour forth now that power which is from thee, the princely Spirit, which thou gavest to thy beloved Son, Jesus Christ, which he gave to the holy Apostles, who established the Church in every place.[26]

The same bid to the people is repeated for the ordination of a presbyter, and then as the other presbyters join in touching him, the ordaining bishop says: "Impart to him the Spirit of grace and counsel for presbyters so that he may support and govern thy people."[27] The prayer for the deacon asks: "Give the Holy Spirit of grace and care and diligence to this thy servant."[28] This *epiclesis* character of these ordination prayers points

---

26. H. Boone Porter, *The Ordination Prayers of the Ancient Western Churches* (London: SPCK, 1967), p. 6.

27. Ibid., p. 8.

28. Ibid., p. 6.

to a theology of beseeching rather than bestowing the Holy Spirit.

In later, highly developed medieval rites like the Sarum Pontifical, the addition of the imperative formula from John's Gospel, "Receive the Holy Spirit" (*Accipe Spiritum Sanctum*), is among the most significant developments from the ancient rites. The increase of sacrificial language and of ceremonial actions further characterizes medieval developments.

In the Eastern churches, the most significant aspect of the ordination rites is the simple declaration of the ordination, which parallels the baptismal proclamation, "The servant of God, *N.,* is baptized in the name of the Father, Amen. And of the Son, Amen. And of the Holy Spirit, Amen."[29] Such avoidance of the first person singular, as in the Western "I baptize you . . . ," is clearly intentional. In the Maronite rite for the ordination of deacons, for example, the bishop says: "For not in the imposition of our sinful hands, but by the rich operation of thy mercies, grace is given them."[30] After the prayer, the bishop proclaims, "He is ordained in the Church of God." John Chrysostom affirms this "impersonal" view of ordination:

> What speak I of priests? I say that neither angel nor archangel can give us any of these things which be given unto us of God; but it is the Father, Son, and the Holy Ghost which is the effectual cause of all these things: the priest doth only put on his hands and his tongue.[31]

According to Gregory of Nyssa, it is "the power of the word" that in ordination transforms an ordinary man into "a guide, a president, a teacher of righteousness, an instructor in hidden mysteries."[32]

At the time of the Reformation, the calling and ordaining of ministers in Wittenberg seems to have been rather fluid until 1535—most of the pastors having already been ordained in the Roman Catholic church.

Luther ordained Georg Roerer in 1525, but there appears to be no record of the rite. In 1526 a Hessian rite appeared that offered alternate formulae: "receive the Spirit" or "receive the keys of the kingdom of heaven."[33]

---

29. *Service Book,* p. 280.

30. W. K. Firminger, "The Ordinal," in *Liturgy and Worship,* ed. W. K. Lowther Clarke and Charles Harris (London: SPCK, 1932), p. 639. Cf. the Syrian Jacobite rite: "for not in the imposition of our sinful hands, but in the visitation of thy copious mercy, grace is given to them." Cf. also the Coptic rite, p. 640.

31. Ibid., p. 641, citing the 85th Homily on St. John.

32. Ibid., p. 642.

33. A. L. Richter, ed., *Die evangelischen Kirchenordnungen des sechszehnten Jahrhunderts,* vol. 1 (Weimar: Verlag des Landes-Industrie-comptoirs, 1846), p. 66.

In 1535 the Elector John Frederick established an order for the examination, calling, and ordination of candidates. Luther was frequently the ordinator, and the order that he prepared became the basis for numerous sixteenth-century rites.[34] The candidates are first examined on the day of the ordination or the preceding day. If they are found worthy, the congregation is to pray "for them and for the whole ministry." Then, at the ordination, all kneeling, the choir sings *"Veni Sancte Spiritus"* (it is not clear whether Luther had in mind the hymn or the antiphon). A versicle and collect for the Holy Spirit are said:

> Create in me a clean heart, O God.
> *And renew a right spirit within me.*
> Lord God, you taught the hearts of your faithful people by sending them the light of your Holy Spirit. Grant that we, by your Spirit, may have a right judgment in all things and evermore rejoice in his holy counsel; through your Son, Jesus Christ our Lord. (202)

First Timothy 3:1-7; Acts 20:28-31; and a charge are read to the ordinands.

> Then while the whole presbytery impose their hands on the heads of the ordinands, the ordinator says the Lord's Prayer in a clear voice. . . .
> And if he desires or time permits, he may add this prayer which explains more fully the three parts of the Lord's Prayer: Merciful God, heavenly Father, thou hast said to us through the mouth of thy dear Son our Lord Jesus Christ: "The harvest truly is plenteous, but the laborers are few. Pray ye therefore the Lord of the harvest, that he will send forth laborers into his harvest" [Matthew 9:37–38]. Upon this thy divine command, we pray heartily that thou wouldst grant thy Holy Spirit richly to these thy servants, to us, and to all those who are called to serve thy Word so that the company of us who publish the good tidings may be great, and that we may stand faithful and firm against the devil, the world, and the flesh, to the end that thy name may be hallowed, thy kingdom grow, and thy will be done. Be also pleased at length to check and stop the detestable abomination of the pope, Mohammed, and other sects which blaspheme thy name, hinder thy kingdom, and oppose thy will. Graciously hear this our prayer, since thou hast so commanded, taught, and promised, even as we believe and trust through thy dear Son, Jesus Christ our Lord, who liveth and reigneth with thee and the Holy Ghost, world without end. Amen.

The prayer begins with the Matthean harvest text, as did Bugenhagen's prayer for ordination. The *epiclesis* form should be noted here as well as the absence of the formula "Receive the Holy Spirit." Following the or-

---

34. *LW*, vol. 53, pp. 124–26.

dination, the ordinator addresses 1 Pet. 5:2–4 to the ordinands. Then the ordinator "shall bless them with the sign of the cross" saying these or other words: "The Lord bless you that you may bring forth much fruit." Finally the hymn "Now Let Us Pray to the Holy Ghost" may be sung.

> This ended, the presbyter chants: Our Father, etc. And first the ordinands shall commune with the congregation, then likewise the ordinator if he so desires.

This rite of Luther's influenced numerous rites that appeared in Germany during the sixteenth century, notably Braunschweig (1543),[35] Mecklenberg (1552),[36] Lueneburg (1564)[37] and (1575),[38] Mansfeld (1580),[39] Hoya (1581),[40] Hanneberg (1582),[41] and Lauenberg (1585).[42]

The seventeenth-century Lutheran orthodox theologians formalized the declarative character of ordination, which recognizes rather than constitutes.[43] It is called a "public testimony whereby the fact of vocation is recognized, witnessed, and confirmed . . . and committed to him on behalf of God and the Church and entrusted to him with a public witness."[44] In the rite of ordination, "God is being asked to give and confirm the gifts the minister needs for his office."[45]

In 1844 Wilhelm Loehe published an Agenda which he dedicated and sent to Friedrich Wyneken in Fort Wayne, Indiana. The Agenda and the ordination rite were destined to have a profound and far-reaching effect on Lutheranism in America. The rite begins with the words of Jesus from John 20. After the candidate's promise, the ordinator addresses the candidate and says:

> We ask God the Father of our Lord Jesus Christ, the only Lord of the

35. Richter, *Evangelischen Kirchenordnungen,* vol. 2, pp. 60ff.

36. Emil Sehling, ed., *Die evangelischen Kirchenordnungen des XVI. Jahrhunderts,* vol. V (6 vols.; vols. I–V—Leipzig: Reisland, 1902-13; vol. VI—Tübingen: J. C. B. Mohr [Paul Siebeck], 1955-), p. 194.

37. Ibid., vol. VI, part 1, p. 535.

38. Ibid., pp. 655ff.

39. Ibid., vol. I, part 2, pp. 243ff.

40. Ibid., vol. VI, part 2, pp. 1132ff.

41. Ibid., vol. I, part 2, pp. 321–24.

42. Ibid., vol. V, pp. 407ff.

43. Friedrich Kalb, *Theology of Worship in 17th Century Lutheranism,* trans. H. P. A. Hamann (St. Louis: Concordia Publishing House, 1965), p. 128.

44. Ludwig Dunte, *Decisiones mille et sex casuum conscientiae* (1628), p. 657, cited in Kalb, *Theology of Worship.*

45. Andreas Kesler, *Theologia casuum conscientiae etc.* (1683), p. 5, cited in Kalb, *Theology of Worship.*

harvest, that he who called you to this office would make you qualified for it through his Holy Spirit.[46]

After citing the ordeal St. Paul mentions in 2 Corinthians 6, the ordinator continues:

The Lord grant that you may suffer and do the work of an evangelical preacher.

At the laying on of hands, the ordinator says:

We commit to you herewith, through the laying on of our hands, the holy office of the Word and Sacraments of the triune God, and ordain and consecrate you a minister of the holy Church in the name of the Father, Son, and Holy Spirit.

Then follows the Lord's Prayer and a prayer which is essentially Luther's prayer.

The *Lutheran Agenda* of the Synodical Conference (undated, but published in the 1940s) has the ordinator lay his right hand on the kneeling ordinand and say:

I now commit unto thee the holy office of the Word and the Sacraments; I ordain and consecrate thee a minister of the Church and install thee as pastor of this congregation in the name of the Father and of the Son and of the Holy Ghost. The Lord pour out upon thee His Holy Spirit for the office and the work committed unto thee by the call, that thou mayest be a faithful dispenser of the means of grace.[47]

The ordination rite in the *Occasional Services* (1962—but prepared and approved by the churches in 1950) drops the Loehe formula and adopts a formula which has important similarities to the *Lutheran Agenda* form and the then-current Anglican ordinal:

The Lord bestow upon thee the Holy Ghost for the office and work of a Minister in the Church of God, now committed unto thee by the authority of the Church through the imposition of our hands: in the Name of the Father, and of the Son, and of the Holy Ghost.[48]

The twentieth-century Lutheran adaptation of the late medieval formula

46. Wilhelm Loehe, ed., *Agende für Christliche Gemeinden des lutherischen Bekenntnisses* (Nördlingen: Beck'schen Buchhandlung, 1844), pp. 248f.

47. *The Lutheran Agenda,* the Evangelical Lutheran Synodical Conference (St. Louis: Concordia Publishing House, n.d.), p. 107.

48. *Occasional Services* (1962), p. 98.

"Receive the Holy Spirit" is a positive attempt to give a more sacramental character to ordination (see the Apology to the Augsburg Confession, Article XIII, which suggests that ordination can be understood to be a sacrament). It seeks to take seriously the need for the operation of the Spirit through Word and Sacrament.

In the last part of the twentieth century the *epiclesis* form seems to be preferable because it accomplishes the same thing and is, moreover, in accord with the growing ecumenical consensus and the practice of the early Lutherans as well as the early Christians. Praying for the Spirit avoids the apparent presumption of the ordinator "giving" the Spirit, who blows where he wills (John 3:8), just as he works faith where he pleases (The Augsburg Confession, Article V).

Preparation for the Service

The ordinands vest in the basic liturgical vesture, which increasingly in North America is the alb. Since the surplice has been the traditional vestment for the daily prayer services, its use in ordination is perhaps less desirable unless it is the custom of the parish.

The ordinand sits with the congregation until the presentation. This is to make clear that the ordinand is called from among the people to be ordained to serve the church.

Since everywhere in the ecumenical tradition the ordinand kneels to receive the laying on of hands, provision should be made for a place to kneel. A kneeling desk, even in a church which has a communion rail, helps give focus to the place of laying on of hands and prayer by locating the action in the center of the chancel. A kneeling desk, moreover, enables a group of clergy to gather around the person being ordained more conveniently than when there is a communion rail in the way.

When a group of ordinands is to be ordained at one time, the presiding minister may move along the line of ordinands kneeling at the rail, in much the same manner as at the Affirmation of Baptism (Confirmation) or at the distribution of Holy Communion. A more desirable practice, however, is for the presiding minister to remain in the center and for each ordinand in turn to come to the center and kneel there at the kneeling desk for the laying on of hands. This enables the group of pastors to gather around the ordinand, and it also makes the action equally visible for all ordinands.

Survey of the Service

Although the rubric (p. 192, no. 1) does not exclude setting Ordination within a service other than the Holy Communion, no provision is made for other settings. It is difficult to see why Ordination should be set within a service other than the principal service of the Christian community, that service which ministers the Word and Sacrament to which the ordinand is called. Luther, in his order, directed the ordinands and the congregation to commune; the *Church Book* and the *Common Service Book* required a celebration of the Holy Communion; and the ecumenical tradition everywhere preserved the relationship between ordination and the Holy Communion. With all their variety, ordination rites in the catholic tradition preserve one constant: ordination always takes place during the celebration of the Holy Communion.

The 1962 *Occasional Services* made Holy Communion optional at Ordination (although it was required at the Setting Apart of a Deaconess), apparently reflecting the varied practice of the participating churches. Ordination, however, took place within The Service whether or not Holy Communion was celebrated.

If Holy Communion is not celebrated, Ordination should at least be set within ante-communion. No other service—Morning Prayer, Evening Prayer, Service of the Word—is appropriate.

The Prayer of the Day for Ordination ⟨538⟩ is a new composition. The *Common Service Book* and *Occasional Services* (1962) had this collect, based on Acts 4:24, 29-30 in the King James Version:

> O Lord God, which hast made heaven, and earth, and the sea, and all that in them is: Grant unto thy servants, that with all boldness they may speak thy Word, that wonders of thy grace may be wrought by the Name of thy Holy Child Jesus; who liveth and reigneth with thee and the Holy Ghost, one God, world without end.

The 1979 *Book of Common Prayer* permits the prayer of the day (as did the *Church Book*) or this prayer, which the *Service Book and Hymnal* gave as no. 1 under Collects and Prayers (p. 218):

> O God of unchangeable power and eternal light: Look favorably on your whole Church, that wonderful and sacred mystery; by the effectual working of your providence, carry out in tranquility the plan of salvation; let the whole world see and know that things which were cast down are being raised up, and things which had grown old are being made new, and that all things are being brought to their perfection by him through whom all things were made, your Son Jesus Christ our Lord; who lives and reigns with you, in the unity of the Holy Spirit, one God, for ever and ever.

The prayer is from the Gelasian Sacramentary (no. 432). The translation is based on that of William Bright in *Ancient Collects* (pp. 98–99).

The *Common Service Book* appointed two lessons, the Epistle (Rom. 10:6-15) and the Gospel (Luke 10:2-11, 16). *Occasional Services* (1962) added an Old Testament lesson (Jer. 23:1–4), shortened the Epistle to verses 8 through 15 and provided an alternate (1 Cor. 4:1–5), and gave two alternate Gospels (Matt. 9:36–38 or John 21:15–17). *Occasional Services* (1982), like the Roman Catholic rite, provides a great number of suggested readings from which a selection may be made.

Lessons at Ordination

ROMAN CATHOLIC	LUTHERAN	EPISCOPAL
	Exod. 3:13–15	
Num. 3:5–9		
	Num. 6:22–27	
Num. 11:11b–12, 14–17, 24–25a	Num. 11:16–17, 14–15b	Num. 11:16–17, 24–25b (Priest)
	Isa. 6:1–8	Isa. 6:1–8 (Priest)
	Isa. 40:1–11	
	Isa. 42:5–9	Isa. 42:1–9 (Bishop)
	Isa. 57:7–10	
Isa. 61:1–3a		Isa. 61:1–8 (Bishop)
Jer. 1:4–9		Jer. 1:4–9 (Deacon)
	Jer. 23:1–5	
	Jer. 23:25–28a	
	Ezek. 3:16–21	
		Ecclus. 39:1–8 (Deacon)
Acts 6:1–7a		Acts 6:2–7 (Deacon)
Acts 8:26–40		
Acts 10:37–43		
Acts 20:17–18a, 28–32, 36	Acts 20:28–35	
	Rom. 10:13–17	
Rom. 12:4–8	Rom. 12:4–8	
		2 Cor. 3:4–9 (Bishop)
2 Cor. 4:1–2, 5–7	2 Cor. 4:1–7 (8–12)	2 Cor. 4:1–6 (Deacons)
2 Cor. 5:14–20	2 Cor. 5:11–21	
Eph. 4:1–7, 11–13	Eph. 4:4–16	Eph. 4:7, 11–16 (Priests)
		Phil. 4:4–9 (Priests)

Lessons at Ordination (continued)

Roman Catholic	Lutheran	Episcopal
	1 Tim. 3:1–7	1 Tim. 3:1–7 (Bishops)
1 Tim. 3:8–13		1 Tim. 3:8–13 (Deacons)
1 Tim. 4:12–16	1 Tim. 4:14–16	
2 Tim. 1:6–14		
	2 Tim. 4:1–5	
Heb. 5:1–10		Heb. 5:1–10 (Bishops)
1 Pet. 4:7b–11		
1 Pet. 5:1–4	1 Pet. 5:2–4	1 Pet. 5:1–4 (Priests)
Matt. 5:13–16		
	Matt. 9:1–8	
Matt. 9:35–38	Matt. 9:35–38	Matt. 9:35–38 (Priests)
Matt. 10:1–5a		
	Matt. 16:13–19	
Matt. 20:25–28		
	Mark 4:1–9	
	Mark 10:42–45	
Luke 10:1–9	Luke 10:1–12, 16–20	
Luke 12:35–44		Luke 12:35–38 (Deacons)
Luke 22:14–20, 24–30		Luke 22:24–27 (Deacons)
	Luke 24:44–49a	Luke 24:44–49a (Bishops)
		John 6:35–38 (Priests)
John 10:11–16	John 10:7–18	John 10:11–18 (Priests)
John 12:24–26		
	John 13:(3–11), 12–17, 20	
John 15:9–17		
John 17:6, 14–19	John 17:6–19	John 17:1–9, 18–21 (Bishops)
John 20:19–23		John 20:19–23 (Bishops)
John 21:15–17	John 21:15–17	

The hymn of the day, "To God the Holy Spirit Let Us Pray," (317) is suggested by Luther at the conclusion of his "Ordination of Ministers of the Word" (1539). The other suggested hymn of the day, "Come, Holy Ghost, God and Lord," (163) may be what he means when he directs the choir to sing "*Veni Sancte Spiritus*" while all kneel at the beginning of his order.[49]

The Creed may be omitted (as it is in the Roman Catholic rite; it is required in the Episcopal rite), for the service has abundant credal material. If it seems odd to declare allegiance to the ecumenical creeds and not use one of them in the service, the response may be that, in any case, two of the creeds will not be said and the Lutheran confessions, to which allegiance is also affirmed, will not be read. To preserve the connection between the hymn of the day which invokes the Holy Spirit and the ordination, the Creed—if it is used—is said between the sermon and the hymn of the day.

Following the hymn of the day, the ordinand is brought from the congregation and presented to the presiding minister. In the *Church Book* rite and in the *Forms for Ministerial Acts* of the General Synod (1900), the candidates presented themselves before the altar. The *Common Service Book* had the secretary of the synod or another appointed minister present the candidates:

> The following brethren have been duly approved by (the name of the synod and the day and place of the meeting) as those to whom the Ministry of the Gospel should be committed. By direction of the Synod, therefore, I present these brethren for Ordination to the Holy Ministry.

Then two prayers were appointed, the first from Luther's order, reflecting widespread medieval practice:

> Create in me a clean heart, O God:
> *And renew a right spirit within me.*
> O God Who dist teach the hearts of Thy faithful people, by sending to them the light of Thy Holy Spirit: Grant us by the same Spirit to have a right judgment in all things, and evermore to rejoice in His holy comfort; through Jesus Christ, Thy Son, our Lord. *Amen.*
> Their sound went into all the earth:
> *And their words unto the end of the world.*
> O God the Giver of every good and perfect gift: Pour, we beseech Thee, upon these Thy servants Thy heavenly benediction; and so replenish them with the truth of Thy doctrine and adorn them with holiness of life, that, meditating upon Thy law day and night, they may believe what they read,

---

49. *LW,* vol. 53, pp. 126, 124.

teach what they believe, show forth in their lives what they teach, and, faithfully serving Thee in their office, may keep that which has been committed to their trust blameless unto the day of Christ Jesus, Who liveth and reigneth with Thee and the Holy Ghost, ever One God, world without end. *Amen.*

In the *Occasional Services* (1982) rite, when the ordination takes place in the ordinand's home congregation, the presenter may be an officer of that congregation or an official of the district or synod. When several people are ordained in connection with a district/synod convention, it is desirable that each ordinand have a sponsoring pastor who may also serve as presenter. At a district/synod convention, the secretary of the district/synod may present all the ordinands. The words of the presentation may be altered to fit the circumstances of the authorization and the call.

In the current Roman Catholic rite, the deacon calls the candidate forward and a priest designated by the bishop asks the bishop to ordain the candidate:

Most Reverend Father, holy mother Church asks you to ordain this man, our brother, for service as a priest.

The bishop asks, "Do you judge him to be worthy?" The presenter answers:

After inquiry among the people of Christ and upon recommendation of those concerned with his training, I testify that he has been found worthy.

Then follows the Election by the Bishop and the Consent of the People. The Bishop says:

We rely on the help of the Lord God and our Savior Jesus Christ, and we choose this man, our brother, for priesthood in the presbyteral order.

All present say "Thanks be to God" or "give their assent to the choice in some other way, according to local custom."[50]

In the 1979 *Book of Common Prayer* form for the ordination of a priest, a priest and a layperson (and other presenters) present the ordinand to the bishop:

N., Bishop in the Church of God, on behalf of the clergy and people of the Diocese of N., we present to you N.N. to be ordained a priest in Christ's holy catholic Church. (p. 526)

---

50. *Roman Pontifical,* vol. 1, pp. 206–7.

The presenters, in response to the bishop's question, certify that the candidate has satisfied all the requirements of the canons and that the candidate's manner of life is suitable to the exercise of this ministry.[51]

In the Ordination rite in *Occasional Services* (1982), the presiding minister's address, which has its origins in the *Common Service Book,* testifies to the antiquity of the tradition which is being continued in this service—"according to apostolic usage," which is ordination by the laying on of hands and prayer. The address also makes clear that the candidate is not to be ordained "a Lutheran pastor" (any more than one is "baptized a Lutheran"). Ordination confers "the office of Word and Sacrament in the one holy catholic Church."

The use of scriptural passages to make up the body of the presiding minister's address to the ordinand has deep roots in Lutheran practice. It has seemed right to generation after generation of Lutherans to describe the church's ministry by means of Scripture.

John 20:21-23 appears in most North American Lutheran rites, as does Matt. 28:18-20. The *Church Book* and the *Common Service Book* then use 1 Tim. 3:1-7 ("If a man desire the office of a bishop, he desireth a good work . . . ," KJV) and Acts 20:28 ("Take heed therefore unto yourselves, and to all the flock, over which the Holy Ghost hath made you overseers . . . ," KJV). These two texts, which speak of bishops and of oversight, suggest the Lutheran understanding that pastors are bishops and that when Lutherans ordain pastors they are in fact ordaining bishops.[52]

The following table shows the various biblical texts used in several orders in the address to the ordinand.

Lutheran Agenda	General Synod (1881)	General Synod (1900)	*Church Book* (1892)	*Common Service Book* (1919)	*Occasional Services* (1962)	*Occasional Services* (1982)
	Ezek. 33:2-7					
	(John 10:1-16)					
			John 20:21-23	John 20:21-23	John 20:21-23	John 20:21-23

---

51. *Book of Common Prayer* (1979), p. 526.

52. The "priesthood of all believers" is matched by the "episcopacy of all priests." All believers are priests, and all pastors (priests) are bishops. Thus everyone is elevated one step.

Lutheran Agenda	General Synod (1881)	General Synod (1900)	Church Book (1892)	Common Service Book (1919)	Occasional Services (1962)	Occasional Services (1982)
		Matt. 28:18–20		Matt. 28:18–20	Matt. 28:18–20	Matt. 28:18–20
		John 20:21–23				
						1 Cor. 11:23–26
	(2 Tim. 2:1–4;					
1 Tim. 3:1	1 Tim. 3:2;	1 Tim. 3:1–7	1 Tim. 3:1–7	1 Tim. 3:1–7	1 Tim. 3:1–7	
1 Cor. 4:1	Titus 1:7;					
	1 Tim. 3:6–7; 4:12–15;					
2 Tim. 2:15	2 Tim. 2:15;					
2 Tim. 4:2	4:16;					
Titus 2:1	2:7)					
Titus 2:7a						
Titus 1:7–9						
1 Cor. 4:2						
1 Tim. 4:16						
		Acts 20:28–32	Acts 20:28–32	Acts 20:28–32	[Acts 20:28 incorporated into conclusion of the Address]	

An examination of this table reveals some interesting aspects of the Lutheran use of Scripture. The *Lutheran Agenda* uses only texts which are attributed to St. Paul. (They are introduced, "Thus saith St. Paul.") There are no Gospel texts. Also, the list shows a distinct preference for a series of brief verses — "proof texts" is a less charitable description. The General Synod rite of 1881 is the only one to provide (and require) an Old Testament reading in the address to the ordinands. In addition, this rite, contrary to the usual Lutheran preference for readings which retain the integrity of the individual texts, fashions an address from a pastiche of portions of the pastoral Epistles. *Occasional Services* (1962) uses two traditional Lutheran texts and adds to them a third to give a threefold description of the work of the ministry: the office of the keys (absolution is accounted a sacrament in the Apology of the Augsburg Confession, Articles XII and XIII), Holy Baptism, and the Holy Communion. Thus each reading describes a separate sacramental action which the ordinand is being ordained to perform.

The examination of the candidate follows. The first question seeks recognition of the divine dimension of the call to the ministry of Word and Sacrament; the call that comes through the church is in reality the call by the Holy Spirit. The second question recognizes that the church by whose hands the ordinand is to enter the Christian ministry has its own identity and is bound to three descending categories of documents: Scripture, the three ecumenical creeds, and the Lutheran confessions. That is to say, the church in which the candidate is to be ordained acknowledges itself to be Christian, catholic, and Lutheran. The third question deals with the quality of the ordinand's spiritual life. The fourth question recognizes that the life of the Christian pastor is not simply inward but is also directed outward as a witness to the world (traditionally, the primary responsibility of the deacon).

The response to each question could appropriately be a simple, "I will," as it was in earlier drafts of the rite. The concluding blessing by the presiding minister (p. 194) clearly indicates that the ordinand must rely on God's help to fulfill the promises:

> Almighty God, who has given you the will to do these things, graciously give you the strength and compassion to perform them.

But Lutheran piety is such that Lutherans expect a reply that will explicitly ask God's help. In the Roman Catholic rite for Ordination of a Priest, the reliance of the ordinand upon God's help is indicated in various ways—in certain questions, in certain answers, in the bishop's blessing at the end:

> Are you resolved, with the help of the Holy Spirit, to discharge without fail the office of priesthood in the presbyteral order as a conscientious fellow worker with the bishops in caring for the Lord's flock?
> *I am.*
> Are you resolved to celebrate the mysteries of Christ faithfully and religiously as the Church has handed them down to us for the glory of God and the sanctification of Christ's people?
> *I am.*
> Are you resolved to exercise the ministry of the word worthily and wisely, preaching the Gospel and explaining the Catholic faith?
> *I am.*
> Are you resolved to consecrate your life to God for the salvation of his people, and to unite yourself more closely every day to Christ the High Priest, who offered himself for us to the Father as a perfect sacrifice?
> *I am, with the help of God.*
> . . . May God who has begun the good work in you bring it to fulfillment.[53]

---

53. *Roman Pontifical,* vol. 1, pp. 209–11.

The Episcopal rite for the Ordination of a Priest, in the questions which explain "this trust and responsibility," requires a simple and consistent answer by the ordinand:

> My *brother*, do you believe that you are truly called by God and his Church to this priesthood?
> *I believe I am so called.*
> Do you now in the presence of the Church commit yourself to this trust and responsibility?
> *I do.*
> Will you respect and be guided by the pastoral direction and leadership of your bishop?
> *I will.*
> Will you be diligent in the reading and study of the Holy Scriptures . . . ?
> *I will.*
> Will you endeavor so to minister the Word of God and the sacraments of the New Covenant, that the reconciling love of Christ may be known and received?
> *I will.*
> Will you undertake to be a faithful pastor . . . ?
> *I will.*
> Will you do your best to pattern your life . . . in accordance with the teachings of Christ . . . ?
> *I will.*
> Will you persevere in prayer . . . ?
> *I will.*
> May the Lord who has given you the will to do these things give you the grace and power to perform them.
> *Amen.*[54]

In the North American Lutheran tradition the four questions of *Occasional Services* (1982) have developed from one twofold question in the *Church Book:*

> Are you now ready to take upon you this Holy Ministry, and faithfully to serve in it? Will you preach and teach the pure Word of God in accordance with the Confessions of the Evangelical Lutheran Church, and adorn the doctrine of our Saviour by a holy life and godly conversation?
> *Yes, with my whole heart, the Lord helping me through the power and grace of His Holy Spirit.*[55]

In the *Common Service Book,* this double question becomes a triple question:

---

54. *Book of Common Prayer* (1979), pp. 531–32.
55. *Church Book,* pp. 423–24.

Are you now ready to take upon you this Holy Ministry, and faithfully to serve in it?
Will you preach and teach the pure Word of God in accordance with the Confession of the Evangelical Lutheran Church?
Will you adorn the doctrine of our Saviour by a holy life and conversation?[56]

The candidate's answer is the same as in the *Church Book*. In *Occasional Services* (1962) the question is divided into four separate questions:

Are you now ready to take upon you this Holy Ministry, and faithfully to serve therein?
Yes, by the help of God.
Will you preach and teach the Word of God in accordance with the Confessions of the Church, and will you administer the Holy Sacraments after the ordinance of Christ?
Yes, by the help of God.
Will you be diligent in the study of Holy Scripture, instant in prayer, and faithful in the use of the means of grace?
Yes, by the help of God.
Will you adorn the doctrine of God our Saviour by a holy life and conversation?
Yes, by the help of God.

Moreover, an additional optional oath is provided:

Before God and the Lord Jesus Christ, who shall judge the quick and the dead at his appearing, I *(N.N.)* do promise, with his grace and help, to fulfill these sacred obligations. Amen.[57]

Then the officiating minister says:

Almighty God, who hath chosen you to be his *ministers*, enable you to fulfill by his help what you have begun in his favor. Amen.[58]

The examination concluded, the prayers of intercession follow with particular reference to the ordinand. In the Roman Catholic rite the Litany of the Saints, which takes the place of the intercessions, is sung or said at this point as a way of inviting all the saints, especially those whose names the ordinand bears, to join the prayers of the assembly. The Litany concludes with the bishop standing and voicing the prayer which all the saints have been invited to share:

---

56. *Common Service Book*, p. 458.
57. *Occasional Services* (1962), p. 97.
58. Ibid., p. 98.

> Hear us, Lord our God,
> and pour out upon this servant of yours
> the blessing of the Holy Spirit
> and the grace and power of the priesthood.
> In your sight we offer this man for ordination:
> support him with your unfailing love.
> We ask this through Christ our Lord.[59]

The prayers in the Lutheran rite echo this use of the Litany of the Saints at the conclusion, "For the glorious company of all the saints . . . " It would be appropriate to name here those saints of particular importance for this ordination: those for whom the ordinand is named, the saint whose name the church building bears. The prayers might take the form of a litany for ordination based on the Litany for Ordinations in the *Book of Common Prayer* or the Western form of the Litany (*LBW*, Min. Ed., p. 86) or the Eastern Litany of Evening Prayer (*LBW*, Min. Ed., pp. 65–68).

After the prayers the ordinand may kneel, and "Come, Holy Ghost, Our Souls Inspire" (472, 473) is sung as a prayer for the presence and power of the Holy Spirit. This hymn, an office hymn at vespers (and terce) on Pentecost and frequently used through the centuries to pray for the presence of the Holy Spirit on any occasion when the invocation of the Spirit was appropriate, has been a traditional prayer at ordination in the Western church since the late medieval period. The location of the hymn varied in different rites: immediately after the laying on of hands, after the Gospel and before the examination and the laying on of hands. In his ordination order Luther required instead another hymn of invocation of the Holy Spirit, *"Veni Sancte Spiritus"* (see Hymn 163), the "golden sequence" used after the alleluia verse on Pentecost.

Following the hymn, the prayers continue with the central prayer of the service, the thanksgiving ⟨536–37⟩. It is deliberately constructed to parallel the Great Thanksgiving in the Holy Communion and the thanksgiving at Holy Baptism. The verse and response of the eucharistic dialogue, "Lift up your hearts: *We lift them to the Lord*," are limited by ancient liturgical custom to the eucharistic preface and so do not appear here, in Holy Baptism, nor in the palm ceremonies of the Sunday of the Passion.

The first phrase of the prayer, calling upon God by three of his titles, is identical with the beginning of the thanksgiving in Holy Baptism and Great Thanksgiving I in the Holy Communion. The sentences which

---

59. *Roman Pontifical*, vol. 1, p. 212. In the Episcopal rite the Litany for Ordinations is said earlier in the service, before the collect which begins the Ministry of the Word.

follow are drawn from Eph. 1:7; Heb. 2:14; Eph. 4:10–12. Calling upon God who has poured out his gifts upon his church, the presiding minister, as the minister authorized to ordain, lays both hands on the head of the ordinand. The focus of attention here is the ordinand; all of the energy of the rite is directed toward that person.

For reasons of convenience and to indicate their auxiliary roles, other clergy may lay their right hands on the head of the ordinand.

> The presiding minister continues the prayer: Eternal God, through your Son, Jesus Christ, pour out your Holy Spirit upon _____ and fill *him/her* with the gifts of grace [for the ministry of Word and Sacrament].

The bracketed phrase indicates a lack of agreement as to whether the ordination formula needs to be explicit in naming the purpose of the gifts of grace implored, some arguing that unless specific mention is made of the pastoral office, such a prayer could be used at any time for any person; and others arguing that the context and the action of laying on of hands makes the intention quite clear.

There is no provision for lay people to participate in the laying on of hands—a custom recently introduced in some places—for that would obscure what is taking place. The people have presented the ordinand to the bishop (or the bishop's representative), and those who have been ordained receive the ordinand into the ministry to which they have previously been admitted.

LUTHERAN

Holy God, mighty Lord, gracious Father, we bless you for your infinite love in Christ our Lord, in whom we have redemption and forgiveness of sins according to the riches of his grace. We thank you that by his death your Son has overcome death and, having been raised by your mighty power, has ascended far above all the heavens, that he might fill all things. We praise you that Christ has poured out his gifts abundantly on the Church, making some apostles, some prophets, some pastors and teachers, to equip your people for their work of

EPISCOPAL

God and Father of all, we praise you for your infinite love in calling us to be a holy people in the kingdom of your Son Jesus our Lord, who is the image of your eternal and invisible glory, the firstborn among many brethren, and the head of the Church. We thank you that by his death he has overcome death, and, having ascended into heaven, has poured his gifts abundantly upon your people, making some apostles, some prophets, some evangelists, some pastors and teachers, to equip the saints for the work of ministry and the

LUTHERAN	EPISCOPAL
ministry for building up the body of Christ.	building up of his body.
The minister lays both hands on the head of the ordinand(s). Other clergy may impose their right hands.	*Here the Bishop lays hands upon the head of the ordained, the Priests who are present also laying on their hands. At the same time the Bishop prays*
Eternal God, through your Son, Jesus Christ, pour out your Holy Spirit upon _____ and fill *him/her* with the gifts of grace [for the ministry of Word and Sacrament].	Therefore, Father, through Jesus Christ your Son, give your Holy Spirit to *N.*, fill *him* with grace and power, and make *him* a priest in your Church.
Following the laying on of hands the ordinand(s) remains kneeling. Bless *his/her* proclamation of your Word and administration of your Sacraments, O Lord, so that your Church may be gathered for praise and strengthened for service. Make *him/her a* faithful *pastor(s)*, patient *teacher(s)*, wise counselor(s). Grant that in all things *he/she* may serve without reproach, that your people may be renewed and your name be glorified in the Church; through Jesus Christ our Lord, who lives and reigns with you and the Holy Spirit, one God, forever.	*The Bishop then continues* May *he* exalt you, O Lord in the midst of your people; offer spiritual sacrifices acceptable to you; boldly proclaim the gospel of salvation; and rightly administer the sacraments of the New Covenant. Make *him* a faithful pastor, a patient teacher, and a wise councilor. Grant that in all things *he* may serve without reproach, so that your people may be strengthened and your Name glorified in all the world. All this we ask through Jesus Christ our Lord, who with you and the Holy Spirit lives and reigns, one God for ever and ever.[60]

The Roman Catholic "Prayer of Consecration" is this:

With his hands extended over the candidate, the bishop sings the prayer of consecration or says it aloud.

---

60. *Book of Common Prayer* (1979), pp. 533–34. Note the different spelling and consequently the different understanding of the pastor/priest as "counsellor" and "councilor."

The Prayer Book prayer at the ordination of a priest "incorporates material from Bucer's prayer (used in prior Anglican ordinals), Eph. 4:11–12, and the new South Indian and English proposed rites. It presents a fuller view of the priesthood than does the prayer of prior rites: a priest is to proclaim the gospel and administer the sacraments, act as pastor and teacher, and share in the councils of the church" (Hatchett, *Commentary on American Prayer Book,* pp. 526–27).

Come to our help,
Lord, holy Father, almighty and eternal God;
you are the source of every honor and dignity,
of all progress and stability.
You watch over the growing family of man
by your gift of wisdom and your pattern of order.
When you had appointed high priests to rule your people,
you chose other men next to them in rank and dignity
to be with them and to help them in their task;
and so there grew up
the ranks of priests and the offices of levites,
established by sacred rites.

In the desert
you extended the spirit of Moses to seventy wise men
who helped him to rule the great company of his people.
You shared among the sons of Aaron
the fullness of their father's power,
to provide worthy priests in sufficient number
for the increasing rites of sacrifice and worship.
With the same loving care
you gave companions to your Son's apostles
to help in teaching the faith:
they preached the Gospel to the whole world.

Lord,
grant also to us such fellow workers,
for we are weak and our need is greater.

Almighty Father,
grant to this servant of yours
the dignity of the priesthood.
Renew within him the Spirit of holiness.
As a co-worker with the order of bishops
may he be faithful in the ministry
that he receives from you, Lord God,
and be to others a model of right conduct.

May he be faithful in working with the order of bishops,
so that the words of the Gospel may reach the ends of the earth,
and the family of nations,
made one in Christ,
may become God's one, holy people.

We ask this through our Lord Jesus Christ, your Son,
who lives and reigns with you and the Holy Spirit,
one God, for ever and ever.[61]

---

61. *Roman Pontifical,* vol. 1, pp. 212–14.

Each of the three ordination prayers—Lutheran, Episcopal, and Roman Catholic—follows a similar structure. The first part is a thankful remembrance of God's work in history (the Roman Catholic prayer centering on the Old Testament, the Lutheran and Episcopal prayers centering on Christ). Each prayer then asks God's blessing on the various aspects of the work of the new priest or pastor. Each prayer concludes with a trinitarian doxology.

In the Orthodox churches the ordination of a priest takes place at the Great Entrance after the gifts have been carried from the credence table to the altar in order that he may participate in their consecration. The rite is remarkable for its simplicity.

The candidate is brought to the altar by a deacon. He kneels before the altar and the bishop "lays his hand upon his head" and says:

> The grace divine, which always healeth that which is infirm, and completeth that which is wanting, elevateth through the laying on of hands N., the most devout Deacon, to be a Priest. Wherefore, let us pray for him, that the grace of the all-holy Spirit may come upon him.[62]

While the priests and choir alternately sing "Lord, have mercy," the bishop prays quietly for the Holy Spirit:

> O God who hast no beginning and no ending; who art older than every created thing; who crownest with the name of Presbyter those whom thou deemest worthy to serve the word of thy truth in the divine ministry of this degree: Do thou, the same Lord of all men, deign to preserve in pureness of life and in unswerving faith this man also, upon whom, through me, thou hast graciously been pleased to lay hands. Be favorably pleased to grant unto him the great grace of thy Holy Spirit, and make him wholly thy servant, in all things acceptable unto thee, and worthily exercising the great honors of the priesthood which thou hast conferred upon him by thy present power.[63]

The bishop concludes the prayer aloud:

> For thine is the majesty, and thine are the kingdom and the power and the glory, of the Father, and of the Son, and of the Holy Spirit, now, and ever, and unto ages of ages.[64]

Then, while the priest says the litany of peace ("In peace let us pray to the Lord"), the bishop, keeping his hand on the ordinand's head, prays silently for the ordinand:

---

62. *Service Book,* p. 316.
63. Ibid., pp. 316–17.
64. Ibid., p. 317.

O God great in might and inscrutable in wisdom, marvelous in counsel above the sons of men: Do thou, the same Lord, fill with the gift of thy Holy Spirit this man whom it hath pleased thee to advance to the degree of Priest; that he may be worthy to stand in innocency before thine Altar: to proclaim the Gospel of thy kingdom; to minister the word of thy truth; to offer unto thee spiritual gifts and sacrifices; to renew thy people through the laver of regeneration. That when he shall go to meet thee, at the Second Coming of our great God and Saviour, Jesus Christ, thine Only-begotten Son, he may receive the reward of a good steward in the degree committed unto him, through the plenitude of thy goodness.[65]

The bishop then exclaims aloud, concluding both his prayer and the litany of peace sung by the priest:

For blessed and glorified is thine all-holy and majestic Name, of the Father, and of the Son, and of the Holy Spirit, now, and ever, and unto ages of ages.[66]

As the cry "Axios!" ("Worthy!") is sung the new priest is vested with the stole, cincture, and chasuble. The peace is shared, and the ordinand "taketh his place among the Priests." The Liturgy of the Faithful continues with the preparation of the Holy Gifts, the Nicene Creed, and the consecration.

In *Occasional Services* (1982), the prayer of thanksgiving ended, the congregation sits down and the ordinand receives an emblem of the office —a stole, understood as signifying the yoke of Christ (Matt. 11:28–30).[67] The Roman Catholic rite at this point calls for the investiture of the new priest with stole and chasuble. The *Book of Common Prayer* (1979) has the rubric: "The new Priest is now vested according to the order of priests" (worded in a general way to accommodate the various traditions within The Episcopal Church). In the Lutheran book's "Notes on the Service," no. 12 permits other symbols of ministry to be given also:

Where local custom indicates that another symbol of ministry (e.g., the Bible) be given, the presenter or assisting minister may hand the item to the newly ordained as the presiding minister says: "Receive this _____ as a sign of your calling to the ministry of Word and Sacrament."

---

65. Ibid.

66. Ibid., p. 318.

67. The stole, which in the twentieth century had been given great prominence in Lutheran practice in North America as *the* liturgical sign of ordination, is receiving less attention in other liturgical traditions. It is the chasuble which is the peculiar vestment of the pastor. See Robert W. Hovda, "The Vesting of Liturgical Ministers," *Worship* 54:2 (March 1980): 98–117.

The Bible is of particular importance, especially in the Lutheran church in view of its history. Giving a series of items—stole, chasuble, Bible, baptismal shell, chalice, and paten—is cumbersome and undesirable, for it requires that these items only pass through the hands of the new pastor so that the next item may be held briefly.

In the Roman Catholic rite, following the investiture, the symbolic action is the anointing of the hands of the new priest with the prayer which emphasizes the priest's responsibility to offer sacrifice:

> The Father anointed our Lord Jesus Christ
> through the power of the Holy Spirit.
> May Jesus preserve you to sanctify the Christian people
> and to offer sacrifice to God.[68]

The Episcopal rite gives a Bible as the symbol of the authority for the work of a priest (which in Lutheran terms is the twofold work of Word and Sacrament, proclamation and celebration). As the Bible is given, the *Book of Common Prayer* has the bishop say:

> Receive the Bible as a sign of the authority given to you to preach the Word of God and to administer his holy Sacraments. Do not forget the trust committed to you as a priest of the Church of God.[69]

In *Occasional Services* (1982) four passages of Scripture together with a new composition form a charge to the ordinand. The first passage, 1 Tim. 6:11-12, is new to the Lutheran order; the second, Acts 20:28, was used in Luther's order and in earlier North American rites (before the ordination); the third passage, 1 Pet. 5:2-4, is used in Luther's order for ordination; the fourth scriptural passage, 1 Cor. 4:1-2, has precedence in the *Lutheran Agenda* of the Synodical Conference.

The blessing is from Heb. 13:20-21.

The congregation receives the newly ordained and acclaims the ordination. This action accomplishes several things. The first question addressed to the congregation elicits the recognition by the congregation of their representative function: they represent the whole church, and the person ordained is not ordained for the service of some but for the service of all. The question also elicits from the congregation a recognition of the divine origin of the ministry.

> Will you, assembled as the people of God and speaking for the whole Church, receive _____ as *a messenger(s)* of Jesus Christ sent to serve

---

68. *Roman Pontifical,* vol. 1, p. 214.
69. *Book of Common Prayer* (1979), p. 534.

God's people with the Gospel of hope and salvation? Will you regard *him/her* as *a servant(s)* of Christ?

The second question requires the congregation to support the ministry and those who labor in it so that all seek to avoid and to overcome differences and quarrels.

Will you pray for *him/her*, help and honor *him/her* for *his/her* work's sake, and in all things strive to live together in the peace and unity of Christ?

The language of this question reflects 1 Thess. 5:13 (KJV) and Eph. 4:3.

This done, the ordination is acclaimed. This acclamation accomplishes the announcement of "the authority to preach the Word and administer the Sacraments," which in earlier North American Lutheran rites was accomplished at the laying on of hands. In earlier books the acclamation was as follows: in the *Church Book:* "We now commit unto thee the Holy Office of the Word and Sacraments of the Triune God . . . "; in the *Common Service Book:* "I now commit unto thee the Holy Office of the Word and Sacraments . . . "; in *Occasional Services* (1962): "The Lord bestow upon thee the Holy Ghost for the office and work of a Minister in the Church of God, now committed unto thee."

In the *Book of Common Prayer* (1979) the questioning of the congregation is done at the beginning of the service, at the Presentation, before the litany, Kyrie, and collect for the day. It consists of one simple and basic question:

Dear friends in Christ, you know the importance of this ministry, and the weight of your responsibility in presenting *N.N.* for ordination to the sacred priesthood. Therefore if any of you know any impediment or crime because of which we should not proceed, come forward now, and make it known. Is it your will that *N.* be ordained a priest?
It is.
Will you uphold *him* in this ministry?
We will.[70]

The congregation has no role in the Roman Catholic rite.

The action of ordination in all three rites — Lutheran, Episcopal, and Roman Catholic — concludes with the sharing of the peace.

The postcommunion prayer ⟨539⟩ is a revision of the prayer "After Communion" provided in the 1979 *Book of Common Prayer* (pp. 523, 535, 546) and originally drafted by H. Boone Porter.

Installation, while clearly related to ordination, is not a part of ordination. There may be situations when an installation on the same occasion

---

70. Ibid., p. 527.

as the ordination may be the best solution to a problem (so the form is provided, pp. 199–200), but such a combined order should be the very rare exception. When it is done, the decision to do so should be logistical and practical, never theological, lest our ecumenical commitments be betrayed.

Comparison of Rites
Ordination

ROMAN CATHOLIC (Ordination of Priests)	LUTHERAN (Ordination)	EPISCOPAL (Ordination of Priests)
		The presentation Questions to ordinand Questions to congregation
		Litany for ordinations
		Collect for the day
Liturgy of the Word		Old Testament Lesson Psalm 43 or 132:8–19
		Epistle
	Gospel	Gospel
Calling and presentation of the candidate		
Election by bishop and consent of people		
Homily	Sermon	Sermon
		Nicene Creed
	Hymn of the day	
	Presentation	
	Address John 20:21–23 Matt. 28:18–20 1 Cor. 11:23–26	
Examination	Examination	Examination
Promise of obedience		
Litany of the Saints	The prayers	
	"Veni Creator Spiritus"	*"Veni Creator Spiritus"* or *"Veni Sancte Spiritus"*

Comparison of Rites (continued)
Ordination

ROMAN CATHOLIC (Ordination of Priests)	LUTHERAN (Ordination)	EPISCOPAL (Ordination of Priests)
Laying on of hands in silence		Silent prayer
Prayer of consecration	The thanksgiving with laying on of hands	Prayer of consecration with laying on of hands
Investiture with stole and chasuble	Giving of stole	Vesting the priest
		Giving of Bible
Anointing the hands *"Veni Creator Spiritus"* or Psalm 110 meanwhile		
	Exhortation 1 Tim. 6:11–12 Acts 20:28 1 Pet. 5:2–4 1 Cor. 4:1–2	
	Blessing	
	Questions to congregation	
The peace	The peace	The peace
Presentation of the gifts	Offering	Offering
The peace		
The Eucharist	(The Eucharist)	The Eucharist

ANNIVERSARY OF AN ORDINATION
(*Occasional Services*, p. 150)

Parallel Rites

Roman Catholic   Renewal of Commitment to Priestly Service, *Sacramentary*, pp. 131–33.

Episcopal   Reaffirmation of Ordination Vows, *Book of Occasional Services*, pp. 212–15.

Characteristics

Provision for the Anniversary of an Ordination as a local celebration is a peculiar Lutheran contribution. The form is simple and suggests a way of celebrating the Holy Communion to give it relevance to the anniversary of the ordination of the individual pastor. Thanksgiving for past service and prayer for continued faithfulness are the themes.

Background

The Roman Catholic rite has renewed an ancient custom by making provision for the renewal of ordination vows at the Maundy Thursday Mass of the Chrism, which the priests of the diocese concelebrate with their bishop in the cathedral church. While not exactly an anniversary of ordination, it is an occasion for the renewal of their dedication to their vocation, and it is done in the context of the celebration of the Eucharist and in union with the bishop.

The Renewal of Commitment to Priestly Service follows the sermon and replaces the Creed and the prayers in the liturgy. The bishop addresses the following questions to the priests and to the congregation and they respond.

My brothers,
today we celebrate the memory of the first eucharist,
at which our Lord Jesus Christ shared with his apostles and with us
his call to the priestly service of his Church.
Now, in the presence of your bishop and God's holy people,
are you ready to renew your own dedication to Christ
as priests of the new covenant?
   I am.
At your ordination
you accepted the responsibilities of the priesthood
out of love for the Lord Jesus and his Church.
Are you resolved to unite yourselves more closely to Christ
and to try to become more like him
by joyfully sacrificing your own pleasure and ambition
to bring his peace and love to your brothers and sisters?
   I am.
Are you resolved
to be faithful ministers of the mysteries of God,
to celebrate the eucharist and the other liturgical services
with sincere devotion?
Are you resolved to imitate Jesus Christ,
the head and shepherd of the Church,
by teaching the Christian faith
without thinking of your own profit,
solely for the well-being of the people
you were sent to serve?
   I am.

My brothers and sisters,
pray for your priests.
Ask the Lord to bless them with the fullness of his love,
to help them be faithful ministers of Christ the High Priest,
so that they will be able to lead you to him,
the fountain of your salvation.
Lord Jesus Christ, hear us and answer our prayer.
Pray also for me
that despite my own unworthiness
I may faithfully fulfill the office of apostle
which Jesus Christ has entrusted to me.
Pray that I may become more like
our High Priest and Good Shepherd,
the teacher and servant of all,
and so be a genuine sign
of Christ's loving presence among you.
Lord Jesus Christ, hear us and answer our prayer.
May the Lord in his love
keep you close to him always,
and may he bring all of us,
his priests and people,
to eternal life.
Amen.

The liturgy then continues with the offering.

The Episcopal *Book of Occasional Services* provides a form for the Reaffirmation of Ordination Vows, "intended for use at a celebration of the Eucharist upon an occasion when the clergy are gathered together with the bishop." The rubrics recognize the tradition that this may be done on Maundy Thursday "at a celebration of the Eucharist other than the Proper Liturgy of the day."

After the sermon (and the Creed), the bishop, sitting in a chair before the altar, addresses those who are to renew their vows.

Dear friends, the ministry we share is none other than the sacrificial ministry of Christ, who gave himself up to death on the cross for the salvation of the world. By his glorious resurrection he has opened for us the way of everlasting life. By the gift of the Holy Spirit he shares with us the riches of his grace.

We are called to proclaim his death and resurrection, to administer the Sacraments of the New Covenant which he sealed with his blood on the cross, and to care for his people in the power of the Spirit.

Do you here, in the presence of Christ and his Church, renew your commitment to your ministry, under the pastoral direction of your bishop?
I do.

203

Do you reaffirm your promise to give yourself to prayer and study?
I do.

Do you reaffirm your promise so to minister the Word of God and the Sacraments of the New Covenant that the reconciling love of Christ may be known and received?
I do.

Do you reaffirm your promise to be a faithful servant of all those committed to your care, patterning your life in accordance with the teachings of Christ, so that you may be a wholesome example to your people?
I do.

The Bishop then stands and makes this affirmation
And now, as your bishop, I, too, before God and you, re-dedicate myself and reaffirm the promises that I made when I was ordained. I ask your prayers.

Bishop and Clergy
May the Lord who has given us the will to do these things, give us also the grace and power to perform them.

The service continues with the peace.

Survey of the Service

The postcommunion prayer ⟨505⟩, like ⟨539⟩, is an adaptation of the prayer "After Communion" provided in the 1979 *Book of Common Prayer* (pp. 523, 535, 546) for the ordinations of a bishop, a priest, and a deacon. It was drafted for the Prayer Book by H. Boone Porter.

SETTING APART OF A DEACONESS
(*Occasional Services*, pp. 210–17)

Parallel Rites

Roman Catholic	See Ordination of a Deacon.
Episcopal	See The Ordination of a Deacon.
Lutheran	Order for the Setting Apart of a Deaconess, *Occasional Services* (1962), pp. 100–105.[71]
	Order for the Consecration of a Deaconess, *Occasional Services* (1930), pp. 119–25.
Methodist	An Office for the Consecration of Deaconesses, *Book of Worship*, pp. 327–29.

---

71. Notice that while Ordination in the 1962 *Occasional Services permits* the celebration of the Holy Communion, the order for the Setting Apart of a Deaconess *requires* it.

Purpose

This service is for the reception of one into the diaconate by an act of consecration. (The deaconesses themselves prefer to describe the act as ordination.) At the present time only the Lutheran Church in America and the Lutheran Deaconess Association in Valparaiso, Indiana, employ such a rite, and only women are admitted to the diaconate. It should be noted, however, that there are in various places in the Lutheran churches groups of men who serve as deacons, some of whom have been ordained to the task. The third general note looks forward to the time when the officially recognized diaconate will admit men as well as women to its membership. As the church has learned to admit women as well as men to the pastorate, so in time it may learn to receive men as well as women into its diaconate.

Characteristics

The service is structured in such a way as to present certain parallels with ordination and with the installation of a bishop.

Installation of a Bishop	Ordination	Setting Apart of a Deaconess
Hymn of the day	Hymn of the day	Hymn of the day
Presentation	Presentation	Presentation
Address with scriptural passages	Address with scriptural passages	Address with scriptural passages
Questions to candidate	Questions to candidate	Questions to candidate
	The prayers	The prayers
	"Come, Holy Ghost, Our Souls Inspire"	
	The thanksgiving with laying on of hands	The thanksgiving with laying on of hands
		Statement of committal of office
	Presentation of stole	Presentation of cross
	Address with scriptural passages	Address with scriptural passages
	Blessing	
Address to congregation	Questions to congregation	Questions to congregation
Bestowal of office		

Installation of a Bishop	Ordination	Setting Apart of a Deaconess
The blessing		
The prayers		
Acclamation	Acclamation	
		Blessing or prayer
The peace	The peace	The peace

Survey of the Service

If the Setting Apart of a Deaconess is scheduled as a service separate from the principal service of a congregation, the appointed propers are used. The appointed propers are also used if this rite is set within the chief service of a congregation on a Sunday for which the color is green ("ordinary" Sundays). If, however, the Setting Apart of a Deaconess is set within the chief service of a congregation on a Sunday of Advent, Christmas, Lent, Easter, or a Festival, the propers for that Sunday or Festival are used. It is therefore most desirable to schedule the Setting Apart of a Deaconess at a time other than at the chief service of a congregation so that full attention may be given to this ministry. Attention is called in the following list to commemorations which are especially appropriate for the consecration of a deaconess:

> January 27 (Lydia, Dorcas, and Phoebe)
> February 25 (Elizabeth Fedde, deaconess)
> April 29 (Catherine of Siena, teacher)
> August 10 (Lawrence, deacon, martyr)
> August 13 (Florence Nightingale and Clara Maass, renewers of society)
> October 4 (Theodor Fliedner, renewer of society)
> December 26 (St. Stephen, deacon and martyr)

The prayer of the day for the Setting Apart of a Deaconess is (196) in the *LBW*. The prayer appeared in the *Service Book and Hymnal* as no. 69 of Collects and Prayers (music ed., p. 228) and was borrowed for that book from *The Ritual of the Methodist Episcopal Church* (1916), Order for the Consecration of a Deaconess, based on a prayer which mentions Old Testament women in the 1908 *Ritual*. The prayer was expanded in the 1944 Methodist *Book of Worship*, and in the 1964 *Book of Worship* it has this form:

> O eternal God, the Father of our Lord Jesus Christ, who didst call Phoebe and Dorcas into the service of thy Church: Look upon *these* thy *servants*

who *are* now to be set apart to the office of deaconess. Give to *them*, we pray thee, such understanding of thy holy Gospel, such firmness of Christian purpose, such diligence in thy service, and such beauty of life in Christ, that *they* may be to all whom *they* teach or serve a worthy revelation of the meaning and power of the Christian life. May *they* so order *their* time and nourish *their minds* and *hearts* that *they* may constantly grow in grace and in the knowledge of our Lord Jesus Christ, and may steadily increase in power to lead others unto him.

Grant that *they* may have strength of body, mind, and soul for the fulfillment of thy will in the holy task to which thou hast called *them;* and grant *them* thy Holy Spirit, that *they* may worthily discharge the work committed to *them*, to the blessing of mankind and to the praise of Christ our Savior.[72]

Occasional Services (1962) provided as the collect for the Setting Apart of a Deaconess the collect appointed for the Twelfth Sunday after Trinity (the Thirteenth Sunday after Pentecost):

Almighty and merciful God, of whose only gift it cometh that thy faithful people do unto thee true and laudable service: Grant, we beseech thee, that we may so faithfully serve thee in this life, that we fail not finally to attain thy heavenly promises; through Jesus Christ, thy Son, our Lord, who liveth and reigneth with thee and the Holy Ghost, one God, world without end.[73]

Occasional Services (1930) had a new composition as the collect:

Almighty God, our Heavenly Father, Whose we are and Whom we serve: Grant that our love may abound more and more in knowledge and in all judgment; that we may approve things that are excellent; that we may be sincere and without offence till the day of Christ; being filled with the fruits of righteousness, which are by Jesus Christ unto Whom with Thee and the Holy Ghost, One God, be all glory and praise evermore.[74]

Occasional Services (1982) is the first Lutheran book to provide Old Testament readings for the Setting Apart of a Deaconess. *Occasional Services* (1962) provided only an Epistle (Phil. 2:5-13 or 1 Cor. 13:1-13 [the 1930 rite appointed Phil. 2:1-13 or Gal. 6:2-10]) and a Gospel (John 15:1-8 [the 1930 book appointed Matt. 6:19-21 or John 15:1-15]), even though the *Service Book and Hymnal* restored the use of the Old Testament lesson.

The hymn of the day may be either "Come, Holy Ghost, Our Souls Inspire" (472, 473), the traditional hymn of invocation of the Holy Spirit, or "Lord, Whose Love in Humble Service" (423), a hymn which de-

---

72. *Book of Worship,* p. 328.

73. *Occasional Services* (1962), p. 100; *Service Book and Hymnal,* p. 99.

74. *Occasional Services* (1930), p. 119.

scribes the work that deaconesses share.[75] Either hymn is appropriate, but it is perhaps desirable to use "Lord, Whose Love in Humble Service" as the hymn of the day and to sing "Come, Holy Ghost, Our Souls Inspire" prior to the thanksgiving. At the conclusion of the hymn, the head of the deaconess community brings the candidate to a place in front of the presiding minister, who stands before the altar.

The rubric (no. 2) governing the designation of the presiding minister allows for a variety of procedures depending upon the practice of the particular community to which the candidate belongs.

The wording of the presentation formula also indicates the Lutheran Church in America's limited experience with deaconesses. In ordination the presenter says:

> I present for ordination to the holy ministry of Word and Sacrament (full name[s]) who *has* been prepared, examined, and certified for this ministry and who has been called by the Church to the office of *pastor*.

The generally accepted process is here set forth: preparation, examination, certification, and a call by the church. In the Setting Apart of a Deaconess the head of the diaconal community says:

> I present for setting apart to the office of deaconess _____, who has been prepared and approved by (church body).

The process of preparation is similar to the preparation for ordinands, but there is no examination of the candidates for the diaconate, no use of "call" to describe the deaconesses' work. The preparation and approval are not that of the whole church but only of the church body to which the candidate belongs.

The presiding minister's address recalls the ministry of three pairs of exemplars. The first pair are two prophetesses: Miriam the prophetess and Deborah the prophetess. Miriam, the sister of Aaron (Exod. 15:20) and of Moses (Num. 26:59), is linked with Moses and Aaron in Mic. 6:4. She was punished for challenging Moses' unique relationship to God according to Num. 12:1-15 (used as a warning in Deut. 24:9). She died in Kadesh (Num. 20:1). Deborah (Judges 4—5) wrought a great victory over the Canaanites, as described in the marvelous ancient poem, the Song of Deborah (Judges 5). The second pair of exemplars are two male deacons,

---

75. The hymnal in the *Service Book and Hymnal* appointed Hymn 549 ("Saviour, thee my heart I tender") for deaconesses. *Occasional Services* (1962) directed: "The Order shall follow the Sermon, and shall begin with a hymn of Invocation of the Holy Ghost" (p. 100). *Occasional Services* (1930) directed that after the General Prayer "*shall follow the* Hymn: Veni Creator Spiritus (No. 142) *or the* Hymn: Nunc Sancte nobis Spiritus (No. 148)."

Stephen and Philip. Stephen was the first Christian martyr (Acts 6–7) and is commemorated on December 26. Philip the Deacon (not to be confused with Philip the Apostle, who is commemorated with St. James the Less on May 1) was chosen with Stephen (and Prochorus, Nicanor, Timon, Parmenas, and Nicolaus [Acts 6:5]). His ministry is described in Acts 8:5-8, 26-40. The inclusion of these two males in a rite for women (the prayer of the day speaks of how God through the ages has "called women to the diaconate in the Church") may seem odd, but it is there to broaden the view of those who would limit the diaconate to women. Note the rubric: "If men are certified for the diaconal community, the language of this order is to be modified accordingly." The third pair of exemplars are two coworkers with the apostles: Phoebe and Priscilla. Phoebe is described by St. Paul as "a deaconess of the church at Cenchreae" (Rom. 16:1). She was perhaps a widow and is commemorated on January 27. Priscilla, with her husband Aquilla, was called by St. Paul "my fellow workers in Christ Jesus" (Rom. 16:3). Their work is described in Acts 18:2-4, 18-26. Priscilla seems to be the same person as Prisca in 1 Cor. 16:19. This diverse collection of representative deacons and deaconesses—Old Testament and New Testament, married and (perhaps) widowed and perhaps single, preachers and evangelists and "helpers," political and military leaders—serves as background for the text from 1 Corinthians 12 on the diversity of gifts.

Historically, deacons—whose responsibility is to serve the world in the name of Christ—have been the activists in the church. So the presiding minister's summary of the work of the diaconate speaks of serving the needy, caring for the sick, comforting the distressed, and by words and work bringing God's love to all.

The questions in the examination parallel those in Ordination:

Ordination	*Setting Apart of a Deaconess*
Will you assume this office, believing that the Church's call is God's call to the ministry of Word and Sacrament?	Will you assume this ministry, and as a servant of God perform the work of a deaconess in the Church?
The Church in which you are to be ordained confesses that the Holy Scriptures are the Word of God and are the norm of its faith and life. We accept, teach, and confess the Apostles', the Nicene, and the Athanasian Creeds. We	The Church in which you will serve confesses that the Holy Scriptures are the Word of God and are the norm of its faith and life. We accept, teach, and confess the Apostles', the Nicene, and the Athanasian Creeds. We also

Ordination	*Setting Apart of a Deaconess*
also acknowledge the Lutheran Confessions as true witnesses and faithful expositions of the Holy Scriptures. Will you therefore preach and teach in accordance with the Holy Scriptures and these creeds and confessions?	acknowledge the Lutheran Confessions as true witnesses and faithful expositions of the Holy Scriptures. Will you serve in accordance with the Holy Scriptures and these creeds and confessions?
Will you be diligent in your study of the Holy Scriptures and in your use of the means of grace? Will you pray for God's people, nourish them with the Word and the Holy Sacraments, and lead them by your own example in faithful service and holy living?	Will you be diligent in your study of the Holy Scriptures and faithful in your use of the means of grace and in prayer?
Will you give faithful witness in the world, that God's love may be known in all that you do? (pp. 193-94)	Will you witness in word and deed, and by your own example encourage God's people in faithful service and holy living? (p. 211)

The prayers are similar to those in Ordination. To underscore the parallel with ordination the optional hymn before the thanksgiving could be *"Veni Creator Spiritus"* (472, 473), the hymn-prayer traditionally associated with the invocation of the Holy Spirit.

The beginning of the thanksgiving ⟨540⟩ emphasizes service, by following the pattern of Christ, making reference to Phil. 2:7 and Matt. 20:26 (Luke 22:24-27; Mark 10:42-45), and acknowledging the variety of ministries in the church.

The candidate kneels for the thanksgiving ⟨540-41⟩ and for the statement of committal of office which follows. The two actions are separated in this rite for clarity; in *Occasional Services* (1962) they were joined:

> The office of Deaconess is now committed unto you, and by the laying on of hands you are set apart for this service in the Church: In the Name of the Father, and of the Son, and of the Holy Ghost.[76]

The new deaconess then stands for the giving of the cross—among Lutherans the traditional emblem of the deaconess. The language of the bestowal is similar to that of the previous books, but with an emphasis on the resurrection as well as the death of Christ.

---

76. *Occasional Services* (1962), p. 104.

Common Service Book	Occasional Services (1962)	Occasional Services (1982)
Receive and wear this Cross, a symbol of your office of Deaconess. Be not ashamed to confess the faith of Christ crucified and ever bear in your heart the remembrance of His love Who died on the Cross for you.	Receive and wear this Cross, symbol of your office of Deaconess. Be not ashamed to confess the faith of Christ crucified and ever to bear in your heart the remembrance of his love who died on the Cross for you.	Receive and wear this cross as a sign of your calling to serve the Lord and his people. Confess your faith in the risen Christ, and bear in your heart the love of him who died on the cross for you.

Where customary, a verse of Scripture selected for the deaconess is read by the head of the deaconess community and is thus given to the new deaconess.

Again, as in Ordination, the congregation is questioned about its intention to help support and honor the deaconess. The consecration of the deaconess is not dependent upon the reception by the congregation any more than the ordination of a pastor is dependent upon the reaction of the congregation (see Ezek. 3:16–21; 33:1–16).

The support having been pledged, the deaconess may kneel for the blessing (Heb. 13:20–21). The "fourth century prayer" ⟨542⟩ given in the notes on "The Service in Detail" is from the *Apostolic Constitutions* of ca. 380 and is perhaps therefore to be preferred to the blessing from Hebrews 13 which is used frequently elsewhere.

The deaconess then stands, and the peace is shared by all.

Development of the Rite
Setting Apart/Consecration
of a Deaconess

General Synod (1900)	Occasional Services (1930)	Occasional Services (1962)	Occasional Services (1982)
(The Setting Apart of Deaconesses)	(Order for the Consecration of a Deaconess)	(Order for the Setting Apart of a Deaconess)	(The Setting Apart of a Deaconess)
	Invocation	Invocation	
	Introit	Introit	

Development of the Rite (continued)
Setting Apart/Consecration
of a Deaconess

General Synod (1900)	*Occasional Services* (1930)	*Occasional Services* (1962)	*Occasional Services* (1982)
(The Setting Apart of Deaconesses)	(Order for the Consecration of a Deaconess)	(Order for the Setting Apart of a Deaconess)	(The Setting Apart of a Deaconess)
	Collect	Collect	Prayer of the day
			First lesson
			Psalm
	Epistle	Epistle	Second lesson
	Gradual	Gradual	Verse
	Gospel	Gospel	Gospel
	Creed	Creed	
	Hymn	Hymn	Sermon
After the Sermon	Sermon	Sermon	Hymn of the day
	Offering	Offering	
or at Vespers after the hymn:	General thanksgiving, instead of the general prayer		
		Prayer of the church	
	Hymn	Hymn	
	Presentation	Presentation	Presentation
	Collect		
Address	Address with Rom. 16:1-2 1 Cor. 1:3-9	1 Cor. 12:4-6 Description of diaconate	1 Cor. 12:4-7 Description of diaconate
Examination	Examination	Examination	Examination
			The prayers
			(Hymn)
Laying on of hands	Laying on of hands	Laying on of hands	Thanksgiving and Laying on of hands

212

Development of the Rite (continued)
Setting Apart/Consecration
of a Deaconess

General Synod (1900)	Occasional Services (1930)	Occasional Services (1962)	Occasional Services (1982)
(The Setting Apart of Deaconesses)	(Order for the Consecration of a Deaconess)	(Order for the Setting Apart of a Deaconess)	(The Setting Apart of a Deaconess)
	Blessing	Blessing	
Magnificat			
Salutation and response			
Kyrie			
Our Father	Our Father	Our Father	
	Prayer from *Apostolic Constitutions*	Prayer from *Apostolic Constitutions*	
Four collects	Prayer		
(Hymn)			
	Blessing Heb. 13:20–21		
	Giving of cross	Giving of cross	Giving of cross
			Questions to congregation
Aaronic benediction		Blessing Heb. 13:20–21	Blessing Heb. 13:20–21
			or Prayer from *Apostolic Constitutions*
	Hymn		
			The peace
	Preface and Holy Communion	Preface and Holy Communion	

Comparison of Rites
Ordination of a Deacon

Roman Catholic	Lutheran (Setting Apart of a Deaconess)	Episcopal
		Collect
		Presentation
		Questions to candidate
		Questions to people
		Litany
		Collect for the day
		First lesson
		Psalm 84 or 119:33–40
		Epistle
Service of the Word through the Gospel		
		Gospel
		Sermon
	Hymn of the day	Creed
Calling of candidate		
Presentation	Presentation	
Election by bishop and consent of people		
Homily	Address	
(Commitment to celibacy)		
Examination	Examination	Examination
Promise of obedience		
Invitation to prayer and Litany of Saints	The prayers	
	(Hymn)	*"Veni Creator Spiritus"* or *"Veni Sancte Spiritus"*
Laying on of hands in silence	Laying on of hands during	Laying on of hands during
Prayer of consecration*	Thanksgiving	Prayer of consecration†

*The candidate kneels before the bishop. With his hands extended over the can-

Comparison of Rites (continued)
Ordination of a Deacon

ROMAN CATHOLIC	LUTHERAN (Setting Apart of a Deaconess)	EPISCOPAL
Investiture with stole and dalmatic	Giving of cross	Giving of Bible

---

didate, he sings the prayer of consecration or says it aloud.
Almighty God,
be present with us by your power.
You are the source of all honor,
you assign to each his rank,
you give to each his ministry.

You remain unchanged,
but you watch over all creation and make it new
through your Son, Jesus Christ, our Lord:
he is your Word, your power, and your wisdom.
You foresee all things in your eternal providence
and make due provision for every age.
You make the Church, Christ's body,
grow to its full stature as a new and greater temple.
You enrich it with every kind of grace
and perfect it with a diversity of members
to serve the whole body in a wonderful pattern of unity.

You established a threefold ministry of worship and service
for the glory of your name.
As ministers of your tabernacle you chose the sons of Levi
and gave them your blessing as their everlasting inheritance.
In the first days of your Church
under the inspiration of the Holy Spirit
the apostles of your Son appointed seven men of good repute
to assist them in the daily ministry,
so that they themselves might be more free for prayer and preaching.
By prayer and the laying on of hands
the apostles entrusted to those men the ministry of serving at tables.

Lord,
look with favor on this servant of yours,
whom we now dedicate to the office of deacon,
to minister at your holy altar.

Lord,
send forth upon him the Holy Spirit,
that he may be strengthened
by the gift of your sevenfold grace
to carry out faithfully the work of the ministry.

May he excel in every virtue:
in love that is sincere,
in concern for the sick and the poor,

Comparison of Rites (continued)
Ordination of a Deacon

ROMAN CATHOLIC	LUTHERAN (Setting Apart of a Deaconess)	EPISCOPAL
Presentation of Gospels		
	Questions to congregation	
	Blessing or prayer	
The peace	The peace	The peace

---

in unassuming authority,
in self-discipline,
and in holiness of life.
May his conduct exemplify your commandments
and lead your people to imitate his purity of life.
May he remain strong and steadfast in Christ,
giving to the world the witness of a pure conscience.
May he in this life imitate your Son,
who came, not to be served but to serve,
and one day reign with him in heaven.

We ask this through our Lord Jesus Christ, your Son,
who lives and reigns with you and the Holy Spirit,
one God, for ever and ever.

† O God, most merciful Father, we praise you for sending your Son Jesus Christ, who took on himself the form of a servant, and humbled himself, becoming obedient even to death on the cross. We praise you that you have highly exalted him, and made him Lord of all; and that, through him, we know that whoever would be great must be servant of all. We praise you for the many ministries in your Church, and for calling this your servant to the order of deacons.
Here the Bishop lays hands upon the head of the ordinand, and prays.
Therefore, Father, through Jesus Christ your Son, give your Holy Spirit to *N.;* fill *him* with grace and power, and make *him* a deacon in your Church.
The Bishop then continues
Make *him*, O Lord, modest and humble, strong and constant, to observe the discipline of Christ. Let *his* life and teaching so reflect your commandments, that through *him* many may come to know you and love you. As your Son came not to be served but to serve, may this deacon share in Christ's service, and come to the unending glory of him who, with you and the Holy Spirit, lives and reigns, one God, for ever and ever.

Marion Hatchett in his *Commentary on the American Prayer Book* observes that this prayer of consecration for the deacon "is similar to that of the South Indian and English proposed rites. It incorporates allusions to Phil. 2:5–11 and Luke 22:27 and phrases from the super populum of prior Anglican rites which had been derived from the ancient Roman prayer, thus restoring these phrases to their original use" (p. 527).

In the Orthodox church the ordination of a deacon takes place after the consecration of the holy gifts because the deacon does not celebrate the Eucharist but only serves at it.[77]

The candidate is brought to the bishop and kneels before the altar (on one knee "in token that the fullness of the sacred ministry is not conferred upon the Deacon but only a portion thereof").[78] While "Lord have mercy" is chanted, the bishop prays quietly:

O Lord our God, who by thy foreknowledge dost send down the fullness of the Holy Spirit upon those who are ordained by thine inscrutable power to be thy servitors, and to administer thy spotless Sacraments: Do thou, the same Sovereign Master, preserve also this man, whom thou hast been pleased to ordain, through me, by the Laying-on of Hands, to the service of the Diaconate, in all soberness of life, holding the mystery of the faith in a pure conscience. Vouchsafe unto him the grace which thou didst grant unto Stephen, thy first Martyr, whom, also, thou didst call to be the first in the work of thy ministry; and make him worthy to administer after thy good pleasure the degree which it hath seemed good to thee to confer upon him. For they who minister well prepare for themselves a good degree. And manifest him as wholly thy servant.

Then the bishop says aloud:

For thine are the kingdom and the power and the glory, of the Father, and of the Son, and of the Holy Spirit, now, and ever, and unto ages of ages. Amen.[79]

While the litany "In peace let us pray to the Lord" is sung, the bishop, his hand still on the head of the candidate, prays quietly:

O God our Saviour, who by thine incorruptible voice didst appoint unto thine Apostles the law of the Diaconate, and didst manifest the first Martyr, Stephen, to be of the same; and didst proclaim him the first who should exercise the office of a Deacon, as it is written in thy Holy Gospel: Whosoever desireth to be first among you, let him be your servant: Do thou, O Master of all men, fill also this thy servant, whom thou hast graciously permitted to enter upon the ministry of a Deacon, with all faith, and love, and power, and holiness, through the inspiration of thy holy and life-giving Spirit; for not through the Laying-on of my hands, but through the visitation of thy rich bounties, is grace bestowed upon thy worthy ones: That he, being devoid of sin, may stand blameless before thee in the terrible Day of Judgment, and receive the unfailing reward of thy promise.

---

77. *Service Book,* p. 605.
78. Ibid., p. 606.
79. Ibid., p. 312.

Then, aloud, the bishop exclaims:

> For thou art our God, and unto thee we do ascribe glory, to the Father, and
> to the Son, and to the Holy Spirit, now, and ever, and unto ages of ages.[80]

The new deacon then receives the stole on the left shoulder while "Axios!"
("Worthy!") is sung, and the Liturgy continues with the Lord's Prayer
and the breaking of the bread.

INSTALLATION OF A BISHOP
(*Occasional Services*, pp. 218–23)

Parallel Rites

Roman Catholic	Ordination of a Bishop, Ordination of Bishops (see also Reception of a Bishop in the Cathedral Church and Blessing of Pontifical Insignia), *Roman Pontifical*, vol. 1, pp. 217–54, 380–83.
Orthodox	The Order of Electing and Consecrating a Bishop, *Service Book*, pp. 323–31.
Episcopal	The Ordination of a Bishop, *Book of Common Prayer*, pp. 511–23.
	Recognition and Investiture of a Diocesan Bishop, Welcoming and Seating of a Bishop in the Cathedral, *Book of Occasional Services*, pp. 216–27.
Lutheran	Order for the Induction of a President, *Occasional Services* (1962), pp. 134–38.
	Order for the Induction of a President, *Occasional Services* (1930), pp. 137–41.
	Formulary for the Induction of the President and Vice-Presidents of Synod, *Lutheran Agenda*, pp. 195–97.
Methodist	The Order for the Consecration of Bishops, *Book of Worship*, pp. 53–58; *An Ordinal*, pp. 88–122.
Church of South India	The Consecration of Bishops, *Book of Common Worship*, pp. 173–79.

Purpose

In general North American Lutheran understanding, bishop is regarded

---

80. Ibid., pp. 313–14.

not as a rank but simply as an office that a pastor may hold. Therefore this service is not an ordination or consecration of the person elected bishop. The bishop does not kneel for the statement of bestowal of the office, nor is there a laying on of hands during that action. There is simply the permissive rubric (p. 222, not in the text of the service), "The presiding minister may lay his/her right hand on the head of the bishop" while the blessing (no. 9) is said. The service does, however, have obvious parallels with the forms for the ordination of a bishop in the various churches with an episcopal polity.

Characteristics

The structures of the Installation of a Bishop and the Installation of a Pastor are parallel, and both installation rites recall the structure of ordination.

Ordination	Installation of a Bishop	Installation of a Pastor
Hymn of the day	Hymn of the day	Hymn of the day
Presentation	Presentation	Presentation
Address	Address	Address
John 20:21–23	John 20:21–23	John 20:21–23
Matt. 28:18–20	Matt. 28:18–20	Matt. 28:18–20
	Acts 20:28	
1 Cor. 11:23–36		
		1 Tim. 4:12–16
	2 Tim. 2:15	
	2 Tim. 1:13–14	
Questions to candidate	Questions to candidate	Questions to candidate
The prayers		
"Come, Holy Ghost, Our Souls Inspire"		
Thanksgiving with the laying on of hands		
Presentation of stole		
Address		
Blessing (Heb. 13:20–21)		
Questions to congregation	Questions to congregation	Questions to congregation
	Bestowal of office	Bestowal of office

Ordination	Installation of a Bishop	Installation of a Pastor
	Blessing (Heb. 13:20–21)	Blessing (Heb. 13:20–21)
	The prayers	The prayers
	(Presentation of pectoral cross)	(Procession to or presentation of symbols of office)
Acclamation by people	Acclamation by people	Acclamation by people
The peace	The peace	The peace

Background

The development of this rite through the twentieth century in North America indicates the growing understanding of the role of oversight in the church as well as the overcoming, or outgrowing, of the prejudices of the immigrants from European churches. The 1918 *Common Service Book* made no provision for a rite of installation for the president of a synod. The person chosen simply took up his new job and began work. (Women were not ordained in those days.)

The 1930 *Occasional Services* provided an Order for the Induction of a President, and the 1962 *Occasional Services* followed with the Order for the Induction of a President "for the induction into office of a President of a Synod or District, or of a general ecclesiastical Body." The order had certain similarities to the Form of Ordaining or Consecrating a Bishop given in the 1928 American *Book of Common Prayer*. At the center of the action, the president-elect knelt before the officiating minister to receive the office but there was no laying on of hands. The language of the bestowal of the office was remarkably similar in the Episcopal and Lutheran orders:

Book of Common Prayer (1928)	*Occasional Services* (1962)
Receive the Holy Ghost for the Office and Work of a Bishop in the Church of God, now committed unto thee by the Imposition of our hands; In the Name of the Father, and of the Son, and of the Holy Ghost. Amen. And remember that thou stir up the grace of God, which is given thee by this	The Office of President of _____ is now committed unto you: In the Name of the Father, and of the Son, and of the Holy Ghost. Amen. Remember that thou stir up the gift of God which is in thee. For God hath not given us the spirit of fear, but of power, and of love,

Book of Common Prayer (1928)	*Occasional Services* (1962)
imposition of our hands; for God hath not given us the spirit of fear, but of power, and love, and soberness. (p. 558)	and of a sound mind. Amen. (pp. 136–37)

Occasional Services (1982) uses the title "bishop" rather than "president" because "bishop" is now in common use throughout the Lutheran churches in North America.

Survey of the Service

The Prayer of the Day for the Installation of a Bishop ⟨543⟩ was originally composed for the Day of St. Peter (June 29) in the 1549 *Book of Common Prayer*. In the 1662 Prayer Book a variant of it was included as the collect for the Consecration of a Bishop. The prayer (without the reference to St. Peter, as in the adaptation for the Consecration of a Bishop) was included in the *Common Service Book* as one of six collects for Apostles' Days and was included in the *Service Book and Hymnal* as the Collect for the Feast of St. Peter and St. Paul (June 29).

After the hymn of the day and the presentation, the presiding minister addresses the bishop-elect with five passages of Scripture. The first three (John 20:21–23; Matt. 28:18–20; Acts 20:28) have been used frequently in Lutheran ordination services; the first two are the first two passages used in the address in Ordination. The last two (2 Tim. 2:15 and 2 Tim. 1:13–14) are new selections.

The questions in the examination parallel those of Ordination:

Ordination	*Installation of a Bishop*
1. Will you assume this office?	1. Will you assume the office?
2. Will you preach and teach in accordance with the Scriptures, Creeds, and Confessions?	2. Will you discharge your duties in accordance with the Scriptures and Confessions in harmony with constitution?
3. Will you study Scripture, pray, nourish, lead?	3. Will you study Scripture, pray, nourish, lead?
4. Will you witness in the world?	4. Will you witness in the world?
	5. Will you guide, encourage, support pastors and congregations?

The concluding blessing is the same in Ordination and Installation of a Bishop:

> Almighty God, who has given you the will to do these things, graciously give you the strength and compassion to perform them.

In Ordination the examination leads to the prayers and to the ordination itself. However, since in contemporary North American Lutheran understanding the bishop-elect is not being ordained but is simply being installed in a new office, the direction of this service changes and the congregation is asked two questions to encourage its reception of the bishop-elect and their support of the new shepherd. The order of examination of the candidate followed by examination of the congregation is parallel to that of the Installation of a Pastor. Then, in both rites, following the questions, the office is committed to the candidate with similar formulas:

Installation of a Bishop	*Installation of a Pastor*
The office of bishop is now committed to you in the name of the Father, and of the Son, and of the Holy Spirit. Amen.	The office of _____ is now committed to you in the name of the Father, and of the Son, and of the Holy Spirit. Amen.

The new bishop may then kneel for the blessing from Heb. 13:20–21 (during which the presiding minister may lay the right hand—not both hands so as not to imply an ordination—on the head of the new bishop). The new bishop remains kneeling for the prayers.

At the conclusion of the prayers of intercession, a final admonition is given to the new bishop from 2 Tim. 1:6–7 (with the reference to "the laying on of my hands" deleted, since it does not apply): "Remember to rekindle the gift of God that is within you."

When a pectoral cross is given to the new bishop, the cross may be kept on a credence table until the time of its presentation (no. 12). At the conclusion of the prayers, a server or an assisting minister may bring the cross to the presiding minister, who places it around the bishop's neck and says:

> Receive this cross as a sign of your calling to serve the Lord and his people, and as an emblem of the office to which you have been elected.

It is perhaps curious that the emblem of a bishop among North American Lutherans is a pectoral cross (perhaps because some pastors choose to wear a pectoral cross also, and thus a cross does not necessarily imply a distinction between pastor and bishop, although it does elsewhere in

Lutheranism). In the Roman rite the three distinctive emblems of the bishop are the ring, the miter, and the pastoral staff (crozier). The ring is given with the words:

> Take this ring, the seal of your fidelity.
> With faith and love protect the bride of Christ his holy Church.

It is an apt concept so long as bishops are celibate. The miter is placed on the bishop's head in silence. The pastoral staff is given with these words:

> Take this staff as a sign of your pastoral office:
> keep watch over the whole flock
> in which the Holy Spirit has appointed you
> to shepherd in the Church of God.[81]

In the Episcopal rite the principal symbol of office to the bishop is the Bible as it is for the priest. The Bible is presented to the new bishop with these words:

> Receive the Holy Scriptures. Feed the flock of Christ committed to your charge, guard and defend them in his truth, and be a faithful steward of his holy Word and Sacraments.
> *After this other symbols of office may be given.*[82]

Before the presentation of the Bible, "the new Bishop is now vested according to the order of bishops," but the vesture of that rank is not specified to allow for varieties of practice within The Episcopal Church. In the *Book of Occasional Services* a rite is provided for Recognition and Investiture of a Diocesan Bishop in which reference is made to the option of giving a pastoral staff and to the required giving of a Bible. In both the Roman Catholic and Episcopal rites the investiture leads to the seating of the bishop in the chair designated for the bishop of the diocese (the *cathedra*).

In the Orthodox church, the consecration of a bishop is in three stages. First, there is the election, which includes the selection of the candidate and his nomination to the synod, accompanied by hymns and prayers. The second and third parts belong to the consecration itself and take place in the cathedral church. The second part of the rite is the examination of the faith of the candidate and elevation to the status of bishop-elect. It takes place at the vigil of the liturgy. The candidate recites three confessions of faith, the first of which is the Nicene Creed. After the third confession of faith, the presiding bishop blesses him:

---

81. *Roman Pontifical*, vol. 1, p. 233.
82. *Book of Common Prayer* (1979), p. 521.

> The grace of the Holy Spirit, through my humility, exalteth thee, most God-beloved Archimandrite (*or* Hiero-monk), *N.*, to be the Bishop-elect of the God-saved cities *N.N.*[83]

As always in the Orthodox rites, here and elsewhere, there is no direct declaration "I elevate you . . ." or "I ordain you . . ." or "I baptize you . . ." Rather, the Orthodox liturgy is more reticent and indirect and acts as a witness to what is being accomplished by the Holy Spirit. The participants watch what is being done in their midst by the holy and life-creating Spirit of God.

The bishop-elect then stands aside in the deacon's chapel or the chapel to the south of the altar, vested as a priest.

The consecration itself takes place during the Divine Liturgy, near the beginning of the service, after the singing of the "thrice holy" ("Holy God, holy mighty One, holy immortal One, have mercy on us").

> The Consecration takes place at this point because the Little Entrance typifies the coming to earth of the Lord incarnate, who suffered for us, and rose again, and was received up into heaven. Thereafter the Holy Spirit consecrated the first successors of the Saviour, and revealed them as enthroned and reigning with Christ. Therefore, when the Chief Bishop enters the Sanctuary, as it were heaven, with the other ecclesiastics, the candidate for Consecration is led thither, and the Sacrament of Laying-on of Hands is conferred upon him before they all take their places on the episcopal thrones . . . and thus he, also, becomes a throned Bishop, and sits with them as their equal.[84]

The bishop-elect is led to the bishops. The candidate kneels in the midst of the bishops, who take the Book of the Gospels and lay it open, with the writing downward, upon his head. The presiding bishop says:

> By the election and approbation of the most God-loving Bishops, and of all the consecrated Council, the grace divine, which always healeth that which is infirm, and completeth that which is wanting, through the laying-on of hands elevateth thee, the most God-loving Archimandrite (*or* Hiero-monk) *N.*, duly elected, to be the Bishop of the God-saved cities, *NN.* Wherefore let us pray for him, that the grace of the all-holy Spirit may come upon him.[85]

While the bishops hold the Book of the Gospels, the presiding bishop makes three crosses above the head of the one being consecrated, saying:

---

83. *Service Book,* p. 328.
84. Ibid., p. 607.
85. Ibid., p. 329.

In the name of the Father, and of the Son, and of the Holy Spirit, now and ever and unto ages of ages.

While the bishops lay their right hands on the bishop-elect's head, the presiding bishop says:

> O Master, Lord our God, who through thine all-laudable Apostle Paul hast established for us an ordinance of degrees and ranks, unto the service and divine celebration of thine august and all-spotless Mysteries upon thy holy Altar; first, Apostles, secondly, Prophets, thirdly, teachers: Do thou, the same Lord of all, who also hast graciously enabled this chosen person to come under the yoke of the Gospel and the dignity of a Bishop through the laying-on of hands of us, his fellow Bishops here present, strengthen him by the inspiration and power and grace of thy Holy Spirit, as thou didst strengthen thy holy Apostles and Prophets; as thou didst anoint Kings; as thou hast consecrated Bishops: And make his bishopric to be blameless; and adorning him with all dignity, present thou him holy, that he may be worthy to ask those things which are for the salvation of the people, and that thou mayest give ear unto him. For blessed is thy Name, and glorified thy Kingdom, of the Father, and of the Son, and of the Holy Spirit, now, and ever, and unto ages of ages. Amen.[86]

After a litany "In peace let us pray to the Lord" led by one of the consecrating bishops, the presiding bishop prays for the new bishop, who then is vested while the presiding bishop and choir sing "Axios!" ("Worthy!").[87] The liturgy continues with the Epistle. At the conclusion of the liturgy the new bishop receives the bishop's cassock, pectoral icon, mantle, and cowl, is led to his *kathedra*, and receives the pastoral staff *(posokh).*

Comparison of Rites
Installation/Ordination of a Bishop

ROMAN CATHOLIC (Ordination of Bishop)	LUTHERAN (Installation of Bishop)	EPISCOPAL (Ordination of Bishop)
		Collect
		Presentation
		Testimonials of election
		Promise of conformity

---

86. Ibid., pp. 329–30.
87. Ibid., p. 607.

Comparison of Rites (continued)
Installation/Ordination of a Bishop

ROMAN CATHOLIC (Ordination of Bishop)	LUTHERAN (Installation of Bishop)	EPISCOPAL (Ordination of Bishop)
		Consent of people
		Litany
		Kyries
Liturgy of the Word	Liturgy of the Word	Collect for the Day
		Old Testament
		Epistle
Gospel	Gospel	Gospel
	Sermon	Sermon
"Veni Creator Spiritus"	Hymn of the day	
Presentation	Presentation	
Apostolic letter	Address	
Consent of the people		
Homily		
Examination	Examination	Examination
	Questions to congregation	
		Creed
		"Veni Creator Spiritus" or *"Veni Sancte Spiritus"*
Litany of Saints		Silent prayer
Laying on of hands in silence	Bestowal of the office	Laying on of hands and Prayer of Consecration*

---

*God and Father of our Lord Jesus Christ, Father of mercies and God of all comfort, dwelling on high but having regard for the lowly, knowing all things before they come to pass: We give you thanks that from the beginning you have gathered and prepared a people to be heirs of the covenant of Abraham, and have raised up prophets, kings, and priests, never leaving your temple untended. We praise you also that from the creation you have graciously accepted the ministry of those whom you have chosen.

The Presiding Bishop and other Bishops now lay their hands upon the head of the bishop-elect, and say together
Therefore, Father, make N. a bishop in your Church. Pour out upon *him* the power of your princely Spirit, whom you bestowed upon your beloved Son Jesus

Comparison of Rites (continued)
Installation/Ordination of a Bishop

ROMAN CATHOLIC	LUTHERAN	EPISCOPAL
(Ordination of Bishop)	(Installation of Bishop)	(Ordination of Bishop)
	Blessing	
Book of the Gospels		
Prayer of Consecration†	The prayers	

Christ, with whom he endowed the apostles, and by whom your Church is built up in every place, to the glory and unceasing praise of your Name.

The Presiding Bishop continues
To you, O Father, all hearts are open; fill, we pray, the heart of this your servant whom you have chosen to be a bishop in your Church, with such love of you and of all the people, that *he* may feed and tend the flock of Christ, and exercise without reproach the high priesthood to which you have called *him*, serving before you day and night in the ministry of reconciliation, declaring pardon in your Name, offering the holy gifts, and wisely overseeing the life and work of the Church. In all things may *he* present before you the acceptable offering of a pure, and gentle, and holy life; through Jesus Christ your Son, to whom, with you and the Holy Spirit, be honor and power and glory in the Church, now and for ever.

†God the Father of our Lord Jesus Christ,
Father of mercies and God of all consolation,
you dwell in heaven,
yet look with compassion on all that is humble.
You know all things before they come to be;
by your gracious word
you have established the plan of your Church.
From the beginning
you chose the descendents of Abraham to be your holy nation.
You established rulers and priests,
and did not leave your sanctuary without ministers to serve you.
From the creation of the world
you have been pleased to be glorified
by those whom you have chosen.

The following part of the prayer is recited by all the consecrating bishops,
with hands joined:
So now pour out upon this chosen one
that power which is from you,
the governing Spirit
whom you gave to your beloved Son, Jesus Christ,
the Spirit given by him to the holy apostles,
who founded the Church in every place to be your temple
for the unceasing glory and praise of your name.

Then the principal consecrator continues alone:
Father, you know all hearts.
You have chosen your servant for the office of bishop.
May he be a shepherd to your holy flock,

227

Comparison of Rites (continued)
Installation/Ordination of a Bishop

ROMAN CATHOLIC	LUTHERAN	EPISCOPAL
(Ordination of Bishop)	(Installation of Bishop)	(Ordination of Bishop)
Anointing Bishop's head		
Presentation of Gospels		
Investiture	Presentation of pectoral cross	Vesting the bishop
		Presentation of Bible
	Acclamation	Acclamation
Seating the Bishop		
The peace	The peace	The peace

INSTALLATION OF A PASTOR
(Occasional Services, pp. 224–31)

Parallel Rites

Episcopal

Letter of Institution of a Minister, Celebration of a New Ministry, *Book of Common Prayer*, pp. 557, 558–65.

Reaffirmation of Ordination Vows, *Book of Occasional Services*, pp. 212–15.

Lutheran

Order for the Installation of a Pastor, *Occasional Services* (1962), pp. 125–28.

---

and a high priest blameless in your sight,
ministering to you night and day;
may he always gain the blessing of your favor
and offer the gifts of your holy Church.
Through the Spirit who gives the grace of high priesthood
grant him the power
to forgive sins as you have commanded,
to assign ministries as you have decreed,
and to loose every bond by the authority which you gave to your apostles.
May he be pleasing to you by his gentleness and purity of heart,
presenting a fragrant offering to you,
through Jesus Christ, your Son,
through whom glory and power and honor are yours
with the Holy Spirit
in your holy Church
now and for ever.

Both prayers of consecration are very close to the prayer of Hippolytus for the ordination of a bishop, as is the Orthodox prayer also.

The Order for the Installation of a Minister, *Lutheran Agenda*, pp. 110–16.

Order for the Installation of a Pastor, *Common Service Book* (text ed.), pp. 460–63.

The Installation of a Chaplain, *Occasional Services* (1962), pp. 205–7.

Presbyterian   A Service for Ordination and Installation, *Worshipbook*, pp. 89–95.

Purpose

This service is to recognize and celebrate the beginning of a person's ministry in a particular place or particular role. The Installation of a Pastor is intended to include the installation of chaplains in the military services, hospitals, colleges, and schools.

Characteristics

Again, the parallels with the service of Ordination are to be noted:

Ordination	*Installation*
Hymn of the day	Hymn of the day
Presentation	Presentation and certification
Address with scriptural passages	Address with scriptural passages
Questions to ordinand	Questions to pastor
	Questions to congregation
	Committal of office
	Blessing
The prayers	The prayers
"Come, Holy Ghost, Our Souls Inspire"	
Thanksgiving with laying on of hands	
Giving of stole	Statements by font, pulpit, altar *or* Giving of instruments of office
Address with scriptural passages	
Blessing	
Questions to congregation	
Acclamation by congregation	Acclamation by congregation
The peace	The peace

229

Background

In churches which assign pastors to their duties such as the Roman Catholic and Methodist churches, there is no installation, no ratification of the ministry on the part of the congregation.

In churches which operate with a call system, in which the congregation has a voice in the selection of a pastor, a service of installation is customary. By ordination one enters the ministry of the Christian church ritually and in fact. By installation one ritually becomes responsible for a particular focus of the church's ministry — a congregation, a hospital, a school, a branch of military service. The actual responsibility for such ministry usually will have been undertaken some time earlier.

Development of the Rite
Installation of a Pastor

General Synod (1881)	Church Book (1892)	General Synod (1900)	Common Service Book (1918)	Occasional Services (1962)	Occasional Services (1982)
"A religious service" recommended but not actually required		Religious service required			
Sermon		Sermon*			Sermon
					Hymn of Day
	Certification of call	Testimonial to election	Certification of call	Certification of call	Certification of call
	Address—	Address— John 20:21–23	Address— John 20:21–23	Address— John 20:21–23	Address— John 20:21–23
	Matt. 28:19–20	Matt. 28:19–20	Matt. 28:19–20		Matt. 28:18–20
	1 Tim. 3:1–7	1 Tim. 3:1–7	1 Tim. 4:12–16	1 Tim. 4:12–16	1 Tim. 4:12–16
	Acts 20:28–31	Acts 20:28			
Examination of pastor	Acceptance by pastor	Acceptance by pastor	Acceptance by pastor	Acceptance by pastor	Promises by pastor
Examination of people			Acceptance by people	Acceptance by people	Promises by people
Declaration that A.B. is pastor	Installation and blessing	Declaration	Declaration	Declaration	Committal of office
	Address to congregation— Eph. 6:4 1 Thess. 5:12–13	Address to congregation— 1 Thess. 5:12–13 Eph. 6:4			

*If the candidate is to preach, the installation precedes the sermon.

Development of the Rite (continued)
Installation of a Pastor

General Synod (1881)	Church Book (1892)	General Synod (1900)	Common Service Book (1918)	Occasional Services (1962)	Occasional Services (1982)
	Luke 10:7 1 Cor. 9:11 Heb. 13:17	Luke 10:7 Heb. 13:17			
					Blessing Heb. 13:20–21
Hymn					
Charge to pastor					
Charge to people					
"Singing"					
				Salutation	
Prayer	Prayer	Prayer	Prayer for pastor for people	Prayer for pastor for people	The prayers
	Our Father	Our Father	Our Father	Our Father	
					Symbols of office
	Hymn of praise or doxology	Hymn of praise or doxology			
			Blessing John 15:16	Blessing John 15:16	
	Hymn of praise or doxology	Hymn of praise or doxology	Hymn	Hymn	
Benediction by new pastor	Benediction by new pastor	Benediction by new pastor	Blessing by new pastor	Blessing by new pastor	
Welcome by heads of families					Acclamation by people
					The peace

Survey of the Service

The prayer of the day ⟨543⟩—the same as for the Installation of a Bishop—is from the *LBW* (Min. Ed., p. 109) for "Ministers of the Word" (194). It originated in the 1549 *Book of Common Prayer* for St. Peter's Day (June 29) and was incorporated into the *Common Service Book* as one of the collects for the Apostles' Days and into the *Service Book and Hymnal* for the Feast of St. Peter and St. Paul (June 29).

The 1979 *Book of Common Prayer* appoints the same collect for Ordination and for the Celebration of a New Ministry: the prayer which the

Service Book and Hymnal gave as no. 1 under Collects and Prayers (music ed., p. 218). It is from the Gelasian Sacramentary, translated by William Bright in *Ancient Collects* (p. 92).

It is perhaps desirable to select a hymn of the day other than *"Veni Creator Spiritus"* (472, 473) so as not to suggest that installation is a second ordination or a rite comparable to ordination.

The rather stilted language of the request for certification has been in Lutheran use through four books. In the *Forms for Ministerial Acts* of the General Synod (1900):

> Dearly Beloved: We have been duly authorized to install *N.N.*, our esteemed brother and fellow laborer in the gospel, as Pastor of this Congregation. Before so doing we need to be assured that he has been regularly elected, and now ask for the proper testimonials.[88]

The *Common Service Book* (1918) has the officiating minister say:

> Dearly Beloved: Having been authorized to install, as Pastor of this Congregation, the Reverend *N.N.*, our fellow-laborer in the Gospel of Christ, I now ask for the certification of his call.[89]

The *Occasional Services* (1962) has the officiating minister say:

> Dearly Beloved: Having been authorized by the Church to install our fellow-laborer in the Gospel as Pastor of this Parish (*or,* Congregation), I now ask for the certification of his call.[90]

That flat formula, however, is hardly clearer than the language of the *Church Book* (1892):

> Dearly Beloved! We have been called to install *N.N.*, our esteemed brother and fellow-laborer in the Gospel, as Pastor of this Parish. But we need first to be assured that he has been regularly chosen to become your Minister, and therefore now ask for the proper testimonials.

A statement by the representative of the congregation may seem sufficient, but those who argue for the retention of a request by the presiding minister point to its reference to the authorization by the church. This helps to overcome the notion that the congregation acts independently of the larger church.

---

88. *Forms for Ministerial Acts* published by the General Synod of the Evangelical Lutheran Church in the United States (Philadelphia: Lutheran Publication Society, 1900), p. 79.

89. *Common Service Book,* text ed. (1919), p. 460.

90. *Occasional Services* (1962), p. 125.

The address to the pastor uses texts traditional in Lutheran rites of installation. The questions to the pastor (and to the congregation) are elaborated in this rite (a return to the style of the 1881 General Synod liturgy) to clarify to the pastor and the congregation the tasks that a pastor is called to perform. This can prevent unrealistic and incorrect expectations on the part of the pastor and the congregation.

If the presentation of the symbols of office to the pastor by representatives of the congregation (no. 12) is to be effective, the rubric directing movement from place to place must be observed. Merely to read the lines while the ministers remain in one place is not only far less effective, it is confusing to the congregation who can have no idea of why the lines are being said.

The presiding minister and the pastor (led by the processional cross, perhaps flanked by torches) may go to the font. A layperson, walking up from the congregation to make clear the representative function of this action, meets them there, makes the presentation, says the line provided, and returns to the congregation.

The presiding minister and the pastor, led by the processional cross and torches, go to the pulpit. A layperson, coming from the congregation, meets them there, makes the presentation, says the words provided, and returns to the congregation.

The cross leads the presiding minister and the pastor to the altar, where a representative of the congregation meets them, makes the presentation, says the words provided, and returns to the congregation. (The text of the statement at the altar is perhaps unfortunate and may be misleading for the pastor leads worship not only from the altar, but from the font and the pulpit as well. The altar is the table on which the Holy Communion is celebrated: that is part of worship but not all of it.)

An alternative procedure is for the pastor to receive symbols of the pastoral office from the presiding minister. This procedure is perhaps less desirable, for the call to minister in this place comes not from the jurisdiction represented by the presiding minister but from the congregation. Nonetheless, in certain situations the alternative practice may be preferable. Since the pastor cannot at once hold all of the items being presented, a server should bring them one by one from a credence table to the presiding minister who gives each to the pastor, who then gives each to another server who takes it to the appropriate place; a baptismal shell is received and placed on or by the font; a Bible is received and placed on the pulpit; a chalice and paten are received and placed on the altar in preparation for the Offertory.

The presentation of symbols is appropriate only when the ministry to which the pastor is being installed is directly one of Word and Sacrament.

The presiding minister and the pastor remain before the congregation for the welcome by a representative of the congregation. This representative should come from the congregation to welcome the pastor and should not be a vested assisting minister or a member of the choir.

This welcome may be expressed briefly in words or it may be simply a handshake or an embrace. (The custom of the congregation and not the gender of the new pastor should determine whether a handshake or an embrace is suitable.)

Following the welcome, the newly installed pastor assumes the role of presiding minister and greets the congregation with the peace. During the remainder of the service, the installing pastor may serve as an assisting minister or, perhaps better, so that lay people from the congregation may assist in the Holy Communion, the installing pastor may move to a chair near the altar and remain there for the rest of the service.

The rubrics (p. 229) indicate how this order may be adapted when a pastor who had resigned or had been removed from the clergy roster is reinstated or when a pastor-elect who had been ordained by another denomination is about to begin ministry in the Lutheran church. (Of the churches cooperating in the development of the 1982 *Occasional Services* only the Lutheran Church in America at this writing has a policy of reordination, in which case the installation order need not be modified to accommodate one ordained in another communion.)

One who is being reinstated affirms God's call and declares a willingness to resume the duties of the office. One entering the Lutheran ministry subscribes publicly to the Scriptures, the Creeds, and the Lutheran Confessions.

The Episcopal Church in the *Book of Occasional Services* provides for the Reaffirmation of Ordination Vows, intended "for use at a celebration of the Eucharist upon an occasion when the clergy are gathered together with the bishop."[91] The rite may be used on Maundy Thursday when it has been traditional for the clergy (priests and deacons) of a diocese with their bishop to reaffirm their ordination vows. This often takes place at the Mass of Chrism and "should be done at a celebration of the Eucharist other than the Proper Liturgy of the day."[92] The rite—adapted as necessary—"may also be used on the occasion of the reception of a priest from another Communion or of a restoration to the ministry."[93]

---

91. *Book of Occasional Services* (1979), p. 212.
92. Ibid.
93. Ibid., pp. 214, 212.

Adaptation of the Rite
Installation of a Pastor

Installation	*Reinstatement*	*Reception Beginning Ministry in the Lutheran Church*
Hymn of the day	Hymn of the day	Hymn of the day
	N., having been ordained a pastor in the Church of Jesus Christ by _____, has been examined and approved by _____ to resume the ministry of Word and Sacrament.	N., having been ordained a pastor in the Church of Jesus Christ, has been examined and approved by _____ for service in the ministry of Word and Sacrament.
Certification of call	Certification of call	Certification of call
Address	Address	Address
	Before Almighty God and in the presence of this congregation, I ask you: Will you affirm that the Lord has called you to the ministry of Word and Sacrament, and will you resume the duties of this office? *I will, and I ask God to help me.*	The Church in which you are to minister confesses that the Holy Scriptures are the Word of God and are the norm of its faith and life. We accept, teach, and confess the Apostles', Nicene, and Athanasian Creeds. We also acknowledge the Lutheran Confessions as true witnesses and faithful expositions of the Holy Scriptures. Is this your confession?
Questions of pastor	Questions of pastor	Questions of pastor
Questions of people	Questions of people	Questions of people
Committal of office	Committal of office	Committal of office
Blessing	Blessing	Blessing
Prayers	Prayers	Prayers
Symbols of office	Symbols of office	Symbols of office
Welcome and acclamation	Welcome and acclamation	Welcome and acclamation
The peace	The peace	The peace

Comparison of Rites
Installation of a Bishop/Pastor

LUTHERAN (Installation of a Bishop)	LUTHERAN (Installation of a Pastor)	EPISCOPAL (Celebration of a New Ministry)
Hymn of the day	Hymn of the day	(hymn/psalm/anthem)
		1. The Institution
	Certification of call	
Presentation	Presentation	Presentation
Address	Address	
Examination	Examination	Examination
Questions to people	Questions to people	Questions to people
		Litany
		Collect
		Old Testament Lesson
		Psalm
		Epistle
		Gospel
		Sermon
		Hymn
Committal of office	Committal of office	2. The Induction
Blessing	Blessing	
Prayers	Prayers	
Giving of pectoral cross	Giving of symbols	Giving of symbols
		Prayer
	Greeting	Greeting
The peace	The peace	The peace

INSTALLATION TO A REGIONAL OR CHURCHWIDE OFFICE
(*Occasional Services*, pp. 232–34)

Parallel Rites

Lutheran

The Installation of a Pastor Called to the General Work of the Church is listed (p. 157) in the contents of the first printing of *Occasional Services* (1962), but such a service does not appear in the text of the book. Instead, there is a "Prayer at the Installation of One Called to General Service in the Church" on p. 214. The error was subsequently corrected by the deletion of the entry in the table of contents.

Purpose

This service is for the installation of such people as district deans, secretaries, and others "whose election or appointment . . . does not constitute a call or a major occupational commitment." It is therefore for the installation of people to a part-time office or function. It is not for congregational officers nor for full-time church workers; for these two kinds of workers two other services are provided.

Those called to the general work of the church are installed with the order for the Installation of a Pastor.

Characteristics

This office is simple in format — a reading from Romans 12, an optional description of the duties of the office, a question of the person elected and of the assembly, the committal of office in the name of the Holy Trinity, a prayer ⟨544⟩ (newly composed) for grace and strength, the blessing from Heb. 13:20–21. When used as a separate service, additional prayers may be said and the service concludes with the blessing from Morning Prayer: "The Lord Almighty bless us and direct our days and our deeds in his peace." It is simple in form and general in language since it is designed to serve a variety of offices.

Background

The Lutheran church in North America seems to be unique in providing such an order. It has become part of Lutheran liturgical piety to expect a rite to mark the beginning of every office and function within the church at all levels. This is not necessarily a development to be applauded.

It may betray a formalism which relies upon the performance of a rite to begin a work and thus to insure that the work will be pleasing to God. This formalism may therefore reveal a deficient understanding of Holy Baptism, which is the basic commissioning service for Christian people.

COMMISSIONING OF MISSIONARIES
(*Occasional Services*, pp. 204–9)

Parallel Rites

Roman Catholic	The *Sacramentary* provides Propers for a Mass For the Spread of the Gospel, pp. 894–95.
Episcopal	The *Book of Common Prayer* provides Propers for a Eucharist "For the Mission of the Church," pp. 257, 930.
Lutheran	Order for Sending Forth of a Missionary, *Occasional Services* (1962), pp. 129–33. Order for the Commissioning of a Foreign Missionary, *Occasional Services* (1930), pp. 128–33. The Order for the Ordination and Commissioning of a Missionary, *Lutheran Agenda*, pp. 126–31.
Methodist	An Office for the Commissioning of Missionaries and Deaconesses, *Book of Worship*, pp. 330–33.

Purpose

This rite is used to send a missionary off to the mission field. It is in effect a kind of itinerarium (prayer before travel) and service of Godspeed. An installation is often held in the place of ministry once the missionary has arrived.

This rite is not limited to the commissioning of those missionaries who are being sent abroad. It is also appropriate for those missionaries who remain in North America for their work.

Characteristics

There is very little ecumenical precedent to follow in forming such a service. The Lutheran church and the United Methodist Church appear to be alone in providing such a rite. Its use, however, has for decades been a Lutheran custom, based on the practice described in the New Testament (Acts 13:3). The additional Orders and Offices of 1930 which supplemented the occasional services in the *Common Service Book* of 1918 introduced the service.

The rite shows the changing understanding of the role of missionaries and of the culture of other nations and peoples. This rite, it should be noted, is less condescending toward others than its predecessor in the 1962 book. In *Occasional Services* (1962) the third prayer after the laying on of hands is:

> O God of all the nations of the earth, remember the multitudes of the heathen, who, though created in thine image, are ignorant of thy love; and, according to the propitiation of thy Son Jesus Christ, grant that by the prayers and labors of thy holy Church they may be delivered from all superstition and unbelief, and brought to worship thee; through him whom thou hast sent to be our salvation, the Resurrection and the Life of all the faithful, the same thy Son Jesus Christ our Lord.[94]

These three prayers in the 1962 rite correspond to the three prayers used in the 1930 rite to replace the General Prayer. However, the third prayer in the 1930 rite is less self-righteous:

> O Lord, make ready the Way in the dark lands, in the hearts which know Thee not; that those who, consecrated to the fulfilling of Thy last command, are carrying the message of Thy Cross to the souls of men, may, constantly aided and uplifted by Thee, labor to the enriching of Thy great harvest: Who livest and reignest with the Father, in the unity of the Holy Ghost, One God, world without end.[95]

Increasingly it is urged by many that the work of evangelization should be carried on by indigenous Christians. In areas in which Christianity is growing most, North American missionaries may have a limited role.

Few churches abroad are now considered "younger churches"[96] to be nurtured and directed by foreigners. Some of those churches in fact now send missionaries to the countries which first evangelized them. The flow of the gospel is reversing itself. The churches established by earlier generations of missionaries have their own leaders and are developing forms of Christianity rooted in local cultures rather than in the culture from which the missionaries came.

Rather than winning converts to Christianity, the primary task of many missionaries is now to render other forms of assistance—agricul-

---

94. *Occasional Services* (1962), p. 131.
95. *Occasional Services* (1930), p. 131.
96. See the Prayer of the Church in the *Service Book and Hymnal,* music ed., p. 7:

> According to thy merciful goodness, O God, extend thy saving health to the younger Churches. Grant that they may rejoice in a rich harvest of souls for thy kingdom. Support them in times of trial and weakness, and make them steadfast, abounding in the work of the Lord.
> *We beseech thee to hear us, good Lord.*

tural and health care, training indigenous pastors to work under the direction of a native church leader.

The need for ecumenical cooperation has long been recognized in the mission fields, often ahead of ecumenical progress at home.

Development of the Rite
Commissioning of Missionaries

Occasional Services (1930)	Lutheran Agenda	Occasional Services (1962)	Occasional Services (1982)
Introit		Introit	
Collect		Collect	
Epistle: 1 Cor. 1:18–31		Epistle: 1 Cor. 1:18–31	
Gospel: Matt. 28:18–20		Gospel: Matt. 28:18–20	
Sermon		Sermon	Sermon
			Hymn of the day
Prayers			
Hymn	Offering	(Hymn)	
Certification of call and presentation	Address— Matt. 28:18–20 Eph. 4:10–12	Address	Address
			Lesson: Rom. 12:4–8 1 Pet. 4:8–11 Matt. 20:25–28 Acts 13:2–3
Acceptance by missionary	Examination	Acceptance by missionary	Examination
			Questions to people
			Prayer
Laying on of hands*	Laying on of right hand	Laying on of hands†	(Laying on of right hand)

*In the Name and Faith of Jesus Christ, Amen.
N.N. is sent forth as His ambassador and witness.
The Father in Heaven guard and keep you in His love, enrich and strengthen you with the grace of His dear Son, comfort and uphold you with the presence of His Holy Spirit. Amen.

†In the Name of the Father, and of the Son, and of the Holy Ghost. Amen. The ser-

Development of the Rite (continued)
Commissioning of Missionaries

Occasional Services (1930)	Lutheran Agenda	Occasional Services (1962)	Occasional Services (1982)
Blessing	Blessing		
Our Father		Our Father	
Prayer	Prayer	Prayers	The prayers
Blessing	Blessing 1 Pet. 5:2–4	Blessing	
Hymn		(Hymn)	
Holy Communion		Holy Communion	The peace

Survey of the Service

While other settings are permitted, the Commissioning of Missionaries is most appropriately set within the Holy Communion. An action as important to the proclamation of the gospel as this seems to deserve to be set within the church's principal act of worship.

Rubric (no. 2) is designed to allow for the varied practices of the several cooperating churches, for the practices of calling, sending, and commissioning missionaries are not uniform.

It is desirable that the same person serve as presiding minister throughout the service. Those who are newly commissioned may assist in the Holy Communion as assisting ministers when that seems desirable and appropriate. It may be most natural, however, for the missionaries to be the recipients of this service rather than participants in its ministration.

The families of the missionaries may stand with them and answer the questions addressed to the missionaries (no. 6). Care must be taken, however, not to require or coerce the participation of unwilling members of the family or of those young persons who have had little say in the decision to accept a call to the mission field.

The first two questions are similar to the two questions asked of the candidate in the 1962 rite and close to the 1930 rite before it:

---

vant of God, *N.N.,* is sent forth as his ambassador and witness.
Almighty God, our heavenly Father, guide and keep you in all your ways, and enable you to spread abroad the riches of his grace in Christ, by the power and comfort of his Holy Spirit. Amen.

Occasional Services (1930)	Occasional Services (1962)	Occasional Services (1982)
Are you ready to take upon you this ministry?	Are you ready to take upon you this ministry and to serve the Church in accordance with its teaching and practice?	Will you accept this commission and carry it out in accordance with the Holy Scriptures?
Will you in all things and in all your ways strive to acquit yourself an ambassador and servant of Jesus Christ? (p. 132)	Will you in all things live as becometh an ambassador and servant of Jesus Christ? (p. 130)	Will you endeavor in all things to conduct yourselves as is fitting for ambassadors and servants of Jesus Christ? (p. 205)

The third question—"Will you be faithful, understanding, and loving to the people among whom you will live and work?"—reflects an appreciation of the people to whom the missionary is sent. This recognition has been absent from earlier rites.

The fourth question—"Will you serve under the assignment and jurisdiction of the church to which you are sent?"—is to be omitted when it is not relevant, as the line in the left margin indicates.

The standard formula is used at the conclusion of the questions: "Almighty God, who has given you the will to do these things, graciously give you the strength and compassion to perform them." (See Ordination, p. 194; Setting Apart of a Deaconess, p. 212; Installation of a Bishop, p. 220; Installation of a Pastor, p. 226.)

The people, who are understood to represent the whole church and to speak for it, should be made aware of their representative function by means of an announcement, an explanation in the service leaflet, or instruction in the sermon. The question to the congregation asks their help, prayer, and support for those who are sent as missionaries.

The most noticeable difference between the 1982 rite and its predecessors is that the 1982 rite does not require kneeling or the laying on of hands. The intention of this change is to avoid the suggestion that this rite is an ordination. The candidates, however, may kneel, and in the context of prayer the presiding minister may lay the right hand upon the head of the missionaries.

The prayer (no. 8) has a triune shape, blessing in order the Father, the Son, and the Holy Spirit for the work of salvation, freedom, and power. The presiding minister, perhaps with the gesture of the laying on of the right hand, says the blessing. Again, the prayer is other-directed. It speaks not of bringing the people to whom the missionary is sent into the church and of winning converts but of showing God's love to them. The emphasis is less on result and more on the process. The missionary task of the church is to reflect and emulate the self-giving love of Christ without counting the cost or the benefits to the giver.

A notable prayer from the 1930 and 1962 rites has not been carried into the 1982 rite but may be incorporated into the prayers:

> Almighty God, heavenly Father, who through thy Son Jesus Christ hast given commandment unto thy people to go into all the world and preach the Gospel to every creature: Grant us a ready will to obey thy word; and, as we have entered into the labors of other men, help us to serve thee, that others may enter into our labors; and that we with them, and they with us, may attain unto everlasting life; through the same Jesus Christ, thy Son, our Lord.[97]

(The phrase "the labors of other men" could become simply "the labors of others.") The thought is another example of humility in the service of God. It recognizes our debt to past generations and our responsibility to future generations with the hope that together we all may one day rejoice in the kingdom of God.

---

97. *Occasional Services* (1962), p. 130. See also Hymn 248 in the *Service Book and Hymnal,* "Our Father, by whose servants/ Our house was built of old," stanza 3.

7

DEDICATIONS
AND BLESSINGS

INTRODUCTION

Rites of dedication, blessing, and consecration assist Christians in acknowledging God's creative and redemptive purpose in the world. Such rites have their roots in Hebrew worship.[1] At the beginning of the Christian movement, "thanksgiving" was the dominant term in rites of blessing, based on the Hebrew *Berakah*. In Hebrew and early Christian use to bless meant essentially to thank God. The familiar Benedicamus ("Let us bless the Lord. *Thanks be to God")* embodies this rich understanding of the action of blessing. It is at once an expression of thanksgiving to God and a proclamation of his deeds. On the basis of his past actions for his creation, his people are bold to ask for his continued work.

In the longer *Berakah* upon which the later Christian blessings are patterned there are four elements: (1) God's creative saving act; (2) the recalling of God's mighty deeds for his people; (3) a petition that his creative and saving activity may continue and bring to completion what he has begun; and (4) a concluding doxology. The *Berakah* therefore is a doxological event in which God is confessed and praised for his might and his goodness to his creatures followed by a specific petition and concluded with a final expression of praise. In such prayer God's people praise the Creator for his work in history and claim his promises for the future.

Through the centuries the language and the understanding of blessing in the practice of the church has been inconsistent. Christian tradition has sometimes enthusiastically embraced quasi-magical concepts of blessing, consecration, and dedication; and it has sometimes rejected all blessing as not only unnecessary but as a subversion of the gospel. The more common Lutheran positions, as one might expect, lie somewhat uncertainly between these two extremes, reluctant to discard traditional language but reluctant also to embrace wholeheartedly and unreservedly a

---

1. 1 Kings 8:63; Num. 7:10; Exod. 40:10.

theology of blessing.[2]

It is perhaps possible to distinguish between three terms: (1) to *consecrate* is to make holy, to hallow; (2) to *dedicate* is to reserve for special use; (3) to *bless* is in English usually synonymous with consecrate, dedicate, or hallow. It can mean "prosper";[3] following Hebrew use and the Greek New Testament, to *bless* is to thank God (*eulogeō*).

Actual practice, however, has not generally reflected any such distinction. Lutheran service books, often following medieval (and earlier) practice, have tended to use the three terms—consecrate, dedicate, bless—almost interchangeably, and elaborate formulas (like legal documents) use all three terms: "Blessed, hallowed, and dedicated be this Ground to be used as part of God's Acre in this Parish."[4]

The richness of Scripture may not admit of a simple solution, but two aspects of the universe are clear in the Bible and in Lutheran theology: the goodness of creation and the fact of sin.

The refrain of Genesis 1 punctuates the acts of creation: "and God saw that it was good"[5] and, finally, the seventh time, "And God saw everything that he had made, and behold, it was very good."[6] The goodness of creation is affirmed grandly at the outset of the story, and it is reaffirmed in the vision of Isaiah, echoed by the church in its celebration of the Holy Communion:

> Holy, holy, holy is the Lord of hosts;
> the whole earth is full of his glory.[7]

In the Large Catechism Luther reflects this understanding of the natural world in his explanation of the third article of the Apostles' Creed:

> I hold and believe that I am a creature of God; that is, that he has given and constantly sustains my body, soul, and life, my members great and small, all

---

2. Luther's most intemperate blast is in the Smalcald Articles, Part III, Article XV in Tappert, ed., *Book of Concord,* p. 316:

> Finally, there remains the pope's bag of magic tricks which contains silly and childish articles, such as the consecration of churches, the baptism of bells, the baptism of altar stones, the invitation to such ceremonies of sponsors who might make gifts, etc. Such baptizing is a ridicule and mockery of holy Baptism which should not be tolerated. In addition, there are blessings of candles, palms, spices, oats, cakes, etc. These cannot be called blessings, and they are not, but are mere mockery and fraud. Such frauds, which are without number, we commend for adoration to their god and to themselves until they tire of them. We do not wish to have anything to do with them.

3. *Occasional Services* (1962), p. 111.
4. Ibid., p. 124; see also p. 118.
5. Gen. 1:10b, 12b, 18b, 21b, 25b.
6. Gen. 1:31a.
7. Isa. 6:3.

the faculties of my mind, my reason and understanding. . . . Besides, he makes all creation help provide the comforts and necessities of life—sun, moon, and stars in the heavens, day and night, air, fire, water, the earth and all that it brings forth, birds and fish, beasts, grain and all kinds of produce.[8]

For here we see how the Father has given himself to us, with all his creatures, has abundantly provided for us in this life, and, further, has showered us with inexpressible eternal treasures through his Son and the Holy Spirit.[9]

Christians have consistently maintained that the creation is capable of bearing the Creator to us; "the finite is capable of the Infinite." Catholic Christianity, of which Lutheranism is a part, is a sacramental religion.

The other aspect of creation that the Bible and Lutheran theology insist upon is the defilement of the creation by sin. Genesis 3 describes how after the act of pride, disobedience, and rebellion, all relationships were distorted: man and woman, woman and childbearing, man and work, humans and animals. The primal sin infected not only those who did it and their descendents, but it corrupts the rest of creation as well:

Cursed is the ground because of you;
in toil you shall eat of it all the days of your life;
thorns and thistles it shall bring forth to you . . .
In the sweat of your face
you shall eat bread . . .[10]

St. Paul echoes this profound understanding of the depths of sin when he writes of nature's future share in the freedom from bondage to decay and in the glorious liberty:

For the creation waits with eager longing for the revealing of the sons of God . . . because the creation itself will be set free from its bondage to decay and obtain the glorious liberty of the children of God. We know that the whole creation has been groaning in travail together until now . . .[11]

Sin is not limited to people but infects and corrupts all of creation, and the promised triumph of God over sin and death will transform not only people but all creation.

The apostle advised Timothy, in words which have often been used to support the practice of blessing people and things:

---

8. Tappert, ed., *Book of Concord*, p. 412.
9. Ibid., p. 413.
10. Gen. 3:17–19.
11. Rom. 8:19–22.

> Everything created by God is good, and nothing is to be rejected if it is received with thanksgiving; for then it is consecrated by the word of God and prayer.[12]

The blessing of people and objects, therefore, is a way of expressing God's redemptive claim on all creation. The blessing of people is seldom disputed; the benediction is the expected conclusion of nearly every religious service of every Christian denomination. The blessing of things, however, raises some objections. Sometimes the Reformers expressed a dislike of blessing material objects, suggesting that blessing could properly be invoked only upon people, not things. Thus the rubric in *Occasional Services* (1962) before the prayers for the blessing of palms, fishing boats, and wedding rings warns:

> In the use of the following forms of blessing, it must be clear that all of God's creation is good, and that these forms are intended to set apart certain things for specific use, and that the principal blessing is upon those that use them for the specific purpose.[13]

The blessing of spaces, buildings, and objects is a recognition that nothing is outside God's sphere of concern. It is a recognition of our corruption of the good creation since nothing can serve God without a cleansing; it is a confession of the depth of sin. But it is also a sign of the promise of the redemption of all creation. Thus the blessing of people, objects, spaces, and buildings is an act of confession and an act of hope.

All of this is not for the sake of the space or the building or the object itself, but it is done so that all of life and all of creation—things seen and unseen—may praise God and give him glory.

Is everything therefore to be blessed? Should there be blessings of animals, bees, silkworms, stables, stretchers, ambulances, wheelchairs, medicine, bread, cakes, ale, cheese, butter, lard, fowl, grapes, seed, fire, crops, vineyards, fields, pastures, granaries, mills, wells, fountains, bridges, archives, libraries, limekilns, blast furnaces, ships, automobiles, railways, trains, airplanes, tools used in scaling mountains, fire engines, electric dynamos, printing presses, typewriters, telegraph instruments, and seismographs (an actual list, in fact, of the blessings in the now superseded *Roman Ritual*)?[14] In reaction to such a list it is not difficult to

---

12. 1 Tim. 4:4–5.
13. *Occasional Services* (1962), p. 215.
14. *The Roman Ritual*, vol. 3, *The Blessings*, trans. Philip T. Weller (Milwaukee: Bruce, 1952), pp. 331–421. The Anglo-Catholics, not to be outdone and to be relevant to the new age, in *A Manual for Priests of the American Church: Complementary to the Occasional Offices of the Book of Common Prayer* (Cambridge, Mass.: Society of St. John the Evangelist, 1978), have provided even for "the blessing of a space-craft."

sympathize with the inclination to discourage the category of blessing altogether.

To convert the whole world into a temple by attempting to bless everything in it is not only impossible, but it divides the world into two realms of "sacred" and "secular" and excludes one from the other. That which is blessed is holy and sacred; that which is not is secular, profane, unholy. The incarnation is the clearest rejection of such a position, showing that the world and the things in it are capable of revealing the Creator to us. The incarnation, most of all, opens all creation to the encounter between God and humanity. Devout and attentive people have been able to find "tongues in trees, books in the running brooks, sermons in stones, and good in everything."[15] In blessing, therefore, we seek to transform not the object, space, or building but our perception of it. Its significance has been enriched. By blessing, dedicating, and consecrating we present a special offering to God which, we pray in the blessing, may find special use or significance in the church's ministry.

The object, space, or building embodies our responsive gesture of offering, and it is our use of the object that changes our perception of it.[16] We invest the object, space, or building with a new significance. It becomes a symbol, a particularization which points beyond itself to the rest of creation and to the Creator. It moves to include. A particular space marked out as "sacred" becomes a point of reference for understanding all creation. Sacred space makes all space sacred. We pray, therefore, that the symbolic potential may be realized by us and be effective in us.

For Further Reading

A Book of Blessings. Ottawa, Canada: Canadian Conference of Catholic Bishops, 1981.
Clarke, W. K. Lowther. "The Consecration of Churches and Other Occasional Services." In Liturgy and Worship, edited by W. K. Lowther Clarke and Charles Harris, pp. 703–28. London: SPCK, 1932.
Cohn, Robert L. The Shape of Sacred Space: Four Biblical Studies. Missoula, Mont.: Scholars Press, 1981.
Crichton, J. D. The Dedication of a Church: A Commentary. Dublin: Veritas Publications, 1980.

---

15. William Shakespeare, As You Like It, act 2, sc. 1, lines 16–17. John Mole, "Nourishing Conundrums," Times Literary Supplement (December 19, 1980), observes, "naming, redemption of the commonplace, and the making of sacred objects are the essence of poetry" (p. 1428).
16. F. Lochner, Liturgische Monatschrifte, 1884.

Eliade, Mircea. *The Sacred and the Profane*. New York: Harcourt, Brace & World, 1959.

Guardini, Romano. *Sacred Signs*. Wilmington, Del.: Michael Glazier, 1979.

Hatchett, Marion. *Sanctifying Life, Time, Space: An Introduction to Liturgical Study*. New York: Seabury Press, 1976.

Parabola: Myth and the Quest for Meaning 3:1 (1978). An issue devoted to Sacred Space.

Simons, Thomas G. *Blessings: A Reappraisal of Their Nature, Purpose, and Celebration*. Saratoga, Calif.: Resource Publications, 1981.

Sövik, Edward A. "Notes on Sacred Space." *Christian Century* 99:11 (March 31, 1982): 363–66.

Westermann, Claus. *Blessing in the Bible and the Life of the Church*. Translated by Keith Crim. Philadelphia: Fortress Press, 1978.

THE DEDICATION OF A CHURCH BUILDING

The Dedication of a Church Building is to be understood as a three-part action—groundbreaking, cornerstone laying, and dedicating the completed building. In this unified rite, progressive attention is paid to the stages of the construction of the edifice.

The rite of dedication should ultimately direct attention not to the building but to those who will use the building. A helpful example is Solomon's prayer at the dedication of the Temple in Jerusalem (1 Kings 8). God's name is there in the Temple, yet he dwells in heaven (8:27–30). Nonetheless, even the heaven of heavens cannot contain him. In the remainder of the prayer Solomon emphasizes what will be done in the building rather than the building itself. The prayer concludes with a blessing of the people (8:54–61), which has no direct reference to the house at all. The Temple is a sign of God's presence with his people, who are in turn obliged to live a life of obedience to him (8:61).

The New Testament generally refrains from applying cultic terminology in traditional ways. So the Temple is not a building, but it is the baptized people.

When buildings specifically for Christian use were first erected, the church structure was understood as "the house of the church," that is, the house built to shelter the people of God, who are themselves the church.

This primacy of the people who use the house is always to be maintained and understood. The point is not to slight the dedication but to give it proper focus and direction.

DEDICATION OF A CHURCH BUILDING: GROUNDBREAKING
(*Occasional Services*, pp. 158–61)

Parallel Rites

Roman Catholic   Laying of a Foundation Stone or Commencement of Work on the Building of a Church, *Dedication of a Church and an Altar,* pp. 1–10.[17]

Episcopal   Founding of a Church: Groundbreaking, *Book of Occasional Services,* pp. 195–200.

Lutheran   The Blessing of a Church-Site and Ground Breaking, *Occasional Services* (1962), pp. 159–61.
Order for the Blessing of a Church Site and Ground Breaking, *Occasional Services* (1930), pp. 103–6.
The Order for the Ground Breaking for a Church or School, *Lutheran Agenda,* pp. 145–48.

Methodist   An Office for the Breaking of Ground for a Church Building, *Book of Worship,* pp. 344–47.

Purpose

This service is chiefly to begin the work of the construction of the house of the church in the name of God the Holy Trinity and to ask his blessing on the work of construction.

> When the building of a new church begins, it is desirable to celebrate a rite to ask God's blessing on the work which is to be undertaken and to remind the people that the structure built of stone will be a visible sign of the living Church, God's building, which is formed of the people themselves.[18]

A secondary purpose is to set apart a portion of ground on which the church will be built. Thirdly, the service gives the congregation an opportunity to visualize their new building.

Characteristics

The 1982 rite is a departure from the pattern established in the 1930 and 1962 *Occasional Services*. It follows instead the structure of the recent Roman Catholic and Episcopal rites.

---

17. *Dedication of a Church and an Altar* (Toronto: International Committee on English in the Liturgy, 1978).
18. Ibid., p. 1, no. 1.

The service is a simple one at the site of the new building. A hymn is sung; a lesson (or lessons) from the Bible is read; a prayer of thanksgiving is said; the service concludes with a brief prayer, the Lord's Prayer, and the dismissal.

There is no benediction, for this is but the beginning of the work of building a church. This first part of the three-part dedication leads directly to the second: the ground is broken so that the excavation and construction can take place.

Background

It has long been customary to bless the site of a new church building (note the titles of the parallel rites in the two previous Lutheran books, 1930 and 1962, which preserved this emphasis), and the new *Roman Pontifical* continues the tradition.

Ceremonial groundbreaking, however, appears to be a relatively new action in Christian history. It was introduced to North American Lutheran churches in the *Occasional Services* of 1930. There is no parallel in the 1928 *Book of Common Prayer* (although it was in the *Book of Offices*), nor is there a parallel in the Orthodox churches. It is a secondary service in the new Episcopal liturgy, appearing not in the Prayer Book but in the *Book of Occasional Services.*

Preparation for the Service

"Insofar as possible, the area for the erection of the church should be marked out well. It should be possible to walk around it conveniently."[19]

To help the congregation visualize the new building, the outline of the church may be indicated with stakes, white lime, or cord. Cords may also be stretched diagonally across the space in the shape of an X, the monogram in Greek for Christ.

The Episcopal *Book of Occasional Services* (drawing on its predecessor *Book of Offices* [1949]) gives more specific directions for the stretching of the cords, incorporating the action into the service of groundbreaking as a dramatic enactment of enclosing the portion of ground on which the church will rise.

Before the service, four stakes are set in the ground, at the corners of the proposed building. Three cords are prepared, two to extend diagonally from corner to corner, a third to enclose the space. A spade is placed at the site of the Altar.[20]

---

19. Ibid., p. 1, no. 5.
20. *Book of Occasional Services,* p. 195.

The lesson is Gen. 28:10–17, after which a sermon may follow, and then Ps. 132:1–9 (10–19). During the singing of the Psalm,

> persons appointed stretch two cords diagonally across the space, from the northeast to the southwest, and from the southeast to the northwest, securing them to the stakes, thus forming the Greek letter X (chi), the symbol both of the cross and of the name of Christ.[21]

Then Ps. 48:1–3, 7–13 is sung, during which

> persons appointed stretch the third cord completely around the four stakes, enclosing the area. They move clockwise, beginning and ending at the southeast corner. The ministers and people may follow in procession.[22]

This stretching of diagonal cords is an Episcopal adaptation of a medieval custom in which the letters of the alphabet were drawn diagonally across the floor of the church by the bishop with the crozier. The manner of doing so varied. The Roman Pontifical of Clement VIII and Urban VIII (1596) required the bishop to trace the letters of the Greek alphabet beginning at the northwest corner and moving to the southeast corner; then to trace the letters of the Latin alphabet beginning at the southwest corner and moving to the northeast corner. Other traditions did not use the Greek but rather the Latin alphabet for both diagonals. The Gregorian Sacramentary and ancient English rites have the bishop move from the northeast to the southwest and from the southeast to the northwest. In all the books the bishop is directed to trace the letters in silence.

The meaning is uncertain. The action has similarities to Jesus' writing in the dust (John 8:6, 8). The practice may suggest the use of all the letters of the common languages which will be spoken in the place. It is therefore the act of giving the material needed for this communication.[23]

The 1930 and 1962 *Occasional Services* suggested the construction of a "temporary Altar, properly dressed and furnished."[24] This represented the understanding of the altar as a focus for worship, a sign of the presence of God in the midst of his people.[25] The 1982 rite speaks only of the site of the altar, saying nothing about a "temporary altar." The primary purpose of an altar is to be the table on which the Holy Com-

---

21. Ibid., p. 198.
22. Ibid.
23. There is a discussion — in Latin — of the actions in the *Pontificale Romanum Clementis VIII ac Urbani VIII*, vol. 2, ed. Joseph Catalano (Paris, 1851), pp. 91–95.
24. *Occasional Services* (1930), p. 103; *Occasional Services* (1962), p. 159.
25. Lutherans used to boast that theirs was a God-centered liturgy, shown by the central altar, as opposed to the "man-centered" worship of the Reformed churches, shown by the central pulpit.

munion is celebrated, and since there is no celebration of the Eucharist in groundbreaking, an altar seems unnecessary. The primary sign of God's presence is the assembly of his baptized people.

The *Roman Pontifical* directs: "In the place where the altar will be located, a wooden cross of appropriate height is placed."[26] The Orthodox practice is similar: "A large wooden cross is prepared, and this cross is planted in a trench dug at the spot where the altar is to be."[27] The erection of such a cross would also be appropriate in Lutheran use.

Survey of the Service

It has been traditional in the Christian church for the bishop to preside at the various services connected with the dedication of a church building.[28] Consideration may be given to maintaining that tradition, but circumstances will probably suggest that the pastor of the congregation should preside. In churches with an episcopal polity, ownership of the buildings of the diocese is vested in the bishop, and thus the bishop's role in their dedication is appropriate. The Lutheran churches in North America are adopting the title "bishop" but have not adopted episcopal polity. Ownership of property and buildings is congregational. Moreover, congregations do not identify with the bishop as they might if they were under episcopal government: Lutheran bishops are called "pastors of pastors," not "pastors of congregations" or "pastors of synods or districts." The pastor *loci* therefore would seem to be the natural presider at the rites of dedication.

The ministers and members of neighboring congregations should be invited to participate in the service so that the ecumenical nature of the church may be made clear.

If there is a procession to the new site, the processional cross, perhaps flanked on either side by torches, may lead the procession. Instead of the usual processional cross, a large wooden cross may be carried in procession and set up at the site of the altar. The servers follow in procession, behind them the choir, then the assisting ministers, then the presiding minister. The congregation follows the presiding minister.

---

26. *Dedication of a Church and an Altar,* p. 2, no. 6.

27. *Service Book,* p. 479.

28. "Since the bishop has been entrusted with the care of the particular Church, it is his responsibility to dedicate to God new churches built in his diocese" (*Dedication of a Church and an Altar,* p. 12, no. 6). The Orthodox rule is more forceful:

> No one may found a church, either of stone or of wood, except the Bishop himself, or an Archpriest or one of the Priests whom it shall please him to send, with his special blessing, for that purpose. But if any one shall dare to begin the building of a church without the Bishop's blessing, he shall incur the penalty of being deposed, as a contemner of the Bishop's authority. (*Service Book,* p. 479)

Appropriate lessons are read, and an address may follow. After the lessons (and the address), cords may be stretched diagonally across the entire space that the church building will occupy. Then the presiding minister begins the prayer of blessing ⟨510⟩. The second sentence of the prayer has been taken from the Roman Catholic Blessing of the Site of the New Church.

If desired, during the course of the prayer, the presiding minister may trace the sign of the cross in the earth at the approximate site of the altar. (This action may be less appropriate if the processional cross or a large wooden cross already marks the site.) Cords may be used to indicate this site, stretched diagonally across the site of the altar, the cross thus formed being an X-shaped St. Andrew's cross rather than a traditional Latin (†) cross. An alternate practice is for the presiding minister to mark a cross on the ground with lime or simply gesture with the hand. If the presiding minister is a bishop who carries a crozier, the cross may be traced with the foot of the staff.

It is inappropriate to turn the earth with a spade at this point, for that would render less effective the act of groundbreaking which occurs after the prayer and which is the principal reason for the assembly.

The prayer of thanksgiving is notable for its attention to the people who are to use the site rather than for its attention to the site itself. It is in contrast with the prayers in the earlier occasional service books.

Occasional Services (1930)	*Occasional Services* (1962)	*Occasional Services* (1982)
Accept, O Lord God Almighty, this Ground: Let Thy blessing descend upon it as the dew from heaven that here may rise adoration, thanksgiving, and the praise of Thy Holy Name; that here Thy Word may be declared and Thy Way revealed and taught; that here may be Thy House and the Place where Thine honor dwelleth; and, we beseech Thee, let Thy benediction ever abide upon this Place	Accept, O Lord, this place and let thy blessing descend upon it as the dew from heaven, that hence may arise adoration, thanksgiving and praise of thy holy Name; that here thy Word may be proclaimed and thy way revealed; that this may be thy House and the Place where thine honor dwelleth. Let thy gracious benediction ever abide here and upon all who shall gather here to worship thee; through Jesus Christ our Lord.	Blessed are you, O Lord our God, king of the universe. You fill the entire world with your presence; your name is to be hallowed through all the earth. Bless all who have worked or contributed to provide this site which today we set apart for the building of a church. *The minister may trace the sign of the cross. . . .* May this be a place

DEDICATIONS AND BLESSINGS

Occasional Services (1930)	Occasional Services (1962)	Occasional Services (1982)
and all who gather here to worship and commune with Thee; through Jesus Christ our Lord. Let the beauty of the Lord our God be upon us, and establish thou the work of our hands upon us; that as, in Thy Name, we undertake the building of an House to Thy praise, we may be blessed of Thee in the beginning, prospered and protected by Thee in the continuance, and established and accepted in the completion; through Jesus Christ our Lord.	Let the beauty of the Lord our God be upon us, and establish thou the work of our hands upon us; that as, in thy Name, we undertake the building of a House to thy glory, we may of thee be blessed in its beginning, prospered in its continuance, and established in its completion; through Jesus Christ our Lord.	where your glory dwells and where your way is revealed in Word and Sacrament. May your gracious blessing descend like the dew from heaven upon this place and upon all who shall gather here to worship you. You have given us joy in a work begun in your name; may we soon celebrate your presence in the house of your Church, and, in the time to come, praise you forever in our eternal home; through Jesus Christ our Lord, who lives and reigns with you and the Holy Spirit, one God, now and forever. ⟨510⟩

The statement at the turning of the earth and the prayer following are abbreviations of the 1930–62 rite:

Occasional Services (1930)	Occasional Services (1962)	Occasional Services (1982)
In the Faith of Jesus Christ this work is begun and this ground is broken, In the Name and to the glory of the Father, and of the Son, and of the Holy Ghost: That true faith may	In the faith of Jesus Christ this work is begun and this ground is broken: In the Name of the Father, and of the Son, and of the Holy Ghost. May true faith, the fear of God and love of the	With faith in Jesus Christ this work is begun and this ground is broken in the name of the Father, and of the Son, and of the Holy Spirit. Amen.

Occasional Services (1930)	*Occasional Services* (1962)	*Occasional Services* (1982)
flourish here and the fear of God and love of the brethren; and that this may be a place destined for prayer and the invocation and adoration of the Name of our Lord Jesus Christ, Who with the Father, and the Holy Ghost, liveth and reigneth, One God, world without end.	brethren flourish here; and may this place be set apart for the invocation and adoration of the Name of our Lord Jesus Christ, who with the Father, and the Holy Ghost, liveth and reigneth, one God, world without end.	
		Our Father . . .

The minister may say:	*The minister may say:*	
O God, from Whom every good thing taketh its beginning and through Whom it gathereth rich growth, always advancing to better things: Grant to us suppliants, we beseech Thee, that this which we undertake to the praise of Thy Name, we may, by the help of Thy Fatherly wisdom, carry through to completion; through Jesus Christ our Lord.	O God, in whom every good thing has its beginning, and by whom it increases and advances to greater worth: Grant us, thy servants, that what we have this day undertaken to the glory of thy Name, may, by the aid of thy Fatherly wisdom, be successfully completed; through Jesus Christ Our Lord.	O Lord our God, in you every good work has its beginning. Grant that what we have undertaken this day to the glory of your name may be successfully completed to the good of all your people; through Jesus Christ our Lord. ⟨511⟩

The placement of the Lord's Prayer before the final prayer is unusual and follows the older patterns of the *Common Service Book* and the *Service Book and Hymnal*. Elsewhere in the *Lutheran Book of Worship* and *Occasional Services* (1982) the Our Father is the conclusion of the prayers.

The dismissal replaces the benediction in this service, for the work of building the church has just begun.

Development of the Rite
Dedication of a Church Building:
Groundbreaking

Lutheran Agenda	Occasional Services (1930)	Occasional Services (1962)	Occasional Services (1982)
			(Procession)
			Hymn
			Address
Vesper versicles	Verses*	Verses†	
	Psalm 100 or 122	Psalm 100 or 122	
Lesson(s)	Lesson	Lesson	Lesson(s)
Gen. 28:10–17	Exod. 3:1–6 or	Exod. 3:1–6 or	Exod. 3:1–6
Psalms 46, 84, 121	2 Sam. 24:18–25 or	2 Sam. 24:18–25 or	
Matt. 28:18–20	Luke 6:47–49	Luke 6:47–49 or	Luke 6:47–49
Eph. 4:1–6		1 Cor. 3:10–14 or	1 Cor. 3:10–14
			Eph. 2:19–22
		Heb. 11:8–10	Heb. 11:8–10

---

*In the Name of the Father, and of the Son, and of the Holy Ghost.
  Amen.
O Lord, open Thou my lips:
  And my mouth shall show forth Thy praise.
Make haste, O God, to deliver me:
  Make haste to help me, O Lord.
Our help is in the Name of the Lord:
  Who made heaven and earth.
Except the Lord build the house:
  They labor in vain that build it.
Blessed are they that dwell in Thy house:
  They will be still praising Thee.
Glory be to the Father, and to the Son, and to the Holy Ghost:
  As it was in the beginning, is now, and ever shall be, world without end.
  Amen.

†In the Name of the Father, and of the Son, and of the Holy Ghost.
  Amen.
O Lord, open thou my lips.
  And my mouth shall show forth thy praise.
Make haste, O God, to deliver me.
  Make haste to help me, O Lord.
Except the Lord build the house:
  They labor in vain that build it.
Glory be to the Father, and to the Son, and to the Holy Ghost:
  As it was in the beginning, is now, and ever shall be, world without end.
  Amen.

Development of the Rite (continued)
Dedication of a Church Building:
Groundbreaking

Lutheran Agenda	*Occasional Services* (1930)	*Occasional Services* (1962)	*Occasional Services* (1982)
Apostles' Creed			
(Hymn)			
(Sermon)	(Address)	(Address)	(Address)
(Offering)			
	Kyrie	Kyrie	
	Our Father	Our Father	
	Salutation and response	Salutation and response	Salutation and response
	2 Prayers	2 Prayers	(Prayer[s])
Groundbreaking‡	Groundbreaking	Groundbreaking	Groundbreaking
Kyrie			
Our Father			Our Father
Salutation and response			
Collect	Prayer	Prayer	Prayer
Collect for peace			
Benedicamus	Benedicamus	Benedicamus	
Blessing	Blessing	Blessing	
			Dismissal

---

‡The Ceremony of the Ground Breaking
The Chairman of the Building Committee shall step forward and give to the Minister a spade. The Minister, taking the spade, shall say:
Whereas, by the grace of God, we are permitted this day to begin the erection of a church (school) at this place, with this spade I now break this ground in the name of the Father and of the Son and of the Holy Ghost in order that the building which shall be constructed here may serve as a place where our God will record His name, where His honor will dwell, and where He will come unto His children and bless them.
As the Minister turns over the first spadeful of ground, he may say:
Other foundation can no man lay than that is laid, which is Jesus Christ, our Lord and Savior, blessed forever.
Then may the members of the Building Committee, in order, take the spade and turn over a piece of ground, accompanying the act with a suitable word of Scripture.

Comparison of Rites
Dedication of a Church Building:
Groundbreaking

ROMAN CATHOLIC	LUTHERAN	EPISCOPAL
		Preparation of cords
Greeting		
Instruction		
Prayer*		
Procession	Procession	Procession
		Litany for the Church
	Hymn	(Hymn)
	Address	
Lesson(s)	Lessons(s)	Lesson: Gen. 28:10–17
1 Kings 5:2–18		
Isa. 28:16–17		
Acts 4:8–12		
1 Cor. 10:1–6		
Psalm 24		
Pss. 42:3, 5; 43:3–4		
Psalm 87		
Psalm 100		
Ps. 118:1–2, 16–17, 22–23		
Matt. 7:21–29		
Matt. 16:13–18		
Mark 12:1–12		
Luke 6:46–49		
Homily	(Address)	(Address)
		Stretching cords

---

*Let us pray.
silence
Lord,
you built a holy Church,
founded upon the apostles
with Jesus Christ as its cornerstone.
Grant that your people,
gathered in your name,
may fear and love you
and grow as the temple of your glory.
May they always follow you,
until, with you at their head,
they arrive at last in your heavenly city.
We ask this through Christ our Lord. (p. 5, no. 17)

Comparison of Rites (continued)
Dedication of a Church Building:
Groundbreaking

ROMAN CATHOLIC	LUTHERAN	EPISCOPAL
	Salutation and response	
	Prayer	
	(Psalm[s])	
Blessing the Site†	Groundbreaking	Groundbreaking‡
Prayer		Salutation and response
Our Father	Our Father	Our Father
		Preces
		and
Prayer§	Prayer	prayer//

---

†Lord,
  you fill the entire world with your presence
  that your name may be hallowed through all the earth.
  Bless all those
  who have worked or contributed
  to provide this site (property, land)
  on which a church will be built.
  Today may they rejoice in a work just begun,
  soon may they celebrate the sacraments in your temple,
  and in time to come may they praise you for ever in heaven.
  We ask this through Christ our Lord. (p. 7, no. 24)

‡*Then the Celebrant, standing at the site of the Altar, says*
  Since faithful people desire to build a house of prayer,
  dedicated to the glory of God [and in honor of _____]
  [to be known as _____,] on this ground, now marked with
  the symbol of Christ;
  Then taking the spade, and breaking the ground, the Celebrant continues
  Therefore, I break ground for this building, in the Name of
  the Father, and of the Son, and of the Holy Spirit.

  May the Gospel be preached,
  the Sacraments administered,
  and prayers and praises offered
  in this place, from generation to generation. *Amen.* (*Book of Occasional
  Services*, p. 199)

§See below, Laying of a Cornerstone, pp. 265-66.

//How wonderful is God in his holy places!
  Establish, O God, what you have wrought in us.
  Be favorable and gracious to Zion:

261

Comparison of Rites (continued)
Dedication of a Church Building:
Groundbreaking

ROMAN CATHOLIC	LUTHERAN	EPISCOPAL
Blessing		
Dismissal	Dismissal	Dismissal

DEDICATION OF A CHURCH BUILDING:
LAYING OF A CORNERSTONE
(Occasional Services, pp. 162–65)

Parallel Rites

Roman Catholic	Laying of a Foundation Stone or Commencement of Work on the Building of a Church, *Dedication of a Church and an Altar,* pp. 1–10.
Episcopal	The Founding of a Church: Laying of a Cornerstone, *Book of Occasional Services,* pp. 200–201.
Lutheran	Order for Laying the Cornerstone of a Church, *Occasional Services* (1962), pp. 106–12. Order for Laying the Corner-stone of a Church, *Common Service Book* (text ed.), pp. 464–67. The Order for the Laying of the Cornerstone of a Church or a School, *Lutheran Agenda,* pp. 149–56. The Laying of a Corner-Stone, *Church Book,* pp. 432–35.
Orthodox	The Office Used at the Founding of a Church (The Laying of a Cornerstone), *Service Book,* pp. 479–92.
Methodist	An Office for the Laying of a Cornerstone of a Church Building, *Book of Worship,* pp. 348–50.

Build up the walls of Jerusalem.

Celebrant Let us pray.

O Lord God of Israel, the heavens cannot contain you, yet you are pleased to dwell in the midst of your people, and have moved us to set apart a space on which to build a house of prayer: Accept and bless the work which we have now begun that it may be brought to completion, to the honor and glory of your holy Name; through Jesus Christ our Lord, who lives and reigns with you in the unity of the Holy Spirit, one God, for ever and ever. *Amen.*

262

DEDICATION OF A CHURCH BUILDING: LAYING OF A CORNERSTONE

Purpose

This service is to thank God for building his church, a spiritual house made of his people, and to ask his grace to serve him as his holy priesthood. In gratitude, the cornerstone of the house of the church is laid.

If the design and construction of the church is such that there is no cornerstone or foundation stone, this part of the dedication is omitted.

Characteristics

This continuation of the three-part dedication, like the groundbreaking, is a simple rite: a psalm is sung or said; a lesson is read; verses are said; the cornerstone is sealed as the Nicene Creed is confessed; the thanksgiving is said; and the stone is set in place. As in groundbreaking, there is no benediction, for although this is the continuation, it is not yet the completion of the dedication of the church. The cornerstone is laid so that the walls of the house may rise.

Background

In the Roman Catholic rite, there is one form for the Blessing of a Church Site and the Laying of the Foundation Stone. In the Episcopal *Book of Occasional Services* there is a brief outline of a form for laying the cornerstone.

The order for the Laying of the Corner Stone of a Church has been in North American Lutheran service books at least since the *Book of Worship* of the General Synod (1867).

Preparation for the Service

The cornerstone, which in the tradition of the West is rectangular (but in the Orthodox tradition of the East is square),[29] is prepared together with cement and the tools for placing the stone in the foundation. The workers who will set the stone in place need to be at hand and alerted as to when they will perform their duty.

---

29. If the church is to be of stone, trenches are dug at the place where the cornerstone is to be laid, and stones and mortar shall be prepared; and on one square stone there shall be depicted or carved a cross; and below the cross . . . a place shall be prepared for the insertion of Holy Relics. And the following inscription shall be put on the stone: In the Name of the Father, and of the Son, and of the Holy Spirit this church is founded . . .

   A church may be founded without the Relics of a Saint and the above-mentioned inscription, but not without the square stone.

   But if the church is to be of wood, no excavations are made, with the exception of one under the wall of the Sanctuary, at the eastern extremity, wherein to set the square stone . . . (*Service Book,* p. 479)

263

The proper color for the occasion is red[30] for the Holy Spirit, the "soul of the Church."[31]

Survey of the Service

It has been traditional in the Christian church for the bishop to preside at the various services connected with the dedication of a church building.[32] Consideration may be given to maintaining that tradition, but circumstances will probably suggest that the pastor of the congregation should preside.

The ministers and members of neighboring congregations should be invited to participate in the service so that the ecumenical nature of the church is clear.

If there is a procession to the new site, the processional cross, perhaps flanked by torches, may lead the procession. The servers follow, behind them the choir, then the assisting ministers, then the presiding minister. The congregation follows behind the presiding minister.

Appropriate lessons are read. The Roman Catholic rite not only requires a sermon, but it tells the preacher what to say:

> When the readings are finished the homily is given, in which the biblical readings are elucidated and the significance of the rite explained: Christ is the cornerstone of the Church, and the temple that is going to be built by the living Church of the community of believers will be at once the house of God and the house of God's people.[33]

The verses said by the presiding minister are from the Psalms. The translation of the first two verses is from the Revised Standard Version; the third is from the Grail translation.[34]

Our help is in the name of the Lord,	
Who made heaven and earth.	124:8
Blessed be the name of the Lord,	
from this time forth and forevermore.	113:2
The stone which the builders rejected	
has become the cornerstone.	118:22

---

30. See Dedication and Anniversary, *LBW,* Min. Ed., p. 185.

31. *Dedication of a Church and an Altar,* p. 2, no. 8, directs, "The vestments are of white or of some festive color." The Episcopal books do not indicate proper colors.

32. See n. 28.

33. *Dedication of a Church and an Altar,* p. 7, no. 22.

34. *The Psalms: A New Translation* (Philadelphia: Westminster Press, 1964), p. 204. While this translation of the third of the verses is more felicitous in this context than that of the *LBW* Psalter, the use of a translation other than that of the *LBW* should not be accorded any significance other than familiarity with the older translation from previous books and some carelessness on the part of the committee. Elsewhere in *Occasional Services* the psalm translation is that of the *LBW* (which was borrowed from the *Book of Common Prayer).*

The items placed in a cornerstone are usually chosen to show the faith of the Christian church upon which the building rests; so a Bible and the *Book of Concord* are often included. Other items reflect the life of the church at the time of the laying of the cornerstone; so a service book, a list of members, a copy of the church newsletter are often included.[35]

Since the action of placing the items in the stone is confined and not many will therefore be able to see clearly what is being done, a minister (who does not need to be the presiding minister) may name each item as it is placed in the cornerstone by the presiding minister so that the congregation can at least hear what is happening.

The principal prayer at this stage of the dedication (p. 164, ⟨512⟩) is noteworthy, for it clearly indicates the church's understanding of itself and its work. The church is the people of God, built as living stones into a spiritual house; the head cornerstone is Jesus Christ (1 Pet. 2:5; Eph. 2:20). This church, this people, builds itself a house. So too in the Roman rite, the concluding prayer directs its attention almost entirely to the people:

The bishop . . . invites the people to pray the general intercessions, in these or similar words:

Brothers and sisters, now that we have laid the cornerstone of our new church, let us pray to God, our Father.
  All pray in silence for a brief period.
  That he may transform into a living temple of his glory all whom he has gathered here and who look upon Christ as the cornerstone of their faith, let us pray to the Lord:
  Bless and watch over your Church, O Lord.
  That God in his power may overcome the division and sin which separate his people so that they may ultimately worship as one, let us pray to the Lord:
  Bless and watch over your Church, O Lord.
  That he may ground upon the bedrock of his Church the faith of all those who have undertaken to work on this building, let us pray to the Lord:

---

35. The *Lutheran Agenda* (p. 150) has this rubric:

The contents of the box may embrace: The constitution and history of the congregation, a Catechism, a Hymnal, the *Concordia Triglotta,* a list containing the names of the church officers, the pastor, the teachers, the building committee, etc.; synodical reports and other church publications; also the names of the President of the country, the Governor of the State, and the Mayor of the city at the time; and lastly, newspapers of the city or state, etc.

The Orthodox church gives elaborate attention to the placement of relics beneath the altar of a church at the time of the dedication. The Roman Catholic rite preserves the custom but with somewhat less emphasis. (*Dedication of a Church and an Altar,* p. 12, no. 5.b: "The greatest care must be taken to determine whether relics intended for deposition are authentic. It is better for an altar to be dedicated without relics than to have relics of doubtful credibility placed beneath it.") The recent Lutheran tradition gives similar attention to the placement of items in the cornerstone.

Bless and watch over your Church, O Lord.

That those who are prevented from building places of worship may bear witness to the Lord by conducting themselves as living temples of glory and faith, let us pray to the Lord:

Bless and watch over your Church, O Lord.

That all here present may be cleansed by his divine power and come to share in the celebration of his holy mysteries, let us pray to the Lord:

Bless and watch over your Church, O Lord.

Our Father . . .

God of love,
we praise your holy name,
for you have made us your temple by baptism
and inspire us to build on earth
churches dedicated to your worship.
Look favorably upon your children,
for they have come with joy
to begin work on this new church.
Enable them to grow into the temple of your glory,
until, shaped anew by your grace,
they are gathered by your hand into your heavenly city.
We ask this through Christ our Lord.[36]

Following the prayer "Blessed are you, O Lord our God, king of the universe" (no. 11), workers spread the mortar and set the stone in place. As the action of laying the stone is being completed, the presiding minister says:

In thanksgiving to God we lay this stone, on which a house for the Church will rise, in the name of the Father, and of the Son, and of the Holy Spirit.

This announcement of the actual setting of the stone is similar to that suggested in the Roman Catholic rite:

The bishop lays the stone on the foundation in
silence or, if he wishes, saying these or similar words:
With faith in Jesus Christ
we lay this stone
on which a church will rise.
May it be a place of sacrament
and a source of grace
to the glory of the Father
who with the Son and Holy Spirit
lives and reigns for ever and ever.[37]

---

36. *Dedication of a Church and an Altar,* pp. 9–10, no. 30.
37. Ibid., p. 9, no. 28.

The acclamation with which this part of the dedication concludes is drawn from the Episcopal *Book of Occasional Services:* "Praise the Lord, because the foundation of the house of the Lord is laid!"[38] The Roman rite suggests the antiphon, "The house of the Lord is firmly built on solid rock. (Alleluia)."[39] In the Episcopal rite the people respond, "Alleluia! Alleluia! Alleluia!" But since the Alleluia demands music and falls flat when merely spoken, and since music may be difficult to manage outdoors at the site of the church, the Lutheran rite concludes with a simple spoken "Thanks be to God."

The minister's words as the stone is set in place assume that the walls of the church have not yet been built and that the cornerstone is treated as more than merely ornamental. If the construction of the building is well along or completed, there is little point to laying the cornerstone. If it is desired nonetheless, the minister may simply set the stone in place in silence or delete the words "on which a house for the church will rise." The conclusion may then be adapted to something similar to the following: "Praise the Lord. The cornerstone of the house has been laid."

Development of the Rite
Dedication of a Church Building:
Laying of a Cornerstone

Lutheran Agenda	Church Book	Common Service Book	Occasional Services (1962)	Occasional Services (1982)
				Procession
				Hymn
		Invocation	Invocation	
Vesper Versicles	Psalm verses*	Psalm verses*	Psalm 48	Psalm

---

38. *Book of Occasional Services,* p. 201. See Ezra 3:11.
39. *Dedication of a Church and an Altar,* p. 9, no. 29.
*Our help is in the Name of the Lord;
  Who made heaven and earth.
How amiable are Thy tabernacles, O Lord of hosts!
  My soul longeth, yea, even fainteth for the courts of the Lord.
His foundation is in the holy mountains.
  The Lord loveth the gates of Zion more than all the dwellings of Jacob.
I was glad when they said unto me, Let us go into the house of the Lord.
  Our feet shall stand within thy gates, O Jerusalem.
Except the Lord build the house, they labor in vain that build it.
  Except the Lord keep the city, the watchman waketh but in vain.
Glory be to the Father, and to the Son, and to the Holy Ghost:
  As it was in the beginning, is now, and ever shall be, world without end.
  Amen.

Development of the Rite (continued)
Dedication of a Church Building:
Laying of a Cornerstone

Lutheran Agenda	Church Book	Common Service Book	Occasional Services (1962)	Occasional Services (1982)
			Psalm 84 Psalm 87 Psalm 127	
Lesson(s) e.g., Gen. 28: 10–22	Lessons Gen. 28:16–22	Lessons	Lesson(s)	Lesson(s)
			1 Chron. 29: 10–18	
Psalm 84 Psalm 87 Psalm 122				
	Isa. 28:16	Isa. 28:16 Ezra 3:10–11		
Matt. 16:13–19 1 Cor. 3:9–23 Eph. 2:19–22 1 Pet. 2:1–9	Eph. 2:19–22	Eph. 2:19–22	Eph. 2:19–22 1 Pet. 2:1–7	
Apostles' Creed	Apostles' Creed	Apostles' Creed	Apostles' Creed	
(Hymn)				
(Sermon)		(Address)	(Address)	(Address)
		(Hymn)	(Hymn)	
(Offering)				
		(List of contents)	(List of contents)	(List of contents)
				Nicene Creed
		Salutation and response	Salutation and response	Salutation and response
	3 Prayers†	3 Prayers†	Prayer 1†	

† Church Book	Common Service Book	Occasional Services (1962)
O Lord God, heavenly Father, Whom the heavens cannot contain, but Whose will it is to have a House upon the earth wherein prayer and praise to Thy Name may	O Lord God, Heavenly Father, Whom the heavens cannot contain, but Whose will it is to have a house upon earth wherein prayer and praise to Thy Name	O Lord God, who although the Heaven of heavens cannot contain thee, yet dost vouchsafe to dwell with thy Church here on earth: Visit, we beseech thee, with thy

Development of the Rite (continued)
Dedication of a Church Building:
Laying of a Cornerstone

Lutheran Agenda	Church Book	Common Service Book	Occasional Services (1962)	Occasional Services (1982)
			Psalm verses	
			Prayer 2†	

Church Book	Common Service Book	Occasional Services (1962)
continually be made: Let Thine eyes be toward this place; and as Thou didst fulfill the devout wish of Thy servant David by the building of the Temple by Solomon his son, do Thou graciously also fulfill the desire of our hearts in the completion of what we here begin; through Jesus Christ our Lord.	may continually be made: Look graciously toward this place; and as Thou didst move Thine ancient people to build for Thee an house of worship, do Thou fulfill also the desire of our hearts, and bless and prosper what we have undertaken in Thy Name.	lovingkindness, this place whereon we lay the foundation of a house to the praise and honor of thy holy Name. And as thou didst fulfill the desire of thy servant David, so likewise grant that our purpose may be accomplished, that thy servants may see thy work, and their children thy glory; through Jesus Christ, our Lord, who liveth and reigneth with thee and the Holy Ghost, one God, world without end.
O Lord Jesus Christ, Thou Son of the living God, Who art the elect and precious Cornerstone and the immutable Foundation of Thy Church: We pray Thee, let the stone which we here lay in Thy Name be a firm foundation; and as Thou art Thyself the Beginning and the Ending, be also the beginning, continuance, and completion of what we here commence for Thine honor and glory.	O Lord Jesus Christ, Thou Son of the Living God, Who art the elect and precious Cornerstone and the immutable Foundation of Thy Church: We pray Thee, let the stone which we here lay in Thy Name be a firm foundation; and as Thou art Thyself the Beginning and the Ending, be also the beginning, continuance, and completion of what we here commence for Thine honor and glory.	O Lord Jesus Christ, Son of the Living God, who art the one Foundation, and the Chief Cornerstone of the Holy Church: Bless what we do now in laying this stone in thy Name, and be thou, we beseech thee, the beginning, the increase, and the consummation of this our work, which is undertaken to thy glory; who with the Father and the Holy Ghost livest and reignest, one God, world without end.
O Lord God, Who makest the assembly of Thy saints an everlasting dwelling-place for Thy Majesty: Bless	O Lord God, Holy Ghost, Who makest the assembly of Thy saints Thy dwelling place: Bless and prosper the	O Lord God, who makest the assembly of thy saints an everlasting dwelling-place for thy Majesty: Bless and

269

Development of the Rite (continued)
Dedication of a Church Building:
Laying of a Cornerstone

Lutheran Agenda	Church Book	Common Service Book	Occasional Services (1962)	Occasional Services (1982)
Cornerstone laying‡	Cornerstone laying§	Cornerstone laying//	Cornerstone laying//	Cornerstone laying
			Prayer 3†	
			Collects	
Our Father	Our Father (List of contents)	Our Father	Our Father	
Salutation and response				
Collect				

Church Book	Common Service Book	Occasional Services (1962)
and prosper the building of this edifice, and grant that in like manner we also, as lively stones, may be built up into a spiritual house and an abiding Temple of Thy glory; through Jesus Christ our Lord, Who liveth and reigneth with Thee and the Holy Ghost, ever one God, world without end.	building of this edifice, and grant that in like manner we also, as living stones, may be built up into a spiritual house and an abiding temple of Thy Glory; Who with the Father and the Son livest and reignest, One God, world without end.	prosper the building of this edifice, and grant that in like manner we also, as living stones, may be built up into a spiritual house and an abiding temple of thy glory; through Jesus Christ our Lord.

‡Our help is in the name of the Lord, who made heaven and earth. Except the Lord build the house, they labor in vain that build it. I lay the cornerstone of an edifice to be here erected under the name of _____ Church and devoted to the worship of the one and only living and true God, to the proclamation of His Gospel, and to the ministry of His holy Sacraments in the name (he strikes the stone) of the Father (he strikes the stone) and of the Son (he strikes the stone) and of the Holy Ghost. Amen.

The Stone which the builders rejected is become the Head of the corner.

Other foundation can no man lay than that is laid, which is Jesus Christ, true God and Man, blessed forever.

Glory be to the Father and to the Son and to the Holy Ghost; as it was in the beginning, is now, and ever shall be, world without end. Amen.

§*The Stone having been adjusted in its place, the Minister shall strike it with a trowel or hammer at the mention of each Name in the Trinity, saying:*

Development of the Rite (continued)
Dedication of a Church Building:
Laying of a Cornerstone

Lutheran Agenda	Church Book	Common Service Book	Occasional Services (1962)	Occasional Services (1982)
Collect for peace				
	(Doxology or hymn)		(Hymn)	
		Salutation and response	Salutation and response	
Benedicamus		Benedicamus	Benedicamus	
Benediction	Benediction	Benediction	Benediction	
				Concluding verse

I do now lay this Corner-stone of the Evangelical Lutheran Church of _____:
In the Name of the Father, — and of the Son, — and of the Holy Ghost —.
Amen.

//The Corner-stone having been placed, the Minister shall strike it with a trowel or hammer at the mention of each Name in the Holy Trinity, saying:

Common Service Book	Occasional Services (1962)
In the Faith of Jesus Christ, I do now lay this Corner-Stone: In the Name of the Father, and of the Son, and of the Holy Ghost; that here true faith, the fear of God and brotherly love may abide; and that this place may be set apart to the preaching of the Gospel, the administration of the Holy Sacraments, and the invocation and praise of the Name of our Lord Jesus Christ, Who with the Father and the Holy Ghost liveth and reigneth, ever One God, world without end.	In the faith of Jesus Christ I do now lay this Cornerstone: In the Name of the Father, and of the Son, and of the Holy Ghost. Amen. Here may true faith and the fear of God, and brotherly love ever abide; and let this place be set apart to the preaching of the Gospel, the administration of the Holy Sacraments, and the invocation and praise of the Name of our Lord Jesus Christ, who with the Father and the Holy Ghost liveth and reigneth, one God, world without end.
Amen. Amen. Amen.	*Amen.*

271

DEDICATIONS AND BLESSINGS

Comparison of Rites
Dedication of a Church Building:
Laying of a Cornerstone

ORTHODOX	ROMAN CATHOLIC	LUTHERAN	EPISCOPAL
	Greeting		
	Instruction		
	Prayer		
Procession	Procession	Procession	
Invocation			
Our Father			
	Lesson		
Psalm 143	Psalm	Psalm	
	Gospel	Lesson(s)	Lesson e.g., Eph. 2:19–22
	Homily	(Address)	Address
Litany			
Hymn			
Blessing of water			
Blessing of oil			
Planting cross			
Prayers			Prayer (of Patron or Title of church)
Psalm 84		Verses	
		(List of contents)	
		Nicene Creed	
	Blessing of site		
Blessing of stone	Blessing of stone*		

---

*Father,
the prophet Daniel spoke of your Son,
as a stone wondrously hewn from a mountain.
The apostle Paul spoke of him,
as a stone firmly founded.
Bless + this foundation stone
to be laid in Christ's name.
You appointed him
the beginning and end of all things.
May this work begun, continue,
and be brought to fulfillment in him,
for he is Lord for ever and ever. (p. 8, no. 27)

Comparison of Rites (continued)
Dedication of a Church Building:
Laying of a Cornerstone

ORTHODOX	ROMAN CATHOLIC	LUTHERAN	EPISCOPAL
		Salutation and response	
		Prayer	
Laying stone†	Laying stone	Laying stone	Laying stone
Sprinkling of foundations	Sprinkling of foundations		Prayer‡
north			
west			
south			
east			
	Prayer		
	Our Father		
	Prayer		
			Hymn
Blessing	Blessing		Blessing
			Dismissal
		Concluding verses	

---

†This Church is founded to the glory of our great God and
Saviour Jesus Christ, in honor and memory of (the name of the
Feast of the Lord, or of the Birth-giver of God, or of the Patron Saint
of the Temple), in the Name of the Father, and of the Son, and of
the Holy Spirit. Amen.
   Then, taking oil, he saith:
The Most High God, who hath founded this Church, is in the midst
of it, and it shall not be removed. God shall help it, and that
right early.
   And he poureth the oil on the stone, set in its place, saying:
Blessed and illustrious be this place for a house of prayer, to
the honour and glory of God, glorified in the Holy Trinity, of
the Father, and of the Son, and of the Holy Spirit. Amen. (*Service Book,* p. 487)

‡Lord Jesus Christ, Son of the living God, you are the brightness
of the Father's glory and the express image of his person, the
one foundation and the chief cornerstone: Bless what we have now
done in the laying of this stone. Be the beginning, the increase,
and the consummation of this work undertaken to the glory of
your Name; who with the Father and the Holy Spirit live and reign,
one God, for ever and ever. (*Book of Occasional Services,* p. 201)

DEDICATION OF A CHURCH BUILDING:
THE COMPLETED BUILDING
(*Occasional Services*, pp. 166–72)

Parallel Rites

Roman Catholic   Dedication of a Church, Dedication of an Altar, *Dedication of a Church and an Altar*, pp. 11–40, 59–81.

Episcopal   Dedication and Consecration of a Church, *Book of Common Prayer*, pp. 566–79.

Lutheran   Order for the Dedication of a Church, *Occasional Services* (1962), pp. 113–20.
Order for the Dedication of a Church, *Common Service Book* (text ed.), pp. 468–74.
The Order for the Dedication of a Church, *Lutheran Agenda*, pp. 157–67.
The Consecration of a Church, *Church Book*, pp. 435–39.

Orthodox   The Office at the Consecration of a Church When Performed by a Bishop, *Service Book*, pp. 493–511.

Methodist   An Office for the Opening or Consecrating of a Church Building, *Book of Worship*, pp. 351–54.
An Office for the Dedication of a Church Building, *Book of Worship*, pp. 355–60.

Purpose

The act of dedicating a church invests the completed church building with significance for the pilgrim people of God as a sign of God's presence among his people here and a promise of the church triumphant rejoicing in his presence in the courts of heaven.

This service is also to be used with suitable modification for the dedication of a remodeled or a reclaimed church building.

Characteristics

This rite completes the three-part work of dedication and is the culmination of the dedication.

The celebration of the Holy Communion is one of the primary tasks of the church, a principal focus and source of its identity. The Dedication of a Church Building, therefore, is set within the context of a celebration of the Eucharist.

274

There are two forms of the action of dedication. In the first form, given in the text of the service, the ministers and congregation enter the church, and in an elaborate entrance rite the minister blesses in order the font, the pulpit, the altar, and the building. With the building thus entered and hallowed, the celebration of Holy Communion follows, beginning with the prayer of the day.

The second form of the dedication is given in outline in the notes. This form integrates the actions of dedication into the structure of the Holy Communion and perhaps more clearly indicates that what consecrates an object is not prayer but the use to which the object is put. Moreover, the impact of the successive elements of the service is heightened by placing the Bible on the reading desk at the time of the blessing of the desk; then the readings and sermon follow. At the blessing of the altar, the table is vested; the communion vessels placed on it; and the offertory and Great Thanksgiving follow. As each place in the church is dedicated, it may be decorated by members of the congregation with flowers, candles, or banners.

If the organ or other musical instruments are to be blessed at the time of the dedication of the church, this may appropriately be done just before the hymn of praise. Then the instruments sound for the first time.

The vessels, paraments, linens, candles, crosses, banners, and other such ornaments are not dedicated in this service but are simply put in place at the appropriate time. The *Book of Common Prayer* form for the Dedication and Consecration of a Church provides a general prayer for the dedication of such items:

> We give you thanks, O God, for the gifts of your people, and for the work of many hands, which have beautified this place and furnished it for the celebration of your holy mysteries. Accept and bless all we have done, and grant that in these earthly things we may behold the order and beauty of things heavenly; through Jesus Christ our Lord.[40]

In the Lutheran rite similar general mention of the donors may be made in the prayers.

Background

From the time of Constantine, when Christians began to erect buildings for use as churches, the consecration was apparently accomplished by the celebration of the Holy Communion within the building. Later, dedication rites were developed and elaborated and became common. In the past, the Protestant tradition generally preferred the title "dedica-

---

40. *Book of Common Prayer* (1979), p. 573.

tion" for this service; the Roman Catholic tradition preferred "consecration." "Consecration" suggests calling down God's blessing to alter the character of the building; "dedication" suggests offering it to God for his use. Today the *Roman Pontifical* calls the service The Dedication of a Church and an Altar.

Preparation for the Service

It may be appropriate for the bishop or a representative of the bishop to participate in the dedication of a church.[41]

It is still more appropriate for representatives of other churches and denominations to be invited to participate in the service as an expression of ecumenical solidarity. The church is larger than any one denomination, and the service of dedication should make that clear.

The proper color for the dedication of a church is red, the color of the Holy Spirit, "the soul of the church," whose fire fills the holy community. (The Roman rite calls for vestments of "white or of some festive color."[42])

It is appropriate that the communion vessels, pulpit and lectern Bibles, crosses and crucifixes, candlesticks, and other ornaments be carried in procession by their donors or other representatives of the congregation. It may also be fitting that blueprints, construction plans, and tools used in the construction be carried by appropriate people and placed in the altar area for the duration of the service.

Survey of the Service

The congregation gathers outside the new building or at another convenient place such as the parish house, or the former or a neighboring church building. When necessary, because of inclement weather or other circumstances, the congregation may assemble inside the church, but the ministers will enter in procession.

The procession may be led by a processional cross (and torches); banners may also be carried in the procession. The servers lead the procession; the choir follows the cross; the assisting ministers (carrying the communion vessels, Bibles, ornaments, and decorations) and finally the presiding minister bring up the end. The congregation follows. When it is convenient, the procession may walk around the building(s) to be dedicated and then go to the main entrance.

When all have gathered at the door of the church, the presiding

---

41. *Dedication of a Church and an Altar,* p. 12, no. 6; *Book of Common Prayer* (1979), p. 566. See n. 28.
42. *Dedication of a Church and an Altar,* p. 18, no. 23.

minister gives the apostolic greeting, the address, and the prayer.

The address is based on the address and prayer at the beginning of the *Book of Common Prayer* rite:

LUTHERAN	EPISCOPAL
Brothers and sisters: We have come together to dedicate this church for the worship of almighty God and for the building up of the body of Christ. From this day forward let it be a place for the gathering of the people of God, a place for proclaiming the Gospel through Word and Sacrament, a place for bringing life and hope to us and to this community.	Through the ages, Almighty God has moved his people to build houses of prayer and praise, and to set apart places for the ministry of his holy Word and Sacraments. With gratitude for the building (rebuilding, *or* adornment) of (*name of church*), we are now gathered to dedicate and consecrate it in God's Name. Let us pray. Almighty God, we thank you for making us in your image, to share in the ordering of your world. Receive the work of our hands in this place, now to be set apart for your worship, the building up of the living, and the remembrance of the dead, to the praise and glory of your Name; through Jesus Christ our Lord.[43]

The prayer which follows in the Lutheran rite, "Direct us, O Lord, in all our doings" (220), is frequently used in the services of the church and was used at this point before the door of the church by the *Church Book,* the Liturgy of the Joint Synod of Ohio (1912), and *Occasional Services* (1962).

The building is then symbolically given over to the congregation as the builder delivers the keys to the minister, who in turn gives them to a representative of the congregation who unlocks and opens the doors. The handing over of the church is an important act in the Roman Catholic rite, in which "representatives of those who have been involved in the building of the church hand it over to the bishop."[44] There is no parallel act in the Episcopal rite. Other symbols of possession may be given and received: the plan of the building, legal documents for possession of the building, a "book in which the progress of the work is described and the names of those in charge of it and the names of the workers recorded."[45]

43. *Book of Common Prayer* (1979), p. 567.
44. *Dedication of a Church and an Altar,* p. 22, no. 33.
45. Ibid., p. 25, no. 47.

DEDICATIONS AND BLESSINGS

After the verse, "Peace be to this house *and to all who enter here*" (a traditional greeting and in Lutheran use since the *Common Service Book* of 1919), the servers and ministers stand aside, and the choir and people enter the church (led by the processional cross and torches) and move to their places.[46] The cross and torches go to the font, the choir to its place, and the people to the chairs or pews. The servers, assisting ministers, and the presiding minister enter the building last, while Psalm 122 is sung or said, and move to the font where the processional cross and torches stand. The representatives of the congregation (here the assisting ministers) carry such baptismal vessels as a ewer and baptismal shell in the procession and put the vessels on a table, or shelf, by the font. Flowers, candles, and banners may be placed by the font.

The minister and people say the verse, "All your works praise you, O Lord, *and your faithful servants bless you*" (Ps. 145:10). The representative of the congregation who carries the ewer may fill the font at this point by pouring the water from the ewer into it.

The prayer of dedication of the font ⟨513⟩ is basically a condensation of the thanksgiving from Holy Baptism (with a different opening drawn from the Jewish tradition, "Blessed are you, O Lord our God, king of the universe").

Following the blessing of the font, the cross and torches lead the servers, assisting ministers, and presiding minister to the pulpit. An assisting minister who carries the Bible places it on the pulpit (another assisting minister places another Bible on the lectern if there are two places for reading and preaching).

The prayer at the dedication of the pulpit ⟨514⟩ is a new composition drawing a phrase from the Episcopal dedication of the pulpit:

LUTHERAN	EPISCOPAL
Blessed are you, O Lord our God, king of the universe. You have revealed your love for your creation in your Word, our Lord Jesus Christ. Inspired by him, we seek to hold fast the truth and	Father, in every age you have spoken through the voices of prophets, pastors, and teachers. Purify the lives and the lips of those who speak here, that your word only may be proclaimed,

---

46. In the Canadian *Book of Common Prayer* (1959), after the initial greeting of peace (in this form: "Peace be to this House from God our heavenly Father. Peace be to this House from his Son who is our Peace. Peace be to this House from the Holy Ghost, the Comforter"):

the Bishop with his Staff may trace the sign of the Cross upon the floor, together with the Alpha and the Omega. Then he shall say: "I claim this place for Christ crucified, who is the First and the Last, and the Lord of all. Amen." (pp. 683-84)

LUTHERAN

to know your purposes. Purify
the lips of those who speak here,
and grant us grace to hear your
love in all that is proclaimed from
this pulpit which today we set
apart; through our Lord Jesus
Christ, who lives and reigns with
you and the Holy Spirit, one God
forever.

EPISCOPAL

and your word only may be
heard.
Your word is a lantern to
our feet,
And a light to our path.
We dedicate this pulpit in the
Name of the Father, and of the
Son, and of the Holy Spirit.
Amen.[47]

The pulpit (and lectern) hanging may be set in place and a crucifix,
or cross, hung near the pulpit to remind the preacher of what is to be
proclaimed.

After the blessing of the pulpit, the cross and torches lead the servers,
assisting ministers, and the presiding minister to the altar. The assisting
ministers carrying the sacramental vessels place them on the credence
table. The prayer of dedication of the altar ⟨515⟩ is drawn from the blessing of an altar in *Occasional Services* (1962):

Occasional Services
(1962)

O God, who dost continually
nourish thy Church with the
heavenly Bread in Christ Jesus:
Grant unto all, who at this Altar
receive thy precious gifts, the
grace to walk in faith and love
throughout their lives, until they
finally behold thee face to face in
thine eternal kingdom; through
the same Jesus Christ, thy Son,
our Lord.[48]

Occasional Services
(1982)

Blessed are you, O Lord our God,
king of the universe. You nourish
your people with the heavenly
bread in Jesus Christ. Bless and
sanctify all who receive his body
and blood at this altar which
today we set apart. Give them
grace to live in faith and love
throughout their lives, until at last
we all behold you face to face
at the heavenly altar where your
saints and angels praise you
forever; through our Lord Jesus
Christ, who lives and reigns with
you and the Holy Spirit, one
God forever.

At the dedication of the altar, the presiding minister may lay a hand on
the altar. If the mensa is prepared in the traditional manner with five

---

47. *Book of Common Prayer* (1979), p. 571.
48. *Occasional Services* (1962), p. 175.

crosses (for the five wounds of Christ) inscribed in it (one in each corner and a fifth in the center), the minister may trace with a finger these five crosses, beginning with the one in the center, while saying the prayer:

> Blessed are you, O Lord our God, king of the universe. You nourish your people (+) with the heavenly bread in Jesus Christ. Bless and sanctify all (+) who receive his body and blood at this altar which today we set apart. Give them grace (+) to live in faith and love throughout their lives, until at last (+) we all behold you face to face at the heavenly altar where your saints and angels praise you forever (+); through our Lord Jesus Christ, who lives and reigns with you and the Holy Spirit, one God, forever.

The prayer at its conclusion looks beyond this earthly house to "the heavenly altar"—a thought which was expressed in the conclusion of the prayer of dedication in the *Common Service Book*:

> And so prepare Thy servants who worship here, that when their earthly pilgrimage is ended, they may be received into the House not made with hands, eternal in the heavens, there to behold Thy glory, O Everlasting God, Father, Son, and Holy Spirit, and to adore and praise Thee, One God, world without end.[49]

The thought was simplified at the end of the prayer provided in *Occasional Services* (1962) for matins and vespers on the day of dedication:

> O God, who dost call all men unto thee, and who dost graciously receive all them that come: Vouchsafe thy pardon to all those who here confess their sins; bestow the comfort of thy Spirit on those who humbly and faithfully bring thee their needs and sorrows; accept the praise and worship that are offered here; and grant that many may find thee in this place, and, finding thee, be filled in soul and body with all things needful; and finally, with all thine own, be united in that communion with thee which is eternal in the heavens, where thou livest and reignest, one God, world without end.[50]

After the blessing of the altar, the frontal (if there is one) and the fair linen are spread on it. The crucifix, or cross, and candles are set in place, and the candles are lit. As a further sign of rejoicing, flowers may be placed around the altar at this time.

The "Lighting of the Altar and the Church" is a separate section of the Roman Catholic rite for the Dedication of a Church.[51] The bishop gives the deacon a lighted candle and says:

---

49. *Common Service Book,* text ed. (1919), p. 471.
50. *Occasional Services* (1962), p. 120.
51. *Dedication of a Church and an Altar,* pp. 33–34, nos. 69–71.

DEDICATION OF A CHURCH BUILDING: THE COMPLETED BUILDING

> Light of Christ,
> shine forth in the Church
> and bring all nations
> to the fullness of truth.

Then the bishop sits, and the deacon lights the altar candles for the celebration of the Eucharist, "and the other lamps are lit as a sign of rejoicing." Meanwhile the song of Tobias from the apocryphal book of Tobit is sung (Tob. 13:10, 13–15, 17), with the antiphon:

> Your light will come, Jerusalem; upon you the glory of the Lord will dawn and all nations will walk in your light, alleluia.

(During Lent, the antiphon is "Jerusalem, city of God, you will shine with the light of God's splendor; all people on earth will pay you homage.") A rubric allows that "another appropriate song may be sung, especially one in honor of Christ, the light of the world." Thus, in yet another way, the eschatological dimension of the dedication and of the building is shown.

After the dedication and vesting of the altar, the cross and torches lead the servers, assisting ministers, and presiding minister to the midst of the people. This location is intended to be not the chancel but a place such as halfway down the center aisle. This indicates that the church is not an auditorium with a stage for a performance, but that the building is the house of the church and the church is the people.

The prayer of dedication ⟨516⟩ makes use of the opening of King Solomon's prayer at the dedication of the Temple in Jerusalem, which was recalled in earlier Lutheran prayers of dedication in the *Church Book,* the *Common Service Book,* and *Occasional Services* (1962):

> Almighty and everlasting God, whom the Heaven of heavens cannot contain, yet who art willing to have an House fashioned by man, wherein thine honor dwelleth and where men may worship thee . . . [52]

The prayer of the day ⟨148⟩ also employs the same reference.

The minister says the prayer with arms extended in the ancient posture of prayer and in imitation of Solomon (1 Kings 8:22).

After the prayer from the midst of the people, the servers and ministers go to their places. The assisting ministers, depending on whether they have a further role in the service, return to their places in the congregation or in the altar area.

---

52. *Church Book* (1892), p. 438; *Common Service Book,* text ed. (1919), p. 472; *Occasional Services* (1962), p. 117.

The proper Preface for the Dedication of a Church is taken from the *Book of Common Prayer* (1979):

LUTHERAN

Through Jesus Christ, our great high priest, in whom we are built up as living stones of a holy temple, that we might offer before you the sacrifice of thanksgiving.

EPISCOPAL

Through Jesus Christ our great High Priest, in whom we are built up as living stones of a holy temple, that we might offer before you a sacrifice of praise and prayer which is holy and pleasing in your sight.[53]

The Roman Catholic rite provides a solemn blessing at the conclusion of the Mass.[54] The bishop extends his hands over the people and blesses them saying:

The Lord of earth and heaven
has assembled you before him this day
to dedicate this house of prayer.
May he fill you with the blessings of heaven.
  Amen.
God the Father wills that all his children
scattered through the world
become one family in his Son.
May he make you his temple,
the dwelling place of his Holy Spirit.
  Amen.
May God free you from every bond of sin,
dwell within you and give you joy.
May you live with him for ever
in the company of all his saints.
  Amen.
The bishop takes the pastoral staff and continues.
May almighty God bless you,
the Father, and the Son, + and the Holy Spirit.
  Amen.[55]

It is desirable that the anniversary of the dedication of a church be celebrated annually as an occasion to review its history and to discover anew its nature and purpose. The propers for the dedication and anniversary are in the Ministers Edition of the *LBW* (p. 185). See also the Litany

---

53. *Book of Common Prayer* (1979), p. 381.
54. *Dedication of a Church and an Altar*, pp. 39–40, no. 84.
55. Ibid.

of Thanksgiving for a Church in the *Book of Common Prayer* (pp. 578–79).

Moreover, congregations should not overlook the observance of the festival day of their patron or title (for example, St. John on December 27 or June 24; St. Paul on January 25 or June 29; Trinity on Trinity Sunday; Christ the King on the Last Sunday after Pentecost; Incarnation on the First Sunday after Christmas).

For a congregation whose name is less obviously connected with the church calendar, it can be a useful exercise to examine with care the calendar and lectionary to find a day which seems appropriate for its patronal or titular festival. These days may be appropriate celebrations for congregations bearing the more common names of Lutheran churches in North America: Advocate, Holy Spirit, Holy Comforter—Pentecost, Vigil of Pentecost, or in year B the First Sunday after Pentecost, which in year B is observed as the Octave of Pentecost; Atonement, Reconciliation—Wednesday in Holy Week or in year A the Fourth Sunday after Pentecost (Second Lesson, see KJV), in year B Second Sunday in Lent (Second Lesson, see KJV), in year C the First Sunday after Christmas (Second Lesson, see KJV); Bethany—July 29, the commemoration of Mary, Martha, and Lazarus of Bethany; Calvary—the Sunday of the Passion; Christ—the Baptism of Our Lord (see especially the Second Lesson); Concordia—June 25, the Presentation of the Augsburg Confession; Emmanuel, Immanuel—December 23 when the proper antiphon to the Magnificat is "O Emmanuel" or, especially in year A, the Fourth Sunday in Advent; Faith—Reformation Day (see especially the Second Lesson); Gethsemane—the Sunday of the Passion; Gloria Dei—Trinity Sunday or Transfiguration (last Sunday after the Epiphany or August 6); Good Shepherd, Shepherd of the Hills, Shepherd of the Valley, Shepherd of the Desert—the Fourth Sunday of Easter; Grace—the Second Sunday after Christmas; Hope—the Fourth Sunday in Advent; Mediator—Monday in Holy Week or in year C the Eighteenth Sunday after Pentecost; Messiah—Baptism of Our Lord or in year A the Second Sunday after the Epiphany or the Second Sunday in Lent; Peace, Prince of Peace, Friedens, Salem—Christmas Day; Redeemer, Savior—the Fourth Sunday in Advent, especially in year A; Transfiguration—the Last Sunday after the Epiphany or August 6 (see Notes on the Liturgy, *LBW,* Min. Ed., p. 14); Zion—the Fourth Sunday in Lent, especially in year C.

Development of the Rite
Dedication of a Church

General Synod (1867)	Joint Synod of Ohio (1912)	General Synod (1881)	General Synod (1900)	*Lutheran Agenda*
	Procession		Procession	
	Ps. 124:8			
	Prayer			
	Hymn			
	Psalm 100			
	Opening doors			
	Peace be to this house . . .			Prayer at door
	Entrance			Entrance
	Psalm 122	Anthem		Psalm 124 or 100 or 122
Psalm 84	Ps. 84: 1, 10a			
Psalm 24	Ps. 24:9–10	Psalm 24	Psalm 24	
			Prayer and entrance	Entrance
			Psalm 122	
			Psalm 43	
Gloria Patri	Gloria Patri		Hymn	
Salutation and response				
Prayer	Prayer			
Address				Address
Lessons	Lessons Rev. 21:1–5 and Luke 19:1–10	Lessons	Lessons	
				[Morning service through offertory]
1 Kings 8: 22–30, 54–58	*or* 1 Kings 8:1–13, 22–30		1 Kings 8:1–13 22–30	

Development of the Rite
Dedication of a Church

Church Book (1892)	Common Service Book (1919)	Occasional Services (1962)	Occasional Services (1982)
(Procession)	Procession	Procession	Procession
	Invocation	Invocation	Greeting
Ps. 124:8	Ps. 124:8	Ps. 124:8	
			Address
Prayer		Prayer	Prayer
Psalm 24	Psalm 24	Psalm 24	
Prayer	Peace be to this house . . .	Peace be to this house . . .	Peace be to this house . . .
Entrance	Entrance	Entrance	Entrance
Psalm 122	Psalm 122	Psalm 122	Psalm 122
Entering chancel:	Entering chancel:	Entering chancel:	
Ps. 43:3–4	Ps. 43:3–4	Psalm 43:3–4	
Hymn	*"Veni Creator Spiritus"*	*"Veni Creator Spiritus"*	
Lesson	Lessons	Lessons	
		Gen. 28:10–17	
1 Kings 8:1–13, 22–30	1 Kings 8:12–30	1 Kings 8:12–30	

Development of the Rite (continued)
Dedication of a Church

General Synod (1867)	Joint Synod of Ohio (1912)	General Synod (1881)	General Synod (1900)	*Lutheran Agenda*
Eph. 2:11–22				
		2 Chron. 6:18–33		
		Psalm 48 or 122		
Heb. 10:19–29		Heb. 10:19–26	Heb. 10:19–25	
		Anthem or hymn		
		Prayer		2 Prayers
		Hymn		
		Presentation		
Apostles' Creed	Apostles' Creed			
Consecration*	Consecration*	Dedication†	Dedication‡ Threefold Amen	Dedication of altar of pulpit of ornaments

---

* And now, in this faith, and with hearts lifted up to Almighty God, from whom cometh down every blessing, we, ministers of the Church of Christ here assembled, do set apart and consecrate this edifice as a house of God, as a place of assembly for the Christian Church under the name of _____ Evangelical Lutheran Church, separating it henceforth from all unhallowed, ordinary, and common uses. We do consecrate it, with its pulpit, its altar, its baptismal font, and all its parts to the honor of Almighty God our heavenly Father, for the offering up to Him of praise and thanksgiving, of prayer and intercession. We consecrate it to the preservation and furtherance of the Gospel of His only-begotten Son, our Lord Jesus Christ, the Enlightener and Redeemer of the world, that in it the Word of the cross may be preached according to the Confessions of our Evangelical Lutheran Church, His holy sacraments may be rightly administered to God's believing people, and His teachings handed down to the latest generations. We consecrate it to the gracious work of the Holy Ghost, that in it, through His influence, the hearts of men may be enlightened, sanctified and sealed unto salvation, and Christian unity, love and happiness may be promoted. To these holy purposes we do set apart and consecrate this house, in the name of the Father, and of the Son, and of the Holy Ghost. Amen.
During the last sentence all the ministers participating in the consecration shall raise the right hand.
But, inasmuch as the consecration of the temple erected by human hands is

Development of the Rite (continued)
Dedication of a Church

Church Book (1892)	Common Service Book (1919)	Occasional Services (1962)	Occasional Services (1982)
		Matt. 16:13–18	
	Heb. 10:19–25	Heb. 10:10–25	
	Eph. 2:13–22	Eph. 2:13–22	
	1 Cor. 3:9–17	1 Cor. 3:9–17	
Prayer	Prayer		
Dedication	Dedication	Dedication of altar of pulpit of font	Dedication of font of pulpit of altar

vain and ineffectual, if not followed by another consecration, even the consecration of those who intend to worship therein, I call upon all of you, who are here present, now to consecrate yourselves anew with all you are and have to the service of God. To Him let our souls be consecrated with all their powers and affections, that they may be renewed after the image of Him who hath created them in righteousness and true holiness! To Him let our bodies be consecrated, that they may be the temples of the Holy Ghost, and all their members and senses be vessels and instruments sanctified unto God! To Him let our calling and station in life be consecrated, that we may faithfully employ them in doing good and glorifying our Father who is in heaven! To Him let our whole life be consecrated, that every day may bear witness that we have not received His grace in vain, but that we are living to His glory! Thus may the consecration of this house be accompanied by the consecration of ourselves. And let all the people say, Amen. (Joint Synod of Ohio, pp. 171–72)

† Dearly beloved in the Lord: Forasmuch as devout and holy men, as well under the law as under the gospel, moved either by the express command of God, or by the secret inspiration of the blessed Spirit, and acting agreeably to their own reason and a sense of holy veneration, have erected houses for the public worship of God, and separated them from all unhallowed, worldly, and common uses, in order to fill men's minds with greater reverence for his glorious Majesty, and affect their hearts with more devotion and humility in His service; which pious works have been approved of and graciously accepted by

Development of the Rite (continued)
Dedication of a Church

General Synod (1867)	Joint Synod of Ohio (1912)	General Synod (1881)	General Synod (1900)	*Lutheran Agenda*
Prayer	Prayer			
		Nicene Creed		
			General prayer	
Our Father		Te Deum		
				Holy Communion

---

our Heavenly Father: Let us not doubt but that He will also favorably approve our godly purpose of setting apart this place in solemn manner, for the performance of the several offices of religious worship, and bestow His blessing upon this our undertaking.

I therefore pronounce this _____ Evangelical Lutheran Church to be set apart henceforth for offices sacred and divine.

Unto Thee, O God, the Father of our Lord Jesus Christ, and the Creator of all things, we dedicate this house.

Unto Thee, O Christ, the everlasting Son of the Father, and the Redeemer of the world, we dedicate this house.

Unto Thee, O Holy Ghost, proceeding from the Father and the Son, the Sanctifier of the saints, we dedicate this house.

We dedicate it for the offering up of praise and prayer; for the administration of the sacraments; for the preaching of the word. We dedicate it to the extension of the Gospel of Christ, and the salvation of man. We dedicate it to the gracious work of the Holy Spirit, and the promotion of unity, charity, and peace throughout the world.

To these holy purposes, and the furtherance of the will of God in all things, we set apart and consecrate this house, in the name of the Father, and of the Son, and of the Holy Ghost, One God, world without end. Amen. (pp. 146–48)

‡ O Lord, our God, we thank Thee for Thy great goodness in moving us to build this house wherein to proclaim Thy Holy Word and to praise Thy name. We pray Thee with our whole heart, let Thy holy Baptism be efficacious at this font. Let Thy saving Gospel be proclaimed from this pulpit. Let this altar be spread with the gracious gifts of Thy Table. Let this organ resound with Thy praise. Preserve Thy Word and Sacrament pure and uncorrupted in this place, and through the same enlighten and sanctify those whom Thou dost now and hereafter gather to Thyself here, that they may become the temple of the Holy Ghost. Remember, according to Thy mercy, the congregation which has erected this house. As they have builded for Thee a house to the honor of Thy name, build Thou them into a spiritual house, a dwelling of Thy Holy Spirit. Send hither at all times faithful pastors and teachers. Awaken the hearts of the

Development of the Rite (continued)
Dedication of a Church

Church Book (1892)	Common Service Book (1919)	Occasional Services (1962)	Occasional Services (1982)
		Prayer	
The dedication*	The dedication†	The dedication‡	The dedication
Nicene Creed			
	Introit and The Service	Introit and The Service	Hymn
			Holy Communion

---

congregation, that they may ever gladly obey the call to Thy sanctuary. Graciously hear us when we offer Thee here our thanks and our petitions. Bless the marriages which shall here be solemnized. Forgive us our sins as we here confess them. And prepare us in this Thy house, that when our pilgrimage is ended, we may depart in peace to our Father's house not made with hands, there to unite in Thy praise, with all the angels and the saints, through Jesus Christ our Lord. Amen.

And now this _____ Evangelical Lutheran Church, being dedicated by the Word of God and prayer to be a sanctuary, is henceforth set apart with its pulpit, its altar and font, and all its vessels and furniture to the service of God: In the name of the Father, and of the Son, and of the Holy Ghost.
                    Amen. Amen. Amen.   (pp. 135–36)

* And now, we do set apart and consecrate this Edifice of the Evangelical Lutheran Church of _____ as a House of God: In the Name of the Father, and of the Son, and of the Holy Ghost.
Amen. Amen. Amen.   (p. 439)

† I do now set apart this _____ Evangelical Lutheran Church as a House of God; and dedicate it to the glory and honor of Almighty God, and to the service of His holy Church: In the Name of the Father, and of the Son, and of the Holy Ghost. Amen.
Amen. Amen. Amen.   (pp. 471–72)

‡ Blest and dedicate be this Evangelical Lutheran Church of _____ to the glory and honor of Almighty God, and to the service of his Holy Church: In the Name of the Father, and of the Son, and of the Holy Ghost. Amen.
Amen. Amen. Amen.   (p. 118)

Comparison of Rites
Dedication of a Church

Orthodox	Roman Catholic	Lutheran	Lutheran (alternate)	Episcopal
				Address
				Prayer
Entrance of the bishop	Entrance	Procession	Procession	Procession
		Greeting	Greeting	
		Address	Address	
		Prayer	Prayer	
	Giving church to bishop	Giving church to congregation	Giving church to congregation	
		Peace be . . .	Peace be . . .	Peace be . . .
		Psalm 122	Psalm 122	Psalm 122
				Prayer by bishop layperson rector
	Sprinkling people and building with prayer	Dedication of font of pulpit of altar of church	Dedication of font	Dedication of font (Baptism)
	Gloria		Hymn of praise	
	Opening prayer	Prayer of the day	Prayer of the day	
			Dedication of pulpit	Dedication of pulpit
	Lessons		Lessons	Lessons
				(Dedication of musical instrument)
	Gospel	Gospel	Gospel	Gospel
	Homily	Sermon	Sermon	Sermon
		Hymn of the day	Hymn of the day	
	Creed	Creed	Creed	Creed
	Litany of Saints	Prayers	Prayers	Prayers
		The peace	The peace	
Preparation of columns of altar				
Prayer				
Placing altar table on columns				
Psalms 145, 23	Depositing relics			
Prayer	Prayer of dedication		Dedication of altar	Dedication of altar
Litany				
Washing and vesting altar	Anointing altar and walls of church			

290

Comparison of Rites (continued)
Dedication of a Church

ORTHODOX	ROMAN CATHOLIC	LUTHERAN	LUTHERAN (alternate)	EPISCOPAL
Psalms 84, 51, 132	Incensing altar and church			
Prayer	Vesting altar			
Lighting candles	Lighting altar and church			
Bringing relics, icons, Gospels				
Psalm 24				
Prayer				
Litany				
				The peace
	Offering	Offering	Offering	Offering
		Great Thanksgiving	Great Thanksgiving	Great Thanksgiving
		Communion	Communion	Communion
		Postcommunion	Postcommunion	Postcommunion
			Dedicatory prayer	
		Benediction	Benediction	Benediction

DEDICATION OF A FACILITY
FOR CHURCH USE
(*Occasional Services*, pp. 178–79)

Parallel Rites

Episcopal

Celebration for a Home, *Book of Occasional Services,* pp. 131–41, could be adapted.

Lutheran

Dedication of a Parish House, Church House, School, or Hospital, *Occasional Services* (1962), pp. 164–67.

Order for the Dedication of a Church House, *Occasional Services* (1930), pp. 109–12.

Office for the Dedication of a Hospital—House of Mercy, *Occasional Services* (1930), pp. 176–79.

The Order for the Dedication of a Parish House, *Lutheran Agenda*, pp. 181–82.

The Order for the Dedication of a School, *Lutheran Agenda,* pp. 168–71.

Methodist   An Office for the Dedication of a School, College, or University Building, *Book of Worship*, pp. 361–64.
An Office for the Dedication of a Hospital, *Book of Worship*, pp. 365–69.

Purpose

This rite is to dedicate any church facility other than the church building itself.

Characteristics

The order is simple in order to be applicable to the variety of uses to which it may be put. A one-sentence statement, a lesson, a verse and response, and a prayer are all that are required. A psalm or canticle and hymns may also be added to this simple form.

The Holy Communion may be celebrated following the dedication, or the rite may stand by itself. The nature of the facility will help determine whether or not the Holy Communion is appropriate.

Background

For many centuries church buildings were used only for worship, and the rites of dedication separated them "from all unhallowed, ordinary, and common uses."[56] In recent decades, however, church buildings are often not so set off from the rest of life and may in fact shelter several functions.

In the past, therefore, one expected rites of dedication for a variety of church facilities in addition to the dedication of a church. But modern rites lay much less emphasis on the separation of these functions. The *Book of Common Prayer* and the *Book of Occasional Services,* for example, make no provision for the blessing of a church facility other than a church or chapel. However, the *Book of Offices* (1949) provided prayers for the dedication of a parish house; a school, college, or seminary; a hospital; a conventual house—all within the structure of the blessing of houses. *Occasional Services* (1930) provided for the dedication of a church house and the dedication of a hospital or house of mercy. The *Lutheran Agenda* provided orders for the dedication of a school, a parish house, and a parsonage. *Occasional Services* (1962) had one

---

56. *The Book of Worship* published by Order of the Evangelical Lutheran General Synod in North America (1867), p. 119 (see also p. 117); *The Liturgy of the Evangelical Lutheran Church* prepared and published by order of the General Synod (1881), p. 147; *A Liturgy for the Use of Evangelical Lutheran Pastors* prepared by a committee appointed by the Evangelical Lutheran Joint Synod of Ohio and other states (1912), p. 171.

omnibus order for The Dedication of a Parish House, Church House, School or Hospital.

Survey of the Service

When appropriate, the congregation may go in procession from the place of worship to the site of the dedication. The processional cross (flanked by torches) may lead the way. Then follow the servers, choir, assisting ministers, the presiding minister, and then the congregation. A hymn may be sung in procession or at the site.

A psalm or canticle may follow the opening statement by the presiding minister. Then a lesson is read. *Occasional Services* (1930) appointed Ps. 119:1-6 or Psalm 34 for the dedication of a church house and appointed this list of lessons: Exod. 20:1-17; Deut. 6:4-9; Isa. 55:1-3, 6-13; Matt. 13:1-9; Luke 2:40-52; John 21:15-17; 2 Tim. 2:1-15; 1 John 1:1-10. It made no provision for psalms or lessons in the Office for the Dedication of a Hospital—House of Mercy. The *Lutheran Agenda* suggested for the dedication of a school: Deut. 6:1-9; 1 Sam. 3:1-10; Psalm 8; Matt. 21:10-16; Mark 10:13-16; Luke 2:42-52; 19:1-10. *Occasional Services* (1962) for its general rite for the Dedication of a Parish House, Church House, School or Hospital suggested Psalms 6, 23, 34, 46, 48; 119:1-16; 130; and suggested as lessons Exod. 20:1-17; Deut. 6:4-9; Isa. 55:6-13; Mark 1:23-34; Luke 2:40-52; John 21:15-17; Heb. 12:11-15; 2 Tim. 2:1-15; 1 John 1:1-10; James 5:13-16; Eph. 2:13-22. (These last two citations, which are out of biblical order, were apparently late additions to the list.)

Prayer ⟨519⟩, cast in general terms, is a new composition.

Appropriate prayers (no. 8) when there is no Holy Communion may be selected from the collection of Petitions, Intercessions, and Thanksgivings (*LBW*, Min. Ed., pp. 105-15):

    For a camp: Use of Leisure (188)[57]

      Conservation of Natural Resources (216)[58]

    For a retreat center: Self-Dedication (203)[59]

    For a school: Schools (184)[60]

---

57. A prayer adapted from the 1979 *Book of Common Prayer* (p. 825, no. 32) and written for that book by James G. Birney.

58. A prayer adapted from the 1979 *Book of Common Prayer* (p. 827, no. 41), drafted by Charles W. F. Smith.

59. A prayer borrowed from the 1979 *Book of Common Prayer* (pp. 832-33, no. 61) and written by William Temple, archbishop of Canterbury (1942-44). See *The Living Church* (June 8, 1935).

60. A prayer borrowed from the 1979 *Book of Common Prayer* (p. 824, no. 31), which is a revision of a prayer in the 1928 American Prayer Book. The 1928 prayer was a revision of a prayer in the 1912 Scottish Prayer Book.

Grace to Receive the Word (201)[61]
The Care of Children (232)[62]
Prayer of the Church, "Bless the schools of the Church . . ."[63]
For a retirement home: The Aged (229)[64]
For a parish hall: The Mission of the Church (192)[65]
For a resource center: Spread of the Gospel (190)[66]
For a youth center: Young Persons (233)[67]
For a gymnasium: Use of Leisure (188)[68]
For a hospital: Renewers of Society (141)[69]
Those in Affliction (223)[70]
The Poor and the Neglected (181)[71]

These prayers from the *LBW* will help to suggest ideas for other prayers
and intercessions.

DEDICATION OF A CEMETERY

(*Occasional Services*, pp. 180–82)

Parallel Rites

Anglican   Form of Consecration of Church-yard or Cemetery
                            separately, Canadian *Book of Common Prayer*
                            (1959), pp. 691–92.

---

61. The Collect for the Second Sunday in Advent in the 1549 *Book of Common Prayer*
and carried forward into subsequent prayer books. In the 1979 Prayer Book it is appointed
for "Proper 28," the Sunday closest to November 16. It was used in the *Lutheran Hymnal*
as the Collect for the Word (p. 14).

62. The prayer is adapted from the 1979 *Book of Common Prayer* (p. 829, no. 46) and
originally appeared in the 1928 American Prayer Book. It was written by John W. Suter,
Jr., and based on a much longer prayer by William Austin Smith. The biblical allusion
is to Phil. 4:8.

63. The Prayer of the Church, *Service Book and Hymnal,* music ed., p. 7.

64. A prayer written for the 1979 *Book of Common Prayer* (p. 830, no. 49) by Charles
W. F. Smith and Ivy Watkins Smith.

65. A prayer written for the 1979 *Book of Common Prayer* (pp. 816–17, no. 8) by Caroline Rose.

66. A prayer adapted from the *Service Book and Hymnal* (p. 219, no. 10), which was
adapted from the *Book of Common Worship* of the Presbyterian Church in the U.S.A.
(1906), p. 133.

67. A prayer written for the 1979 *Book of Common Prayer* (p. 829, no. 7) by Sister Ann
Brooke Bushong of the Church Army.

68. See n. 57.

69. New.

70. Adapted from the *Service Book and Hymnal* (p. 223, no. 24) which adapted the
prayer from the Church of Scotland's *Prayers for Divine Service* (2d ed., 1929), p. 239.

71. Adapted from the 1979 *Book of Common Prayer* (p. 826, no. 35), which revised a
prayer in the 1928 American Prayer Book, first published among proposals for revision of
1892 in *The Book Annexed.*

Lutheran   Order for the Blessing of a Cemetery, *Occasional Services* (1962), pp. 121–24.

Order for the Blessing of a Cemetery, *Occasional Services* (1930), pp. 112–18.

Order for the Dedication of a Burial Ground, *Lutheran Agenda,* pp. 178–80.

Dedication of the God's Acre, *Forms for Ministerial Acts,* General Synod (1900), pp. 137–42.

Order for the Consecration of a Burial Ground, *Liturgy of the Evangelical Lutheran Church,* General Synod (1881), pp. 151–56.

Purpose

This order is to mark out a plot of ground as a burying place for God's people and to set it aside from other uses as "God's acre."

This order may also be used to dedicate a mausoleum.

Characteristics

The rite is simple and direct. There is a reading, a hymn, a prayer beginning with verses from Psalm 91, and the benediction.

The service may be used alone or, if the cemetery is near the place of worship, it may be used in connection with a celebration of the Holy Communion.

Background

The dedication of a cemetery, which had been a relatively common practice as evidenced by the incorporation of rites for the dedication of a cemetery in most Lutheran service books since the nineteenth century, is apparently falling into disuse. It is no longer common for churches to set aside their own cemeteries.

There is no comparable rite in the current Episcopal books. When needed, presumably an adaptation of the Burial of the Dead would serve. The Episcopal *Book of Offices* (1949) provided a simple rite for the Benediction of a Grave or Cemetery as part of a section on Benediction of Church Ornaments. In its entirety, the form was:

> *Antiphon.* In the place where he was crucified there was a garden: + and in the garden a new sepulchre, wherein was never man yet laid.
>
> The eternal God is thy refuge;
> *And underneath are the everlasting arms.*
>
> Let us pray.
>
> O God, whose blessed Son was laid in the holy sepulchre in the garden;

> Bless, we beseech thee, this *Grave,* that *he* whose *body* is buried here may dwell with Christ in paradise, and may come to thy heavenly kingdom; through the same Jesus Christ our Lord. *Amen.*[72]

The Form of Consecration of a Church-yard or Cemetery provided in the Canadian Prayer Book (1959) is in large measure a legal transaction. The religious ceremonies are primarily a procession around the portion of ground to be consecrated and these prayers:

> O God, who by the example of thy holy servants in all ages, hast taught us to assign particular places, where the bodies of thy saints may rest in peace, whilst their souls are kept in the hands of their faithful Redeemer: Accept, we beseech thee, this charitable work of ours, in separating this portion of ground to that good purpose; and give us grace that, by the frequent instances of mortality which we behold, we may so number our days as to apply our hearts unto wisdom; so that by thy mercy we may have our part in the resurrection to eternal life, with him who died for our sins and rose again for our justification, and now liveth and reigneth with thee and the Holy Spirit, one God, world without end. *Amen.*
>
> O Lord Jesu Christ, who by thy death hast overcome death, and by thy rising to life again hast restored to us everlasting life: Grant to all thy servants, who shall here be buried, that their bodies may rest in peace, and that through the grave and gate of death they may pass to a joyful resurrection; through thy merits, who livest with the Father and the Holy Spirit, one God, world without end. *Amen.* [73]

The bishop then says the Collect for All Saints' Day. A hymn may be sung and an address given; the service then concludes with the benediction.

There is no modern Roman Catholic rite available in English.

The word "cemetery," from the Greek *koimeterion,* a "resting/sleeping place" (cf. "dormitory," which is from the Latin equivalent, and the German *Friedhof,* a resting place, literally, a "house of peace"), seems to have been used exclusively of Christian burial grounds. Christian cemeteries appear to have been blessed from the ninth century. Roman Catholic canon law required each parish to have its own cemetery, although the bishop could allow several parishes to use an interparochial cemetery, and required cemeteries to be blessed. Two forms were provided. The preferred form was the Rite of Solemn Blessing, sometimes called the consecration, which was conducted by a bishop. This was an elaborate order in which the cemetery was marked with five crosses, tying

---

72. *Book of Offices* (2d ed., 1949), p. 70.
73. Canadian *Book of Common Prayer* (1959), p. 691.

it symbolically to the body of the crucified and risen Lord with his five wounds. The other form was the simple blessing in the *Roman Ritual* which is conducted by a priest authorized by a bishop. This form can also be used to bless a single grave when burial is in a cemetery that has not been blessed.

Since the Reformation the Lutheran churches have followed no uniform practice. The later agendas provide for the blessing of cemeteries. In the judgment of the *Encyclopedia of the Lutheran Church* (I, 384):

> Lutheran congregations . . . should, where they do not possess cemeteries of their own, at least insist on blessing the individual graves of their members. The intent and purpose of such a consecration is not to add a new quality to the grave, but to bear public witness to the distinction between the baptized and the unbaptized, between members of the church and such as have severed their connection with the church.

Such a distinction makes more sense, perhaps, in a country with a state church in which nearly everyone at least begins with a "connection with the church."

The Agenda of the United Evangelical Lutheran Church (Part IV) contains an order for the blessing of a cemetery:

Introduction
Address
Lesson
Our Father
Collect
Consecration
> (Hallowed be this ground as a resting place for such as have died according to God's will. In the name of the Father, and of the Son, and of the Holy Spirit.)

Preparation for the Service

A large wooden cross may be set up in the middle of the cemetery in preparation for the dedication.

Legal requirements, such as the enclosure of the cemetery, must be satisfied.[74]

Survey of the Service

Occasional Services (1962) said that "the President of the Synod or District, or the Pastor of the Parish, may officiate at the Blessing of a

---

74. Ibid. "Before the Consecration of the Church-yard or Cemetery takes place, the Bishop shall make certain that the ground is sufficiently enclosed and that reasonable provision has been made for its maintenance."

Cemetery." *Occasional Services* (1982) does not make any reference to who may appropriately lead the service except that the person is expected to be ordained, as indicated by the (P) for presiding minister.

During the hymn (no. 4) it may be possible and desirable for the ministers and people to go in procession around the perimeter of the cemetery. More than one hymn may be necessary to accompany the action.

The versicles before the prayer (no. 5) are from Ps. 91: 1, 4, 11. They are a remnant of a psalm which has in Lutheran use often been associated with the blessing of a cemetery. The translation is that of the psalter in the *LBW*.

The prayer of dedication ⟨520⟩ is a new composition praising God's eternity, remembering the lives of those who have gone before us, and recognizing that the graves of the faithful have already been sanctified by Jesus' rest in the tomb. (See the prayer (287) in the committal service, *LBW,* Min. Ed., p. 337, which is in part a recognition of the blessing of the grave.) The prayer concludes with the promise of new life.

The older Lutheran rites (1930, 1962) contained a marvelous prefacial blessing, drawn from the Roman Catholic solemn rite, which it would be a pity to lose:

> Blessing and honor, and thanksgiving and glory, be unto thee, O Lord, Holy Father, Almighty, Everlasting God, through Christ our Lord, who is the everlasting, unwaning Day, the eternal Glory; who commanded his followers so to walk that they may escape the darkness of everlasting night, and come happily to the land of brightness; who, in the Manhood which he took upon him, wept over Lazarus, and by the power of his Godhead restored him to life; and who brought salvation unto mankind crushed under the weight of sin; through whom we humbly beseech thee, O Lord, that we and all who sleep in Jesus may be numbered in the assembly of the saints; may come to thee, who art the Everlasting Life; and may joyfully praise thee with all thine elect for evermore; who livest and reignest, God, world without end.[75]

It may perhaps be used after the prayer of dedication (no. 5).

Congregations fortunate enough to have a cemetery adjacent to the church building (for the presence of the graves reminds the living of the shortness of life and points to the hope of the resurrection) should be encouraged to celebrate brief rites in the cemetery annually. An appropriate time is All Saints' Day (or the Sunday following). After the service, the congregation can go in procession to the cemetery, say or sing Psalm 91, hear a brief lesson, and offer appropriate prayers such as (235) and (222) (*LBW*, Min. Ed., pp. 115, 113).

---

75. *Occasional Services* (1962), p. 124; *Occasional Services* (1930), p. 118.

Development of the Rite
Dedication of a Cemetery

General Synod (1881)	General Synod (1900)	*Lutheran Agenda*	*Occasional Services* (1930)*	*Occasional Services* (1962)	*Occasional Services* (1982)
	(Hymn)		Hymn	Hymn	(Procession)
Invocation		Invocation	Invocation	Invocation	
		(Hymn)			
	Kyrie	(Kyrie)			
Prayer		Prayer	Verses	Verses	
	Psalm 90	(Psalm 90)	Psalm 23	Psalm 91 (or 23 or 142)	
Lessons Genesis 23	Lessons Genesis 23	Lesson(s)	Lessons Gen. 23: 1–20	Lessons Gen. 23: 1–20	Lesson(s)
	1 Thess. 4: 13–18		1 Thess. 4: 13–18	1 Thess. 4: 13–18	
1 Cor. 15: 12–26				1 Cor. 15: 51–57	
			John 14: 1–6 or 19:38–42	John 14:1–6 John 19: 38–42	
		(Hymn)	Hymn		
Address		(Address)			(Address)
					Hymn
		Verses			Verses
			Litany		
			Kyrie		
	Prayer				
	Our Father		Our Father		
			5 prayers	3 prayers	
Dedication Prayer	Dedication	Dedication	Dedication	Dedication	Dedication
Our Father			Our Father		
	(Hymn)	Hymn	(Hymn)	(Hymn)	
			(Address)	(Address)	
			Benedicamus		Benedicamus
Benediction	Benediction	Benediction	Benediction	Benediction	Benediction
			Hymn	Hymn	

*The structure of the 1930 rite follows that of matins and vespers.

Comparison of Rites
Dedication of a Cemetery

ROMAN CATHOLIC (solemn)	ROMAN CATHOLIC (simple)	*Occasional Services* (1930)	*Occasional Services* (1962)	*Occasional Services* (1982)
Placing 5 wooden crosses*	Placing one wooden cross			Placing one wooden cross
		Hymn	(Hymn)	Procession
		Invocation	Invocation	
		Vesper verses	Vesper verses	
		Psalm 23		
		Hymn		
Sermon		Lessons	Lessons	Lessons
Prayer			Hymn	Hymn
Litany of the Saints	Litany of the Saints	Litany		
		Kyrie		
Psalm 51, circling and sprinkling cemetery		Our Father		
1. At front cross Prayer Fixing 3 candles	Prayer Fixing 3 candles	Prayer		
2. To rear cross Psalms 6, 32 Prayer Fixing 3 candles				

---

*The five crosses are arranged in the form of a cross (as on the Easter Candle) at the borders of the cemetery and in the center:

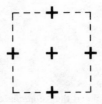

Comparison of Rites (continued)
Dedication of a Cemetery

ROMAN CATHOLIC (solemn)	ROMAN CATHOLIC (simple)	Occasional Services (1930)	Occasional Services (1962)	Occasional Services (1982)
3. To right cross Psalm 38 Prayer Fixing 3 candles				
4. To left cross Psalm 102 Prayer Fixing 3 candles				
5. To center cross Psalms 130, 143		Prayer		Versicles and prayer
Preface		Preface and blessing	Preface and blessing	
Fixing 3 candles				
Prayer		(Hymn)	(Hymn)	
		(Address)	(Address)	
		Benedicamus		Benedicamus
Blessing		Blessing	Blessing	Blessing
Eucharist in the church				

DEDICATION OF AN ORGAN
OR OTHER MUSICAL INSTRUMENT
(*Occasional Services*, pp. 173–75)

Parallel Rites

Episcopal   Dedication of Church Furnishings and Ornaments:
4. A Bell (traditionally reserved to the Bishop);
17. An Organ or Other Musical Instrument, *Book of Occasional Services*, pp. 182, 189.

Lutheran   The Blessing of Instruments of Music for Use in the Church, *Occasional Services* (1962), pp. 184–85.

Office for the Blessing of an Organ, Office for the Blessing of a Tower Bell, *Occasional Services* (1930), pp. 165–67, 167–70.

The Order for the Dedication of an Organ, The Order for the Dedication of a Bell, *Lutheran Agenda*, pp. 172–74, 175–77.

The Dedication of an Organ, The Dedication of a Bell, *Forms for Ministerial Acts*, General Synod (1900), pp. 142–44, 145–46.

Methodist   An Office for the Dedication of a Church Organ or Other Instruments of Sacred Music, *Book of Worship*, pp. 370–71.

Purpose

This rite is intended only for the dedication of an instrument permanently installed in the worship space for use there. Such instruments are the organ, piano, harpsichord, and handbells.

This rite is not for the blessing of such things as a new piano for the church school or an instrument for personal use.

This rite, like the parallel rite in the 1962 *Occasional Services*, may also be used for the dedication of church bells. (In liturgical books, the blessing of bells usually follows next after the blessing of an organ.)

Characteristics

When the organ or other musical instrument is dedicated at the same time as the church building, this rite is integrated into the service of dedication.

It is presented separately since the installation of an organ usually takes place some months, or years, after the completion of the building.

Survey of the Service

The instrument is not played for worship until the dedication is completed.

When an organ is dedicated, it is appropriate for a burst of praise from the instrument to follow the prayer of dedication. When other instruments are dedicated, they may be played similarly where possible.

The antiphon to the psalm (Job 21:12) is suggested by the *Book of Occasional Services* (p. 189).

The versicles introducing the prayer of dedication (no. 6) are from Ps. 81:1–2. The translation is that of the psalter in the *LBW*. The dedicatory prayer ⟨517⟩ is a new composition; the phrase "Be with us now as we dedicate this _____ to your praise and glory" is from the Episcopal *Book of Occasional Services* (p. 193).

The concluding prayer when there is no Holy Communion ⟨518⟩ is from the Episcopal form for the dedication of An Organ or Other Musical Instrument in the *Book of Occasional Services* (p. 189, changing "temple" to "church").

Development of the Rite
Dedication of an Organ

General Synod (1900)	*Lutheran Agenda*	*Occasional Services* (1930)	*Occasional Services* (1962)	*Occasional Services* (1982)
		(Before The Service)	(Before The Service)	(Before the Holy Communion)
		Invocation	Invocation	Address
		Ps. 124:8	Ps. 124:8	Psalm
		Psalm 150	Ps. 150:1–2	
		Ps. 92:1		
Collect	Collect			
Lessons	Lessons			Lessons
2 Chron. 29:25–31	2 Chron. 29:25–31			2 Chron. 29:25–30
Psalms 93, 150	Psalms 98, 150			
Eph. 5: 19–29	Eph. 5: 19–29			Eph. 5: 18b–20
Rev. 5:6–14	Rev. 5:6–14			Rev. 5: (6–10), 11–14
Sermon				
Offertory	Offertory			
	Address			
		Salutation and response	Salutation and response	Versicles and
Prayer*	Prayer*	2 prayers†	Prayer‡	Prayer

---

*General Synod (1900)	*Lutheran Agenda* (194?)
Almighty and everlasting God, Who dwellest in the heavens, surrounded	Almighty and everlasting God, who dwellest in the heavens, surrounded

Development of the Rite (continued)
Dedication of an Organ

General Synod (1900)	Lutheran Agenda	Occasional Services (1930)	Occasional Services (1962)	Occasional Services (1982)
Our Father	Our Father			
Dedication§	Dedication§	Dedication//	Dedication#	Dedication

*General Synod (1900)

by angels and archangels, who worship Thee, saying Holy, holy, holy, Lord God of Hosts: we bless Thee that thou also inhabitest the praises of Israel. Accept, we beseech Thee, the sacrifice of praise which we bring Thee for all Thy mercies, and especially for the gift of Thy Son, for the founding of Thy Church, for the fellowship of Thy saints, and for the joy of Thy service. We thank Thee that we are permitted this day to set apart this organ to Thy praise. Be pleased to accept and to sanctify this offering. Grant us Thy grace, that by its right use we may be assisted in singing the songs of Zion. Pour out Thy Holy Spirit upon all who shall here assemble, that they may sing with the spirit and with the understanding also. Attune our hearts to sing Thy praise on earth that at length we may join with the innumerable company before Thy throne in the unending praise of heaven, through Jesus Christ, to Whom with Thee and the Holy Ghost, ever one God, be glory and dominion and power, world without end. Amen. (pp. 143-44)

Lutheran Agenda (194?)

by angels and archangels that worship Thee, saying: Holy, holy, holy, Lord God of Hosts, we bless Thee that Thou also inhabitest the praises of Thy people here on earth. Accept, we beseech Thee, the sacrifice of praise which we bring Thee for all Thy mercies, especially for the gift of Thy Son, for the founding of Thy Church, for the fellowship of Thy saints, and for the joy of Thy service. We thank Thee that thou hast of Thy goodness given us this organ, which we this day desire to set apart for Thy praise. Help us so to use it that it may serve only to glorify Thy name and to edify Thy people. May it be sanctified art that awakens its harmonies, that we may at all times with our hearts and mouths sing unto Thee in psalms and hymns and spiritual songs. Even as the tones of this organ peal forth in pleasing unity and concord, so give us all unity of spirit and harmony of faith, that we may here in time with one mind and one mouth glorify Thee, until at length we join with the innumerable company before Thy throne in the unending praise of heaven; through Jesus Christ, to whom, with Thee and the Holy Ghost, be glory and dominion and power, world without end. Amen. (pp. 172-73)

†O God, Who by Thy servant Moses didst command that trumpets should be made and blown at the making of sacrifices to Thy Name and Who didst desire the praise of Thy Name to be chanted by the children of Israel with trumpets and cymbals: Bless, we beseech Thee, this Organ, which we dedicate to Thy Worship; and grant that Thy faithful ones joyfully praising Thee in spiritual songs here on earth may at length enter into the eternal joys in heaven; through Jesus Christ,

Development of the Rite (continued)
Dedication of an Organ

General Synod (1900)	Lutheran Agenda	Occasional Services (1930)	Occasional Services (1962)	Occasional Services (1982)
Hymn		Hymn		
		Blessing	Blessing	
		The Service begins with the introit	The Service begins with the introit	The Holy Communion begins with entrance hymn
		Before Epistle: 2 Chron. 29:25–28 Eph. 5: 15–21	Before Epistle: 2 Chron. 29:25–28	

Thy Son, our Lord. *Amen.*

O God, to Whom the Cherubim and Seraphim adoringly sing, Holy, Holy, Holy: Grant that as our voices are uplifted to Thy praise, so we may continually sing and make melody in our hearts unto Thee, Who livest and reignest, One God, world without end. *Amen.* (p. 166)

‡O Lord our God, who by Thy servant David didst appoint for the Levites instruments of music of the Lord to praise thee, because thy mercy endureth forever: Graciously receive at our hands this Organ (*or*, Bell, *or*, Instrument) which we now dedicate to thy service. Grant unto thy people that they may sing their songs unto thee all the days of their lives in the House of the Lord; and help them so to do with the spirit and with the understanding also, that they may be numbered among those who shall sing the New Song before thy throne; through Jesus Christ our Lord, who liveth and reigneth with thee and the Holy Ghost, one God, world without end. *Amen.* (p. 185)

§And now this organ, set apart by the Word of God and prayer, is henceforth dedicated to the worship of God: In the name of the Father, and of the Son, and of the Holy Ghost. Amen. (pp. 173–74)

//Blest and dedicate be this Organ to the praise of Almighty God, to His honor and glory, and to the uplift of our hearts and minds in the services of His House, In the Name of the Father, and of the Son, and of the Holy Ghost. Amen.

O Come, let us sing unto the Lord: let us make a joyful noise unto the Rock of our salvation. Alleluia. Amen. (p. 166)

#Blest and dedicate be this Organ (*or* Bell, *or* Instrument) to the praise, honor and glory of Almighty God, and to the edification of his holy people: In the Name of the Father, and of the Son, and of the Holy Ghost. Amen. (p. 185)

Development of the Rite
Blessing of a Bell

Roman Ritual	General Synod (1900)	Lutheran Agenda	Occasional Services (1930)
	After Creed:	(Before Epistle: Num. 10:1–10; Psalm 100)	(Before Epistle: Num. 10:1–10)
			After Creed:
			Hymn
Ps. 124:8			Ps. 124:8
Psalm 51			Ps. 150:1
Psalm 54			Ps. 29:2
Psalm 57			
Psalm 67			
Psalm 70			
Psalm 86			
Psalm 130			
		Sermon	
	Address	Address	
Kyrie			
Our Father			
Preces			
Prayer*	Prayer†	Prayer†	Prayer*

*O God Who by Thy servant Moses didst command that silver trumpets should be made to call the people to holy assemblies: Bless, we beseech Thee, *this Bell,* dedicated to Thine honor and glory, and grant that *its voice* may sound forth from generation to generation, ever calling Thy children to holy convocation in praise and worship of Thy glorious Name; through Jesus Christ, Thy Son, our Lord. Blest and dedicate be *this Bell* to the honor and glory of Almighty God: In the Name of the Father, and of the Son, and of the Holy Ghost. Amen. (p. 168)

† General Synod (1900)	*Lutheran Agenda*
O Lord, our God, we praise Thee and give thanks unto Thy name that Thou hast established among us a place where we may worship Thee, and where Thy Word may be proclaimed. We thank Thee for the privilege of adorning Thy house with a bell, and we beseech Thee to bless us in the use thereof, that its sound may go forth to Thy glory and to the edification of the congregation. Grant that we may gladly	O Lord, our God, we praise Thee and give thanks unto Thy name that Thou hast established among us a place where we may worship Thee and where Thy Word may be proclaimed. We thank Thee for the privilege of adorning Thy house with a bell, and we beseech Thee to bless its use unto us, that its sound may go forth to Thy glory and to the edification of the congregation. Grant that we may gladly obey the

Development of the Rite (continued)
Blessing of a Bell

Roman Ritual	General Synod (1900)	*Lutheran Agenda*	*Occasional Services* (1930)
Sprinkling bell		Striking bell 3 times "In the name . . ."	
Incensing bell			
Prayer			
		Our Father	

General Synod (1900)	*Lutheran Agenda*
obey the voice of the bell when it calls us to Thy house, and not neglect its admonition to adore Thy grace and glory. Preserve this house from all danger, especially from false doctrine and service, and may the sound of this bell go forth from generation to generation to Thy praise, to the glory of Thy name and to the admonition and edification of all who live in this place. To Thee, O Triune God, be praise and dominion, here in the Church of Thy redeemed, and in heaven in the blessed company of saints and angels, from everlasting to everlasting. Amen. (pp. 145–46)	voice of the bell when it calls us to Thy house, and not neglect its admonition to adore Thy grace and glory. Preserve this house from all danger, especially from false doctrine and practice, and may the sound of this bell go forth from generation to generation to Thy praise, to the glory of Thy name, and to the admonition and edification of all who live in this place. To Thee, O Triune God, be praise and dominion, here in the Church of Thy redeemed and in heaven in the blessed company of saints and angels, from everlasting to everlasting. Amen. O Lord, forasmuch as Thou hast said in Thy Word that every creature is sanctified by Thy Word and our prayer, we call upon Thee as concerning this bell, which is now to sound forth to the glory of Thy holy name. It is, indeed, but sounding brass and knoweth not what it doth proclaim. But we beseech Thee, be pleased to accept its song of praise, and grant that it may call us also to repentance. Let the voice of the bell admonish us that we are strangers and pilgrims on the earth, seeking the city to come. Do Thou arouse us, when the bell calleth us, to watch and pray. And graciously help us that, when we shall

Development of the Rite (continued)
Blessing of a Bell

Roman Ritual	General Synod (1900)	Lutheran Agenda	Occasional Services (1930)
Signing bell with cross			
	Sermon with reference to significance of bells in church use	(Hymn) Benediction	

DEDICATION OF WORSHIP FURNISHINGS
(*Occasional Services*, pp. 176–77)

Parallel Rites

CROSS/CRUCIFIX

Roman Catholic *Roman Ritual: Complete Edition* (1964), pp. 543–49.

Episcopal *Book of Occasional Services,* pp. 182–83.

Lutheran *Occasional Services* (1962), pp. 180–81.
Occasional Services (1930), pp. 157–58 (altar cross); pp. 173–74 (steeple cross).

CANDLES/CANDLESTICKS/LAMPS

Roman Catholic *Roman Ritual: Complete Edition*, p. 557.

Episcopal *Book of Occasional Services,* p. 183.

Lutheran *Occasional Services* (1962), pp. 182–84.
Occasional Services (1930), pp. 163–64.
Lutheran Agenda, pp. 165–67.

General Synod (1900) *Lutheran Agenda*

be borne to our graves, this bell may ring in Thy great Sabbath, which Thou hast prepared for Thy people; through Jesus Christ, our Lord. Amen.
The bell may be struck three times, while the Minister says:
In the name of the Father, and of the Son and of the Holy Ghost. (pp. 175–76)

PATEN/CHALICE

Roman Catholic — *Dedication of a Church and an Altar,* pp. 97–103.

Episcopal — *Book of Occasional Services,* pp. 181–82.

Lutheran — *Occasional Services* (1962), pp. 181–82.
Occasional Services (1930), pp. 159–62.
Lutheran Agenda, pp. 165–67.

PARAMENTS

Roman Catholic — *Roman Ritual: Complete Edition,* pp. 539–43.

Episcopal — *Book of Occasional Services,* pp. 183–84.

Lutheran — *Occasional Services* (1962), pp. 182–84.
Occasional Services (1930), pp. 163–64.

FUNERAL PALL

Episcopal — *Book of Occasional Services,* pp. 191–92.

WINDOW

Episcopal — *Book of Occasional Services,* p. 188.

Lutheran — *Occasional Services* (1962), pp. 186–87.
Occasional Services (1930), pp. 171–72.

OIL

Roman Catholic — *The Rites,* pp. 521–27.

Episcopal — *Book of Common Prayer,* p. 455.
Book of Occasional Services, pp. 186–87 (blessing an aumbry for the oils).

GENERAL

Episcopal — Any Church Ornament, *Book of Occasional Services,* p. 192.

Lutheran — A General Order of Benediction, *Occasional Services* (1962), pp. 187–88.

Orthodox — For the Blessing of Any Object, *Service Book,* pp. 557–58.

Methodist — An Office for the Dedication of a Memorial, *Book of Worship,* p. 372.

Purpose

This rite is for the dedication of worship furnishings, including depletable items such as candles and oil, not simply church furnishings and ornaments.

Characteristics

The blessing of worship furnishings is not a necessary action nor even a traditional one. The *Book of Occasional Services* of The Episcopal Church observes (p. 177):

> In accordance with a venerable tradition, church furnishings and ornaments are consecrated by being put to the use for which they were intended. If a rite of dedication is desired, one of the following forms may be used . . .

Twenty-two items, including a general form for the dedication of "Any Church Ornament," are provided for.[76]

The Roman Catholic church has provided English translations only of rites for the blessing of oil and of a chalice and paten.[77]

The Lutheran rite for the Dedication of Worship Furnishings consists simply of an offertory prayer said after the presentation of the gifts (no. 25) and prior to the offertory prayer (no. 26) of the Holy Communion. When circumstances suggest a longer form of dedication, the appropriate petition from this order may replace the prayer (no. 8) in the General Order of Blessing (p. 184).

Survey of the Service

Movable objects such as candles, sacramental vessels, or a cross should be placed on a credence table or other table until the dedication. At the presentation of the gifts (no. 25) in the Holy Communion, the object is brought to the altar by a server or brought in the offertory procession by the donor and presented to the presiding minister.

When the object to be dedicated is fixed in place, as to a wall, or is im-

---

76. 1. An Altar (Reserved to the Bishop); 2. A Font (Reserved to the Bishop); 3. Chalices and Patens (Traditionally reserved to the Bishop); 4. A Bell (Traditionally reserved to the Bishop); 5. A Cross; 6. Candlesticks and Lamps; 7. Altar Cloths and Hangings; 8. A Service Book; 9. A Bible, Lectionary, or Gospel Book; 10. A Repository for the Scriptures; 11. An Aumbry or Tabernacle for the Sacrament; 12. An Aumbry for the Oils; 13. An Ambo (Lectern-Pulpit); 14. Chairs, Benches, and Prayer Desks; 15. A Stained Glass Window; 16. Pictures and Statues; 17. An Organ or Other Musical Instrument; 18. A Vessel for Incense; 19. Surplices and Albs; 20. Vestments for the Liturgy; 21. A Funeral Pall; 22. Any Church Ornament.

77. The Canadian Conference of Catholic Bishops has compiled *A Book of Blessings* (Ottawa, 1981) that provides for the blessing of a great variety of people, places, and things.

movable, there should be a procession (processional cross, servers, assisting ministers, presiding minister) to the object. An appropriate hymn stanza or appropriate psalm verses or other biblical verses may be sung or said as the procession moves toward the object to be dedicated.

Oil is kept in a cruet, or a bottle, for the dedication and afterward.

The traditional date for the blessing of candles is Candlemas, February 2, the Presentation of Our Lord in the Temple[78] — see the Gospel for the Day.

The paschal candle is not dedicated with this rite but is blessed in connection with the celebration of the Vigil of Easter each year.[79]

A funeral pall may be spread over the communion rail for the dedication (and then removed for the distribution of Holy Communion), or it may be spread over a table or a coffin-shaped frame placed before the altar at the head of the center aisle, as if at a funeral.

Comparison of Rites
Dedication of Worship Furnishings

CROSS/CRUCIFIX

LUTHERAN — *Occasional Services* (1930)

The Office *shall be administered at* The Service. *It shall follow the* Hymn *after the* Creed. *The Cross shall be placed on a side table against its use in the Office. No memorial or gift inscription should be placed upon the front side of the cross or upon its base.*[80]

The Hymn ended, the officiating Minister shall remove the Cross from the side table to the Altar. He shall place it on the Mensa *immediately in the middle. Then he shall say:*

Our help is in the Name of the Lord:
Who made heaven and earth.

God forbid that I should glory, save in the Cross of our Lord Jesus Christ:
By whom the world is crucified unto me, and I unto the world.

The Lord be with you.
And with thy spirit.

Lift up your hearts.
We lift them up unto the Lord.

Let us give thanks unto the Lord our God.
It is meet and right so to do.

---

78. See Philip H. Pfatteicher, *Festivals and Commemorations* (Minneapolis: Augsburg Publishing House, 1980), pp. 67–70.

79. *LBW,* Min. Ed., pp. 27, 143–46.

80. This wise counsel, widely disregarded, was dropped in the 1962 *Occasional Services.* It should, nonetheless, still be remembered, for the cross is and should clearly be the cross of Christ.

It is truly meet, right, and salutary, that we should give thanks unto Thee, O Lord, Holy Father, Almighty, Everlasting God, Who on the Tree of the Cross didst give salvation unto mankind through Christ our Lord:

We therefore pray Thee, O Holy Lord, Father Almighty, Eternal God, that Thou wouldest deign to bless this Cross, that it may ever be to us the reminder of our salvation, the foundation of our faith, an incitement to good works, a comfort in all this mortal life: that all who look upon it may love and serve Thee in this life and by Thy mercy, through the Blood of the Cross, enter into life eternal; through Him Who loved us and gave himself for us, Jesus Christ, Thy Son, our Lord. *Amen.*

Bless and hallow, O Lord Jesus Christ, this Memorial-Standard of Thy Passion and Death, which we place upon Thy Altar this day, that all beholding it may adore Thee and give thanks to Thee for that victory which, through Thy obedience unto death, Thou hast obtained for us and for all who rest in Thee, Who with the Father and the Holy Ghost art One God evermore. *Amen.*

Then the officiating Minister shall place the Cross in its place upon the Altar, and all shall say:

Glory be to the Father, and to the Son, and to the Holy Ghost; as it was in the beginning, is now, and ever shall be, world without end. Amen.[81] (pp. 157–58)

LUTHERAN — *Occasional Services* (1962)

Our help is in the Name of the Lord.
Who made heaven and earth.
We adore thee, O Christ, and we bless thee.
Because by thy Cross thou hast redeemed us.
The Lord be with you.
And with thy spirit.
Let us pray.
Then the Minister shall say one or more of the following Collects:
O Almighty Father, eternal God, bless this Cross and grant that all who look upon it may have life through Jesus Christ our Lord. *Amen.*

Bless, O God, this standard wrought and set up for the recollection of thy faithful people, as a remembrance of that Cross upon which thou didst triumph through the sacrifice of thine only Son; and grant that, as often as we behold and call to mind the victorious symbol of thy divine humility, we

---

81. This form with the preface dialogue is adapted from the "More Solemn Blessing of a Cross" in the *Roman Ritual: Complete Edition* by P. Weller (pp. 544–49). Notable too is the phrase "O Holy Lord, Father Almighty, Eternal God," which has been suggested as the accurate grouping of these titles, each noun thus having its adjective, rather than the more familiar "O Lord, holy Father, almighty and everliving God" (which the prayer also uses). The directions for placing the cross at the time of the dedication on the middle of the mensa (the top of the altar table) and then, at the conclusion, setting it back in its intended place upon the altar (or gradine or retable) is helpful still.

may fight with surer confidence against the foe, and bow in deeper humility in thy presence; through the same Jesus Christ our Lord. *Amen.*

O Lord Jesus Christ, who in the Cross hast fashioned a memorial of thy victory and our redemption, and by thy sacrifice hast made it a sign of thine eternal love: Grant that it may be our protection and assurance, the strength of our faith, and the bond of peace and love in both time and eternity; who with the Father and the Holy Ghost art one God, world without end. *Amen.* (p. 180)

LUTHERAN — *Occasional Services* (1982)

Accept this *cross/crucifix* which we offer in thanksgiving; may this sign of your Son's triumph draw us to him who leads us with his banner of salvation. (p. 176)

EPISCOPAL — *Book of Occasional Services*

We will glory in the cross of our Lord Jesus Christ, in whom is our salvation, our life and resurrection.

Christ for us became obedient unto death:
Even death on a cross.
Let us pray. (*Silence*)
O gracious God, who in your mercy ordained that your Son should suffer death on a cross of shame: We thank you that it has become for us the sign of his triumph and the banner of our salvation; and we pray that this cross may draw our hearts to him, who leads us to the glory of your kingdom; where you live and reign for ever and ever. *Amen.* (p. 182)

CANDLES

LUTHERAN — *Occasional Services* (1982)

Accept these *candles/candlesticks/lamps* which we offer in thanksgiving; may they be to us a sign of Christ, the light of the world, the light no darkness can overcome. (p. 176)

EPISCOPAL — *Book of Occasional Services*

Before the throne burn seven lamps of fire, which are the seven spirits of God.

You, O Lord, are my lamp:
My God, you make my darkness bright.
Let us pray. (*Silence*)
O heavenly Father, who revealed to us the vision of your Son in the midst of the candlesticks, and of your Spirit in seven lamps of fire before your throne: Grant that *these lights (lamps),* to be kindled for your glory, may be to us a sign of your presence and the promise of eternal light; through Jesus Christ our Lord. *Amen.* (p. 183)

DEDICATIONS AND BLESSINGS

CHALICE/PATEN

ROMAN CATHOLIC—*Dedication of a Church and Altar*

> *Any bishop or priest may bless a chalice and paten.*
> I will take the cup of salvation and call on the
> name of the Lord.
> Let us pray. (*Silence*)
> Lord,
> with joy we place on your altar
> this cup and this paten,
> vessels with which we will celebrate
> the sacrifice of Christ's new covenant.
> May they be sanctified,
> for in them the body and blood of Christ
> will be offered, consecrated, and received.
> Lord,
> when we celebrate Christ's faultless sacrifice on earth,
> may we be renewed in strength
> and filled with your Spirit,
> until we join with your saints
> at your table in heaven.
> Glory and honor be yours for ever and ever.
> *Blessed be God for ever.* (pp. 97–103)

LUTHERAN—*Occasional Services* (1930)

> Our help is in the Name of the Lord:
> *Who made heaven and earth.*
> The bread which we break, is it not the communion of the Body of Christ?
> *The cup of blessing which we bless, is it not the communion of the Blood of Christ?*
> As oft as ye eat this bread and drink this cup, ye do show the Lord's death till He come.
> *I will offer to Thee the sacrifices of thanksgiving, and will call upon the Name of the Lord.*
> The Lord be with you.
> *And with thy spirit.*
> Let us pray.
> Almighty, Everlasting God, bless and hallow these vessels, we beseech Thee, which we present to Thee for the administration of Thy Holy Sacrament, that all who partake of the precious Body and Blood of our Lord Jesus Christ in this present life, may in the life to come be united with Him in eternal peace and joy; through the same Jesus Christ, our Lord. *Amen.*
> Blest and dedicate be these Vessels for the administration of the Holy Sacrament of our Lord and Saviour Jesus Christ, Who liveth and reigneth with God the Father in the unity of the Holy Spirit, One God, world without end. Amen. (pp. 161–62)

LUTHERAN — *Occasional Services* (1962)

> Our help is in the Name of the Lord.
> *Who made heaven and earth.*
> Honor and majesty are before him.
> *Strength and beauty are in his sanctuary.*
> The Lord be with you.
> *And with thy spirit.*
> Let us pray.
> O Lord our God, who under the old Covenant didst appoint the use of vessels of gold and silver for the service of thy sanctuary, and for the offerings brought unto thee: Graciously accept this Vessel (*these Vessels*) which we present unto thee for the service of thine Altar; and grant that all who partake of the blessed Sacrament in this place may be united to thy beloved Son, and grow up to the fullness of life in thy holy Church. Blessed art thou, O Lord our God, through Jesus Christ our Lord, who liveth and reigneth with thee and the Holy Spirit, one God, world without end. *Amen.*
> Blest and dedicate be this Paten (*or* Ciborium, *or* Chalice, *or* these Vessels) for the service of the Altar of God: In the Name of the Father, and of the Son, and of the Holy Ghost. Amen. (pp. 181–82)

LUTHERAN — *Occasional Services* (1982)

> Accept this *paten/chalice* which we offer in thanksgiving; may all who receive the heavenly *food and drink* be sustained by your grace and power. (p. 177)

EPISCOPAL — *Book of Occasional Services*

> *(Traditionally reserved to the Bishop)*
> Taste and see that the Lord is good; happy are they who trust in him.
> The cup of blessing which we bless is a sharing in the Blood of Christ.
> *The bread which we break is a sharing in the Body of Christ.*
> Let us pray. *(Silence)*
> Almighty God, whose blessed Son instituted the Sacrament of his Body and Blood: Grant that all who receive the holy Mysteries from *these vessels,* which we now consecrate for use in your Church, may be sustained by his presence and enjoy for ever his heavenly benediction; who lives and reigns in glory everlasting. *Amen.* (pp. 181–82)

PARAMENTS

LUTHERAN — *Occasional Services* (1962)

> Our help is in the Name of the Lord.
> *Who made heaven and earth.*
> O worship the Lord in the beauty of holiness.
> *I will offer unto thee the sacrifices of thanksgiving, and will call upon the Name of the Lord.*

The Lord be with you.
 And with thy spirit.
Let us pray.
(Paraments, Linens, Hangings)
O Lord God Almighty, who didst command Moses, thy servant, during the forty days in the Mount, to make hangings and fine linens which Miriam wove and prepared for thy service in the Tabernacle: Bless and hallow these Paraments *(or* Linens, Hangings, Coverings) for the vesting and covering of the Altar of thine adorable Son, our Lord Jesus Christ, who liveth and reigneth with thee in the unity of the Holy Spirit, one God, world without end. *Amen.*
(Ornaments)
Hear our prayers, O Lord, merciful Father, and graciously bless and hallow these Ornaments prepared for the service of thy Sanctuary; through Jesus Christ, thy Son, our Lord. *Amen.*
(Vestments)
O Lord God Almighty, who didst command Moses, thy servant, to provide vestments for the High Priest, the Priests and the Levites, required in the services of the Tabernacle, and who didst bestow the spirit of wisdom in the fulfilling of thy command: Bless and hallow, we beseech thee, these Vestments for use in thy worship; and graciously grant that they who are clothed therewith and who minister before thee may bear the yoke of Christ in humbleness of heart, and be clothed in the garments of salvation; through the same thy Son, Jesus Christ, our Lord. *Amen.* (pp. 182–84)

LUTHERAN — *Occasional Services* (1982)

Accept these paraments which we offer in thanksgiving; may they adorn this house, show us the beauty of holiness, and so proclaim the glory of your majesty. (p. 177)

EPISCOPAL — *Book of Occasional Services* (altar cloths and hangings)

This is the offering which you shall receive from the people: gold, silver, and bronze, blue and purple and scarlet cloth, and finely woven linen.
 O Lord my God, how excellent is your greatness:
 You are clothed with majesty and splendor.
Let us pray. *(Silence)*
O glorious God, all your works proclaim your perfect beauty: Accept our offering of this _____, and grant that it may adorn this sanctuary and show forth your glory; through Jesus Christ our Lord. *Amen.* (pp. 183–84)

FUNERAL PALL

LUTHERAN — *Occasional Services* (1982)

Accept this pall which we offer in thanksgiving; may it be a reminder that in

Baptism we have been clothed in the righteousness of Christ, that we may know that those who have departed this earthly life are received into the arms of your mercy. (p. 177)

EPISCOPAL — *Book of Occasional Services*

I will greatly rejoice in the Lord; my soul shall exult in my God.
He has clothed me with the garments of salvation;
He has covered me with the robe of righteousness.
Let us pray. (*Silence*)
O God, who baptized us into the Body of your Son Jesus Christ, and made us members with different functions, all necessary and all to be honored: Make this pall a sign of our common membership in Christ, that we may know those who have departed this earthly life, not as the world esteems them, but as you know and love them; through Jesus Christ our Lord. *Amen.* (pp. 191–92)

WINDOW

LUTHERAN — *Occasional Services* (1930)

Our help is in the Name of the Lord:
Who made heaven and earth.
The Dayspring from on high hath visited us; to give light to them that sit in darkness, and in the shadow of death;
To guide our feet into the way of peace.
Our Lord Jesus said: I am the Light of the world; he that followeth me shall not walk in darkness, but shall have the light of life.
The Lord is my light and my salvation: whom shall I fear?
Glory be to the Father, and to the Son, and to the Holy Ghost:
As it was in the beginning, is now, and ever shall be, world without end. Amen.

Arise, shine, for thy Light is come, and the glory of the Lord is risen upon thee. Alleluia.
Blest and dedicate be this Window to the glory of Almighty God, In the Name of the Father, and of the Son, and of the Holy Ghost. Amen.
Hallowed also be this Window as a memorial to _____.
The memory of the just is blessed.
Let us pray.
O God, Who commanded the Light to shine out of darkness and didst send Thy Son to be the Light of Life: Accept this window which we humbly dedicate to the enrichment of Thy House; and as the light which Thou hast created illuminates it, shedding its radiance in this Holy Place, so may the light of the knowledge of Thy glory in Thy dear Son shine in our hearts and nourish us in all holy living; through the same Thy Son, Jesus Christ, our Lord. *Amen.* (pp. 171–72)

DEDICATIONS AND BLESSINGS

LUTHERAN — *Occasional Services* (1962)

Our help is in the Name of the Lord.
Who made heaven and earth.
O worship the Lord in the beauty of holiness.
Fear before him, all the earth.
The Lord be with you.
And with thy spirit.
Let us pray.

O God, who commanded the light to shine out of darkness, and didst send thy Son to be the Light of Life: Bless and accept this Window placed for the adornment of thy House, and as the light which thou hast created shows forth its beauty, so may the light of the knowledge of thy Son shine in our hearts; through the same thy Son, Jesus Christ our Lord. *Amen.*

Almighty God, the light of faithful souls and the brightness of thy saints: Graciously receive of our hands this Window which we dedicate to thee (and in memory of thy servant, *N.N.*) for the beauty of thy House, the edifying of thy people, and the glory of thy Name; through Jesus Christ our Lord. *Amen.*

Blest and dedicate be this Window to the glory of Almighty God: In the Name of the Father, and of the Son, and of the Holy Ghost. *Amen.* (pp. 186–87)

EPISCOPAL — *Book of Occasional Services*

I will make your windows of agates, and all your borders of pleasant stones.
Look upon the rainbow, and praise him who made it:
How beautiful it is in its brightness.
Let us pray. (*Silence*)

O Lord God, the whole world is filled with the radiance of your glory: Accept our offering of this window which we now dedicate to you for the adornment of this place and the inspiration of your people. Grant that as the light shines through it in many colors, so our lives may show forth the beauty of your manifold gifts of grace; through Jesus Christ our Lord. *Amen.* (p. 188)

LUTHERAN — *Occasional Services* (1982)

Accept this window which we offer in thanksgiving; as the light which shines through it is transformed into still greater splendor, so may our lives show the beauty of your manifold gifts of grace. (p. 177)

OIL

LUTHERAN — *Occasional Services* (1982)

Accept this oil which we offer in thanksgiving; may those who look to you for health and salvation be filled with the power of your Holy Spirit and become radiant with the goodness of life which has its source in you. (p. 177)

ROMAN CATHOLIC — *The Rites* (Blessing of the Oil of the Sick)

Lord God, loving Father,
you bring healing to the sick
through your Son Jesus Christ.
Hear us as we pray to you in faith,
and send the Holy Spirit, man's Helper and Friend,
upon this oil, which nature has provided
to serve the needs of men.
May your blessing +
come upon all who are anointed with this oil,
that they may be freed from pain and illness
and be made well again in body, mind, and soul.
Father, may this oil be blessed for our use
in the name of our Lord Jesus Christ
(who lives and reigns with you for ever and ever.
    Amen). (pp. 522–23)

EPISCOPAL — *Book of Common Prayer*

O Lord, holy Father, giver of health and salvation: Send your Holy Spirit to sanctify this oil; that, as your holy apostles anointed many that were sick and healed them, so may those who in faith and repentance receive this holy unction be made whole; through Jesus Christ our Lord, who lives and reigns with you and the Holy Spirit, one God, for ever and ever. *Amen.* (p. 455)

GENERAL

LUTHERAN — *Occasional Services* (1930)

Our help is in the Name of the Lord:
    Who made heaven and earth.
God is not unrighteous to forget your work and labor of love, which ye have showed toward His Name.
    To do good and to communicate forget not; for with such sacrifices God
    is well pleased.
The Lord be with you.
    And with thy spirit.
Let us pray.
O Lord God, Who hast commanded every man to offer unto Thee of Thine own gifts according to the purpose of his heart, and Who dost abundantly requite them from Thine eternal bounty: Be pleased to accept, we beseech Thee, this offering now made unto Thee by Thy servants, and grant that it may be used unto Thy glory, through Jesus Christ, our Lord. Amen.
O God, by Whose Word all things are sanctified: Pour out Thy benediction upon this _____ (*or,* offering), that whoever shall use it according to Thy purpose and will in thanksgiving unto Thee, may glorify Thy Holy Name; through Jesus Christ Thy Son, our Lord. Amen. (p. 175)

The order in *Occasional Services* (1962) is similar.

EPISCOPAL — *Book of Occasional Services*

> Solomon beautified the sanctuary, and multiplied the vessels of the temple.
> Oh, the majesty and magnificence of God's presence!
> *Oh, the power and the splendor of his sanctuary!*
> Let us pray. (*Silence*)
> O God, whose blessed Son has sanctified and transfigured the use of material things: Receive *this* _____ which we offer, and grant that *it* may proclaim your love, benefit your Church, and minister grace and joy to those who use *it;* through Jesus Christ our Lord. *Amen.* (p. 192)

LUTHERAN — *Occasional Services* (1982)

> Accept this _____ which we offer in thanksgiving; may it serve to increase our vision of your glory, to remind us of your goodness, and to support our calling to worship you in spirit and truth.
>
> *or,*
>
> Accept this _____ which we offer in thanksgiving; may those who use it do so in reverence and love, giving honor and glory to your holy name. (p. 177)

BLESSING OF A DWELLING
(Occasional Services, pp. 186–91)

Parallel Rites

Episcopal

Celebration for a Home, *Book of Occasional Services,* pp. 131–41.

Blessing in Homes at Epiphany; Blessing in Homes at Easter, *Book of Occasional Services,* pp. 45–48, 97–100.

Lutheran

Order for the Blessing of a Dwelling, *Occasional Services* (1962), pp. 151–53. See also The Blessing of a Room or an Apartment, The Blessing of a Family Altar, p. 211.

The Order for the Dedication of a Dwelling, *Lutheran Agenda,* pp. 185–86.

Orthodox

Prayers at the Founding of a House, When One is About to Take Up Abode in a New House, *Service Book,* p. 557.

Methodist

An Office for the Blessing of a Dwelling, *Book of Worship,* pp. 373–74.

Purpose

This rite is to invoke God's blessing on the inhabitants of a dwelling (a house or an apartment) and to celebrate the various aspects of family life as a new beginning in a new place.

This is not a rite to mark off and identify sacred space.

Background

A traditional prayer for the protection of those who live in a house is the prayer in Compline, "Visit our dwellings, O Lord . . . " (262).

The popular Christian tradition has used brief rites for the blessing of the places where people live. Sometimes these rites were connected with the church year. A favorite time for such blessing—especially in Germany—was the Epiphany, when the Wise Men entered "the house" to offer their gifts to the infant Jesus (Matt. 2:11). Chalk was blessed with a versicle and prayer:

> Our help is in the name of the Lord.
> *Who made heaven and earth.*
> The Lord be with you.
> *May he also be with you.*
> Bless + O Lord God, this creature, chalk, to let it be a help to mankind. Grant that those who will use it with faith in your holy name, and with it inscribe on the doors of their homes the names of your saints Caspar, Melchior, and Balthassar, may through their merits and intercession enjoy health in body and protection of soul; through Christ our Lord.[82]

The chalk was sprinkled with holy water and distributed to the congregation so that they could mark on the lintels of their houses the year and the initials of the traditional names of the Magi—Kaspar (Caspar), Melchior, and Balthassar—separated by three crosses:

19 + K + M + B 83

Behind this religious practice lay a secular custom. Down through Renaissance times, a royal "progress" was often preceded by messengers, called harbingers, who rode ahead of the main party to commandeer lodging places for the night. The doors of the lodgings thus selected were customarily marked with chalk.[83] The Christian custom of marking the doors of houses with chalk at Epiphany therefore is a way of declaring a welcome to one's home of the three kings as they journey to the King of kings.

---

82. See the *Roman Ritual*, p. 410.
83. See George Herbert's poem "The Forerunners."

BLESSING OF A DWELLING

In the *Roman Ritual* a simple form was provided for use by a priest to bless houses on the Epiphany, and the Episcopal *Book of Occasional Services* has provided a similar form:

Roman Ritual	*Book of Occasional Services*
God's peace be in this house. *And in all who live here.* Antiphon: Magi from the East came to Bethlehem to adore the Lord; and opening their treasure chests, they presented Him with precious gifts: gold for the great King, incense for the true God, and myrrh in symbol of His burial. Alleluia.	Peace be to this house, and to all who dwell in it. *Antiphon:* The Lord has shown forth his glory: Come let us adore him. *or,* I saw water proceeding out of the temple; from the right side it flowed, alleluia; and all those to whom that water came shall be saved, and shall say, alleluia, alleluia.
The Magnificat Our Father . . . and lead us not into temptation *But deliver us from evil.* Many shall come from Saba *Bearing gold and incense.* Lord, heed my prayer *And let my cry be heard by you.* The Lord be with you. *May he also be with you.* Let us pray.	The Magnificat — — — — — The Lord be with you. *And also with you.* Let us pray.
God, who on this day revealed your only-begotten Son to all nations by the guidance of a star, grant that we who now know you by faith may finally behold you in your heavenly majesty; through Christ our Lord.	O God, by the leading of a star you manifested your only Son to the peoples of the earth: Lead us, who know you now by faith, to your presence, where we may see your glory face to face; through Jesus Christ our Lord, who lives and reigns with you and the Holy Spirit, one God, now and for ever. *Amen.*
Responsory: Be enlightened and shine forth, O Jerusalem, for your light is come; and upon you is risen the glory of the Lord Jesus Christ born of the Virgin Mary. Nations shall walk in your	*or,* Father in heaven, who at the baptism of Jesus in the River Jordan proclaimed him your beloved Son and anointed him with the Holy Spirit: Grant that all who are baptized into his Name may keep the covenant

Roman Ritual	*Book of Occasional Services*
light, and kings in the splendor of your birth. *And the glory of the Lord is risen upon you.* Let us pray. Lord God almighty, bless + this home, and under its shelter let there be health, chastity, self-conquest, humility, goodness, mildness, obedience to your commandments, and thanks-giving to God the Father, Son, and Holy Spirit. May your blessing remain always in this home and on those who live here; through Christ our Lord.[84]	they have made, and boldly confess him as Lord and Savior; who with you and the Holy Spirit lives and reigns, one God, in glory everlasting. *Amen.* *Then:* Visit, O blessed Lord, this home with the gladness of your presence. Bless *all* who *live* here with the gift of your love; and grant that *they* may manifest your love [to each other and] to all whose lives *they touch.* May *they* grow in grace and in the knowledge and love of you; guide, comfort, and strengthen *them;* and preserve *them* in peace, O Jesus Christ, now and for ever. *Amen.* Blessing.[85]

Easter was another customary time for the blessing of houses, when a physical connection, was made by the sprinkling of the houses with Easter water. The Episcopal *Book of Occasional Services* has provided a rite for places "where it is customary to invite the parish priest to the homes of parishioners during the Fifty Days of Easter," which parallels the older rite in the *Roman Ritual:*

Roman Ritual	*Book of Occasional Services*
God's peace be in this home. *And in all who live here.* *Antiphon:* I saw water flowing out from beneath the threshold of the temple, alleluia; and all to whom this water came were saved, and they shall say, alleluia, alleluia. Psalm 117:1 Glory be to the Father . . . I saw water . . . Lord, show us your mercy,	Peace be to this house, and to all who dwell in it. *Antiphon:* Alleluia. The Lord is risen indeed: Come let us adore him. Alleluia. *or,* I saw water proceeding out of the temple; from the right side it flowed, alleluia; and all those to whom that water came shall be saved and shall say, alleluia, alleluia.

---

84. *Roman Ritual*, pp. 410–12.
85. *Book of Occasional Services*, pp. 45–48.

Roman Ritual	*Book of Occasional Services*
alleluia.	Psalm 114 (or another psalm)
And grant us your salvation, alleluia.	
Lord, heed my prayer.	
And let my cry be heard by you.	
The Lord be with you.	The Lord be with you.
May He also be with you.	*And also with you.*
Let us pray.	Let us pray.
Hear us, holy Lord and Father, almighty everlasting God; and as you guarded the homes of the Israelites from the avenging angel on their flight from Egypt, if their homes were signed with the blood of a lamb—therein prefiguring our Easter sacrifice in which Christ is the victim— so likewise in your goodness send your holy angel to watch over and protect all who live in this home, to be with them and give them comfort and encouragement; through Christ our Lord.[86]	(a collect of the Easter season) *Then:* Visit: O blessed Lord, this home with the gladness of your presence. Bless *all* who *live* here with the gift of your love; and grant that *they* may manifest your love [to each other and] to all whose lives *they touch.* May *they* grow in grace and in the knowledge and love of you; guide, comfort, and strengthen *them;* and preserve *them* in peace, O Jesus Christ, now and for ever. *Amen.*
	Blessing.[87]

It is to be noted that the *Book of Occasional Services* does not call these rites the blessing *of* homes but rather the blessing *in* homes at Epiphany and at Easter.

Liturgical books also sometimes provided a simple form for the blessing of houses at times other than during Easter or at the Epiphany. The *Roman Ritual* provided three such forms—two for the blessing of houses and one for the blessing of an apartment or a home:

Blessing of Homes outside of Eastertime	Another Blessing of a Home	Blessing of an Apartment or a Home
God's peace be in this home. *And in all who live here.* *Antiphon:* Purify me with hyssop, Lord, and		

---

86. *Roman Ritual,* pp. 415–16.
87. *Book of Occasional Services,* pp. 97–100.

Blessing of Homes outside of Eastertime	Another Blessing of a Home	Blessing of an Apartment or a Home
I shall be clean of sin. Wash me, and I shall be whiter than snow. Psalm 51:1 Glory be to the Father . . . Purify me with hyssop . . .		
Lord, heed my prayer. *And let my cry be heard by you.* The Lord be with you. *May He also be with you.*	Our help is in the name of the Lord. *Who made heaven and earth.* The Lord be with you. *May He also be with you.*	Our help is in the name of the Lord. *Who made heaven and earth.* The Lord be with you. *May He also be with you.*
Let us pray. Hear us, holy Lord and Father, almighty everlasting God, and in your goodness send your holy angel from heaven to watch over and protect all who live in this home, to be with them and give them comfort and encouragement; through Christ our Lord.[88]	Let us pray. God the Father almighty, we fervently implore you for the sake of this home and its occupants and possessions, that you may bless + and sanctify + them, enriching them by your kindness in every way possible. Pour out on them, Lord, heavenly dew in good measure, as well as an abundance of earthly needs. Mercifully listen to their prayers, and grant that their desires be fulfilled. At our lowly coming be pleased to bless + and sanctify + this home, as you once were pleased to bless the home of	Let us pray. Lord God almighty, bless + this apartment (*or* home), that it be the shelter of health, purity, and self-control; that there prevail here a spirit of humility, goodness, mildness, obedience to the commandments, and gratitude to God the Father, Son, and Holy Spirit. May this blessing remain on this place and on those who live here now and always.[89]

---

88. *Roman Ritual,* pp. 460–61.
89. Ibid., p. 460.

Blessing of Homes outside of Eastertime	Another Blessing of a Home	Blessing of an Apartment or a Home
	Abraham, Isaac, and Jacob. Within these walls let your angels of light preside and stand watch over those who live here; through Christ our Lord.[90]	

The Orthodox *Service Book* provides a prayer at the founding of a house:

O God Almighty, who hast made the heavens with wisdom, and hast established the earth upon its firm foundations, the Creator and Author of all men: Look upon thy servant, *N.,* to whom it hath seemed good to set up a house for his dwelling in the dominion of thy power, and to rear it by building. Establish thou the same upon a stable rock, and found it according to thy divine word in the Gospel, so that neither wind nor flood nor any other thing shall be able to harm it. Graciously grant that he may bring it to an ending; and deliver all those who shall wish to dwell therein from every attack of the enemy.

For thine is the dominion, and thine are the kingdom and the power and the glory, of the Father, and of the Son, and of the Holy Spirit, now, and ever, and unto ages of ages.[91]

And the Orthodox *Service Book* provides a prayer when one is about to take up abode in a new home:

O God our Saviour, who didst deign to enter under the roof of Zaccheus, unto the salvation of the same and of all who were in the house: Do thou, the same Lord, keep safe also from all harm those who have now desired to dwell here, and who together with us unworthy ones do offer unto thee prayers and supplications; blessing this their dwelling, and preserving their life free from aspersion. For unto thee are due all glory, honour and worship, together with thy Father who hath no beginning, and thine all-holy, and good, and life-giving Spirit, now, and ever, and unto ages of ages. Amen.[92]

Following in such a tradition, the *Lutheran Agenda* provided a simple Order for the Dedication of a Dwelling:

Our help is in the name of the Lord, who made heaven and earth.
O Lord, open Thou my lips; and my mouth shall show forth Thy praise.

---

90. Ibid., pp. 461–62.
91. *Service Book,* p. 557.
92. Ibid.

Show Thy work unto Thy servants and Thine honor unto their children.
Glory be to the Father . . .
As all things are sanctified by the Word of God and prayer, let us pray:
O Lord, almighty and eternal God, who hast permitted Thy servants to erect
this house, we entreat Thee to enter and abide therein, that the salvation of
Thy kingdom may come to all that inhabit it, to the end that Thy name may
be hallowed and all glory and worship be given unto Thee from this time
forth and even forevermore. Amen.

Lesson, e.g., Luke 19:1–10
(Address)

O Lord, holy Father, bless this household, bless their going in; bless them as
Thou didst bless the house of Thy patriarchs Abraham, Isaac, and Jacob. O
Lord Jesus Christ, who didst say to Thy disciples, When ye enter a house, ye
shall greet it and say, Peace be with this house, let Thy peace come upon this
house, and bless it with the fullness of Thy grace. O Lord God, Holy Ghost,
Thou Spirit of wisdom and truth, of counsel and strength, of knowledge and
the fear of God, come to this household with Thy manifold gifts, and sanctify it unto Thy temple and dwelling place. Bless, O Lord, this house and
what belongs thereto. Bless its inhabitants with true faith and a godly life,
with zeal and faithfulness in Thy service. Bless them with health and strength
in body and soul. Let Thy holy angels encamp around this house both day
and night. Defend it against all danger, against fire and other calamities.
Protect it with Thy mighty hand, and let all that dwell therein live in peace
and happiness all the days of their lives. Unto Thee, the Father, the Son, and
the Holy Ghost, be praise and glory forevermore. Amen.[93]

"Then may the Service close with the Lord's Prayer and the Benediction."
Occasional Services (1962) added to the occasional services approved
in 1950 an Order for the Blessing of a Dwelling (pp. 151–53), modeled on
the order of Matins and Vespers and consisting of psalms, lessons, and
prayers. After the traditional greeting, "Peace be to this house: *and to all
that dwell therein,*" verses from Psalms 124 and 122 were said:

Our help is in the Name of the Lord:
Who made heaven and earth. (124:8)
Peace be within thy walls:
And prosperity within thy palaces. (122:7)
For my brethren and companions' sakes I will now say:
Peace be within thee. (122:8)

The *Gloria Patri* followed. Psalms 34, 90, 91, 127, 128, 145 were suggested; after the psalm(s), one or more of the following lessons were read:

---

93. *Lutheran Agenda,* pp. 185–86.

Exod. 20:1–17; Deut. 6:3–9; 8:10–18; Matt. 7:24–29; Luke 10:38–42;
19:1–10. "At the Blessing of a Parsonage, any of the foregoing, or Acts
18:7–11, or 1 Corinthians 16:13–18, may be read." After each lesson, as at
Matins and Vespers, the response "O Lord, have mercy upon us. *Thanks
be to God*" was suggested. A hymn could follow, and then the prayers.

> Visit, we beseech thee, O Lord, this dwelling-place, and drive far from it all
> the snares of the enemy. Let thy holy angels dwell herein to preserve it in
> peace, and may thy blessing be upon it evermore; through Jesus Christ our
> Lord. *Amen.*
> Blest be this dwelling: In the Name of the Father, and of the Son, and of the
> Holy Ghost. *Amen.*

The Lord's Prayer was said and after it one or more of the following or
the collect "Direct us, O Lord, in all our doings":

> O God, who settest the solitary in families: So bless this home with thy
> gracious presence that thy love may be its inspiration, thy wisdom its guide,
> thy truth its light and thy peace its benediction; through Jesus Christ our
> Lord.

> O God, of whom the whole family in heaven and earth is named: Regard
> with favor thy servants who shall dwell in this place. Watch over their bodies
> and souls, and cause them to show forth thy love and beauty; and grant that,
> in the fellowship of thy holy Church, they may grow into the life that is in
> thee; through Christ our Lord.

> *For the Blessing of a Parsonage*
> O God, our heavenly Father: Let thy blessing rest upon this Parsonage
> which we humbly dedicate to thee. Make it thy habitation and the place
> where thine honor dwelleth. Enkindle those who dwell herein so to shine in
> the world that men may glorify thee; through Jesus Christ, thy Son, our
> Lord.

> Accept of our hands, O Lord, and be pleased to bless this house which we
> have reared to thy glory and to the use of this Parish. Be thou its light by
> night and its shade by day, that in this place men may behold thy glory;
> through Christ our Lord.

The blessing concluded the service.

Occasional Services (1962) also provided a simple general structure,
Prayers and Blessings for Special Occasions, which included two prayers
for homes:

> Our help is in the Name of the Lord.
> *Who made heaven and earth.*
> The Lord be with you.
> *And with thy spirit.*
> Let us pray.

The Blessing of a Room
or Apartment

Visit, O Lord, this dwelling place with thy Presence, that it may be a place of obedience to thy commandments and of thanksgiving to thee. Let thy blessing remain for all time upon this place and those who dwell therein; through Jesus Christ our Lord. *Amen.*

The Blessing of a
Family Altar

O God, whose Son has promised his Presence where two or three are gathered in his Name: Bless this family and this place which it has set apart for thy worship; and as it unites in thy praise, let it be bound together in love and mutual service now and forever; through Jesus Christ our Lord. *Amen.*

The Blessing of Almighty God, the Father, the Son, and the Holy Ghost be with you all. *Amen.*[94]

In recent years popular devotion has taken a fancy to more elaborate blessing of homes and houses in which each room is visited with appropriate verses and prayers. The Episcopal and Lutheran rites are similar.

Characteristics

In these rites a certain reticence is evident in treating certain rooms, notably the bedroom. The Lutheran rite omits the bathroom altogether. The Episcopal rite deals with the bathroom in this way:

Antiphon
I will sprinkle you with clean water, and you will be cleansed.
    Let us hold fast the confession of our hope without wavering:
    Having our bodies washed with pure water.
Let us pray. (*Silence*)
O holy God, in the incarnation of your Son our Lord you made our flesh the instrument of your self-revelation: Give us a proper respect and reverence for our mortal bodies, keeping them clean and fair, whole and sound; that, glorifying you in them, we may confidently await our being clothed upon with spiritual bodies, when that which is mortal is transformed by life; through Jesus Christ our Lord. *Amen.*[95]

Survey of the Service

Depending on the size of the home or apartment, a procession may move from room to room led by the bearer of the candle. The procession may be accompanied by instruments such as bells, tambourines, and finger cymbals.

---

94. *Occasional Services* (1962), pp. 208, 211.
95. *Book of Occasional Services,* p. 136.

Members of the family should participate in the leadership of the service.

The reading at the entrance (Ps. 121:8) is used as the verse and response at the entrance in the Episcopal rite.

The prayers are all new compositions except for four: the prayer for the living room ⟨526⟩ is an abbreviation of the prayer "In the Living Room or Family Room" in the *Book of Occasional Services* (p. 139); the prayer for the kitchen ⟨529⟩ is an adaptation of the prayer in the *Book of Occasional Services* (p. 137); the prayer for the dining room ⟨530⟩ is an adaptation of the Episcopal prayer "In a Dining Room or Area" (p. 138); the prayer for the bedroom(s) ⟨531⟩ is the antiphon to the Gospel Canticle in Compline and is used as the antiphon for the prayer "In a Bedroom" in the *Book of Occasional Services* (p. 134).

The blessing at the conclusion of the rite is from the last verse of Psalm 121. It echoes the verse used at the entrance.

GENERAL ORDER OF BLESSING
(*Occasional Services*, pp. 183–85)

Parallel Rites

Lutheran	Prayers and Blessings for Special Occasions (The Blessing of a New Business Venture, the Blessing of a Family Altar); Forms of Blessing (Palms, Fishing Boat, Wedding Ring), *Occasional Services* (1962), pp. 208, 211, 215.
Orthodox	For the Blessing of Any Object, *Service Book,* pp. 557–58.

Purpose

This general order is to accommodate the various requests which come to pastors from time to time and which ask the pastor to bless an assortment of objects and events.

It may also be appropriate for the blessing of such things as the Christmas crib or crèche.

Characteristics

This form is simple and general. The core is a brief introductory statement, a prayer of blessing, benedicamus and benediction. When appropriate and desired, this form may be expanded by the addition of a psalm or canticle, lesson(s), and hymn.

The effective use of this form therefore requires careful preparation by the pastor so that it will suit the particular occasion for which it is used.

Background

Occasional Services (1962) provided a prayer for the blessing of fishing boats. The inclusion of such a prayer has caused bewilderment for some and merriment for others. To those unfamiliar with the cultural importance of the blessing of fishing boats (the intent is to bless commercial fleets, not pleasure craft), such a practice seems to epitomize liturgical forms at their silliest. Although the blessing of fishing fleets may be foreign to a majority of Lutherans in North America, to many on the coast of New England and the northwest coast of the continent and to some on the Great Lakes, the custom is an honored and an important one. The text of the Blessing of a Fishing Boat given in *Occasional Services* (1962) is:

> O Lord Jesus Christ, whom even the winds and seas obeyed: Bless all those whose business it is to fish in deep waters, and the craft that bear them. Guard and protect them from danger and harm, and grant them a calm voyage and a safe harbor at the last; who, with the Father and the Holy Ghost art one God, for evermore.[96]

The General Order of Blessing is in part designed to accommodate requests for such unusual blessings.

This form may also be used during Rogationtide[97] in those places where on the Days between the Sixth Sunday of Easter and Ascension Day it is customary to bless the fields and to pray for those who labor. On that occasion, a procession may go from the church to a representative field or farm (in this order: processional cross, choir, congregation, servers, assisting ministers, presiding minister) while a hymn is sung or while, more traditionally, the Litany is sung. The propers for the Stewardship of Creation (*LBW,* Min. Ed., pp. 187–88) are intended for the Rogation Days and provide suggestions for psalms, lessons, and prayers.

Current Roman Catholic and Episcopal books do not provide such a general form of blessing, but in the past they did. The *Roman Ritual* has a Form of Blessing for All Things for use "by any priest for the blessing of anything that does not have its own special blessing in the Roman Ritual":

> Our help is in the name of the Lord.
> *Who made heaven and earth.*
> The Lord be with you.
> *May He also be with you.*

---

96. *Occasional Services* (1962), p. 215.
97. So-called from the former name of the Sixth Sunday of Easter (then accounted the Fifth Sunday after Easter), Rogate, from the opening word of the Latin Introit.

Let us pray.

God, whose word suffices to make all things holy, pour out your blessing +
on this object (these objects); and grant that anyone who uses it (them) with
grateful heart and in keeping with your law and will, may receive from you,
its (their) Maker, health in body and protection of soul by calling on your
holy name; through Christ our Lord.[98]

The *Book of Offices* (1949) of the Episcopal Church included a General
Benediction:

Antiphon. Every creature of God is good, and nothing is to be refused, if it
be received with thanksgiving; + for it is sanctified by the word of God and
prayer.
   Thou hast created all things;
   And for thy pleasure they are and were created.
Let us pray.
Almighty God, who giveth us richly all things to enjoy; Bless, we beseech
thee, this _____, that receiving it with thanksgiving, we may use it
for the relief of our necessity and the setting forth of thy glory; through Jesus
Christ our Lord. *Amen.*[99]

Other Anglican books sometimes included a form delightfully called the
"Blessing of Anything Whatsoever."

   The Orthodox *Service Book* includes a prayer "For the Blessing of
Any Object":

After the customary beginning: The Thrice-Holy (Holy God, Holy Mighty).
Then: Our Father, . . . *And after the Exclamation* [the Doxology], *the Priest
saith:*
Let us pray to the Lord. Lord, have mercy.
O Creator and Author of the human race, Giver of spiritual graces and
Bestower of eternal salvation: Do thou, the same Lord, send down thy Holy
Spirit with a blessing from on high upon this object; that fortified by the
might of heavenly protection, it may be potent unto bodily salvation and
succor and aid, unto all who shall desire to make use of it, through Jesus
Christ our Lord. Amen. *He then sprinkleth the object thrice with holy
water, and pronounceth the customary Benediction.*[100]

---

98. *Roman Ritual*, pp. 600–601.
99. *Book of Offices* (2d ed., 1949), p. 71. Although this form was included in the section
headed "Benediction of Church Ornaments," the first rubric under that title broadens the
prospective use of the forms provided: "For use at the Opening of a Church, at the Blessing
of Houses, and at other times when new things are to be blessed" (p. 61).
100. *Service Book*, pp. 557–58.

Survey of the Service

The warning in the first rubric, "Care should be exercised to make certain that God's blessing may properly be asked upon the object, place, or event under consideration," places a burden on the pastor to make what sometimes can be a most difficult decision. While it seems clear that it is inappropriate to ask God's blessing on weapons of war and destruction, such as guns and bombs, the pastor more often will be required to make less clear decisions: to bless or not to bless a tombstone, a factory, a pet, a new business.

The pastor will need to ask why God's blessing is sought on this object or enterprise. If those who request the blessing cannot articulate the reasons convincingly, is it possible to find in the request some connection with the order of creation and/or the gospel? Those who request the blessing may perhaps know instinctively more than they are able to express verbally and more perhaps than the pastor understands. The pastor needs to listen sympathetically to the request. It may be strange, "unheard of in all Christendom" as George Seltzer was wont to exclaim upon learning of another outrageous practice in some congregation, but the request need not necessarily be rejected out of hand. Nor need all requests be honored.

In the service itself the verse at the beginning of the prayers, "All your works praise you, O Lord, *and your faithful servants bless you,*" is from Ps. 145:10. The translation is that of the psalms in the *LBW*.

The prayer ⟨521⟩ begins with the Jewish *Berakah* formula, "Blessed are you, O Lord our God, king of the universe," which is frequently employed in *Occasional Services* (1982). It is a blessing of God in thanksgiving by recounting his acts for his people.

The first paragraph echoes the Sanctus, the Preface of the Holy Communion, and the Nicene Creed ("seen and unseen"). The second paragraph recalls Ps. 104:2; Isa. 40:22; Gen. 1:18, 14; Jer. 1:10; and Eccles. 3:1–8.

The prayer then continues with ⟨522⟩ or ⟨523⟩, both new compositions.

THANKSGIVING AT THE DISPOSITION OF A CHURCH BUILDING
(*Occasional Services*, pp. 155–57)

Parallel Rite

Episcopal   Secularizing a Consecrated Building, *Book of Occasional Services,* pp. 204–6.

Purpose

The rite is to thank God for his past mercies in the house which is now to be vacated and to ask God's continued blessing in the new life of the congregation.

Characteristics

If it is true that a building is consecrated by its use, then when its use ceases or changes, its consecrated nature also ceases. This rite is, therefore, not a de-consecration, an undoing of what was accomplished at the dedication of a building, as if God's blessing which was called down then is now being lifted from the building.

If the congregation is ending its existence as the building is vacated, then the Closing of a Congregation is the appropriate service.

Preparation for the Service

The cornerstone and its contents may be removed.

A bearer should be assigned to each movable object remaining in the church so that as many objects as possible may be carried out of the building at the conclusion of the service. Appropriate places for each object — either in the new church or elsewhere — should be designated.

Care must be taken to estimate as exactly as possible the amount of bread and wine necessary for the Holy Communion at this service so that none will be left over.

Survey of the Service

It is appropriate for the final service in a church building to be a service of Holy Communion in thanksgiving for all the gifts of grace bestowed upon God's people in the place about to be vacated.

At the clearing of the table during the postcommunion canticle, any bread remaining and any wine remaining in the chalice(s) and flagons should be consumed by the ministers (and congregation). The sacramental linens are folded in preparation for carrying them from the building.

Following the postcommunion prayer (no. 40), a hymn may be sung. The presiding minister addresses the congregation and the prayers are said. The first prayer ⟨509⟩, a new composition, begins with the *Berakah* formula, "Blessed are you, O Lord our God, king of the universe," which praises God for past blessings and asks continued mercy. The prayers conclude with prayer (69), which is the Prayer of the Day for the Fifth Sunday of Easter. The translation in the *LBW* is a revision of the translation in the *Common Service Book,* which was taken from the 1549 Prayer Book translation of the Latin original in the Gelasian Sacramentary.

After the benediction and dismissal, those appointed receive from the ministers the various sacramental vessels and linens, ornaments, paraments, and Bibles. An appropriate hymn is sung as the ministers lead the procession of the congregation from the building.

If the new building is nearby, it is appropriate for the procession to move directly there.

As soon as possible after the service, the altar — if it remains in the building and if it is to be preserved — is removed.

Comparison of Rites
Thanksgiving at the Disposition
of a Church Building

LUTHERAN	EPISCOPAL
	Altars and all dedicated objects to be preserved are removed
(Holy Communion)	before service begins
(Hymn)	
Address	Address with the reading of the bishop's Declaration of Secularization
Salutation and response	Salutation and response
	Our Father
Prayer: Blessed are you, O Lord our God, king of the universe. You fill the entire world with your presence; your name is to be hallowed through all the earth. Receive our praise and thanksgiving for the blessings, help, and comfort which you bestowed upon your people in this house. Continue your mercies to your Church, that we may be conscious of your unchanging love as we take leave of this place of worship; through Jesus Christ our Lord.	Prayer: Lord God, in your great goodness you once accepted to your honor and glory this building, now secularized: Receive our praise and thanksgiving for the blessings, help, and comfort which you bestowed upon your people in this place. Continue, we pray, your many mercies in your Church, that we may be conscious at all times of your unchanging love; through Jesus Christ our Lord.
O God, form the minds of your faithful people into a single will. Make us love what you command and desire what you	Assist us mercifully, O Lord, in these our prayers, and dispose the way of your servants towards the attainment of

Comparison of Rites (continued)
Thanksgiving at the Disposition
of a Church Building

LUTHERAN

promise, that, amid all the
changes of this world, our
hearts may be fixed where true
joy is found; through your
Son, Jesus Christ our Lord,
who lives and reigns with you
and the Holy Spirit, one God,
now and forever.*
Benediction

Dismissal

EPISCOPAL

everlasting salvation; that
among the swift and varied
changes of this world, our
hearts may surely there be fixed
where true joys are to be found;
through Jesus Christ our
Lord.†

Benediction

(The peace)

*Prayer of the Day for the Fifth Sunday of Easter. From the Gelasian Sacramentary for the third Sunday after the octave of Easter.
†Based on the collect for the Fifth Sunday in Lent (*Book of Common Prayer,* p. 219).

8

SERVICES RELATED TO
THE MINISTRY OF THE LAITY

This collection of services related to the lay ministry should be understood as extensions of baptism, for it is baptism that commissions Christians for their work in the world. Baptism gives significance to all of one's life. In living out that commission, some Christians work within the congregation by being elected to office, by serving as lay professional leaders, by volunteering for work in a number of capacities. Perhaps even more important than this work within the organization is the work which Christians do in their various vocations in the world. By their faithful attention to their responsibilities they bear witness to the work of God throughout his creation and join in the work of renovating society and the world.

FOR FURTHER READING

Capon, Robert Farrar. *An Offering of Uncles: The Priesthood of Adam and the Shape of the World.* New York: Crossroad, 1982.

Detwiler-Zapp, Diane, and William Caveness Dixon. *Lay Caregiving.* Philadelphia: Fortress Press, 1982.

Floristan, Casiano, and Christian Duquoc. *Charisms in the Church.* Concilium, vol. 109. New York: Seabury Press, 1978.

McElvaney, William K. *The People of God in Ministry.* Nashville: Abingdon Press, 1982.

Nouwen, Henri. *Reaching Out.* Garden City, N.Y.: Doubleday & Co., 1975.

INSTALLATION OF
ELECTED PARISH OFFICERS
(*Occasional Services*, pp. 132–35)

Parallel Rites

Episcopal   Commissioning for Lay Ministries in the Church: 1. Wardens and Members of the Vestry; 15. Officers of Church Organizations, *Book of Occasional Services,* pp. 160–63, 174.

Lutheran   Order for the Installation of the Council or Govern-
ing Body of a Local Church, *Occasional Services*
(1962), pp. 139–41.
Order for the Induction of Office Bearers, *Occasional
Services* (1962), pp. 148–50.
Order for the Installation of a Church Council,
Common Service Book (text ed.), pp. 481–83.
Order for the Installation of a Church Council, *Lu-
theran Agenda*, pp. 141–44.

Methodist   An Office for the Recognition of Officials in the
Church, *Book of Worship*, p. 336.
An Office for the Recognition of Church School
Officers and Teachers, *Book of Worship*, pp.
337–38.

Presbyterian   Recognition of Trustees, *Worshipbook*, pp. 98–99.
A Service for Ordination and Installation (for an
Elder, for a Deacon), *Worshipbook,* pp. 89–95.

Brethren   Consecration of Short-Term Service Workers,
Pastor's Manual, pp. 127–31.

Purpose

This rite is to mark the beginning of the service of the elected governing body of a congregation. The Installation of a Lay Professional Leader is used to install those whose ministries entail major occupational commitments.

Characteristics

Two things are noteworthy in this service: the emphasis on baptism and the emphasis on the role of the laity in the work of the church. Indeed, the two are intimately related, for it is baptism, "the ordination of the laity," which commissions lay people for service in the church.

Background

This order is one that Lutherans have traditionally provided, even in books which included few occasional services. It is an important expression of the Lutheran understanding of the nature of the church and its governance as well as the Lutheran understanding of the nature of baptism.

Survey of the Service

A representative of the congregation, not the pastor, reads the names and offices of those who are to be installed. The baptismal creed is said by all.

The Apostles' Creed is integral to this service, and the Nicene Creed should not be substituted for it, even on those days for which the Nicene Creed is appropriate. It is therefore desirable to schedule the Installation of Parish Officers on days for which the color is green, when the Apostles' Creed is the appointed creed.

The minister's address to those being installed begins with St. Paul's recognition of the variety of gifts and services in the body of Christ.[1] It is desirable to read the description of the duties of those being installed as outlined in the constitution of the congregation. It is an instructive reminder to those elected and to the congregation as well of the duties that are required. Those being installed declare their willingness to serve, and—an innovation in this rite—the congregation in turn declares its support in the "mutual ministry that Christ has given to all the baptized."

The prayers—with specific reference to the newly installed officers— and the peace follow. The exchange of the peace is a version of the handshake which characterized several predecessor rites.[2]

1. Many will gladly note the disappearance of the verse from 1 Cor. 15:58, "Therefore be ye steadfast and unmovable, always abounding in the work of the Lord, forasmuch as ye know that your labor is not in vain in the Lord," which had been used as a concluding blessing in earlier rites (*Church Book,* p. 432; *Common Service Book,* p. 483; *Occasional Services* [1962], p. 141). Pastors frequently complained that too many members of the vestry, or council, heard too clearly and obeyed too well the first phrase of that charge.

2. General Synod rites of 1881 and 1900; *Lutheran Agenda* and the *Common Service Book.*

Development of the Rite
Installation of Elected Parish Officers

General Synod (1881)	*Lutheran Agenda*	General Synod (1900)	*Church Book*
		The grace	
Statement of duties	Statement of duties	Statement of duties	Statement of duties
Acceptance of office	Acceptance of office	Acceptance of office	Acceptance of office
	Handshake	Handshake	
	Charge or Blessing	Blessing	Blessing
Prayer	Prayer	Prayer	Prayer
Handshake and blessing			
		1 Cor. 15:58	1 Cor. 15:58
Address to those leaving office	Address to those leaving office		
		Depart in peace	

Development of the Rite
Installation of Elected Parish Officers

Common Service Book	*Occasional Services* (1962)	*Occasional Services* (1982)
Acts 6:2–3	Acts 6:2–3	1 Cor. 12:4–7
Statement of duties	Statement of duties	(Statement of duties)
Acceptance of office	Acceptance of office	Acceptance of office
		Congregation acceptance
Handshake		
Blessing	Blessing	
	Salutation and response	
Prayer	Prayer	
Our Father	Our Father	
1 Cor. 15:58	1 Cor. 15:58	
		Declaration of installation
		The prayers
		The peace

SERVICES RELATED TO THE MINISTRY OF THE LAITY

INSTALLATION OF
A LAY PROFESSIONAL LEADER
(*Occasional Services*, pp. 136–42)

Parallel Rites

Episcopal Commissioning for Lay Ministries in the Church: 5. Catechists or Teachers; 6. Evangelists; 8. Directors of Music, Organists, or other Musicians, *Book of Occasional Services,* pp. 160–62, 166–68, 169.

Methodist An Office for the Consecration of Directors of Christian Education and Directors of Music, *Book of Worship,* pp. 334–35.

Presbyterian The Installation of a Commissioned Church Worker, *Worshipbook,* pp. 96–97.

Brethren Installation of Church Staff, *Pastor's Manual,* pp. 123–26.

Purpose

This service is to install those whose ministries within the church entail a major occupational commitment, such as medical workers, directors of Christian education, youth workers, church musicians, administrative personnel, and Christian day-school teachers. These people may serve as part of the staff of a congregation, a district/synod, or of a board or agency of the church.

Characteristics

The title used for the person installed by this rite, "Lay Professional Leader," is language used by documents in the American Lutheran Church and in the Lutheran Church in America to describe those certified by the church for service in various tasks.

Survey of the Service

The service is directed to the candidate. The congregation has no direct role because the person being installed may not have a relationship to those served which can be expressed by congregational responses in the service.

The brief reading from Romans is used at the beginning of the order for the Installation of a Commissioned Church Worker in the Presbyterian *Worshipbook* (p. 96).

342

The prayers are all new compositions except for the prayer for a church musician ⟨495⟩, which is adapted from the *Book of Occasional Services.*[3]

COMMISSIONING OF
A LAY PROFESSIONAL LEADER
(*Occasional Services*, pp. 141–42)

Purpose

This adaptation of the installation rite is for use where the polity of the church body permits (as in the American Lutheran Church, but not in the Lutheran Church in America). It marks the beginning of a major occupational commitment to the work of the church and recognizes the achievement of professional certification.

Characteristics

The note in the Episcopal *Book of Occasional Services* represents an understanding of the ministry of lay people which is generally shared throughout the Christian church:

> Lay persons are commissioned for their ministry by the Sacrament of Holy Baptism, and no form of commissioning for special functions is necessary. The form which follows is intended for use when a public recognition of a special function is desired. (p. 160)

Thus the church has generally not provided rites to mark the beginning of even such ministries as require a major commitment of time. The 1982 *Occasional Services* is noteworthy in providing such a variety of services related to the ministry of those other than the clergy.

RECOGNITION OF MINISTRIES
IN THE CONGREGATION
(*Occasional Services*, pp. 143–46)

Parallel Rites

Episcopal   Commissioning for Lay Ministries in the Church: 1. Wardens and Members of the Vestry; 2. Deputies to General Convention, or Delegates to Diocesan Convention; 3. Servers at the Altar; 4. Altar Guild Members and Sacristans; 5. Cate-

---

3. P. 169, the prayer of the Royal School of Church Music. See the *Book of Common Prayer* (1979), p. 819, no. 17.

chists or Teachers; 6. Evangelists; 7. Singers; 8. Directors of Music, Organists, or other Musicians; 9. Lectors; 10. Those Who Administer the Chalice; 11. Licensed Lay Readers; 12. Parish Visitors; 13. Members of Prayer Groups; 14. Parish Canvassers; 15. Officers of Church Organizations; 16. Other Lay Ministries, *Book of Occasional Services,* pp. 160–76.

Lutheran

Commissioning of Parish Visitors, *Occasional Services* (1962), pp. 201–2.

Installation of Teachers, *Occasional Services* (1962), pp. 208–9.

Prayers and Blessings for Special Occasions: Choristers, *Occasional Services* (1962), pp. 208, 210.

Prayers and Blessings for Special Occasions: Acolytes, *Occasional Services* (1962), pp. 208, 211.

A Form for the Induction of Sunday School Officers and Teachers, *Lutheran Agenda,* pp. 138–40.

Methodist

An Office for the Recognition of Officials in the Church, *Book of Worship,* p. 336.

An Office for the Recognition of Church School Officers and Teachers, *Book of Worship,* pp. 337–38.

An Office for the Recognition of Choristers, *Book of Worship,* pp. 339–40.

Presbyterian

Recognition of Church School Teachers, *Worshipbook,* pp. 100–101.

Brethren

Commissioning and Consecration of Church School Teachers and Learners, *Pastor's Manual,* pp. 95–103.

Purpose

This service may be used to install the members of a committee of the congregation (for example, the stewardship committee) or others who serve the congregation (for example, choir members, teachers, evangelism visitors), and so may be used several times during a year.

It may be desirable, however, as the title implies, to use the service as a method of bringing to the attention of the congregation the varied ways in which the ministry which is part of the life of all the baptized is being exercised and as a way of recognizing those who offer themselves in a particular ministry of the congregation.

344

Characteristics

This service is part of the offering, a response to St. Paul's invitation, "Present your bodies as a living sacrifice, holy and acceptable to God, which is your spiritual worship." (The New English Bible translates, "offer your very selves to him.") It makes more explicit what is done at every offering when bread and wine, money, and the congregation are offered to God for his use.

The service therefore consists of brief addresses by the minister and a representative of the congregation who describes the ministries which are recognized. The people being recognized stand in their places (they do not come forward), and the prayer appropriate to their ministry is said.

Survey of the Service

The prayers are all newly composed for *Occasional Services* (1982). See also the prayers given on pages 291–92 of *Occasional Services* for the various committees of the congregation: worship (197), education (198), witness (192), service (190, 141), and stewardship (183).

AFFIRMATION OF THE VOCATION OF CHRISTIANS IN THE WORLD
(*Occasional Services*, pp. 147–49)

Parallel Rites

Episcopal — A Form of Commitment to Christian Service, *Book of Common Prayer* (1979), pp. 420–21.

Lutheran — The Blessing of a New Business Venture, *Occasional Services* (1962), pp. 208, 211.

Purpose

This service is a companion to the Recognition of Ministries in the Congregation. The minister's address in each is similar. Recognition of Ministries in the Congregation acknowledges the varied ministries within the church organization; Affirmation of the Vocation of Christians in the World recognizes the varied ministries beyond the congregation and beyond the church organization. Both orders have their roots and inspiration in baptism.

Characteristics

Like the Recognition of Ministries in the Congregation, this service is part of the action of the offering. The minister and a representative of

345

the congregation describe the areas of service to be affirmed; the persons engaged in that service stand; a prayer may be said. The Holy Communion then continues with the offertory prayer.

Special note should be taken of the rubric suggesting various days when the affirmation of vocations would be appropriate. It may be that the observance of such days in themselves will be a suitable affirmation of the vocations of Christians in the world.

Background

This is a new service and an attempt to recognize in a liturgical way the work which Christians do in the world, giving that work equal standing with the service rendered within the institution of the church.

In his *Commentary on the American Prayer Book* Marion Hatchett observes in connection with the Episcopal Form of Commitment to Christian Service in the 1979 *Book of Common Prayer:* "The chief liturgical model for one who undertakes a special responsibility involving commitment to the service of Christ in the world has been the rite for coronation of a ruler."[4] Throughout Christian history, rites have been devised locally for those who enter various civic offices, or who undertake some special responsibility.

The new Episcopal rite is still more open-ended and brief than the rite in *Occasional Services* (1982). An Act of Commitment is prepared before the service consisting "either of a statement of intention or of a series of questions and answers, but which should include a reaffirmation of baptismal promises."[5] Before the offering of the Eucharist the person comes forward and makes the Act of Commitment. Then the celebrant says "these or similar words":

> May the Holy Spirit guide and strengthen you, that in this, and in all things, you may do God's will in the service of the kingdom of his Christ. *Amen.* In the name of this congregation I commend you to this work, and pledge you our prayers, encouragement, and support.[6]

Then the celebrant says this or some other appropriate prayer:

> Almighty God, look with favor upon *this person* who *has* now reaffirmed *his* commitment to follow Christ and to serve in his name. Give *him* courage, patience, and vision; and strengthen us all in our Christian vocation of witness to the world, and of service to others; through Jesus Christ our Lord.[7]

---

4. Marion Hatchett, *Commentary on American Prayer Book,* p. 425.
5. *Book of Common Prayer* (1979), p. 420.
6. Ibid.
7. Ibid., p. 421.

The service continues with the peace and the offertory.

Survey of the Service

The first rubric indicates in a general way the areas of service that are envisioned in this rite. Service through "family" includes the work of a wife/husband, homemaker, mother/father, and the work of foster parents. "Occupation" includes all those areas of work for which one receives wages and upon which God's blessing can be asked. "Voluntary organizations" include those areas of service for which a person does not receive wages: service clubs, volunteer fire companies, hospital service, rescue corps. Service to the community may overlap these areas and may also include part-time work for which one receives compensation, working in a park or with an athletic team, serving in government at various local levels. "Community" may be generously interpreted to include local-service and state-government programs. Service through the nation includes, among other things, government and military service.

A Sunday appointed for the affirmation of vocation should be carefully chosen not on the basis of the secular calendar, or simply at the convenience of the congregation, but on the basis of the appointed lessons.

On a Sunday appointed for the affirmation of vocation it is the practice of some congregations to invite the members to attend the service dressed in their work clothes as a visible demonstration of the variety of forms of service represented in the membership.

Rubric 5 states, "A representative of the congregation reads a brief description of the area of service to be affirmed." The description may be something like this:

> Those who serve on the Oslo Volunteer Fire Company render us all service. They give of their time to keep the fire equipment in repair. They work to raise money for new equipment. They stand always ready to leave their regular employment or their leisure time to come to the aid of those in distress. They teach us how to make our homes and buildings safer places. In all this, by so doing, they help protect us from danger, give us security, and teach us how to serve one another.

Rubric 7 says, "A prayer appropriate to the area of service may be said." The prayer may be drawn from the collection of Petitions, Intercessions, and Thanksgivings (*LBW,* Min. Ed., pp. 105–15):

Families:

The Human Family (177)[8]

---

8. Borrowed from the 1979 *Book of Common Prayer* (p. 815, no. 3) and written by Charles P. Price.

Families (230)[9]
The Care of Children (232)[10]

Occupation:

Commerce and Industry (178)[11]
Agriculture (185)[12]
Prisons and Correctional Institutions (186)[13]
See also the third paragraph of the Prayer of the Church (*LBW,*
Min. Ed., p. 117), "Let your blessing rest upon . . ."

Voluntary organizations:

The Neighborhood (176)[14]
Social Justice (167)[15]

Community and Nation:

State/Provincial and Local Governments (170)[16]
Those in Civil Authority (172)[17]
Cities (174)[18]
Courts of Justice (173)[19]

Leisure:

Use of Leisure (188)[20]

---

9. An adaptation of no. 45 (pp. 828–29) in the 1979 Prayer Book, written by Frederick Dan Huntington, bishop of Central New York (1869–1904), and included in the 1928 American Prayer Book. The biblical allusions include Ps. 68:6; Heb. 12:15; Gal. 5:26; 2 Pet. 1:5–6; Gen. 2:24; Mal. 4:6.

10. Prayer no. 46 in the 1979 Prayer Book (p. 829), written by John W. Suter, based on a prayer by William Austin Smith, and included in the 1928 American Prayer Book. The biblical allusion is Phil. 4:8.

11. A revision of a prayer "For commerce and industry" appointed for the Rogation Days in the 1979 *Book of Common Prayer* (p. 259), which in turn was modeled on a prayer "For industry" in the Canadian Prayer Book.

12. An adaptation of a prayer dating from 1689 based on phrases in the 1662 Prayer Book and introduced into the American Prayer Book in 1892. It is in the 1979 Prayer Book as no. 29 (p. 824).

13. Prayer no. 37 (p. 826) in the 1979 Prayer Book, written by Charles P. Price.

14. New.

15. Prayer no. 27 (p. 823), new to the 1979 Prayer Book by an unknown author.

16. New.

17. A revision of prayer no. 19 (p. 820) in the 1979 *Book of Common Prayer,* originally included in the 1928 American Prayer Book.

18. Written by J. Robert Zimmerman and included in the 1979 Prayer Book as no. 33 (p. 825).

19. Adaptation of no. 21 (p. 821) in the 1979 Prayer Book, originally included in the 1928 American Prayer Book.

20. Adaptation of no. 32, written by James G. Birney and included in the 1979 Prayer Book (p. 825, no. 32).

Joblessness:

The Unemployed (179)[21]

Specific prayers may be composed for the occasion.

The first concluding prayer ⟨503⟩ is an adaptation of a prayer in the Form of Commitment to Christian Service in the 1979 *Book of Common Prayer* (p. 421), prepared by Bonnell Spencer, O. H. C. The alternate prayer ⟨504⟩ is a new composition.

---

21. Prayer no. 30 (p. 824) in the 1979 Prayer Book, a revision of the prayer of the Industrial Christian Fellowship, published in *The Prayer Manual*, ed. F. B. Macnutt (London: A. R. Mowbray & Co., 1951), no. 117.

9

SERVICES RELATED TO
THE LIFE OF THE CONGREGATION

ORGANIZATION OF A CONGREGATION
(*Occasional Services*, pp. 250-53)

Parallel Rites

Lutheran   The Organization of a Congregation, *Occasional Services* (1962), pp. 208-9.

Methodist   An Office for the Organizing of a Church, *Book of Worship,* pp. 341-43.

Purpose

This rite is to mark within a service of worship the formation of a congregation and the establishment of its relationship to the district/synod and to the church body.

Characteristics

The focus of this rite is embodied in the questions asked of the new congregation: its acceptance of the catholic faith, its work in unity and love, its relationship with the district/synod and the church body to which it belongs.

Background

Occasional Services (1962) provided a prayer at "The Organization of a Congregation."

> O Lord Jesus Christ, who art present wherever two or three are gathered together in thy Name: Bless us thy servants now assembled in this place. Grant us unity of spirit in the bond of peace. Set before us a vision of the doors which thou hast opened unto us. Further our endeavors and make us worthy to bear the banner of thy Cross and the name of thy Church; who livest and reignest with the Father and the Holy Ghost, one God, world without end.[1]

---

1. *Occasional Services* (1962), p. 209.

Survey of the Service

The only parallel rite is the Methodist Office for the Organizing of a Church:[2]

METHODIST	LUTHERAN
Declaration of purpose	
(Hymn)	
Jer. 32:37–41	
A litany	
Reception of members	(Reception of members)
	Creed
	Examination of congregation
Giving a name to the church	
Declaration of organization	Declaration of organization
In accordance with the laws and *Discipline* of The United Methodist Church, I hereby declare that the *N.* United Methodist Church is duly constituted and organized for the glory of God, the proclamation of the Gospel, and the service of humanity.	Upon these your promises, I hereby declare that _____ is a duly organized and constituted congregation of (church body) in the name of the Father, and of the Son, and of the Holy Spirit.
2 Pet. 1:3–10	
(Hymn)	
Sermon	
Prayer[3]	Prayer ⟨546⟩[4]
(Hymn)	
(Blessing)	
	The prayers

---

2. *The Book of Worship* (Nashville: United Methodist Publishing House, 1964), pp. 341–43.

3. The Methodist prayer is an adaptation of the prayer at the Laying of a Cornerstone in *Occasional Services* (1962), p. 110.

4. The Lutheran prayer recalls phrases from the prayer at the Organization of a Congregation, *Occasional Services* (1962), p. 209.

352

RECEPTION OF A CONGREGATION
(*Occasional Services*, p. 254)

Parallel Rites

Lutheran

The Admission of a Congregation, *Occasional Services* (1962), pp. 191–92.

Office for the Admission of a Congregation into Synod, *Occasional Services* (1930), pp. 183–84.

Purpose

By this rite a congregation is received into a district/synod, usually at a meeting of the district/synod.

Characteristics

This simple form—a statement, a question, a sentence declaring the reception—is normally used at a district/synod meeting. The older forms of 1930 and 1962 had the president of the district/synod visit the congregation to receive it. These forms had the virtue of involving more members of the congregation, but they had the disadvantage of focusing on the congregation itself rather than the receiving district/synod.

Survey of the Service

Prayer ⟨547⟩ is a new composition.

Development of the Rite
Reception of a Congregation

Occasional Services (1930)	*Occasional Services* (1962)	*Occasional Services* (1982)
In the Name of the Father . . .	In the Name of the Father . . .	
Address	Address	Address
Promise by congregation*	Promise by congregation*	Promise by congregation

---

*Cleaving to the Faith as expressed and taught by the Church, will you strive to foster the work of the Kingdom in the bond of unity and brotherly love both here at home in this place and in the activities of the Church at large?
We will with God's help.
Having by your application signified your willingness to abide by the Constitution of the Synod and its formal enactments, do you accept your privilege of representation and participation in all its deliberations?
We do.
The language of the 1962 book is nearly identical.

Development of the Rite (continued)
Reception of a Congregation

Occasional Services (1930)	Occasional Services (1962)	Occasional Services (1982)
Declaration of admission†	Declaration of admission	Reception of congregation
Prayer‡	Prayer	Prayer

RECEPTION OF LUTHERANS
BY TRANSFER
(*Occasional Services,* pp. 129-31)

Parallel Rites

Episcopal   Welcoming New People to a Congregation, *Book of Occasional Services,* p. 110 (simply three rubrics).

Lutheran   Admission to Membership (By Transfer, Restoration, or Renewal), *Occasional Services* (1962), pp. 189-90.

                    Office for the Public Reception of Fellow-Members of the Household of Faith, *Occasional Services* (1930), p. 179.

Presbyterian   The Reception of Members from Other Churches, *Worshipbook,* pp. 51-52.

Purpose

This form is for welcoming Christians who transfer membership from another Lutheran congregation.

Lutherans who have not been practicing their faith or who are other-

---

†Upon this your covenant, I declare the (name of church) admitted to union with (name of synod) and authorize you to participate in all privileges of this synodical union.
The language of the 1962 book is nearly identical.

‡Almighty God, Who for the propagation of the Holy Gospel hast established Thy Church among men and hast gathered Thy believing children into congregations for the furtherance of Thy Kingdom and their nourishment and growth in the Way that leadeth to Life: Bless this union into which this church and Synod have entered to Thy glory and to their mutual profit in Thy work, that Thy Name may be hallowed, Thy Kingdom come, and Thy Will be done; through Jesus Christ, Thy Son, our Lord.
The language of the 1962 book is nearly identical.

wise not in good standing are received by the Affirmation of Baptism. Non-Lutherans are received by Affirmation of Baptism (see *LBW,* Min. Ed., p. 35).

Characteristics

A separate service for the reception of Lutherans is assumed by the *Lutheran Book of Worship,* where a distinction is drawn between Lutherans and non-Lutherans. "The reception of Lutherans in good standing from other congregations through letter of transfer may be done in a simple ceremony which acknowledges the community of the total Lutheran family" (*LBW,* Min. Ed., p. 35).

To some, drawing this distinction may appear to be contrary to the ecumenical spirit. The intention, however, is to acknowledge that a Lutheran congregation has a relationship to another Lutheran congregation which is different from its relationship to a congregation of another denomination. Despite a diversity of local taste and practice, Lutheran congregations acknowledge the same Scriptures, creeds, and confessional documents; and it is this subscription that gives them their focus of identity and community.

Background

The *Lutheran Agenda* made such a distinction between Lutherans and non-Lutherans, providing for the Reception of Members (by Transfer) and for the Reception of Converts.[5] *Occasional Services* (1930) divided reception not on the basis of denomination but on the basis of standing in the church. There was an Office for the Public Reception of Fellow-Members of the Household of Faith[6] and an Office for the Restoration of

---

5. *Lutheran Agenda,* pp. 30–31. The Liturgy of the Joint Synod of Ohio (1912) also provided for the Reception of Converts (although there was no form for the Reception of Lutherans).

[When members of other churches desire to be received into our Ev. Lutheran Church, they are to be instructed like other catechumens and, when ready to make a public confession, are to be confirmed according to the usual order. If circumstances, however, render it preferable, the following form may be used:]

Dearly beloved: *N.N.* who was formerly a member of the _____ Church, having become convinced that the doctrines taught in our Catechism and Augsburg Confession are the very truth of God's holy Word, and that the opposite teachings of said _____ Church are errors which it is our duty to reject, has declared such conviction before the pastor and vestry of this congregation, and has upon this renunciation of said errors and confession of the true faith been received as a member of this congregation. (pp. 182–83)

See also a similar renunciation of the former faith by a convert to the Orthodox church, *Service Book,* pp. 455–57.

6. *Occasional Services* (1930), pp. 179–80.

One Who Has Lapsed, to Membership in the Church.[7] *Occasional Services* (1962) avoided such distinctions altogether and provided one rite for Admission to Membership (By Transfer, Restoration, or Renewal).[8]

The Episcopal Church requires episcopal confirmation of those who are received into its membership. It does not require a rite of reception of members who have already received the laying on of hands. The *Book of Occasional Services* provides a rite consisting simply of three rubrics for Welcoming New People to a Congregation:

> If it is desired to welcome new people to the congregation publicly, it is suitable that they be introduced in the following manner.
>
> Immediately before the Peace, the persons are asked to come forward, and are introduced briefly, preferably by a member of the congregation.
>
> The celebrant then begins the exchange of the Peace, in the course of which those who have been introduced are greeted personally by the celebrant and members of the congregation as convenient.[9]

The Presbyterian *Worshipbook* (pp. 51–52) provides a form for The Reception of Members from Other Churches. The reception takes place by the receipt of a letter of transfer. The rite is a public acknowledgement of the reception.

Survey of the Service

It is desirable that the Reception of Lutherans by Transfer take place at a service other than when the Affirmation of Baptism is being used, because the combination of the two rites is awkward.

However, it may be necessary that the two rites take place at the same service. In order to avoid addressing the Affirmation of Baptism to some but not all of the group being received into membership by various means, the simplest procedure is to use the Affirmation of Baptism in its entirety up to (but not including) the peace and then insert the Reception of Lutherans by Transfer immediately before the peace (*LBW*, Min. Ed., p. 327, no. 7). The prayers (*Occasional Services*, p. 130, no. 6), having already been said in the Affirmation of Baptism are in this case omitted from the rite for the Reception of Lutherans by Transfer. The prayer ⟨491⟩ may appropriately be said after those being received by transfer have come forward.

The peace is then shared, and after the peace the service continues with the offering.

---

7. Ibid., pp. 180–82.
8. *Occasional Services* (1962), pp. 189–90.
9. *Book of Occasional Services,* p. 110.

Development of the Rite
Reception of Lutherans

Occasional Services (1930)	*Occasional Services* (1962)	*Occasional Services* (1982)
	The Gospel	
The Creed		The Creed
Presentation	Presentation	Presentation
Address		Welcome
	Ps. 124:8	
	Salutation and response	
Prayer*	Prayer†	The prayers‡
	Creed	
	Promise	
	Blessing	
Hymn	Hymn	
Sermon	Sermon	
		The peace

---

*We give thanks unto Thee, O Father of Jesus Christ our Lord, that Thou hast called us to the Fellowship of the Gospel and dost bind us together in the bonds of love and brotherhood and service in the Church established by Thy dear Son; and we humbly pray that those who are this day united with us and we with them may be one in Thee and grow in grace and walk worthy of the Lord unto all pleasing being fruitful in every good work and increasing in knowledge of Thee always, endeavoring to keep the unity of the Spirit in the bond of peace; and, O Merciful Father, we beseech Thee, complete that good work which Thou hast begun in us that at the Day of Christ we may be welcomed in the Church Triumphant, there ever to glorify Thee with Thy Son in the unity of the Holy Spirit, God blessed for evermore.

†We give thanks to thee, Almighty God, that thou hast called us to the fellowship of the Gospel and dost bind us in love, brotherhood and service in thy holy Church; and we humbly pray that those who are this day united with us and we with them, may be one in thee. Grant that we may together grow in grace, be fruitful in every good work, and endeavor to keep the unity of the Spirit in the bond of peace; that at the day of Christ we may be welcomed in the Church triumphant, there ever to glorify thee with thy Son in the unity of the Holy Spirit, God blessed for evermore.

‡The prayer is a new composition. The language of the final phrase recalls 1 Cor. 15:28 (KJV).

FAREWELL AND GODSPEED

(*Occasional Services*, pp. 151-52)

Parallel Rites

Episcopal   When Members Leave a Congregation, *Book of Occasional Services*, p. 111 (simply two rubrics).

Purpose

This form suggests prayer for those who are moving to another congregation and affirms the corporate nature of the baptismal faith.

The form is also appropriate when a pastor leaves a congregation.

Characteristics

In the past, forms have been provided for the reception of members but nothing provided for when members leave a congregation. The implication was that churches should grow. When new names were added there was cause for public display (to some, proof that the pastor was working), but when members left, the less said about that the better. It was an excessively selfish and parochial understanding of the church.

Both the realities of modern, mobile society and a deeper understanding of the nature of the church suggest that the coming and going of members be recognized. When people leave one congregation for another they are not lost to the church. Always, one congregation's gain is another's loss.

Background

The Episcopal *Book of Occasional Services* provides simply two rubrics for When Members Leave a Congregation:

> When persons leave a congregation, it is suitable that, on their last Sunday, the fact be mentioned before the Prayers of the People, and that they be prayed for by name in those Prayers.

> They are greeted personally by the celebrant and lay officials of the congregation at the time of the Peace, or at the end of the service.[10]

Survey of the Service

When new members are received, they are usually received in groups on stated Sundays. Farewell and Godspeed—when members leave a congregation—is intended for use on the last Sunday of attendance as individuals and families transfer their membership to another congregation. Especially in congregations with a frequent turnover of members, there-

---

10. Ibid., p. 111.

fore, care must be taken not to make the farewell too elaborate or time-consuming.

Moreover, care must be taken to avoid the implication that the congregation which the members are leaving is the locus of the true church. It must be clear to all—beginning with the ministers—that the whole church is one and that the members who transfer their membership will doubtless hear the gospel as clearly in the new congregation as in the old, share in the same Supper, and rejoice in the one church.

When the Holy Communion is celebrated, the preferred place for Farewell and Godspeed is following the prayers, immediately before the peace. Thus the prayers can make reference to the unity of the church and name the members who are leaving. The exchange of the peace can be a visible affirmation of that unity.

When the Holy Communion is not celebrated and the ante-communion concludes with the offering, prayers, and benediction, the preferred place for Farewell and Godspeed is immediately before the benediction. The peace is not shared, for that is only part of the celebration of the Holy Communion.

If Farewell and Godspeed is placed after the postcommunion prayer, the silence for reflection following the prayer must be maintained; it is an integral part of the postcommunion and should not be passed over or slighted.

When a pastor leaves a congregation, the address given in "The Service in Detail" (no. 5) may be said by a member of the congregation instead of the address provided for the presiding minister in the text of the rite. If the pastor has a family, another pastor of the congregation may read paragraph no. 5 provided for the presiding minister. If another ordained person is not available, it is best to delete "In Holy Baptism . . . through you" rather than compromise the principle of having only ordained ministers serve as the presiding minister. To have the departing pastor read the paragraph to his or her family is undesirable for it presumes that the speaker represents the stability of the congregation which received those who are now leaving.

Prayer ⟨506⟩ is a new composition.

THANKSGIVING AT THE RETIREMENT OF A DEBT
(*Occasional Services*, pp. 153–54)

Parallel Rites

Lutheran   The Retirement of an Indebtedness, *Occasional Services* (1962), pp. 199–200.

Purpose

This rite is to mark the fulfillment of a financial obligation by a congregation.

Characteristics

The central action of this rite is twofold: the prayer (no. 4) and the singing of the hymn of thanksgiving (no. 6) look back in gratitude for the past effort at retiring the debt; the second prayer (no. 7) looks ahead, centering attention on the gospel, and asks God's help in a life of thanksgiving and praise.

Background

A mortgage burning is good copy for newspaper publicity, but it is largely a meaningless action. It has its origins in the destruction of the actual note of indebtedness. When the promise to pay was fulfilled, one did not want that note to remain. The claim was cancelled by destroying the note, and burning was the most complete and convenient means.

At the present time, however, most institutions prefer to keep the mortgage document on which the note of fulfillment is made. Burning a *copy* of a mortgage is pointless.

The *Occasional Services* (1962) rite for the Retirement of an Indebtedness followed the hymn after the Creed (the hymn before the sermon). After the versicle from Ps. 124:8 and the salutation and response, three prayers were said:

> O Lord our God, of whose bounty come our gifts: We thank thee for the benevolence by which we are enabled to come to this day, and we beseech thee to raise up in every generation faithful benefactors and stewards, that thy kingdom may advance and the whole world be brought to the knowledge of thy Son; through the same Jesus Christ our Lord.
>
> O Lord our God, the Giver of all good: Behold in our gifts which bring thanksgiving to this day an earnest of our consecration to thy service; and grant that now and at all times our gratitude to thee may be as great as our need of thy mercy; through Jesus Christ our Lord.
>
> Thine, O Lord, is the greatness, and the power, and the victory, and the majesty; for all that is in the heaven and in the earth is thine. Thine is the kingdom, O Lord, and thou art exalted as head above all. Both riches and honor come of thee, and of thine own have we given thee, for the good of thy Church and the glory of thy Name; through Jesus Christ our Lord.[11]

---

11. *Occasional Services* (1962), pp. 199–200. The third prayer is from 1 Chron. 29:11–12.

A hymn of thanksgiving was sung and the service continued with the sermon.

Survey of the Service

Prayer ⟨507⟩ is a new composition.

Prayer ⟨508⟩ is the opening section of the Prayer of the Church (*LBW*, Min. Ed., p. 116), which was originally composed for the *Service Book and Hymnal* (p. 6).

INDUCTION OF A CHRISTIAN DAY SCHOOL TEACHER
(*Occasional Services*, pp. 239–42)

Parallel Rites

Episcopal   Commissioning for Lay Ministries in the Church: 5. Catechists or Teachers, *Book of Occasional Services*, pp. 161–62, 166–67.

Lutheran   The Order for the Installation of a Teacher, *Lutheran Agenda*, pp. 132–35.

Purpose

This service is used to install parochial school teachers in those places where the teachers are extended a call as well as a contract to serve in a congregational day school. In church bodies whose polity makes no such provision, teachers are installed using the rite of Installation of a Lay Professional Leader (pp. 136–42).

Characteristics

The structure of the Induction of a Christian Day School Teacher is identical with that of the Installation of a Lay Professional Leader:

Installation of a Lay Professional Leader	*Induction of a Christian Day School Teacher*
Certification of appointment	Certification of call/appointment
Presentation of candidate	Presentation of candidate
Address with scriptural passages	Address with scriptural passages
Questions to candidate	Questions to candidate
Declaration of installation	Declaration of induction
Prayer	Prayer
Blessing	Blessing
The prayers	The prayers

361

Background

This order is included in *Occasional Services* (1982) largely because of the practice of many congregations of the Association of Evangelical Lutheran Churches. In this practice the teachers are called as well as contracted and, therefore, are accorded a quasi-clerical status.

The Order for the Installation of a Teacher given in the *Lutheran Agenda* includes these rubrics:

> Installation shall be administered under the authorization of the President of a synod and according to its appointment. Installation properly takes place within the congregation to which the candidate has been called.

The order begins:

> Dear brother: _____ Evangelical Lutheran _____ at a regular meeting, asking for God's guidance and acting in His fear, hath duly elected and called thee to be a teacher in our school.

> Whereas, then, by divine guidance, thou hast recognized in this call the voice of God . . . I ask thee . . . [12]

It is assumed in the *Lutheran Agenda* that the teacher is male. Woman teachers have their own rite, which is not called installation but induction. The man is addressed "Brother" and is extended a call. The woman is addressed simply as "Friend" and is appointed to her position.[13]

Comparison of Rites
Induction of a
Christian Day School Teacher

Lutheran Agenda	*Book of Occasional Services*	*Occasional Services* (1982)
Follows General Prayer	Follows sermon (and Creed) in in Eucharist	Follows sermon in Holy Communion
	or after collects in Morning Prayer	
	or separately	
		Hymn of the day
	Presentation	Presentation

------

12. *Lutheran Agenda*, p. 132.
13. Ibid., p. 136.

Comparison of Rites (continued)
Induction of a
Christian Day School Teacher

Lutheran Agenda	*Book of Occasional Services*	*Occasional Services* (1982)
Address	Address	Address
	Testimony of sponsors	
Promise by candidate	Promise by candidate	Promise by candidate
Handshake		
	(Lesson)	
	(Homily)	
(Address to congregation)		
(Address to children of the school)		
	Antiphon*	
	Versicle	
	Prayer	
	Commissioning	Commissioning
Prayer		Prayer†
Our Father		
Charge to teacher		
		Blessing
		The prayers
		The peace

* The words which I command you this day shall be upon your hearts; and you shall teach them diligently to your children, and shall talk of them when you sit in your house, and when you walk by the way, and when you lie down, and when you rise.
  We will recount to generations to come the praiseworthy deeds and the power of the Lord:
  And the wonderful works he has done.
Let us pray. (*Silence*)
God of all wisdom and knowledge, give your blessing and guidance to all who teach in your Church, that by word and example they may lead those whom they teach to the knowledge and love of you; through Jesus Christ our Lord.
  In the Name of God and of this congregation, I commission you [*N.*] as Catechist (Teacher) in this *Parish* [and I give you this _____ as a token of your ministry]. (*Book of Occasional Services*, pp. 166–67)

† The prayer (198) is from the *LBW* and was composed for that book.

GUIDELINES FOR
RINGING CHURCH BELLS
(*Occasional Services*, pp. 260–62)

Parallel Rites

Lutheran   Regulations for the Ringing of a Tower Bell —
                          Peal — Chimes, *Occasional Services* (1930), pp.
                          187–93.

Purpose

Although much of the information provided here may have little
significance in an urban congregation surrounded by the noises of the
city, or in those places where most of the congregation live beyond the
sound of the bells, nonetheless, most churches have a bell or bells. These
guidelines suggest ways in which those bells may be used.[14]

Characteristics

Whether these guidelines are followed or not, they at least suggest how
in the life of the church no action is without significance and how the
church has attempted to find spiritual significance in all that it does.

Background

Occasional Services (1930), in the Office for the Blessing of a Tower
Bell, provided an intercessory prayer for optional use "instead of the
General Prayer in the Service or instead of the Prayer following the Kyrie
at Vespers":

> Almighty God, who dost endow Thy children with manifold gifts and graces,
> blessing their lives with the treasures of beauty and harmony, and dost make
> skillful their hands to the creation of the useful and the beautiful: Accept this
> our offering which we have dedicated to Thy service and grant that its use
> may ever be an hallowed one and that its sound may never cease to call men
> unto Thee;
> *We beseech Thee to hear us, O Lord.*
> We humbly pray that its voice may ever be a joyful sound to Thy children,
> calling them to worship and prayer, that they may enter into Thy gates with
> thanksgiving and into Thy courts with praise;
> *We beseech Thee to hear us, O Lord.*
> We humbly pray that its voice may ever be a calling to remembrance to those
> who have strayed from Thy Way;

---

14. See Merle Kitzman, "The Function of Bell Ringing in the Worship Life of the
Lutheran Church," *Response* 6:1 (Pentecost 1964): 20–24.

That it may call in solemn rebuke to the careless and indifferent;

That it may ring forth a sure welcome to the sinner and to whosoever will come;

We beseech Thee to hear us, O Lord.

We humbly pray for those, who, through the sorrows and sufferings of this present life, are prevented from coming to Thy House, that its sound may bring to mind Thy love and compassion for all who suffer;

Thy courage and help for those who are sore beset;

Thy peace for those who are heavy laden; and

Thy comfort for those who mourn;

We beseech Thee to hear us, O Lord.

We humbly pray that when it tolls for the message of the passing of a soul into the Life that knows no ending, we may rejoice and give thanks for the victory which our Lord Jesus Christ, Thy Son, hath obtained for us and for all who sleep in Him, and ever seek Thy grace that we may so live as to enter the rest prepared for the children of God;

We beseech Thee to hear us, O Lord.

And when it sounds forth, far and wide, in rejoicing and thanksgiving, may we lift up our hearts in adoration and praise to Thee, O God, the Father, the Son, and the Holy Ghost, Who livest and reignest evermore.

Amen. [15]

The themes of this prayer had been popular with Christians for centuries. The bells, with a clear voice, spoke a powerful summons, invitation, admonition, rebuke, and reminder. They called to repentance, summoned to worship, led the Our Father, encouraged faithfulness in married life, invited intercession for the sick and dying, and spoke of the end of our earthly pilgrimage. Indeed, such was the regard for the voice of the bells that in medieval times they were treated as if they were living creatures. To purify and consecrate their voice the bells were given names, often names of saints, and were sometimes baptized. While the Reformers rejected such baptism as an abuse of the sacrament and a mockery of the gospel, the role of the bell remained significant in Lutheran churches and, to those with ears to hear, spoke urgently of the Christian life in its several aspects.

CLOSING OF A CONGREGATION
(*Occasional Services*, pp. 255–59)

Parallel Rites

None.

---

15. *Occasional Services* (1930), pp. 169–70. See also the discussion of the Dedication of a Bell in the section headed Dedication of an Organ or Other Musical Instrument, pp. 301–8.

Purpose

This rite is to conclude the life of a congregation with thanksgiving for past mercies and with a recognition that the church nonetheless continues.

Characteristics

This service seeks to give expression to the deep emotion of an often traumatic event and yet to give thanks and to look ahead to the future.

The bishop or the bishop's representative is directed to preside in order to indicate that the regional church, which naturally rejoices in the formation of new congregations and the dedication of new buildings, is equally involved at the end of the use of a building and the end of the life of a congregation.

Preparation for the Service

Provision should be made for the safekeeping of the records of the congregation. The most desirable repository is usually the synod, district, or national church archives.

People should be appointed to carry the sacramental vessels and ornaments from the church at the end of the service.

Provision should be made for the appropriate disposition of the sacramental vessels, linens, and ornaments. It is desirable that they be given to another congregation, especially one with a historic connection with the congregation being closed. If any of the ornaments have historic value, it may be desirable to place them in the proper archives.

Those who have been appointed to carry the items from the church need to know where to put them when the procession has left the church.

Survey of the Service

The Holy Communion with its thanksgiving for the past and its message of the future is the appropriate service with which to bring to a close the life of a congregation. If such a celebration is not possible or desirable, the Closing of a Congregation may be used alone as a separate service. In that case, the rite begins with the prayer ⟨548⟩ with the references to Holy Communion deleted: "Almighty God . . . turn our sorrow over the closing of this congregation into joy . . . " The prayer is an adaptation of a postcommunion prayer (241) in the *LBW*.

The prayer of the day ⟨549⟩ is a new composition.

The declaration of the death of the congregation is a typical formula in Lutheran rites, which favor such formal announcements of events of all sorts. The declaration completes the life of the congregation with words which complement those with which the congregation was organized:

Organization	*Closing*
Upon these, your promises, I hereby declare that _____ is a duly organized and constituted congregation of the _____ in the name of the Father, and of the Son, and of the Holy Spirit. (p. 253)	With thanks to God for the work accomplished here, I declare this congregation to be closed in the name of the Father, and of the Son, and of the Holy Spirit. May the witness of its people continue undiminished, empowered by Jesus Christ, the Lord of the Church. (p. 256)

After the benediction the persons appointed come forward and prepare to take the vessels, linens, and ornaments from the church. As each item is taken, the person appointed to carry it says the appropriate verse. It will probably be most convenient to remove the appointments in this order:

Baptismal shell, bowl, ewer
Chalice and paten, flagon, ciborium, linens
Altar service book and missal stand
Candles
Cross
Bible(s)

When all of the ornaments have been taken in hand, the minister addresses the people with the verse from 1 Peter. An assisting minister dismisses the people, and a hymn is sung during which the sacramental vessels and ornaments are carried from the church and put in the appointed places.

10

OTHER OCCASIONS

OPENING OF A CONVENTION
(*Occasional Services*, pp. 235-36)

Parallel Rites

Roman Catholic	Propers for a Mass for a Council or Synod, *Sacramentary,* p. 877.
Episcopal	Propers for a Eucharist for a Church Convention, *Book of Common Prayer* (1979), pp. 255, 929.
Lutheran	Order for the Opening of Synods, *Occasional Services* (1962), pp. 142-44.
	Order for the Opening of Synods, *Common Service Book,* text ed. (1919), pp. 474-77.
	The Form for the Opening and Closing of Synods, *Lutheran Agenda,* pp. 190-92.
	Opening and Closing of Synods, *Church Book,* pp. 439-40.

Purpose

The title of this rite with the unmodified "convention" reflects the varied usage of North American Lutherans. The service is for use at the opening of meetings of a district/synod and of the national church body.

The 1962 *Occasional Services* used the word "synod" in its older and more traditional meaning, a meeting of church representatives, not a geographical entity.

Characteristics

This order reflects the understanding that a convention of the church is not just another business meeting, but a "synod," a coming together of representatives of the church.

The traditional way of opening a synod was a celebration of the Holy Communion with an emphasis on the invocation of the Holy Spirit. The order in *Occasional Services* (1982) makes use of that tradition, but also adds the announcement which Lutherans have come to expect in such a form, "I declare this convention to be in session . . . " The announcement functions as a declaration that the synod meets in the name of the Holy Trinity. This was for a long time the beginning of various legal proceedings, such as the custom of beginning a last will and testament with "In the name of God. Amen. I, _____, being of sound mind . . . ," or variations on that style. The declaration also serves to define a precise point at which the convention opens (and closes). This desire to be exact about opening and closing is more compatible with the rules of order governing a business meeting than with liturgical action. Liturgical action is best understood as a continuous movement in which one action flows into the next without sharp division or separation.

Survey of the Service

North American Lutheran books from the *Church Book* (1892) through *Occasional Services* (1962) have consistently required the celebration of the Holy Communion at the beginning of a convention of the church. The *Church Book* declared:

> Synods and General Representative Conventions of the Church are to be opened with the full Morning Service, Sermon, and the Holy Communion.[1]

The first business session was then opened with the order for the opening of synod.

Occasional Services (1982) has begun a departure from that tradition by not explicitly directing the celebration of the Holy Communion.

The versicles are those of *Occasional Services* (1962), slightly altered, which were in turn the verses from the *Common Service Book* rearranged. The first two versicles are from the Revised Standard Version, the third an adaptation of the New International Version of the Bible.

> As there are many members in one body
> *So we, though many, are one body in Christ.* (Rom. 12:4-5)
> Where two or three are gathered together in my name,
> *there am I in the midst of them.* (Matt. 18:20)
> I urge you to live a life worthy of the calling you have
> received, being humble and gentle, eager to maintain
> the unity of the Spirit through the bond of peace. (Eph. 4:1-3)
> *Let us pursue justice and peace, for mutual upbuilding.* (Rom. 14:19 *alt.*)

---

1. *Church Book,* p. 439. There was a practical and spiritual necessity for requiring Holy Communion at meetings of the synod. For pastors who did not commune themselves when they celebrated Holy Communion in their congregations, this was often the only opportunity they had during the year to receive the Sacrament!

The prayer (202) has its origins in the Gregorian Sacramentary where it is appointed for the morning mass at St. Peter's Basilica (no. 526). In earlier Lutheran books (*Church Book, Common Service Book,* and *Service Book and Hymnal*) as well as in the prayer books of the Anglican communion, it is the collect appointed for Pentecost. It is an especially appropriate prayer with which to open the deliberations of a convention of the church. Translation of the name of the gift of the Spirit invoked in this prayer, "Counsel," reflects the Revised Standard Version of the Fourth Gospel (see John 14:16, 26; 15:26; 16:7-11; and esp. 16:13-15). Older translations, and the *Book of Common Prayer* still, use instead the word "comfort" following the KJV. It is the church's present prayer and its continued joy to receive the direction of the Holy Spirit, the Counselor.

The declaration of the opening of the synod has been in the process of simplification since 1867. *Occasional Services* (1962) made the president of the synod/district make the declaration in the (papal?) plural: "We do now declare . . . " *Occasional Services* (1982) has restored the "Amen" to the congregation, as in the *Church Book.* The tables on the following pages illustrate this process of simplification.

Development of the Rite
Opening of a Convention

General Synod (1867)	Joint Synod of Ohio (1912)	*Lutheran Agenda*	*Church Book* (1892)
		Morning Service (Athanasian Creed)	Holy Communion
	In the name of the Father . . .		
	Glory be to the Father . . .		
			Hymn of In-vocation of the Holy Ghost
Salutation and response	Salutation and response		Salutation and response
Holy, holy, holy is the Lord our God.			
Heaven and earth are full of Thy glory.			
Prayer	Prayer		3 Prayers
	Epistle: Psalm 46 or 87 or Eph. 6:10–18		

Development of the Rite
Opening of a Convention

General Synod (1900)	Common Service Book	Occasional Services (1962)	Occasional Services (1982)
Holy Communion	Holy Communion	Holy Communion	
Hymn of Invocation of the Holy Ghost	Hymn of Invocation of the Holy Ghost	Hymn of Invocation of the Holy Ghost	
	Verses*	Verses*	Verses*
Salutation and response	Salutation and response	Salutation and response	Salutation and response
Our Father			
4 Prayers	5 Prayers	3 Prayers	Prayer

---

* Common Service Book (1919)	Occasional Services (1962)	Occasional Services (1982)
Rom. 12:4, 5; 14:19	Rom. 12:4, 5	Rom. 12:4–5
Matt. 18:20	Matt. 18:20	Matt. 18:20
Rev. 3:8b		
Eph. 4:1–2a, 3	Eph. 4:1–2a, 3	Eph. 4:1–3
	Rom. 14:19	Rom. 14:19 (alt.)
	Rev. 3:8b	

Development of the Rite (continued)
Opening of a Convention

General Synod (1867)	Joint Synod of Ohio (1912)	*Lutheran Agenda*	*Church Book* (1892)
	Gospel: John 20: 19–23 *or* Luke 19: 12–27		
Apostles' Creed	Apostles' Creed		
Our Father	Our Father		
		Address with	
Heb. 10: 19–24	Heb. 10: 19–24	Heb. 10: 19–24	Heb. 10: 19–24
Opening*	Opening†	2 Prayers	Opening‡

---

*I do hereby open this Synod, in accordance with the usage and principles of our Evangelical Lutheran Church, for the glory of God, for the welfare of the Church of Jesus Christ, and for the edification of all who believe in His name; In the name of the Father, and of the Son, and of the Holy Ghost. Amen.

The Lord be with us, that we may prove what is that good, and acceptable and perfect will of God. *Amen.* (pp. 124–25)

†I do now declare this Synod open, according to the principles and usages of our Church, for the glory of God, and for the good of His kingdom: in the name of the Father, and of the Son, and of the Holy Ghost. *Amen.* (p. 185)

‡ I do now declare this *Synod* open, according to the principles and usages of our Church, for the glory of God, and for the good of His Kingdom: In the Name of the Father, and of the Son, and of the Holy Ghost. *Amen.* (p. 440)

Development of the Rite (continued)
Opening of a Convention

General Synod (1900)	Common Service Book	Occasional Services (1962)	Occasional Services (1982)
	Opening§	Opening//	Opening#
	Blessing	Blessing	
			(Hymn)

---

§ I do now declare this Convention of the _____ open: In the Name of the Father, and of the Son, and of the Holy Ghost. Amen.

And now may the Father of our Lord Jesus Christ, Who hath called us with an holy calling, and hath committed to our trust the glorious Gospel of the grace of God, make you to increase and abound in love toward one another, and toward all men, that you may be steadfast, unmovable, always abounding in the work of the Lord. *Amen.* (pp. 476–77) [2 Tim. 1:9a; 1 Tim. 1:11; 1 Thess. 3:12; 1 Cor. 15:58]

// We do now declare this Synod (*or* _____) to be in session: In the Name of the Father, and of the Son, and of the Holy Ghost. Amen.

The Father of our Lord Jesus Christ, who hath called you with an holy calling, and hath committed to your trust the glorious Gospel of the grace of God, make you to increase and abound in love toward one another, and toward all men. *Amen.* (pp. 143–44) [2 Tim. 1:9a; 1 Tim. 1:11; 1 Thess. 3:12]

I declare this convention to be in session in the name of the Father, and of the Son, and of the Holy Spirit. (p. 236)

375

CLOSING OF A CONVENTION
(*Occasional Services*, pp. 237–38)

Parallel Rites

Lutheran

Order for the Closing of Synods, *Occasional Services* (1962), pp. 145–47.

Order for the Closing of Synods, *Common Service Book* (text ed.), pp. 478–80.

The Form for the Opening and Closing of Synods, *Lutheran Agenda,* pp. 192–94.

Opening and Closing of Synods, *Church Book,* pp. 441–42.

Purpose

This rite is to conclude a church convention with a prayer for God's protection of those who travel and with a petition for God's continued help.

Characteristics

The note of thanksgiving which appeared in the predecessor rites is absent here, for the synod usually does not settle issues and come to a definite conclusion. Rather, it sets agendas for continued work and witness. This form, therefore, turns the attention of the delegates to the world to which they will return. The first prayer asks God's continued help for work in process, and the second prayer asks safe passage for travelers.

Survey of the Service

The verses are selected from those used in earlier Lutheran rites:

> You will be my witnesses
> *to the ends of the earth.* (Acts 1:8b)
> I chose you and appointed you
> *to bear fruit which abides.* (John 15:16)
> Lo, I will be with you always
> *to the end of time.* (Matt. 28:20)

The translation is basically the Revised Standard Version. The response to the first and the third verses is from the Jerusalem Bible.

Prayer (220) is a favorite in the church's liturgy. It is from the Gregorian Sacramentary; the translation is from the *Book of Common Prayer*.

Prayer (269) is the prayer before travel from Responsive Prayer 2, based on the medieval office of itinerarium, a conclusion to morning prayer for travelers.[2]

The ancient prayers envision an extended journey through many perils and taking a long time. They set the journey in the context of a pilgrimage, evoking the pattern of the deliverance of the Israelites through the Red Sea, the journey of the Magi to the infant Jesus, and the archetypal wanderings of Abraham from Ur of the Chaldees to the land of promise.

The prayer in *Occasional Services* (1982) rearranges these three patterns into a chronological order: Abraham, the Red Sea, and the Magi. The dangers of travel have changed in character since the Middle Ages, but the peril nonetheless remains—whether on the highway or in the air—and a prayer for safety is still appropriate. Moreover, the prayer encourages those who travel to understand their journey not simply as another trip but as a suggestion of their path through this world to the next. The ancient symbolism of the pilgrimage remains charged with potential power.

---

2. See *Roman Ritual: Complete Edition*, pp. 747–48.

Development of the Rite
Closing of a Convention

General Synod (1867)	Church Book	General Synod (1900)	Joint Synod of Ohio (1912)
	Litany *or* Suffrages *or* this form: (Hymn of praise or thanksgiving)	Vespers *or:* (Hymn of praise or thanksgiving)	
Ps. 136:1			Ps. 136:1
	Salutation and response		Salutation and response
Prayer	4 Prayers	Free Prayer or 3 Prayers	Prayer
			Lesson Psalm 111 *or* 133 *or* 134
			Apostles' Creed
	Our Father	Our Father	Our Father
			(Hymn)
Closing*	Closing†		Closing‡

---

* I do now close this Synod in the name of the Lord. And now, dear brethren, let us stand fast in the love of Christ, that when he comes again in His glory, we may not be put to shame, but rejoice before Him. (pp. 125–26)

† Dear brethren: I do now close this Convention, in the Name of the Lord. And let it be our part to stand fast in the love of Christ, that, when He cometh in His glory, we may rejoice before Him with exceeding joy. (*Church Book,* p. 442)

‡ Ps. 28:9a
Isa. 55:11
Acts 1:8b
John 15:16

Development of the Rite
Closing of a Convention

Lutheran Agenda	*Common Service Book*	*Occasional Services (1962)*	*Occasional Services (1982)*
Vespers *or:*			
(Hymn of praise or thanksgiving)	(Hymn of praise or thanksgiving)	(Hymn of praise or thanksgiving)	(Hymn)
	(Litany or Bidding Prayer)		
	Verses	Verses	Verses
	Salutation and response	Salutation and response	Salutation and response
Free Prayer or 2 Prayers	5 Prayers	3 Prayers	2 Prayers
Lesson Psalm 111 *or* 133 *or* 134			
Apostles' Creed			
Our Father	Our Father	Our Father	
	Eph. 3:20–21	Eph. 3:20–21	
Closing‡	Closing§	Closing§	Closing//

---

‡ Matt. 28:20
Gloria Patri

§ I do now declare this Convention closed: In the Name of the Father, and of the Son, and of the Holy Ghost. Amen.

Let us stand fast in the love of Christ, that, when He cometh in His glory, we may rejoice before Him with exceeding joy. *Amen.* (p. 460)

Occasional Services (1962) is identical except the first pronoun is plural: "We do now declare . . . "

// I now declare this convention closed in the name of the Father, and of the Son, and of the Holy Spirit. *Amen.* (p. 238)

Development of the Rite (continued)
Closing of a Convention

General Synod (1867)	Church Book	General Synod (1900)	Joint Synod of Ohio (1912)
Apostles' Creed			
Our Father			
Hymn			
Benediction	The grace . . .	The grace . . .	The grace . . .

OPENING OF A SCHOOL YEAR
(*Occasional Services*, pp. 243–45)

Parallel Rites

Lutheran   A Form for Opening and Closing Christian Schools, *Lutheran Hymnal* (1941), pp. 50–52.[3]

Purpose

This rite is to open the school year with a brief service of worship, thus placing all that will follow throughout the year under the name of the Holy Trinity.

Characteristics

This service will be most useful in Christian day schools and high schools.

Survey of the Service

Each dialogue is drawn from Scripture:

Great are the deeds of the Lord!
They are studied by all who delight in them.

---

3. *The Lutheran Hymnal* (St. Louis: Concordia Publishing House, 1941).

Development of the Rite (continued)
Closing of a Convention

Lutheran Agenda	*Common Service Book*	*Occasional Services* (1962)	*Occasional Services* (1982)
The grace . . .		Let us go forth in peace.	Go in peace. Serve the Lord.
		In the Name of Christ our Lord.	*Thanks be to God.*

His work is full of majesty and splendor.
And his righteousness endures forever.
He makes his marvelous works to be remembered;
the Lord is gracious and full of compassion.   (Ps. 111:2–4)

The fear of the Lord is the beginning of wisdom;
those who act accordingly have a good understanding.
His praise endures forever.   (Ps. 111:10)

Come, children, and listen to me;
I will teach you the fear of the Lord.   (Ps. 34:11)
Teach me, O Lord, your ways.   (Ps. 86:11a)
I will bless the Lord at all times;
his praise shall ever be in my mouth.   (Ps. 34:1)
Teach me, O Lord, your ways.   (Ps. 86:11a)
I will glory in the Lord;
let the humble hear and rejoice.   (Ps. 34:2)
Teach me, O Lord, your ways.   (Ps. 86:11a)

The translation is that of the psalter in the *Lutheran Book of Worship*.
It is desirable to choose the lesson(s) from the Daily Lectionary in the *LBW*. For young children a few appropriate verses may be selected from one of the three lessons appointed for each day. On festival days it is desirable to select the lessons from the readings appointed for the festival.
The prayer ⟨545⟩ is a new composition.

CLOSING OF A SCHOOL YEAR
(*Occasional Services*, pp. 246–49)

Parallel Rite

Lutheran   A Form for Opening and Closing Christian Schools,
                         Lutheran Hymnal, pp. 50–52.

Purpose

This rite is to conclude a school year with thanksgiving and with prayer for God's continued help.

Survey of the Service

Each dialogue is drawn from Scripture:

Great is our Lord and mighty in power
   there is no limit to his wisdom. (Ps. 147:5)
We give you thanks, O God, we give you thanks,
   calling upon your name and
   declaring all your wonderful deeds. (Ps. 75:1)
We will recount to generations to come
the praiseworthy deeds and the power of the Lord,
   and the wonderful works he has done. (Ps. 78:4)

Those who know your name
will put their trust in you. (Ps. 9:10a)
   O Lord, watch over us. (Ps. 12:7a)
You never forsake those who seek you, O Lord. (Ps. 9:10b)
   O Lord, watch over us. (Ps. 12:7a)
Sing praise to the Lord;
proclaim to the peoples the things he has done. (Ps. 9:11a, c)
   O Lord, watch over us. (Ps. 12:7a)

The translation is that of the psalter in the *LBW*.

It is desirable to choose the lesson(s) from the Daily Lectionary in the *LBW*. For young children a few appropriate verses may be selected from one of the three lessons appointed for each day. On festival days it is appropriate to select the lesson(s) from the readings appointed for the festival.

The first prayer (251) is by Eric Milner-White.[4] In the *LBW* it is provided at Morning and Evening Prayer when there is a sermon.

---

4. Eric Milner-White and G. W. Briggs, comps., *Daily Prayer* (London: Oxford University Press, 1941), p. 14.

The second prayer (220) is the familiar prayer for guidance that has been in service books for generations. It is from the Gregorian Sacramentary; the translation is that of the *Book of Common Prayer.*

PRAYERS FOR OTHER OCCASIONS
(*Occasional Services*, pp. 290-95)

Parallel Rites

Lutheran

Prayers and Blessings for Special Occasions, *Occasional Services* (1962), pp. 208-15.

The Form for the Opening of a Congregational Meeting, *Lutheran Agenda,* pp. 187-89.

Sources of the Prayers

CONGREGATIONAL MEETINGS

(202) Gregorian Sacramentary no. 526, appointed for morning masses in St. Peter's Basilica. Used in the *Church Book,* the *Common Service Book,* and the *Service Book and Hymnal,* as well as in the prayer books of the Anglican communion as the collect of the day for Pentecost.

⟨556⟩ New, based on Eph. 2:16.

⟨557⟩ *Lutheran Agenda* (pp. 187-88, revised).

(412) Psalm prayer to Psalm 134, adapted from the Roman Catholic *Liturgy of the Hours.*

CHURCH COUNCIL MEETINGS

⟨558⟩ New, based on the collect for St. James' Day (July 25) in the *Service Book and Hymnal,* from the 1549 Prayer Book for the Day of St. Simon and St. Jude (October 28).

(220) Gregorian Sacramentary no. 198, translated by the 1549 *Book of Common Prayer,* revised by the 1789 American Prayer Book. It is in the 1979 Prayer Book as no. 57.

COMMITTEE MEETINGS

⟨559⟩ New.

STEWARDSHIP

(183) For the Proper Use of Wealth (*LBW,* Min. Ed., p. 108). No. 38 in the 1979 Prayer Book (p. 827); new in the 1928 American Prayer Book; a revision of a prayer "For the Rich" from a Book of Offices proposed

for publication to the General Convention of the Episcopal Church in 1889.

EVANGELISM

(190) The Spread of the Gospel (*LBW,* Min. Ed., p. 109). Collect no. 10 in the *Service Book and Hymnal,* adapted from the *Book of Common Worship* of the Presbyterian Church in the U.S.A. (1906), p. 133.

(192) The Mission of the Church (*LBW,* Min. Ed., p. 109). A revision of the prayer in the *LBW,* which was borrowed from the 1979 *Book of Common Prayer* (pp. 816–17, no. 8), by Caroline Rose.

WORSHIP AND MUSIC

(197) Church Musicians and Artists (*LBW,* Min. Ed., p. 110). The prayer of the Royal School of Church Music, revised by the 1979 Prayer Book to include mention of artists as well as musicians. It is in the Prayer Book as no. 17 (p. 819).

EDUCATION

(198) Teachers (*LBW,* Min. Ed., p. 110). Written for the *LBW.*[5]

SOCIAL MINISTRY

(141) Prayer of the Day for Renewers of Society (*LBW,* Min. Ed., p. 183). A revision of the prayer "For Social Justice" in the 1928 American Prayer Book (p. 44), composed perhaps by James Martineau or Bishop Parsons.

MEMBERSHIP CLASSES[6]

⟨560⟩ New, based on Matt. 28:19–20.
⟨561⟩ New, based on Eph. 3:17–19.

---

5. *Occasional Services* (1962) had this prayer for "The Installation of Teachers" (pp. 208-9), which this prayer is based on:

O God, who in the ministry of thy Son hast taught us how precious are all children in thy sight: We ask thy blessing upon all to whom thou hast committed the care and training of the young, especially these thy servants, who offer themselves in Christ's Name to this holy task. Grant them knowledge of thy Word that their words may bring light to those whom they teach. Guide and direct them that their lives may commend the Master whom they serve, that we may be led in the way everlasting; through Jesus Christ our Lord.

6. *Occasional Services* (1962) has this prayer for "Classes for Membership in the Church" (p. 209):

O God, the Holy Spirit, who dost call, gather, enlighten and sanctify the whole Christian Church, and who dost ever hold before it God revealed in the face of Jesus Christ: Be with and bless those who would come to the knowledge of the Lord, and guide those who teach and those who learn, that they may live and walk in thy Presence evermore; who, with the Father and the Son, art one God, world without end.

WEDDING RECEPTIONS[7]

⟨562⟩ New, based on Matt. 22:2.

⟨563⟩ New.

THOSE LEAVING[8]

⟨564⟩ New.

THOSE RETURNING

⟨565⟩ New. The scriptural allusion is to Ps. 121:8.

TIME OF CONFLICT, CRISIS, DISASTER

⟨566⟩ Adapted from the Church of Scotland, *Book of Common Order* (1962), p. 303. The biblical allusion is to Ps. 46:1.

(312) Psalm prayer to Psalm 34, adapted from the Roman Catholic *Liturgy of the Hours*.

(338) Psalm prayer to Psalm 60, adapted from the Roman Catholic *Liturgy of the Hours*.

EXPECTANT PARENTS

⟨567⟩ New.

BIRTH OF A CHILD

⟨568⟩ New.

---

7. *Occasional Services* (1962) provided this prayer for "At A Wedding Reception" (p. 213):

O God, whose blessed Son, our Saviour Jesus Christ, didst grace with his presence the marriage feast at Cana: Abide now and ever with thy servants who have (*this day*) entered the holy estate of matrimony. And as thou dost bless this high moment in their lives, so bless all those moments which may appear of lesser account, that all their life together may be spent in the consciousness of thy fatherly concern for their eternal welfare; through the same Jesus Christ, thy Son, our Lord.

8. *Occasional Services* (1962) provided three prayers "For One Departing from Home" for college, for employment, or for military service (p. 212). The first is the one given in the *LBW* as (251). The other two are:

O God, our heavenly Father, who art everywhere present, alike to them that are afar off and to them that are nigh: To thy gracious keeping we commend thy *servant* who will be absent from us. Preserve *him* in all danger; uphold *him* in crisis; and ever direct *his* feet in the path of righteousness; that, having thee for *his* Protector and Guide, *he* may be returned to us in peace and safety; through Jesus Christ our Lord.

O God, who art the strength and protector of thy people; Into thy hands we commit thy *servant* about to leave us to enter a new phase of *his* life. Succor and preserve *him* in danger and temptation, assist *him* in every good work, further *him* in the right way, and keep both us and *him* alive in the hope of a joyful reunion; through Jesus Christ our Lord.

OPENING OF A CONVENTION

ADOPTION OF A CHILD

⟨569⟩ New.

⟨570⟩ New.

RETIREMENT

⟨571⟩ New.

RETIREMENT OF A PASTOR[9]

⟨572⟩ New.

ANNIVERSARY OF A DEATH[10]

(235) Remembrance of the Faithful Departed (*LBW,* Min. Ed., p. 115). *Service Book and Hymnal* collect no. 42, adapted from the *Book of Common Order* of the Church of Scotland (1962 [1940, 1952]), p. 59.

(285) Conclusion of the Prayers in the Burial of the Dead (*LBW,* Min. Ed., p. 335), revised from the *Service Book and Hymnal* order for the Burial of the Dead (p. 266), which had adapted the prayer from the *Book of Common Order* of the Church of Scotland (1962 [1940, 1952]), pp. 176 and 22.

---

9. *Occasional Services* (1962) provided a form for The Retirement of a Servant of the Church (pp. 203-4). After the sermon the servant of the church (pastor, board member, organist, superintendent) comes forward. The verse and response from Ps. 124:8 and the salutation and response are said. Three prayers are provided:

O Lord Jesus Christ, who thyself dost call and employ all who labor in thy vineyard: We give thee thanks for all who by their services have set forward thy Holy Gospel among us (*and especially thy servant, N.*), and who are now retired from the burden and heat of the day. Grant them grace still to do thee true and laudable service in their several conditions, and finally to receive the reward which thou hast promised thy faithful servants; who livest and reignest with the Father and the Holy Spirit, one God, world without end.

O Almighty God, who in thy mercy hast redeemed the world by the love of thy dear Son: We give thee hearty thanks for thy servants in the ministry of thy Church, that thou hast endued them richly with the gifts of the Holy Spirit; and we pray that in all their words and deeds they may seek thy glory and the increase of thy kingdom; through Jesus Christ our Lord.

Remember, O Lord, all who have ministered unto thee in ministering to their fellowmen, who, reflecting thy divine compassion, have been guides to the blind, comforters to the sad, and helpers of the weak; and who by their actions and ministrations have advanced the good of souls and the honor of our Lord Jesus Christ.

10. See *Occasional Services* (1962), pp. 173-74; *Occasional Services* (1930), pp. 141-45 for the Order of a Service of Commemoration.

APPENDIX I
OCCASIONAL SERVICES IN THE TABLES OF CONTENTS OF NORTH AMERICAN LUTHERAN SERVICE BOOKS IN ENGLISH

The Liturgy, Gospels and Epistles of the English Evangelical Lutheran Church in New York. **New York: J. C. Totten, 1806.**
The Order of Public Worship
The Ministration of Baptism
Form of Preparation for the Lord's Supper
The Order of the Administration of the Lord's Supper
Burial Service

A Liturgy for the Use of Evangelical Lutheran Churches Published by Order of the Evangelical Lutheran Church of the State of New York. **Philadelphia: G. & D. Billmeyer, 1817.**
    VI. The Ministration of Baptism to Infants
    VII. The Ministration of Baptism to Such As Are of Riper Years
    VIII. The Order of Confirmation
    IX. Order of the Service Preparatory to the Celebration of the Lord's Supper
    X. Administration of the Lord's Supper
    XI. A Form for the Inauguration of the Ruling Officers of a Congregation
    XII. The Solemnization of Matrimony
    XIII. The Burial of the Dead
The 1834 edition of this liturgy added:
A Form for the Consecration of a Church
A Form for the Ordination of a Minister

Liturgy, or Formulary, for the Use of Evangelical Lutheran Churches Compiled by a Committee, appointed by the Synod of Ohio and ordered to be printed. **Lancaster, Ohio: John Herman, 1830.**
    I. Public Worship
    II. The Ministration of Baptism to Infants
    III. The Ministration of Baptism to Such As Are of Riper Years
    IV. Of Catechising, and the Order of Confirmation
    V. Order of the Service Preparatory to the Celebration of the Lord's Supper
    VI. The Order for the Administration of the Lord's Supper
    VII. The Communion of the Sick
    VIII. The Form of Solemnization of Matrimony

IX. Form for the Inauguration of the Ruling Officers of a Congregation
X. Form for the Ordaining of Ministers
XI. Form for Empowering Candidates or Catechists
XII. Form for the Consecration of a Church
XIII. The Burial of the Dead

A Liturgy for the Use of the Evangelical Lutheran Church by Authority of the Ministerium of Pennsylvania and Adjacent States. **Philadelphia: Lindsay & Blackiston, 1860.**
Part Second. The Order of Ministerial Acts
  I. The Order of Holy Baptism
     The Baptism of Infants
     The Baptism of Adults
  II. The Order of Confirmation
  III. The Order of Confession and Absolution
  IV. The Order of Marriage
  V. The Order for the Communion of the Sick
  VI. The Order for the Burial of the Dead
  VII. The Order for the Installation of the Church-Council
  VIII. The Order for Opening and Closing of Synod
  IX. The Order of Ordination to the Office of the Ministry
  X. The Order for the Installation of a Minister
  XI. The Order for the Laying of a Corner-Stone of a Church
  XII. The Order for the Consecration of a Church

The Book of Worship published by Order of the Evangelical Lutheran General Synod of North America. **Columbia, S.C.: Duffie & Chapman, 1867.**
Section II. The Order of Ministerial Acts
  I. The Order of Holy Baptism
    1. The Baptism of Infants
    2. Private Baptism
  II. The Baptism of Adults
  III. The Order of Confirmation
  IV. The Order of Holy Communion
    1. The Order of Confession
    2. The Holy Communion
    3. The Communion of the Sick
  V. The Order of Marriage
  VI. The Order for the Installation of the Church Council
  VII. The Order for the Installation of a Minister
  VIII. The Order of Licensure of Candidates
  IX. The Order of Ordination to the Office of the Ministry
  X. The Order for the Laying of the Corner-Stone of a Church
  XI. The Order for the Consecration of a Church
  XII. The Order for the Opening of Synod

XIII. The Closing of Synod
XIV. The Burial of the Dead

The Liturgy of the Evangelical Lutheran Church Prepared and Published by Order of the General Synod. **Philadelphia: Lutheran Publication Society, 1881.**
Part Second
  Order for the Baptism of Children
  Baptism of Adults
  Order for the Confirmation of Persons Baptized in Infancy
  Order for Receiving Members from Other Congregations
  Order for Confession and Absolution, Preparatory to the Celebration of the
    Lord's Supper
  Sentences for the Collection of Alms and Offerings
  Order for the Holy Communion
  Order for the Solemnization of Holy Matrimony
  Order for the Burial of the Dead
  Order for Licensure
  Order for the Ordination of a Minister
  Order for the Installation of a Pastor
  Order for the Installation of the Church Council
  Order for the Laying of a Corner-Stone of a Church
  Order for the Consecration of a Church
  Order for the Consecration of a Burial Ground
  Benedictions

The Church Book For the Use of Evangelical Lutheran Congregations by the Authority of the General Council of the Evangelical Lutheran Church in North America. **Philadelphia: General Council Publication Board, 1891.**
Orders for Ministerial Acts
  For the Baptism of Infants
  For the Baptism of Adults
  For Confirmation
  For Confession and Absolution
    1. Private
    2. Public
  For the Solemnization of Marriage
  For the Visitation of the Sick
  Lessons and Prayers for the Sick
  Communion of the Sick
  Commendation of the Dying
  For the Burial of the Dead
  For the Ordination of Ministers
  For the Installation of Pastors
  For the Installation of Church Councils

For the Laying of Corner-Stones
For the Consecration of Churches
For the Opening and Closing of Synods

**Church Book of the Evangelical Lutheran Augustana Synod in North America.
Rock Island, Ill.: Lutheran Augustana Book Concern, 1898.**
Order for Infant Baptism
Order for Adult Baptism
Order for Confirmation
Order for Solemnization of Marriage
Order for Burial of the Dead
Order for Reception of Members
Order for Excommunication
Order for Laying of a Corner Stone
Order for Dedication of a New Church
Order for Ordination of Ministers
Order for Installation of Pastor
Order for Induction of Church Officers
Order for Communion of the Sick
Order for the Churching of a Mother

**Forms for Ministerial Acts Published by the General Synod of the Evangelical
Lutheran Church in the United States. Philadelphia: Lutheran Publication
Society, 1900.**
The Baptism of Infants
The Baptism of Adults
Confirmation
The Reception of Members from Other Churches
Confession and Absolution, Preparatory to the Holy Communion
The Holy Communion
Communion of the Sick
The Ordination of Ministers
The Installation of a Pastor
Installation of a Church Council
The Setting Apart of Deaconesses
The Marriage Service
The Burial Service
The Laying of a Corner-Stone
The Dedication of a Church
Dedication of the God's Acre
Dedication of an Organ
Dedication of a Bell
Opening of Synod
Closing of Synod

*A Liturgy for the Use of Evangelical Lutheran Pastors Prepared by a Committee
Appointed by the Evangelical Lutheran Joint Synod of Ohio and Other States.*
Columbus, Ohio: Lutheran Book Concern, 1912.
Order for the Baptism of Infants
Order for the Baptism of Adults
Order for Confirmation
Order for Confession and Absolution (Private)
Public Confession and Absolution
Communion of the Sick
Order for the Solemnization of a Marriage
The Burial of the Dead
The Ordination of Ministers
Installation of a Minister
Installation of Church Officers
Installation of School Teachers
Laying of the Corner Stone of a Church
The Consecration of a Church
The Consecration of a School House
The Dedication of an Organ
Dedication of a Cemetery
Excommunication
Restoration of the Excommunicated
Reception of Converts
Opening and Closing of Synods

Liturgy and Agenda. **St. Louis: Concordia Publishing House, 1916; 2d ed., 1921.**
    I. Baptism
        1. The Baptism of Infants: First Form
            Second Form (Without Sponsors)
            Emergency Baptism
        2. Confirmation of Lay Baptism
        3. The Baptism of Adults
    II. Confirmation
    III. The Reception of Converts
    IV. The Reception of Voting Members
    V. Announcement of Excommunication and of Restoration
    VI. Marriage: First Form
        Second Form
    VII. Anniversary of Marriage
    VIII. The Communion of the Sick
    IX. The Burial of the Dead
        A. At the House: In General
            At the Death of a Child
            At the Death of a Young Person
            At the Death of the Aged

Order for the Closing of Synods
Order for the Installation of a Church Council

The Occasional Services from the **Common Service Book** *of the Lutheran* **Church. Philadelphia: Board of Publication of the United Lutheran Church in America, 1930.**
Additional Orders and Offices (authorized by the United Lutheran Church in 1928)
Order for the Blessing of a Church-Site and Ground-Breaking
Order for the Rededication of a Church
Order for the Dedication of a Church House
Order for the Blessing of a Cemetery
Order for the Consecration of a Deaconess
Order for the Installation of a Parish Deaconess
Order for the Commissioning of a Foreign Missionary
Order for Thanksgiving and Benediction of Women after Childbirth
Order for the Induction of a President
Order for a Service of Commemoration

Office for the Blessing of an Altar
Office for the Blessing of a Pulpit
Office for the Blessing of a Lectern
Office for the Blessing of a Font (Baptistery)
Office for the Blessing of an Altar Cross
Office for the Blessing of a Paten or Ciborium
Office for the Blessing of a Chalice
Office for the Blessing of Sacramental Vessels
Office for the Blessing of Altar Ornaments, Paraments, Vestments
Office for the Blessing of an Organ
Office for the Blessing of a Tower Bell — Peal — Chimes
Office for the Unveiling and Blessing of a Memorial Window
Office for the Blessing of a Steeple Cross
A General Office of Benediction
Office for the Dedication of a Hospital — House of Mercy
Office for the Public Reception of Fellow-Members of the Household of Faith
Office for the Restoration of One Who Has Lapsed, to Membership in the
    Church
Office for the Admission of a Congregation into Synod
Office for the Reception of a Minister into Synod
Regulations for the Ringing of a Tower Bell — Peal — Chimes

The Occasional Services from the **Common Service Book** *of the Lutheran* **Church. Philadelphia: Board of Publication of the United Lutheran Church in America, 1930.**
Identical with the 1930 edition except for the addition at the very end of an
Office for the Reception into Synod of a Minister from Another Denomination.

393

APPENDIX I

The Lutheran Agenda. Authorized by the Synods Constituting the Evangelical Lutheran Synodical Conference of North America. **St. Louis: Concordia Publishing House, n.d. [194?].**

The Order of Holy Baptism, The Baptism of Infants (With Sponsors)
The Order of Holy Baptism, The Baptism of Infants (Without Sponsors)
The Order of Holy Baptism, The Ratification of Lay Baptism
The Order of Holy Baptism, The Baptism of Adults
The Rite of Confirmation
  The Examination
  The Confirmation
The Reception of Converts
The Reception of Members (By Transfer)
The Announcement of Excommunication, of Self-Exclusion, and of Reinstatement
The Order of a Marriage (The Congregation Participating)
The Order of a Marriage (The Congregation Not Participating)
The Order of a Marriage (A Short Form)
The Order of the Consecration of a Civil Marriage
The Order for the Anniversary of a Marriage
The Order for the Communion of the Sick
The Order for the Burial of the Dead
  At the House or the Funeral Home
  At the Church
  At the Grave
A Reading Service for the Burial of the Stillborn
  At the House
  At the Grave
Prayer at the Burial of a Suicide
The Order for the Ordination of a Minister
The Order for the Installation of a Minister
A Pastor's Daily Prayer
The Order for the Installation of a Professor
The Order for the Ordination and Commissioning of a Missionary
The Order for the Installation of a Teacher
A Form for the Induction of Women Teachers
A Form for the Induction of Sunday School Officers and Teachers
The Order for the Installation of a Church Council
The Order for the Ground Breaking for a Church or School
The Order for the Laying of the Cornerstone of a Church or School
The Order for the Dedication of a Church
The Order for the Dedication of a School
The Order for the Dedication of an Organ
The Order for the Dedication of a Bell
The Order for the Dedication of a Burial Ground
The Order for the Dedication of a Parish House
The Order for the Dedication of a Parsonage

The Order for the Dedication of a Dwelling
The Form for the Opening of a Congregational Meeting
The Form for the Opening and Closing of Synods
  The Opening
  The Closing
Formulary for the Induction of the President and Vice-Presidents of Synod

Order of Service of the United Evangelical Lutheran Church. **Blair, Neb.: Lutheran Publishing House, 1945.**
Part II, Ministerial Acts
  Baptism of Infants
  Baptism of Adults
  Emergency Baptism
  Confessional Service
  Communion in the Church
  Communion in the Home
  Marriage Service
  Burial of the Dead
Part III, Special Services
  Ordination to the Holy Ministry
  Consecration of a Church
  Dedication of a Parish House
  Dedication of a Parsonage
  Consecration of a Burial Ground

The Occasional Services from the **Service Book and Hymnal.** Approved by the cooperating churches in 1950.
  Order for the Baptism of Infants
  Order for the Baptism of Adults
  Order for Lay Baptism
  Order for Confirmation
  Order for Adult Baptism and Confirmation at the Same Service
  A Brief Order for Public Confession
  Order for Private Confession and Absolution
  Order for the Visitation of the Sick
  Order for the Communion of the Sick
  Order for the Commendation of the Dying
  Order for the Burial of the Dead
  Order for Marriage
  Order for Ordination
  Order for the Setting Apart of a Deaconess
  Order for Laying the Cornerstone of a Church
  Order for the Dedication of a Church
  Order for the Blessing of a Cemetery
  Order for the Installation of a Pastor
  Order for the Sending Forth of a Missionary

Order for the Induction of a President
Order for the Installation of the Council or Governing Body of a Local
  Church
Order for the Opening of Synods
Order for the Closing of Synods
Order for the Induction of Office-Bearers
Order for the Blessing of a Dwelling

The Occasional Services from the **Service Book and Hymnal** *together with Additional Orders and Offices. For the Use of the Lutheran Churches Cooperating in The Commission on the Liturgy and Hymnal.* **Minneapolis: Augsburg Publishing House; Philadelphia: Board of Publication, Lutheran Church in America, 1962.**
Additional Orders and Offices
  The Blessing of a Church-Site and Groundbreaking
  The Blessing of a Church
  The Dedication of a Parish House, Church House, School or Hospital
  The Induction of a Parish Deaconess
  Thanksgiving after the Birth of a Child
  A Service of Commemoration
  The Blessing of an Altar
  The Blessing of a Font or Baptistery
  The Blessing of a Pulpit or Lectern
  The Blessing of a Cross
  The Blessing of Sacramental Vessels
  The Blessing of Altar Ornaments, Paraments, and Vestments
  The Blessing of Instruments of Music for Use in the Church
  The Blessing of a Church Window
  A General Order of Benediction
  Admission to Membership (By Transfer, Restoration or Renewal)
  The Admission of a Congregation
  The Blessing of a Civil Marriage
  Order for the Reception of Ministers
  The Retirement of an Indebtedness
  The Commissioning of Parish Visitors
  The Retirement of a Servant of the Church
  The Installation of a Chaplain
  Prayers and Blessings for Special Occasions
  Forms of Blessing

APPENDIX II
THE INCLUSION OF
OCCASIONAL SERVICES IN
REPRESENTATIVE NORTH AMERICAN
LUTHERAN SERVICE BOOKS

	New York (1806)	New York (1817)	Ohio (1830)	Ministerium of Pa. (1860)	General Synod (1867)	General Synod (1881)	Church Book (1891)	Augustana (1898)	General Synod (1900)
Affirmation of Marriage Vows									
Affirmation of Vocation									
Anniversary of Baptism									
Anniversary of Marriage									
Anniversary of Ordination									
Baptism	x								
of Infants		x	x	x	x	x	x	x	x
of Adults		x	x	x	x	x	x	x	x
Baptism in an Emergency									
Benedictions						x			
Blessing of an Altar									
Blessing of an Altar Cross									
Blessing of Altar Ornaments, Paraments, Vestments									
Blessing of a Chalice									
Blessing of a Church									
Blessing of a Civil Marriage									
Blessing of a Dwelling									

	Joint Synod of Ohio (1912)	Liturgy and Agenda (1916)	Common Service Book (1919)	Occasional Services (1930)	Lutheran Agenda (194?)	U.E.L.C. (1945)	Occasional Services (1950)	Occasional Services (1962)	Occasional Services (1982)
Affirmation of Marriage Vows									x
Affirmation of Vocation									x
Anniversary of Baptism									x
Anniversary of Marriage		x			x				x
Anniversary of Ordination									x
Baptism									
of Infants	x	x	x		x	x	x		
of Adults	x	x	x		x	x	x		
Baptism in an Emergency						x	x		x
Benedictions									
Blessing of an Altar				x				x	
Blessing of an Altar Cross				x				x	
Blessing of Altar Ornaments, Paraments, Vestments				x				x	
Blessing of a Chalice				x					
Blessing of a Church								x	
Blessing of a Civil Marriage					x			x	x
Blessing of a Dwelling		x			x			x	x

	New York (1806)	New York (1817)	Ohio (1830)	Ministerium of Pa. (1860)	General Synod (1867)	General Synod (1881)	Church Book (1891)	Augustana (1898)	General Synod (1900)
Blessing of a Font (Baptistery)									
Blessing of a Lectern									
Blessing of a Paten/Ciborium									
Blessing of a Pulpit									
Blessing of Sacramental Vessels									
Blessing of a Steeple Cross									
Blessing of a Window									
Blessings for Special Occasions									
Burial of the Dead of the Stillborn of a Suicide	x	x	x	x	x	x	x	x	x
Catechizing			x						
Celebration of Holy Communion with Those in Special Circumstances									
Closing of a Congregation									
Closing of a Convention (Synod)					x	x	x		x
Closing of a School Year									
Comforting the Bereaved									

	Joint Synod of Ohio (1912)	Liturgy and Agenda (1916)	Common Service Book (1919)	Occasional Services (1930)	Lutheran Agenda (194?)	U.E.L.C. (1945)	Occasional Services (1950)	Occasional Services (1962)	Occasional Services (1982)
Blessing of a Font (Baptistery)				x				x	
Blessing of a Lectern				x				x	
Blessing of a Paten/Ciborium				x					
Blessing of a Pulpit				x				x	
Blessing of Sacramental Vessels				x				x	
Blessing of a Steeple Cross				x					
Blessing of a Window				x				x	x
Blessings for Special Occasions								x	
Burial of the Dead	x	x	x		x	x	x		x
of the Stillborn					x				
of a Suicide					x				
Catechizing									
Celebration of Holy Communion with Those in Special Circumstances									x
Closing of a Congregation									x
Closing of a Convention (Synod)	x	x	x		x		x		x
Closing of a School Year									x
Comforting the Bereaved									x

	New York (1806)	New York (1817)	Ohio (1830)	Ministerium of Pa. (1860)	General Synod (1867)	General Synod (1881)	Church Book (1891)	Augustana (1898)	General Synod (1900)
Commendation of the Dying							x		
Commissioning of a Lay Professional Leader									
Commissioning of Missionaries									
Commissioning of Parish Visitors									
Communion of the Sick		x	x	x			x	x	x
Confession and Absolution Preparatory to Holy Communion	x	x	x	x	x	x	x		x
Confirmation		x	x	x	x	x	x	x	x
Confirmation of Lay Baptism									
Dedication of a Bell									x
Dedication of a Cemetery						x			x
Dedication of a Church		x (1834)	x	x	x	x	x	x	x
Dedication of a Church Parish House									
Dedication of a Facility for Church Use									
Dedication of a Hospital									

APPENDIX II

	Joint Synod of Ohio (1912)	Liturgy and Agenda (1916)	Common Service Book (1919)	Occasional Services (1930)	Lutheran Agenda (194?)	U.E.L.C. (1945)	Occasional Services (1950)	Occasional Services (1962)	Occasional Services (1982)
Commendation of the Dying			x				x		x
Commissioning of a Lay Professional Leader									x
Commissioning of Missionaries				x	x		x		x
Commissioning of Parish Visitors								x	
Communion of the Sick	x	x	x		x	x	x		
Confession and Absolution Preparatory to Holy Communion	x		x			x	x		
Confirmation	x	x	x		x		x		
Confirmation of Lay Baptism		x			x				
Dedication of a Bell		x		x	x				
Dedication of a Cemetery	x	x		x	x	x	x		x
Dedication of a Church	x	x	x	x	x	x	x		x
Dedication of a Church Parish House		x		x	x	x		x	
Dedication of a Facility for Church Use									x
Dedication of a Hospital				x				x	

403

	New York (1806)	New York (1817)	Ohio (1830)	Ministerium of Pa. (1860)	General Synod (1867)	General Synod (1881)	Church Book (1891)	Augustana (1898)	General Synod (1900)
Dedication of an Organ/Musical Instruments									x
Dedication of a Parsonage									
Dedication of a School									
Dedication of Worship Furnishings									
Distribution of Communion									
Empowering of Candidates or Catechists			x						
Enrollment of Candidates for Baptism									
Excommunication/ Reinstatement								x	
Farewell and Godspeed									
Forms of Blessing									
General Order of Blessing									
Groundbreaking									
Guidelines for Ringing Church Bells									
Individual Confession and Forgiveness								x	

	Joint Synod of Ohio (1912)	Liturgy and Agenda (1916)	Common Service Book (1919)	Occasional Services (1930)	Lutheran Agenda (194?)	U.E.L.C. (1945)	Occasional Services (1950)	Occasional Services (1962)	Occasional Services (1982)
Dedication of an Organ/Musical Instruments	x	x		x	x			x	x
Dedication of a Parsonage		x			x	x			
Dedication of a School	x				x			x	
Dedication of Worship Furnishings									x
Distribution of Communion									x
Empowering of Candidates or Catechists									
Enrollment of Candidates for Baptism									x
Excommunication/Reinstatement	x	x			x				
Farewell and Godspeed									x
Forms of Blessing							x		
General Order of Blessing				x				x	x
Groundbreaking				x	x			x	x
Guidelines for Ringing Church Bells				x					x
Individual Confession and Forgiveness	x			x			x		x

405

	New York (1806)	New York (1817)	Ohio (1830)	Ministerium of Pa. (1860)	General Synod (1867)	General Synod (1881)	Church Book (1891)	Augustana (1898)	General Synod (1900)
Induction of a Christian Day School Teacher									
Induction of Office Bearers									
Induction of President and Vice-Presidents of Synod									
Induction of Sunday School Teachers									
Induction of Women Teachers									
Installation at an Ordination									
Installation of a Bishop/President									
Installation of a Chaplain									
Installation of a Church Council	x	x	x	x	x	x	x	x	
Installation of Elected Parish Officers									
Installation of a Lay Professional Leader									
Installation of a Parish Deaconess									
Installation of a Pastor				x	x	x	x	x	x

	Joint Synod of Ohio (1912)	Liturgy and Agenda (1916)	Common Service Book (1919)	Occasional Services (1930)	Lutheran Agenda (1947?)	U.E.L.C. (1945)	Occasional Services (1950)	Occasional Services (1962)	Occasional Services (1982)
Induction of a Christian Day School Teacher	x	x			x				x
Induction of Office Bearers							x		
Induction of President and Vice-Presidents of Synod					x				
Induction of Sunday School Teachers					x				
Induction of Women Teachers					x				
Installation at an Ordination		x							x
Installation of a Bishop/President				x			x		x
Installation of a Chaplain								x	
Installation of a Church Council	x	x	x		x		x		
Installation of Elected Parish Officers									x
Installation of a Lay Professional Leader									x
Installation of a Parish Deaconess				x				x	
Installation of a Pastor	x	x	x		x		x		x

	New York (1806)	New York (1817)	Ohio (1830)	Ministerium of Pa. (1860)	General Synod (1867)	General Synod (1881)	Church Book (1891)	Augustana (1898)	General Synod (1900)
Installation of a Professor									
Installation to Regional or Churchwide Office									
Lay Baptism									
Laying of the Cornerstone				x	x	x	x	x	x
Laying on of Hands and Anointing the Sick									
Licensure					x	x			
The Lord's Supper	x	x	x		x	x			x
Marriage		x	x	x	x	x	x	x	x
Opening a Congregational Meeting									
Opening of a Convention (Synod)				x	x		x		x
Opening of a School Year									
Ordination		x (1834)	x	x	x	x	x	x	x
Organization of a Congregation									
Pastor's Daily Prayer									
Prayers During Separation or Divorce									
Prayers for Other Occasions									

	Joint Synod of Ohio (1912)	Liturgy and Agenda (1916)	Common Service Book (1919)	Occasional Services (1930)	Lutheran Agenda (194?)	U.E.L.C. (1945)	Occasional Services (1950)	Occasional Services (1962)	Occasional Services (1982)
Installation of a Professor					X				
Installation to Regional or Churchwide Office									X
Lay Baptism			X					X	
Laying of the Cornerstone	X	X	X		X		X		X
Laying on of Hands and Anointing the Sick									X
Licensure									
The Lord's Supper						X			
Marriage	X	X	X		X	X	X		X
Opening a Congregational Meeting		X			X				
Opening of a Convention (Synod)	X	X	X		X		X		X
Opening of a School Year									X
Ordination	X	X	X		X	X	X		X
Organization of a Congregation									X
Pastor's Daily Prayer					X				
Prayers During Separation or Divorce									X
Prayers for Other Occasions								X	X

	New York (1806)	New York (1817)	Ohio (1830)	Ministerium of Pa. (1860)	General Synod (1867)	General Synod (1881)	Church Book (1891)	Augustana (1898)	General Synod (1900)
Prayers of the Day									
Psalms, Lessons, and Prayers							x		
Reception of a Congregation									
Reception of Converts									
Reception of Lutherans by Transfer									
Reception of Members						x		x	x
Reception of a Minister									
Reception of a Minister of Another Community									
Reception of Voting Members									
Recognition of Ministries in the Congregation									
Rededication of a Church									
Restoration of the Lapsed									
Retirement of a Servant of the Church									
Sentences for Collection of Alms and Offerings						x			

	Joint Synod of Ohio (1912)	Liturgy and Agenda (1916)	Common Service Book (1919)	Occasional Services (1930)	Lutheran Agenda (194?)	U.E.L.C. (1945)	Occasional Services (1950)	Occasional Services (1962)	Occasional Services (1982)
Prayers of the Day									x
Psalms, Lessons, and Prayers			x				x		x
Reception of a Congregation				x				x	x
Reception of Converts	x	x			x				
Reception of Lutherans by Transfer									x
Reception of Members				x	x			x	
Reception of a Minister				x				x	
Reception of a Minister of Another Community				x (1943)					
Reception of Voting Members		x							
Recognition of Ministries in the Congregation									x
Rededication of a Church				x					
Restoration of the Lapsed				x					
Retirement of a Servant of the Church								x	
Sentences for Collection of Alms and Offerings									

411

	New York (1806)	New York (1817)	Ohio (1830)	Ministerium of Pa. (1860)	General Synod (1867)	General Synod (1881)	*Church Book* (1891)	Augustana (1898)	General Synod (1900)
Service of Commemoration									
Service of the Word for Healing									
Setting Apart of a Deaconess									x
Thanksgiving: Childbirth								x	
Thanksgiving at the Disposition of a Church									
Thanksgiving at the Retirement of a Debt									

	Joint Synod of Ohio (1912)	Liturgy and Agenda (1916)	Common Service Book (1919)	Occasional Services (1930)	Lutheran Agenda (194?)	U.E.L.C. (1945)	Occasional Services (1950)	Occasional Services (1962)	Occasional Services (1982)
Service of Commemoration				x				x	
Service of the Word for Healing									x
Setting Apart of a Deaconess				x			x		x
Thanksgiving: Childbirth				x				x	x
Thanksgiving at the Disposition of a Church									x
Thanksgiving at the Retirement of a Debt								x	x

APPENDIX III
PAGE NUMBERS FOR
PRAYERS IN THE
LUTHERAN BOOK OF WORSHIP
AND OCCASIONAL SERVICES

NOTE: Ten prayers within the Burial of the Dead share the same numbers as the Psalm prayers for the Psalms 1−10. This error was to have been corrected in the second printing of the *Lutheran Book of Worship*. However, because such a change would perhaps introduce yet more confusion the custodial committee for the *LBW* decided to let the duplication stand.

Prayer Number	Use	*Page Numbers* *LBW* Ministers Ed.	*LBW* Pew Ed.	*Occasional Services* (1982)
1	Advent 1	121	13	263
2	Advent 2	121	13	263
3	Advent 3	122	13	263
4	Advent 3	122	14	264
5	Advent 4	122	14	264
6	Christmas Day	123	14	264
7	Christmas Day	123	14	264
8	Christmas 1	123	14	264
9	Christmas 2	124	15	264–65
10	The Epiphany	124	15	265
11	Baptism of our Lord (Epiphany 1)	124–25	15	265
12	Epiphany 2	125	15	265
13	Epiphany 3	125	15	265
14	Epiphany 4	126	16	266
15	Epiphany 5	126	16	266
16	Epiphany 6	127	16	266
17	Epiphany 7	127	16	266
18	Epiphany 7	127	16	266
19	Epiphany 8	127	17	266
20	Transfiguration	128	17	267
21	Transfiguration	128	17	267

Prayer Number	Use	Page Numbers LBW Ministers Ed.	LBW Pew Ed.	Occasional Services (1982)
22	Ash Wednesday	128–29	17	267
23	–	–	–	–
24	Lent 1	131	17	267
25	Lent 1	132	17	268
26	Lent 2	132	18	268
27	Lent 2	132	18	268
28	Lent 3	133	18	268
29	Lent 4	133	18	268
30	Lent 5	133	19	269
31	Sunday of the Passion	134	19	269
32	Procession with Palms	135	–	–
33	Blessing of Palms	135	–	–
34	Monday in Holy Week	136	19	269
35	Tuesday in Holy Week	136	19	269
36	Wednesday in Holy Week	136	20	269
37	Maundy Thursday	136–37	20	270
38	Maundy Thursday	137	20	270
39	Good Friday	138, 139	20	270
40	Good Friday	138	20	270
41	–	–	–	–
42	Bidding Prayer	139	–	–
43	Bidding Prayer	140	–	–
44	Bidding Prayer	140	–	–
45	Bidding Prayer	140	–	–
46	Bidding Prayer	140	–	–
47	Bidding Prayer	141	–	–
48	Bidding Prayer	141	–	–
49	Bidding Prayer	141	–	–
50	Bidding Prayer	141	–	–
51	Easter Vigil: First Lesson	147	–	–

Prayer Number	Use	Page Numbers		
		LBW Ministers Ed.	*LBW* Pew Ed.	*Occasional Services* (1982)
52	Easter Vigil: Second Lesson	147	—	—
53	Easter Vigil: Third Lesson	147	—	—
54	Easter Vigil: Fourth Lesson	148	—	—
55	Easter Vigil: Fifth Lesson	148	—	—
56	Easter Vigil: Sixth Lesson	149	—	—
57	Easter Vigil: Seventh Lesson	149	—	—
58	Easter Vigil: Eighth Lesson	149	—	—
59	Easter Vigil: Ninth Lesson	150	—	—
60	Easter Vigil: Tenth Lesson	150	—	—
61	Easter Vigil: Eleventh Lesson	151	—	—
62	Easter Day	153	20	270
63	Easter Day	153	21	270
64	Easter Evening	153	21	270
65	Easter 2	154	21	270
66	Easter 3	154	21	270
67	Easter 4	155	22	270
68	Easter 4	155	22	272
69	Easter 5	155	22	156, 272
70	Easter 6	156	22	272
71	Ascension Day	156	22	272
72	Easter 7	156	23	272
73	Easter 7	157	23	273
74	Vigil of Pentecost	157	23	273
75	Pentecost	158	23	273
76	Pentecost	158	23	273
77	Holy Trinity	158	24	274

Prayer Number	Use	Page Numbers		
		LBW Ministers Ed.	*LBW* Pew Ed.	*Occasional Services* (1982)
78	Holy Trinity	159	24	274
79	Pentecost 2	159	24	274
80	Pentecost 3	159	24	274
81	Pentecost 4	160	24	274
82	Pentecost 5	160	25	275
83	Pentecost 6	161	25	275
84	Pentecost 7	161	25	275
85	Pentecost 8	162	25	275
86	Pentecost 8	162	25	275
87	Pentecost 9	163	26	275
88	Pentecost 9	163	26	276
89	Pentecost 10	163	26	276
90	Pentecost 11	163	26	276
91	Pentecost 11	163	26	276
92	Pentecost 12	163–64	26	276
93	Pentecost 13	164	26	276
94	Pentecost 14	164	27	277
95	Pentecost 15	165	27	277
96	Pentecost 16	165	27	277
97	Pentecost 17	166	27	277
98	Pentecost 18	166	28	277
99	Pentecost 19	166	28	278
100	Pentecost 20	166	28	278
101	Pentecost 21	167	28	278
102	Pentecost 22	168	28	278
103	Pentecost 23	168	29	278
104	Pentecost 24	168–69	29	279
105	Pentecost 25	169	29	279
106	Pentecost 26	169	29	279
107	Pentecost 27	170	30	279
108	Christ the King	170	30	279
109	St. Andrew	171	30	280
110	St. Thomas	171	30	280
111	St. Stephen	171	30–31	280
112	St. John	172	31	280

| Prayer Number | Use | *Page Numbers* | | |
		LBW Ministers Ed.	*LBW* Pew Ed.	*Occasional Services* (1982)
113	Holy Innocents	172	31	281
114	Name of Jesus	172–73	31	281
115	Confession of St. Peter	173	31	281
116	Conversion of St. Paul	173	32	281
117	Presentation	174	32	282
118	St. Matthias	174	32	282
119	Annunciation	174	32	282
120	St. Mark	175	32	282
121	St. Philip and St. James	175	33	283
122	Visitation	175–76	33	283
123	St. Barnabas	176	33	283
124	Nativity of St. John the Baptist	176	33	283
125	St. Peter and St. Paul	177	34	284
126	St. Mary Magdalene	177	34	284
127	St. James the Elder	177	34	284
128	Mary, Mother of Our Lord	178	34	284
129	St. Bartholomew	178	34	285
130	Holy Cross	179	35	285
131	St. Matthew	179	35	285
132	St. Michael and All Angels	179	35	285
133	St. Luke	180	35	286
134	St. Simon and St. Jude	180	36	286
135	Reformation Day	180–81	36	286
136	All Saints' Day	181	36	286
137	Saints	181	36	—
138	Martyrs	182	37	—
139	Missionaries	182	37	208
140	Renewers of the Church	182	37	—
141	Renewers of Society	183	37	292
142	Renewers of Society	183	37	—

Prayer Number	Use	Page Numbers		
		LBW Ministers Ed.	*LBW* Pew Ed.	*Occasional Services* (1982)
143	Pastors and Bishops	183	38	—
144	Pastors and Bishops	183	38	—
145	Theologians	184	38	—
146	Artists and Scientists	184	38	—
147	Unity	184–85	39	—
148	Dedication and Anniversary	185	39	171
149	Dedication and Anniversary	185	39	—
150	Harvest	185	39	—
151	Day of Penitence	186	39	—
152	Day of Penitence	186	40	—
153	National Holiday	186	40	—
154	Peace	187	40	—
155	Thanksgiving	187	40	—
156	Stewardship of Creation	187–88	40	—
157	Stewardship of Creation	188	41	—
158	Stewardship of Creation	188	41	—
159	New Year's Eve	188	41	—
160	Holy Baptism	188	—	—
161	Holy Baptism: Post-Communion	188	—	—
162	Marriage	189, 328	202	27, 31
163	Marriage: Post-Communion	190	—	—
164	Burial: Post-Communion	191	—	—
165	Peace Among the Nations	105	42	—
166	Peace	105	42	—
167	Social Justice	105	42	288
168	The Variety of Races and Cultures	105	42	—
169	Our Country	105–6	42	—

Prayer Number	Use	Page Numbers		
		LBW Ministers Ed.	*LBW* Pew Ed.	*Occasional Services* (1982)
170	State/Provincial and Local Governments	106	43	—
171	Responsible Citizenship	106	43	—
172	Those in Civil Authority	106	43	—
173	Courts of Justice	106	43	—
174	Cities	106	43	—
175	Towns and Rural Areas	106–7	43	—
176	The Neighborhood	107	43	—
177	The Human Family	107	44	288–89
178	Commerce and Industry	107	44	—
179	The Unemployed	107	44	—
180	Our Enemies	107	44	289
181	The Poor and the Neglected	107	44	—
182	The Oppressed	108	44	—
183	The Proper Use of Wealth	108	44	291
184	Schools	108	44	—
185	Agriculture	108	45	—
186	Prisons and Correctional Institutions	108	45	—
187	Those Who Suffer for the Sake of Conscience	108	45	—
188	Use of Leisure	109	45	—
189	The Church	109	45	—
190	Spread of the Gospel	109	45	291
191	Missions	109	45	—
192	The Mission of the Church	109	45	291
193	The Saints	109	46	—
194	Ministers of the Word	109	46	—
195	The Election of a President or Pastor	110	46	—

Prayer Number	Use	Page Numbers		
		LBW Ministers Ed.	*LBW* Pew Ed.	*Occasional Services* (1982)
196	Deaconesses and Deacons	110	46	217
197	Church Musicians and Artists	110	46	292
198	Teachers	110	46	139, 241, 292
199	Renewal	110	47	—
200	Renewal	110	47	—
201	Grace to Receive the Word	110	47	—
202	Enlightenment of the Holy Spirit	110	47	236, 290
203	Self-Dedication	111	47	—
204	Trustfulness	111	47	289
205	Before Worship	111	47	—
206	Before Worship	111	47	—
207	Before Holy Communion	111	47	—
208	Before Holy Communion	111	48	—
209	After Holy Communion	111	48	79, 86
210	After Worship	111	48	—
211	Answer to Prayer	112	48	71
212	Answer to Prayer	112	48	—
213	A Prayer Attributed to St. Francis	112	48	289
214	General Thanksgiving	112	49	—
215	Harvest of Lands and Waters	112–13	49	—
216	Conservation of Natural Resources	113	49	—
217	Thanks for the Harvest	113	49	—
218	In Time of Scarce Rainfall	113	49	—
219	Dangers of Abundance	113	49	—
220	Guidance	113	49	167, 238, 247, 291
221	General Intercession	113	50	—

Prayer Number	Use	*Page Numbers* *LBW* Ministers Ed.	*LBW* Pew Ed.	*Occasional Services* (1982)
222	Protection Through Life	113	50	—
223	Those in Affliction	114	50	62, 92
224	Those in Mental Distress	114	50	—
225	Those in Trouble or Bereavement	114	50	—
226	Recovery from Sickness	114	50	92
227	Those Suffering from Addiction	114	50	57
228	Restoration of Health	114	50	52
229	The Aged	114	51	—
230	Families	115	51	—
231	Birth of a Child	115	51	54
232	The Care of Children	115	51	—
233	Young Persons	115	51	—
234	Those Who Live Alone	115	51	—
235	Remembrance of the Faithful Departed	115	51	110, 295
236	Prayer for Purity	195, 233, 269, 318	56, 77, 98, 193	—
237	—	—	—	—
238	Affirmation of Baptism	326	200	—
239	Offertory	206, 243, 279	67, 87, 109	—
240	Offertory	206, 243, 279	68, 88, 109	—
241	Post-Communion	229, 266, 303	74, 94, 117	79, 87
242	Post-Communion	229, 266, 303	74, 94, 117	—

APPENDIX III

Prayer Number	Use	LBW Ministers Ed.	LBW Pew Ed.	Occasional Services (1982)
		Page Numbers		
243	Post-Communion	229, 266, 303	74, 94, 117	—
244	The Prayer When There Is No Holy Communion	231–32, 267–68, 305–6	75, 96, 118	—
245	Holy Baptism: The Thanksgiving	309	122	—
246	Holy Baptism: Prayer for the Holy Spirit	311	124	20
247	Holy Baptism: When Small Children Are Baptized	312	124	21
248	—	—	—	—
249	Morning Prayer: For Grace	51	136	—
250	Morning and Evening Prayer: For the Word	52, 69	137, 153	—
251	Morning and Evening Prayer: For Faith	52, 69	137, 153	247
252	Morning and Evening Prayer: For God's Help	52, 70	137, 153	—
253	Paschal Blessing	56–57	141	—
254	Evening Prayer: Incense Prayer	62	146	—
255	Prayer for Peace	68, 320	151, 195	—
256	—	—	—	—
257	—	—	—	—
258	—	—	—	—
259	Compline	75	157	—
260	Compline	75	158	74, 107
261	Compline	75	158	—

| Prayer Number | Use | *Page Numbers* | | |
		LBW Ministers Ed.	LBW Pew Ed.	*Occasional Services* (1982)
262	Compline	75	158	—
263	Compline	76	158	—
264	Compline	76	158	—
265	Responsive Prayer 1	84	166	—
266	Responsive Prayer 2: Noon	84	166	—
267	Responsive Prayer 2: Afternoon	84	166	—
268	Responsive Prayer 2: Evening	84	166	—
269	Responsive Prayer 2: Before Travel	85	167	238
270	—	—	—	—
271	Corporate Confession	318	193	—
272	Corporate Confession	320	195	—
273	—	—	—	—
274	Affirmation of Baptism	327	201	—
275	Affirmation of Baptism: Confirmation	327	201	—
276	Marriage: Thanksgiving	329	204	29, 34
277	Marriage: For the Couple	330	204	29
278	Marriage: For Families	330	204	29, 35, 43
279	Burial Psalm 1	332 340	207 —	114 —
280	Burial Psalm 2	332 341	207 —	110, 114 —
281	Burial Psalm 3	332 341	207 —	115 —
282	Burial Psalm 4	333 341	208 —	115 —
283	Burial of a Child Psalm 5	333 342	208 —	56, 111, 115 —
284	Burial: Intercessions Psalm 6	335 342	210 —	74, 112 —
285	Burial: Intercessions Psalm 7	335 343	210 —	112, 295 —

Prayer Number	Use	Page Numbers LBW Ministers Ed.	LBW Pew Ed.	Occasional Services (1982)
286	Burial: Commendation	336	211	107, 123
	Psalm 8	343–44	–	–
287	Burial: Committal	337	212	125
	Psalm 9	344	–	–
288	Burial: Committal	339	213	127
	Psalm 10	345	–	–
289	Psalm 11	345–46	–	–
290	Psalm 12	346	–	–
291	Psalm 13	346	–	–
292	Psalm 14	347	–	–
293	Psalm 15	347	–	–
294	Psalm 16	347	–	–
295	Psalm 17	348	–	–
296	Psalm 18	350	–	–
297	Psalm 19	351	–	–
298	Psalm 20	351	–	–
299	Psalm 21	352	–	–
300	Psalm 22	353	–	–
301	Psalm 23	353	–	–
302	Psalm 24	354	–	–
303	Psalm 25	354	–	–
304	Psalm 26	355	–	–
305	Psalm 27	356	–	–
306	Psalm 28	356	–	–
307	Psalm 29	357	–	–
308	Psalm 30	357	–	–
309	Psalm 31	358	–	–
310	Psalm 32	359	–	–
311	Psalm 33	360	–	–
312	Psalm 34	360	–	293
313	Psalm 35	361	–	–
314	Psalm 36	362	–	–
315	Psalm 37	363	–	–
316	Psalm 38	364	–	–
317	Psalm 39	365	–	–
318	Psalm 40	366	–	–

Prayer Number	Use	*Page Numbers*		
		LBW Ministers Ed.	*LBW* Pew Ed.	*Occasional Services* (1982)
319	Psalm 41	366	—	—
320	Psalm 42	367	—	—
321	Psalm 43	367	—	—
322	Psalm 44	368	—	—
323	Psalm 45	369	—	—
324	Psalm 46	370	—	—
325	Psalm 47	370	—	—
326	Psalm 48	371	—	—
327	Psalm 49	371	—	—
328	Psalm 50	372	—	—
329	Psalm 51	373	—	—
330	Psalm 52	374	—	—
331	Psalm 53	374	—	—
332	Psalm 54	374	—	—
333	Psalm 55	375	—	—
334	Psalm 56	376	—	—
335	Psalm 57	376	—	—
336	Psalm 58	377	—	—
337	Psalm 59	377–78	—	—
338	Psalm 60	378	—	294
339	Psalm 61	378	—	—
340	Psalm 62	379	—	—
341	Psalm 63	379	—	—
342	Psalm 64	380	—	—
343	Psalm 65	380–81	—	—
344	Psalm 66	381	—	—
345	Psalm 67	381	—	—
346	Psalm 68	383	—	—
347	Psalm 69	384	—	—
348	Psalm 70	385	—	—
349	Psalm 71	386	—	—
350	Psalm 72	386	—	—
351	Psalm 73	387	—	—
352	Psalm 74	388	—	—
353	Psalm 75	389	—	—

Prayer Number	Use	*LBW* Ministers Ed.	*LBW* Pew Ed.	*Occasional Services* (1982)
354	Psalm 76	389	–	–
355	Psalm 77	390	–	–
356	Psalm 78	393	–	–
357	Psalm 79	393	–	–
358	Psalm 80	394	–	–
359	Psalm 81	395	–	–
360	Psalm 82	395	–	–
361	Psalm 83	396	–	–
362	Psalm 84	396	–	–
363	Psalm 85	397	–	–
364	Psalm 86	398	–	–
365	Psalm 87	398	–	–
366	Psalm 88	399	–	–
367	Psalm 89	400	–	–
368	Psalm 90	401	–	–
369	Psalm 91	402	–	–
370	Psalm 92	402	–	–
371	Psalm 93	403	–	–
372	Psalm 94	403	–	–
373	Psalm 95	404	–	–
374	Psalm 96	404	–	–
375	Psalm 97	405	–	–
376	Psalm 98	405	–	–
377	Psalm 99	406	–	–
378	Psalm 100	406	–	–
379	Psalm 101	407	–	–
380	Psalm 102	408	–	–
381	Psalm 103	408	–	–
382	Psalm 104	410	–	–
383	Psalm 105	411	–	–
384	Psalm 106	413	–	–
385	Psalm 107	414	–	–
386	Psalm 108	415	–	–
387	Psalm 109	416	–	–
388	Psalm 110	416	–	–

Prayer Number	Use	Page Numbers LBW Ministers Ed.	LBW Pew Ed.	Occasional Services (1982)
389	Psalm 111	417	—	—
390	Psalm 112	417	—	—
391	Psalm 113	418	—	—
392	Psalm 114	418	—	—
393	Psalm 115	419	—	—
394	Psalm 116	419	—	—
395	Psalm 117	419	—	—
396	Psalm 118	420	—	—
397	Psalm 119	426	—	—
398	Psalm 120	427	—	—
399	Psalm 121	427	—	—
400	Psalm 122	427	—	—
401	Psalm 123	427	—	—
402	Psalm 124	428	—	—
403	Psalm 125	428	—	—
404	Psalm 126	428	—	—
405	Psalm 127	428	—	—
406	Psalm 128	429	—	—
407	Psalm 129	429	—	—
408	Psalm 130	429	—	—
409	Psalm 131	430	—	—
410	Psalm 132	430	—	—
411	Psalm 133	431	—	—
412	Psalm 134	431	—	290
413	Psalm 135	432	—	—
414	Psalm 136	432	—	—
415	Psalm 137	433	—	—
416	Psalm 138	433	—	—
417	Psalm 139	434	—	—
418	Psalm 140	435	—	—
419	Psalm 141	435	—	—
420	Psalm 142	436	—	—
421	Psalm 143	436	—	—
422	Psalm 144	437	—	—
423	Psalm 145	438	—	—

Prayer Number	Use	Page Numbers LBW Ministers Ed.	LBW Pew Ed.	Occasional Services (1982)
424	Psalm 146	438	–	–
425	Psalm 147	439	–	–
426	Psalm 148	439	–	–
427	Psalm 149	440	–	–
428	Psalm 150	440	–	–
429	Enrollment of Candidates for Baptism	–	–	14
430	Enrollment of Candidates for Baptism	–	–	14
431	Enrollment of Candidates for Baptism	–	–	14
432	Baptism in an Emergency	–	–	17
433	Baptism in an Emergency: Public Recognition (see 245)	–	–	19
434	Anniversary of a Baptism	–	–	25
435	Blessing of a Civil Marriage (see 162)	–	–	32
436	Blessing of a Civil Marriage (see 277)	–	–	34
437	Anniversary of a Marriage	–	–	37
438	Anniversary of a Marriage	–	–	38
439	Affirmation of Marriage Vows (see 162, 435)	–	–	41
440	Affirmation of Marriage Vows	–	–	42
441	Sickness	–	–	50
442	Sickness	–	–	51
443	Sickness	–	–	51
444	Sickness	–	–	51
445	Sickness	–	–	51
446	Gratitude	–	–	52
447	Before Childbirth	–	–	53
448	Before Childbirth	–	–	53

Prayer Number	Use	*Page Numbers*		
		LBW Ministers Ed.	*LBW* Pew Ed.	*Occasional Services* (1982)
449	Following Childbirth	–	–	54
450	Following Childbirth	–	–	54
451	Following Childbirth	–	–	54
452	Stillbirth or Death Shortly After Birth	–	–	56
453	Stillbirth or Death Shortly After Birth	–	–	56
454	Addiction	–	–	57
455	Anxiety, Apprehension, Fear	–	–	59
456	Anxiety, Apprehension, Fear	–	–	60
457	Anxiety, Apprehension, Fear	–	–	60
458	Before Surgery	–	–	74
459	Before Surgery	–	–	75
460	Before Surgery	–	–	75
461	Following Surgery	–	–	75
462	Guilt	–	–	62
463	Loneliness	–	–	64
464	Loneliness	–	–	65
465	Loneliness	–	–	65
466	Impatience or Boredom	–	–	67
467	Impatience or Boredom	–	–	67
468	Impending Death or Irreversible Illness	–	–	68
469	Impending Death or Irreversible Illness	–	–	68
470	Impending Death or Irreversible Illness	–	–	68
471	Anger, Bitterness, Self-Pity, Turmoil	–	–	71
472	Anger, Bitterness, Self-Pity, Turmoil	–	–	71
473	Acceptance of Inevitable Death	–	–	84
474	Acceptance of Inevitable Death	–	–	84

Prayer Number	Use	*Page Numbers*		
		LBW Ministers Ed.	*LBW* Pew Ed.	*Occasional Services* (1982)
475	Acceptance of Inevitable Death	–	–	84
476	Distribution of Communion	–	–	76
477	Service of the Word for Healing: All Who Suffer	–	–	91
478	Service of the Word for Healing: Those Who Minister in Healing	–	–	92
479	Service of the Word for Healing: Family and Friends	–	–	92
480	Service of the Word for Healing: Those Who Desire Our Prayers	–	–	92
481	Service of the Word for Healing: For Those Making Decisions	–	–	93
482	Service of the Word for Healing: Thanksgiving	–	–	95
483	Laying on of Hands and Anointing the Sick: Thanksgiving (see 482)	–	–	101
484	Laying on of Hands and Anointing the Sick: Preparation of the Oil	–	–	102
485	Commendation of the Dying	–	–	103
486	Commendation of the Dying	–	–	105
487	Commendation of the Dying: When a Life-Support System is Withdrawn	–	–	106
488	Comforting the Bereaved	–	–	110
489	Comforting the Bereaved	–	–	111
490	Comforting the Bereaved	–	–	111

Prayer Number	Use	Page Numbers LBW Ministers Ed.	LBW Pew Ed.	Occasional Services (1982)
491	Reception of Lutherans by Transfer	–	–	130
492	Installation of a Lay Professional Leader: General	–	–	138
493	Installation of a Lay Professional Leader: Medical Worker	–	–	138
494	Installation of a Lay Professional Leader: Director of Christian Education, Youth Minister	–	–	139
495	Installation of a Lay Professional Leader: Church Musician	–	–	139
496	Installation of a Lay Professional Leader: Administrative Personnel	–	–	139
497	Recognition of Ministries in the Congregation: Worship	–	–	144
498	Recognition of Ministries in the Congregation: Education	–	–	144
499	Recognition of Ministries in the Congregation: Witness	–	–	144
500	Recognition of Ministries in the Congregation: Service	–	–	145
501	Recognition of Ministries in the Congregation: Stewardship	–	–	145
502	Recognition of Ministries in the Congregation	–	–	145
503	Affirmation of the Vocation of Christians in the World	–	–	148
504	Affirmation of the Vocation of Christians in the World	–	–	148

Prayer Number	Use	Page Numbers		
		LBW Ministers Ed.	LBW Pew Ed.	Occasional Services (1982)
528	Blessing of a Dwelling: Study or Library	–	–	188
529	Blessing of a Dwelling: Kitchen	–	–	188
530	Blessing of a Dwelling: Dining Room	–	–	188
531	Blessing of a Dwelling: Bedroom(s)	–	–	189
532	Blessing of a Dwelling: Guest Room	–	–	189
533	Blessing of a Dwelling	–	–	189
534	Blessing of a Dwelling	–	–	190
535	Blessing of a Dwelling	–	–	190
536	Ordination: The Thanksgiving	–	–	196
537	Ordination: The Thanksgiving	–	–	196
538	Ordination: Prayer of the Day	–	–	202
539	Ordination: Post-Communion	–	–	203
540	Setting Apart of a Deaconess: The Thanksgiving	–	–	213
541	Setting Apart of a Deaconess: The Thanksgiving	–	–	213–14
542	Setting Apart of a Deaconess: *Apostolic Constitutions* Prayer	–	–	216
543 = 194	Installation of a Bishop, Installation of a Pastor	109	46	223, 231
544	Installation to a Regional or Churchwide Office	–	–	233
545	Opening of a School Year	–	–	244
546	Organization of a Congregation	–	–	253
547	Reception of a Congregation	–	–	254

GLOSSARY

Absolution. The formal act, performed only by an ordained pastor, pronouncing the forgiveness of sin by Christ and wiping the sins away. It is found in two forms in Christianity: the indicative form, "I absolve you," and the precatory form in which the pastor prays for forgiveness for the penitent. The precatory form is the form used in the Eastern Orthodox churches.

Altar (from the Latin "high place"). The holy table on which the Holy Communion is celebrated. It is a focus of devotional and liturgical attention since it is the place where God and his people meet as God gives himself in love and as his people in response offer themselves for his service.

Assisting Minister. A lay or ordained person whose ministry in the liturgy is to assist the presiding minister and thus to share in the liturgical leadership.

Aumbry (AHM-bree). A small safe set in the wall of a church or sacristy in which the sacrament or the sacramental vessels are kept. When set in the wall of the church, the traditional place is in the north wall of the chancel.

Baptistery (or baptistry). (1) The part of a church or a separate building that surrounds the baptismal font; the space where Holy Baptism is administered. (2) The large tank used for baptism by immersion.

Berakah (ber-ah-KAH). The characteristic Jewish prayer form which is a blessing, or thanksgiving to God, recounting his acts of mercy to his creation. The Old Testament provides examples of such a prayer (for example, Gen. 24:27; Job 1:21; Ps. 28:6), which was taken over into Christian use in the New Testament (for example, 2 Cor. 1:3; 1 Pet. 1:3) and other early Christian prayers. Some early eucharistic prayers take the form of the *Berakah*, and the name "Eucharist" (that is, "Thanksgiving") is probably related to this practice. Particularly in rites of blessing, *Occasional Services* (1982) has made frequent use of the *Berakah* form of prayer.

Bishop (an Old English form of the Vulgar Latin *biscopus*, which was a variant of the Late Latin *episcopus*, from the Greek *episkopos*, an overseer or guardian). A church superintendent, or overseer, who has charge of the pastors (and congregations) in a particular area.

Boat. A container for incense, carried by a server in procession for replenishing the thurible, or censer.

Candles. The use of candles in the church grew out of processional lights which in early times stood beside or on the altar. This use of processional candles, or torches, has been recovered in recent times. In the early church candles were used only for illumination. The one exception was the lamp which was lighted at sundown and burned throughout the night, the lighting of which involved ceremonies similar to those of the Service of Light at the beginning of evening prayer.

Catechesis (cat-eh-KEE-sis). The instruction and training given to catechumens.

Catechumen. A person preparing for Holy Baptism by undergoing instruction and training in the Christian life. In Lutheran use, the name was often applied to a person baptized in infancy who was receiving catechetical instruction leading to confirmation (Affirmation of Baptism).

Catechumenate (cat-eh-KEW-men-it). The period of instruction and training that catechumens undergo in preparation for Holy Baptism.

Cathedra. The bishop's chair in the cathedral church. Its original position, which is being recovered in modern times, was behind the main altar in the center of the apse. From this chair the bishop preached and gave formal instruction and teaching. The bishop's chair was therefore a symbol of authority; it remains an important symbol of the office.

Cathedral. The church of a diocese in which the bishop's chair, or cathedra, is located. It is not simply any large or ornate church.

Catholic. Whole; a church that receives the Christian faith intact without alteration or selection in matters of faith. The opposite of catholic is heretic, one who picks and chooses which parts of the faith are acceptable. "Catholic" is thus more specific than "Christian" and is not a synonym for "ecumenical," "worldwide," or "universal."

Censer. A closed container in which incense is burned.

Chalice (from the Latin "cup"). The cup used in the Holy Communion to hold the wine.

Chasuble (from the Latin "little house"). The principal outer garment worn by the presiding minister when celebrating the Holy Communion. It is, therefore, a principal liturgical sign of ordination.

Chrism. Olive oil (or other plant oil), sometimes mixed with an aromatic ingredient such as oil of bergamot or cinnamon, used for anointing in Holy Baptism. Perfumed oil is a sensuous sign of joy and well-being and, moreover, has romantic associations (Song of Sol. 1:3; 1:12; 3:6; see also 2 Cor. 2:15). The ability to smell the perfumed oil was understood to be a symbol of sensitivity to God's presence in the world, a sensitivity to the things of the Spirit. *See* **Oil**.

Ciborium (sib-OR-ee-um). The canopy over an altar. From this original meaning, the use of ciborium to mean a chalice-shaped vessel with a lid (canopy) to hold the bread for Holy Communion developed.

Credence. A serving table, or shelf, on which the sacramental vessels and the missal stand until they are brought to the altar for the Holy Communion.

Cross. The sign of Christ, showing his principal work of redemption. It thus becomes the banner of our salvation.

Crozier. The pastoral staff carried by a bishop as a sign of office. In the East it takes the form of a staff surmounted by a cross between two serpents, recalling Num. 21:4–9. In the West, as a result of later symbolism, it has taken the form of a shepherd's crook.

Crucifer. A person who carries the processional cross.

Crucifix. A cross bearing the image of the crucified Savior. In early times the figure of Christ was clothed as a priest and prophet, crowned as a king, and shown alive in an attitude of blessing and triumph, "reigning from a Tree" (see Hymn 124, stanza 3). In the Middle Ages the figure of Christ was commonly represented in the agony of death, showing the cost of our salvation. This representation passed into common Lutheran use throughout Europe and in many churches in North America.

Cruet. A small pitcher made of glass to hold the wine for the Holy Communion or the water for cleansing the chalice.

Crypt. A vault beneath a church used as a chapel or a burying place.

Deacon. A person devoted to the servant ministry of the church, relating the church to the world.

Deaconess. A woman deacon, charged in the early church with certain functions deemed inappropriate, or inadvisable, for male deacons—ministering to sick and poor women, instructing women catechumens, assisting at the baptism of women. In the nineteenth century, the office was recovered in a revised form by the Moravians and brought into Lutheran use by Theodor Fliedner in Kaiserswerth, Germany.

Elements, eucharistic. The bread and wine of the Holy Communion.

Ewer. A large metal (usually brass) pitcher used to carry water to the baptismal font.

Flagon. A pitcher, usually of silver, in which the wine is kept before being poured into the chalice at the Holy Communion.

Font. A basin, or tank, of metal or stone designed to hold water for the administration of Holy Baptism.

Gradine (from the Latin "step"). A steplike shelf behind the altar on which are placed the crucifix, candles, and flowers. Also called a retable.

Kaddish. A prayer of doxology used in Jewish worship as an expression of praise and hope. The Mourners' Kaddish is recited by relatives of the deceased to praise God. It begins:

> Glorified and sanctified be God's great name throughout the world he has created according to his will. May he establish his kingdom in your lifetime and during your days and within the life of the entire house of Israel, speedily and soon; and say Amen.

The congregation responds with words of praise.

Kind. One of the elements of the Holy Communion, as reception "under one kind," for example, in the form of bread alone without the wine.

Liturgy. The whole body of liturgical texts and music used for the worship of God. The Ministers Edition of the *Lutheran Book of Worship* together with *Occasional Services* (1982) are the Liturgy of the church; the Pew Edition of the *Lutheran Book of Worship*, bound in green, contains selections from the Liturgy for congregational use together with the hymnal.

Ministerial Acts. An older name for the collection of services and orders now called occasional services.

Miter (from the Greek *"mitra,"* a turban). The liturgical hat. The miter, ring, and the pastoral staff comprise the principal insignia of a bishop in the Roman

Catholic rite. In the East the miter takes the form of a crown and apparently was not worn before the fall of Constantinople in 1453. In the West it takes the form of a pointed headpiece (representing the tongues of fire which at Pentecost descended upon the apostles). It is not found before the eleventh century.

Mystagogia (myst-a-GO-gee-a). Instruction in the mysteries, that is, the teachings, of Christianity as a continuation of the instruction given before baptism.

Occasional Services. Services for specific occasions as opposed to the more general services of Holy Communion and daily prayer which are appropriate to a variety of occasions.

Office. (1) The cycle of Morning and Evening Prayer and Prayer at the Close of the Day. Also called the Divine Office. (2) A specially constructed form of worship for a specific occasion, usually less elaborate than an "order."

Oil. In the ancient world, oil was used primarily as a medicine. Oil was also a natural source of light (oil lamps) and thus of joy. Finally oil from the olive tree came to suggest reconciliation and peace. (After the Flood the dove brought an olive branch to Noah to announce forgiveness and reconciliation.) Oil thus was a rich symbol of life, health, light, joy, and reconciliation. Christianity has come to distinguish three kinds of oil: the oil of catechumens is used in the anointing of those who are preparing for Holy Baptism; the oil of the sick is used to anoint those who are seriously ill; the oil of chrism is used in baptismal anointing to show the seal of the Holy Spirit. The oil is olive oil or another plant oil. Chrism has an aromatic ingredient added to it.

Order. A specially constructed form of worship appropriate to particular occasions, more elaborate than an "office."

Pall. (1) A covering for the chalice to keep foreign matter from falling into it. (2) A large cloth which is used to cover the coffin during the Burial of the Dead. It is now often white in order to suggest Easter and the resurrection.

Paraments. A general name for the cloths in the various liturgical colors used on the altar, pulpit, and lectern. Paraments do not include the various linens also used to cover the altar and used in the celebration of the Holy Communion.

Passing Bell. The toll of a bell to announce the death of someone in the parish.

Pastoral staff. *See* **Crozier.**

Pectoral cross. A ceremonial cross worn upon the breast (Latin *pectora*). Since the latter portion of the seventeenth century the pectoral cross has been common to bishops (Roman Catholic, Anglican, and Lutheran). Formerly, such crosses were personal ornaments and, if worn, were ordinarily worn under, rather than over, the vestment.

Pontifical. (1) Pertaining to a bishop, as a "pontifical mass," a mass celebrated by a bishop. (2) The liturgical book of the Western church containing prayers and ceremonies used by a bishop.

Preces (PRAY-sees). A series of verses and responses used as prayers or used to introduce a collect or series of collects as in the responsive prayers.

Preface (from the Latin *"praefatio,"* a religious form of words, a formula). A proclamation of praise which begins the Great Thanksgiving, "The Lord be with you . . . Lift up your hearts . . . It is indeed right and salutary . . . "

Prefacial. Pertaining to the preface; in the style of a solemn religious proclamation.

Presbyter (from the Greek *"presbyteros,"* elder). Traditionally those in the church who advise and counsel the bishop.

Presiding Minister. The person who presides at a liturgical service, especially the Holy Communion. The president of the liturgical assembly must be an ordained minister, a pastor.

Proper(s). That part of the Holy Communion which changes according to the season or festival, in contrast to the fixed parts (the "ordinary") of the service.

Pulpit. A stand for preaching or reading, often elaborately decorated and carved. In early Christian churches the bishop preached while seated in the chair, or cathedra. The pulpit is traditionally placed on the north side of the nave, because beginning in the Middle Ages the Gospel was read from the (liturgical) north corner of the altar.

Purificator. A linen napkin, or serviette, used to wipe the rim of the chalice during the administration of Holy Communion.

Pyx. A receptacle designed to contain the consecrated bread of the Holy Communion.

Reconciliation. A name used in recent years, especially in the Roman Catholic church (and The Episcopal Church), as a more hopeful title for what had been commonly called penance or confession.

Reservation. The practice of keeping ("reserving") some of the bread and wine from one celebration of the Eucharist to the next for the purpose of communing those, such as the dying, who are in need of the sacrament between celebrations of the Eucharist.

Reserved Sacrament. The eucharistic elements which are kept for the purpose of communing the sick.

Retable. *See* **Gradine.**

Ring. With the staff and the miter, a principal insignia of a bishop in the Roman Catholic rite. The episcopal ring is worn on the third finger of the right hand and was first mentioned as part of the bishop's emblems of office in the early seventh century. It came into common use in the ninth and tenth centuries.

Sacrament. An ordinary action which, given power by the Word, distills the essence of the gospel. The Lutheran tradition recognizes two, three, or four sacraments. Baptism and Holy Communion are universally regarded as sacraments. The Apology to the Augsburg Confession (Article XII) calls absolution "a sacrament of penitence" and (Article XIII) allows ordination, properly understood, to be called a sacrament.

Sacrament House. An elaborately carved tower of wood or stone, popular in Germany as a place in which to keep the Sacrament of the Altar so that it was available to transport to the sick.

Sacramentary. The liturgical book containing the text of the Eucharist and the propers (but not the lessons nor those parts which were sung, as for example the gradual). The Sacramentary was replaced from the tenth century onward by the missal and the pontifical. The missal, a book containing everything to be sung or said with rubrical directions for the celebration of the Holy Communion throughout the year, is now sometimes called the Sacramentary.

Sacristy. A room in a church used for keeping the sacred vessels and for the vesting of the clergy and others. For convenience, especially when several ministers are vesting at once, the sacristy should be spacious. In Lutheran practice the sacristy is usually much too small and cramped.

Sanctuary. The area immediately surrounding the altar and, in older churches, within the altar or communion rail. It is not properly a name for the church building itself.

Scrutinies. The formal testing which catechumens were required to undergo before Holy Baptism.

Server. The person who assists the ministers in a service.

Stock. A container, usually a metal cylinder with a tight-fitting top, for carrying oil for anointing.

Stole. A scarf of fabric in the liturgical color worn over the shoulders by ordained ministers. Traditionally, it has been the distinctive vestment of the deacon, who wears it like a sash over the left shoulder and fastened under the right arm. The origin of the stole is uncertain.

Tabernacle. A free-standing safe for the sacrament which, until the reforms of the Second Vatican Council, was placed on the altar of Roman Catholic churches.

Thurible. *See* **Censer.**

Thurifer. One who carries the thurible, or censer, in a procession.

Torches. Candles fitted to a staff so that they may be carried in procession. For outdoor processions the candles should be shielded by a glass chimney. Lanterns on poles may also serve as torches outdoors.

Unction. Anointing with oil. *See* Hymn 456, stanza 5.

Verba institutionis. The words of institution spoken by Jesus at the Last Supper and the surrounding narration, "In the night in which he was betrayed our Lord Jesus took bread . . ." Usually abbreviated to "Verba."

Viaticum (vee-AT-eh-come, a Latin word meaning "provision for a journey"). The Holy Communion given as food to strengthen one near death for the journey from this life to the next.

INDEX

For identification, these abbreviations are used following the titles of orders and offices:

BCP	*The Book of Common Prayer* of The Episcopal Church
BCPCan.	The Canadian *Book of Common Prayer*
BOS	*The Book of Occasional Services* of The Episcopal Church
CB	Church of the Brethren
CSB	*Common Service Book*
CSI	Church of South India
LA	*Lutheran Agenda*
LH	*The Lutheran Hymnal*
Orth.	Eastern Orthodox Church
Presb.	Presbyterian Church
RC	Roman Catholic
SBH	*Service Book and Hymnal*
UMC	United Methodist Church

marking with cross, 21
moment of, 175
parts of service of, 15, 30f., 31f.
preparation for, 18
preparation of candidates for, 18
remembrance of, 17
sealing, 21, 153
Baptism, Short Form for Holy, in Cases of Necessity (*LH*), 30
Baptismal
anointing, 93, 96
candle, 32
covenant, 60
instruction, 21
practice, responsible, 21
preparation as journey, 21
shell as symbol of pastoral office, 198
shell in washing, 34
Baptism in an Emergency, 29ff.
leadership of, 31
legitimacy of, 30
Baptism of Adults, Order for, 4, 6
Baptism of Infants, Order for, 4, 6, 7
Bathroom, blessing of a, 329
Before an operation, prayer, 76, 90, 91
Bell, Office for the Blessing of a Tower, 302
Bells
baptism of, 365
dedication of, 302
development of the rite (chart), 306ff.
given names, 365
in Blessing of a Dwelling, 329
ringing, 364f.
voice of, 364f.
Bender, Frederick, 52
Benedicamus, 133, 245
Benediction(s), 101
Aaronic, 43, 46, 111
absent in Groundbreaking, 252, 257
absent in Laying of a Cornerstone, 263
for certain occasions in church year, 10
of a grave or cemetery, 295f.
of church ornaments, 295
Berakah, 245, 278, 333, 334
Berg, R. David, 9n. 15
Bible, 265
as symbol of pastoral office, 198
in dedication of pulpit, 278
Birney, James G., 293n. 57, 348n. 20

Birth of a child, prayer at the, 385
Birth of a Child, Thanksgiving at the, 70
Bishop, 166
as administrator, 167
as high priest, 167
chief pastor and liturgical officer, 166
emblems of, 222f.
installation of a, 218ff.
office not rank of, 218f.
presides at dedication of a church, 254, 264, 276. *See also* Consecration of Bishops, Order for the
Bishop, Order of Electing and Consecrating a (Orth.), 218
Bless, defined, 246
Blessing
after anointing, 101
for all things, 331
forms of, 330
general form of, 319f.
general order of, 309
of a cemetery, 7, 294ff.
of a church site, 251, 252, 263
of a dwelling, 7, 320ff.
of a family altar, 320
of a fishing boat, 331
of a new business venture, 345
of any object (Orth.), 330, 332
of a parsonage, 328
of a room or apartment, 320
of a tower bell, 364
of a wedding ring, 330
of candles, 308
of Christmas crib/crèche, 330
of fields, 331
of oil, 93, 95
of palms, 192
of people, 248
of things, 248. *See also* Benediction(s)
Blessing in Homes (*BOS*), 324
at Easter, 320
at Epiphany, 320
Blessing of a Cemetery, Order for the, 7, 295
Blessing of a Church-Site and Groundbreaking, 251, 252
Blessing of a Church Site and the Laying of a Foundation Stone (RC), 263
Blessing of a Civil Marriage, 38ff.
Blessing of a Civil Marriage (*BCP*), 38

445

in *Common Service Book,* 4
ministry to non-Christians, 139
1950 rite, 7
Bushong, Ann Brooke, Sister,
294 n. 67

Call to the ministry, 168f., 189
Camp, dedication of a, 293
Canadian *Book of Common Prayer.*
See Book of Common Prayer.
Canada.
Candidacy for Ordination as
Deacons and Priests, Admis-
sion to (RC), 172
Candle, baptismal, 32
Candlemas (February 2), 311
Candles, dedication of, 308, 311, 313
Cape May Point, N.J., 2, 3
Carlstadt (Andreas Rudolf
Bodenstein), 114
Cassock, Orthodox bishop's, 225
Catechumen(s)
death of a, 22
defined, 21
sponsor(s) of, 22
Catechumen(s)
Prayers at the Making of a (Orth.),
20
Prayers at the Reception of
(Orth.), 20
Catechumenate
admission to, 22
choosing a name, 22
Concerning the (*BOS*), 20 n. 18
culmination of, 21
defined, 21
duties of, 22
examination of conscience, 22
fasting, 22
prayer, 22
Roman Catholic practice of, 22f.
stages of the, 21f.
Catherine of Siena, Commemoration
of (April 29), 206
Catholic faith, 351
Celebration and Blessing of a Marriage (*BCP*), 39, 49
Celebration for a Home (*BOS*), 291,
320
Celebration of a New Ministry
(*BCP*), 228, 231
Celebration of Anointing in a Large
Congregation (RC), 104
Celebration of Holy Communion
with Those in Special Circumstances, 117, 135ff.

development of the rite (chart),
137f.
minister of, 135
Cemetery
annual service in, 298
blessing of, 297
derivation of name, 296
legal requirements for, 297
prefacial blessing of a, 298
Chalice and paten
as symbols of pastoral office, 198
dedication of, 309, 314f.
Chalk, blessing of, 321
Chasuble, as symbol of pastoral
office, 197, 198
Child, prayer for a sick, 71f., 75, 76
Childbirth, prayers before and
following, 70, 87
Children, prayer for care of, 294, 348
Chilstrom, Herbert W., 8
Choir members, installation of, 344
Chrism, 93
consecration of, 95
Christ, mystical body of, 120
Christendom, vs. secular society, 17
Christianity, corporateness of, 97,
104, 113, 143 n. 1, 148
Christmas, 117, 206
First Sunday after, 51
Christmas crib, blessing of, 330
Church
as spiritual house, 250, 263, 265
communal nature of, 97, 104, 113,
143 n. 1, 148
significance of every action of, 364
Church Book (1868), x, 1, 2, 2 n. 4,
58, 63, 68, 71, 74, 75, 76, 97,
109, 144, 150, 153, 173, 182,
185, 187, 190, 191, 199, 277,
281, 370, 371, 383, 389
Additional Prayers of, 75, 76
Ministerial Acts in (1891–92), 1, 2,
3, 72
Church Book of the Evangelical
Lutheran Augustana Synod
(1898), 390
Church building
as house of the church, 250
dedication of a reclaimed, 274
dedication of a remodeled, 274
separated from ordinary use, 292
symbols of possession of, 277
Church Council, Order for the Installation of, 4, 7, 338
Church council meetings, prayers
for, 383

Dedication of an Organ, the Order
  for the (*LA*), 302
Dedication of an Organ or Other
  Musical Instrument, 301ff.
development of rite (chart), 303ff.
Dedication of a Parish House,
  Church House, School, or
  Hospital, 293
psalms and lessons, 293
Dedication of a Parish House, Order
  for the (*LA*), 291
Dedication of a School, College, or
  University Buildings, An
  Office for (UMC), 292
Dedication of a School, Order for the
  (*LA*), 291
lessons at, 293
Dedication of the God's Acre, 295
Dedication of the Temple in
  Jerusalem, 250, 281
Dedication of Worship Furnishings,
  380ff.
comparison of rites (chart), 311ff.
not a necessary action, 310
Departed, Eucharist for. *See*
  Eucharist for the Departed
Departed
prayers for the, 161
remembrance of the faithful, 140,
  161
Dialogue, eucharistic, 192
Didache, 113
Directors of Christian education,
  installation of, 342
Distribution of Communion, 117n. 6
formula for, 115
Distribution of Communion to Those
  in Special Circumstances,
  116ff.
comparison of rites (chart), 134
Gospel, 132
prayer of the day, 131f.
precedence of Sundays and
  festivals, 132
preparation for visit by minister of,
  125, 129
preparation of congregation for introduction of, 124f.
principal action, 132
selecting ministers for, 126f.
supplements ministry of pastor,
  117
training ministers of, 127ff.
when used with Laying on of
  Hands and Anointing, 102
Divorce, 37, 52ff.

Prayers at the Time of Separation
  or, 52ff.
Divorced
or separated, prayer for the
  (Presb.), 52
rituals for the, 52
Doberstein, John, 86
Doctors and nurses, prayer for, 107
Donors of ornaments
carry donations in procession at
  dedication, 276
recognition of, 275
Douglas, George W., 90, 155
Dowden, John, 86, 87, 159
Drafting Committee on Occasional
  Services, 9
*Draft Proposed Book of Common
  Prayer* (1976), 55, 56
Dream of Gerontius (John Henry
  Newman, 1865), 147
Dualism of body/soul, 59
Dun, Angus (bishop of
  Washington), 87
Durand, William (bishop of
  Mende), 11
Dwelling, Office for the Blessing of a
  (UMC), 320
Dwelling, Order for the Blessing of a,
  7, 320ff.
Dying
Blessing of the, 142
ministry to the, 139ff.
prayer for the, 76

Easter, 22, 117, 206
blessing in homes at, 323
character of Laying on of Hands
  and Anointing, 106
Fifth Sunday of, 334
Second Sunday of, 121
Sixth Sunday of, 331
Easter Vigil, 22, 25, 32, 34
remembrance of baptism at, 17, 32
Education committee meetings,
  prayer at, 384
Elders. *See* Ordination of Elders,
  Order for the; Presbyters
Elect, The, 23
Elijah, 130
Emergency Baptism (*BCP*), 30
*Encyclopedia of the Lutheran
  Church* (1965), 297
Enrollment of Candidates for Bap-
  tism, 18, 20ff.
address to candidates, 28
as part of continuing ministry, 29

Schlachtenhaufen, Bruno, 8
Schmucker, Beale Melanchthon, 1,
    2, 3
School(s)
    dedication of a, 293
    lessons at, 293
    prayer for, 293
Scrutiny of catechumens
    first, 23f.
    second, 24
    third, 24f.
Seabury, Samuel, 89
Second Vatican Council (1962–64),
    11, 93, 123
Secretaries, installation of district,
    237
Secularizing a Consecrated Church
    Building (*BOS*), 333
Self-dedication, prayer of, 293
Seltzer, George Rise, 333
Sending Forth of a Missionary,
    Order for the, 7, 238
Senn, Frank C., 9n. 15, 23n. 19
Sentences for the Sick, 71, 73f., 75
Servers, 111
Service, 347f.
    through family, 347f.
    through occupation, 347, 348
    through the community, 347, 348
    through the nation, 347, 348
    through voluntary organizations,
        347, 348
Service Book and Hymnal (1958),
    7, 8, 69, 72, 97, 109, 117n. 6,
    133, 136, 157, 207, 231,
    239n. 96, 257, 361, 383, 386
    Burial of the Dead, 90, 164, 386
    Collects and Prayers of, 76
        no. 1, 182, 232
        no. 10, 294n. 66, 384
        no. 24, 294n. 70
        no. 35, 88, 107
        no. 42, 386
        no. 43, 159
        no. 44, 90
        no. 69, 206
    Marriage Service, 39, 42
    text edition (1967), 8
Service of Commemoration, 161,
    162, 386n. 10
    comparison of texts (chart), 162f.
Service of Light at Evening Prayer,
    33
Service of the Word, 105, 182
    blessing from, 33
    dialogue in, 106f.

Enrollment of Candidates for Bap-
    tism at, 28
New Testament canticles, 111
Old Testament canticles, 107
Service of the Word for Healing, 92,
    99, 104ff.
    benediction, 111
    blessing, 111
    comparison of rites (chart), 111f.
    conclusion of prayers, 107f.
    dialogue sources, 106f.
    minister of, 105
    not principal Sunday service, 105
    propers, 105, 107
    stations for laying on of hands, 109
Setting Apart of a Deaconess (1950),
    7, 182, 204
Setting Apart of a Deaconess (1982),
    204ff.
    address, 208
    committal of office, 210
    comparison of rites (chart), 214ff.
    development of rite (chart), 211ff.
    examination of candidate, 209f.
    giving verse of Scripture, 211
    hymn of the day, 207f.
    parallels with installation of bishop
        and ordination (chart), 205f.
    prayers, 210
    presentation of candidate, 208
    presentation of cross, 210f.
    questions of congregation, 211
    the thanksgiving, 210
Shepherd, Massey, *Oxford American
    Prayer Book Commentary*, x
Short Form for Holy Baptism in
    Cases of Necessity (*LH*), 30
Short Rite of Adult Initiation in
    Proximate Danger of Death
    (RC), 29
Sick
    brief lessons for the, 71
    communion of the, 4, 7, 76, 135
    those who minister to the, 76, 83
Sickness, meaning of, 69, 82f.
Sign of the cross, 17, 33, 93, 148, 179,
    255
Silence, 69, 85, 98, 109, 133, 174, 176
Simple Rite of Adult Initiation (RC),
    29
Sin, defiling creation, 247
Sins, enumeration of, 63
Slattery, Charles Lewis (bishop of
    Massachusetts), 158
Smalcald Articles. *See* Luther
Small Catechism. *See* Luther